BOB ÖLMSTE

PRACTICAL HARDWARE DETAILS FOR 8080, 8085, Z80, and 6800 MICROPROCESSOR SYSTEMS

PRENTICE-HALL SERIES
IN MICROPROCESSOR TECHNOLOGY

JAMES W. COFFRON

COFFRON *Understanding and Troubleshooting the Microprocessor*

COFFRON *Practical Hardware Details for the 8080, 8085, Z80, and 6800 Microprocessor Systems*

COFFRON *Practical Troubleshooting Techniques for Microprocessor Systems*

CRANE *Laboratory Experiments for Microprocessor Systems*

PRACTICAL HARDWARE DETAILS FOR 8080, 8085, Z80, and 6800 MICROPROCESSOR SYSTEMS

James W. Coffron

PRENTICE-HALL, INC., Englewood Cliffs, New Jersey 07632

Library of Congress Cataloging in Publication Data

Coffron, James.
Practical hardware details for 8080, 8085, Z80, and 6800 microprocessor systems.

(His Prentice-Hall series in microprocessor technolgoy)
Includes index.
1. INTEL 8080 (Computer) 2. INTEL 8085 (Computer) 3. Zilog Model Z-80 (Computer) 4. Motorola 6800 (Computer) I. Title. II. Series.
TK7895.M5C62 621.3819'58 80-26279
ISBN 0-13-691089-0

Printed in the United States of America

10 9 8 7 6 5

Editorial director/interior design: Margaret McAbee
Cover design: Zeppi Long
Manufacturing buyer: Joyce Levatino

PRENTICE-HALL INTERNATIONAL, INC., *LONDON*
PRENTICE-HALL OF AUSTRALIA PTY. LIMITED, *SYDNEY*
PRENTICE-HALL OF CANADA, LTD., *TORONTO*
PRENTICE-HALL OF INDIA PRIVATE LIMITED, *NEW DELHI*
PRENTICE-HALL OF JAPAN, INC., *TOKYO*
PRENTICE-HALL OF SOUTHEAST ASIA PTE. LTD., *SINGAPORE*
WHITEHALL BOOKS LIMITED, *WELLINGTON, NEW ZEALAND*

CONTENTS

Dedication

For Carol Ann (Carlson) Coffron.
Daughter of Andy and Helene Carlson, older sister of Andrea Jean (Carlson) Norcia.
Former Worthy Advisor of Rainbow girls, DeMolay sweetheart, and Eastern Star member.
St. Joseph's School of Nursing graduate,
wonderful mother to Jeff and Kelly,
loving companion, and great wife.
For Carol—who thinks this dedication is absolutely perfect.

FOREWORD

If you have found yourself wishing at times for more detailed practical information about microprocessor systems, you are certain to be delighted with James Coffron's new book, *Practical Hardware Details for 8080, 8085, Z80, and 6800 Microprocessor Systems*.

Beginning with the 3-bus system architecture common to 8-bit microprocessors, Coffron makes the whole structure so understandable in the way he presents microprocessor system organization, the reasons why a system takes the form it has, and how it all works. He writes in clear language, he explains each topic step by step, and his pace is just right for the person who is learning. At the conclusion of each topic he leaves the reader *with a feeling of understanding*, a *feeling of confidence* from knowing that one can refer to the text for review when one needs to, should one forget.

Practical Hardware Details for 8080, 8085, Z80, and 6800 Microprocessor Systems is unique in that it includes the complete schematics for these four systems with all ICs clearly identified, and shows *all pin numbers* to which circuit lines connect. It presents specifications, appropriate timing diagrams, and explanations for convenient reference. Another unique feature is a clear, step-by-step debugging procedure that does not require "reading between the lines" to follow and use effectively. Anyone who learns and follows Coffron's techniques will be able to troubleshoot the microprocessors in common use today.

This book is a worthy follow-up to *Understanding and Troubleshooting the Microprocessor*, in which James Coffron gave us an introduction to microprocessor systems for those who have a digital background. The thing that I find most amazing about this present book is that the author has, if that is possible, been able to find a way to sharpen and improve his focus on microprocessor system hardware, to make this an exceptionally practical and useful book.

Most of us, I think, will want this book on our shelves as a valuable reference for practical hardware details of the leading microprocessors and their systems.

WILLIAM E. LONG

Professor of Electronics
Foothill College
Los Altos Hills, California

PREFACE

Usually, when a student completes a first course in microprocessors many questions still remain to be answered. The truth is that there is so much new material to deal with that more time is required to build experience. If, after a first course is completed, a beginner has a good general idea of how a processor system operates and how the software and the hardware interact with each other, then that first course has been a success.

This book is written to cover the "details" of how a microprocessor system operates. These details are often alluded to in a general course, but are seldom confronted head-on. This text discusses actual systems constructed to include a microprocessor. As we examine a system we will discuss *exactly* how each component in it relates to another.

Our discussion focuses on the same basic system, but with four different microprocessors as the heart of it. The microprocessors used are the 8080, 8085, Z80, and the 6800. The system is modified for each microprocessor to fit the particular demands the microprocessor imposes, although the basic system function remains unchanged overall. This permits a clear comparison of similarities and differences between the various microprocessors.

The main thrust of this book is to understand hardware. Software is discussed, but only in the most direct and economical manner that permits the software to control the hardware. We do not discuss software "tricks" or simplifications. These are topics for a text on software.

A key objective of this book is to provide enough information about using the four microprocessors to enable a reader to build and troubleshoot the hardware that comprises the entire system.

All of the systems described in this text have been built and tested. They *do* work. The integrated circuits used are standard, commercially available, off-the-shelf items. This ensures that anyone who wishes to do so can construct these circuits, test them for proper operation, and use them.

Some time is spent discussing how to debug and troubleshoot the various microprocessor systems. This is necessary because we *must* be able to tell if the hardware is actually performing as it was designed to do. A hardware checkout process called "Static Stimulus Testing" is employed as the major troubleshooting technique. We also discuss several simple troubleshooting techniques and tools that can be readily applied to most systems as we proceed.

All data sheets for the ICs used in the various circuits are readily available in a manufacturer's data book. Nothing in a schematic, we hope, will be left "up to the reader." All circuits given are exact, and all component values are correct, subject to human error. Pin numbers of all ICs are labeled, and every circuit is discussed in detail.

The variety of circuits chosen for discussion throughout this text are calculated to provide the reader with an understanding of how to use a microprocessor. As soon as the beginner in microprocessor systems understands how to use a microprocessor in a way that can perform a useful function, then the fun begins. After that only the creativity, imagination, and resourcefulness of the designer, technician, or engineer limit what can be done with the microprocessor.

The years ahead will see many new and novel uses of microprocessors in ways that are undreamed of today. Let's take a front seat near the action where we can watch an epoch unfold!

JAMES W. COFFRON

1

INTRODUCTION TO 3-BUS ARCHITECTURE

In this chapter we will discuss the general architecture of microprocessor systems. The view of the system that we will present is of particular value for the beginner. After providing a general understanding of how a microprocessor system is usually organized we will then show how to realize this typical system by using four different microprocessors: the 8080, the 8085, the Z80, and the 6800.

As a technology grows toward maturity, preferred or "best" ways of dealing with all aspects of the particular technology gradually emerge. That is, more or less standard methods evolve for designing, manufacturing, testing, troubleshooting, installing, and using technological products. So it is with microprocessors. Though yet in its infancy, the field of microprocessors has already adopted a number of standard responses to questions of organization, structure and architecture, ways of handling data, logical voltage levels, fault analysis, and interfacing to input and output devices, even though the number of uses and systems in the field is still evolving and growing rapidly. It is this commonality that makes it possible (and desirable) to deal with the 8080, 8085, Z80, and 6800 in a single book. Beginning with the 3-bus system architecture, the thread of commonality runs throughout every chapter as we discuss other aspects of systems that use these different microprocessors.

To realize the actual circuits using different microprocessors, we will incorporate those special integrated circuits (ICs) designed for use with a particular microprocessor only where it will add to an overall understanding of the system.

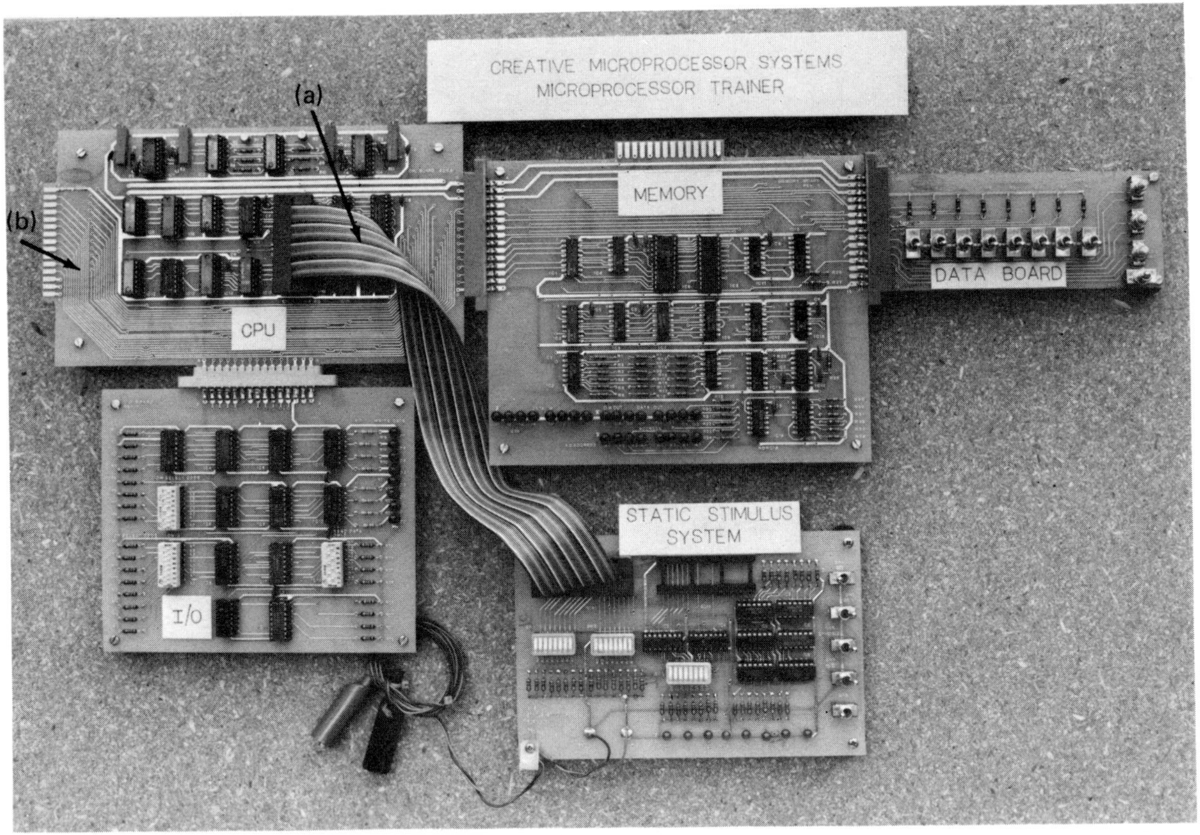

Figure 1-1 Two examples of how a system bus is achieved physically: (a) a specially fabricated bus composed of flexible wires; (b) a bus structure realized in printed circuit board traces instead of wire.

As much as possible, common readily available, off-the-shelf ICs will be utilized. If we are able to comprehend how a microprocessor system works by using standard logic blocks, then adapting this same system to unique logic blocks will be an easy matter.

1-1 The 3-Bus System Architecture

A general system architecture that accurately describes most microprocessor systems is the "3-bus system" architecture. *A system bus* is defined as a physical group of signal lines that have related functions within the system. For example, a particular group of lines may be used to carry the memory address signals. This group could be called the *address bus*. Figure 1-1 shows the physical appearance of two different bus structures. The 3 busses are unique in their electrical function. They are labeled:

1. SYSTEM ADDRESS BUS
2. SYSTEM DATA BUS
3. SYSTEM CONTROL BUS

The logical state of these 3 system busses will describe the system communication path at any instant in time. The *communication path* refers to the route that data will electrically travel from one point to another within the system.

1-2 System Address Bus

The system address bus is an *output only* bus that originates at the microprocessor address pins. The "job" of the system address bus is to enable or select the correct path for electrical communication within the microprocessor system. For now, we will assume that all electrical communication within the microprocessor system is between the microprocessor and the unit enabled by the address bus. For our purpose, a *unit* is any electrical device that accepts data from the microprocessor or provides data to the microprocessor.

For convenience, we further assume that all electrical communication in the microprocessor system is between the microprocessor and the unit enabled by the address bus. (Later in this book we will show that this is not always the case in a microprocessor controlled system.) For beginners in microprocessor systems it is best to limit the communication paths initially to this single one for easier comprehension. Once a solid understanding of this communication path is attained, other possible communication paths that may exist within a microprocessor system are readily explained.

Another important fact concerning the system address bus is its size. The size of a bus indicates how many separate physical electrical lines comprise the bus.

For the 8080, 8085, Z80, and the 6800 microprocessors the address bus is 16 bits wide. This means that there are 16 physical lines that comprize the address bus of the systems built around these microprocessors.

1-3 System Data Bus

The system data bus is a "bi-directional" bus. The term *bi-directional* indicates that data flow can be in either direction. Sometimes the data is generated by the microprocessor and moves from it to a destination elsewhere within the system. The *destination* in the system is the unit that is enabled to receive the data on the system data bus by the logical state of the lines of the system address bus.

At other times data is generated by some other source and sent to the microprocessor via the system data bus. This data is generated by the particular unit in the system that is enabled by the address bus. When data on the data bus is in this mode it is said to be *input* to the microprocessor.

Although data can move in both directions on the data bus, it can never be in both directions at the same instant in time. That means the microprocessor will be set in a mode either to transmit data to the system or to receive data from the system at any given instant. Further, *all bits of the data bus will move data in the same direction at the same time*. This means that all data bus bits must be inputs or all must be outputs at any given instant.

The number of data bits common to the 8080, 8085, Z80, and 6800 microprocessors is eight. Because of this, the data bus is said to be "8 bits wide" and can process 8 bits in parallel. That is why these microprocessors are *labeled 8-bit microprocessors*.

1-4 System Control Bus

The data on the system control bus is comprised of these four signals:

1. MEMORY READ ACTIVE
2. MEMORY WRITE ACTIVE
3. INPUT DEVICE READ ACTIVE
4. OUTPUT DEVICE WRITE ACTIVE

We will add some additional signals to this bus later. It is helpful for understanding if the system control bus is limited at this time to the four signals listed, however. After the function of these four signals is clearly understood, then the functions of additional signals are easier to follow.

The control bus is an *output only* bus. That is, it is uni-directional in the output mode. By contrast, we recall that the data bus was bi-directional.

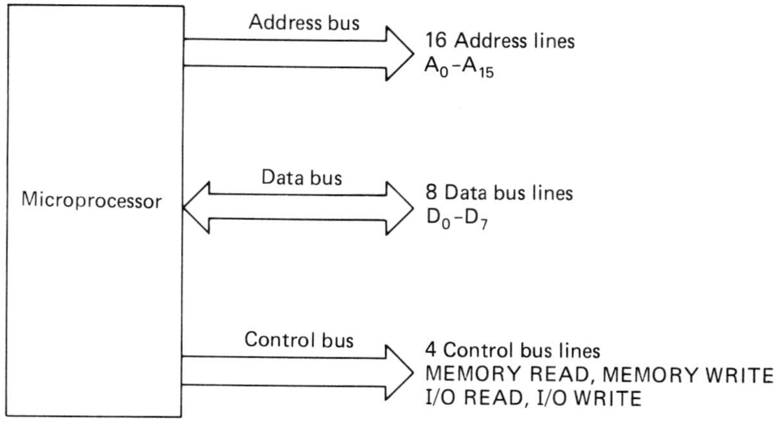

Figure 1-2 Three-bus microprocessor system architecture in block diagram form. The address bus and control bus are output only (uni-directional). The data bus is bi-directional as denoted by the arrowheads pointing in both directions on the data bus.

The use of the term "active" means that when the event called for by the control bus line is happening within the system, that control line is active logical 1 or active logical 0. In microprocessor systems the active state of the control bus lines can be either logical 1 or logical 0. In fact, different lines within the system may be active in different logical states. For example, the MEMORY READ control line can be an active logical 1 and the MEMORY WRITE control line can be an active logical 0.

It is the function of the control bus signal to determine and initiate the type of electrical communication that is taking place on the system data bus. It should be noted that even though the control line may be active logical 1 or active logical 0 within the system, when the line is active the line is said to be "asserted," regardless of the active state.

Figure 1-2 shows the 3-bus architecture in block diagram form. In this Figure we see that the address bus and the control bus have arrows pointing in one direction only. This indicates that these busses are uni-directional. The data bus shown in Figure 1-2 has an arrow on each end pointing in different directions. This indicates a bi-directional bus. The notation we have shown is used often in the literature to describe these busses.

1-5 Using 3-Bus Architecture

We will now discuss in general terms how the 3-bus microprocessor system architecture can adequately process communication in the system. To begin, we must clarify what tasks are performed in a microprocessor system. We can then examine how the 3-bus architecture enables these tasks to be accomplished.

For an initial understanding of microprocessors it is helpful to assign only the following tasks to the system at first, then add to them later. These five tasks represent a good first order approximation of the possible events performed within a microprocessor system. They are:

1. write data to system memory,
2. read data from system memory,
3. write data to an input/output (I/O)device,
4. read data from an I/O device, and
5. perform internal register manipulation within the microprocessor chip.

These five possible events that may occur within a microprocessor system permit many useful and effective systems to be designed. Let us now examine how these five major events can be realized in the 3-bus microprocessor system architecture.

1-6 Writing Data to Memory

In order to understand how a microprocessor system writes data to memory, we must first understand how a memory receives data from *any* input source. To achieve this understanding, we will show a timing diagram representation of how data is written to a semiconductor memory in general terms.* Then it will be an easy matter to show how the 3-bus system architecture accomodates to the specific requirements for this task.

The following discussion refers to Figure 1-3. Notice in Figure 1-3 that the address inputs to the memory are labeled A_0–A_n, where A_n is used to denote the maximum number of address lines required by the memory. For example, if the memory were organized as 1024×1, it would require 10 address lines to access uniquely any location for storage within the memory. The address input lines to the memory would be denoted A_0–A_9.

The data lines of Figure 1-3 are labeled D_0–D_n, where D_n refers to the maximum number of data lines required by memory. For example, if it is organized as a 256×4 bit memory, four data lines will be required. The data lines for this memory are designated D_0–D_3.

The important point to note in the timing diagram of Figure 1-3 is that both the address inputs and the data inputs must be valid prior to the write enable signal being asserted to the memory. The term *valid* means that the address lines and data lines are at a legitimate and acceptable logical 1 or logical 0 voltage level for the family of logic the system is designed to use. For example, if the system is designed around the TTL family of devices, a valid logical 1 is 2.4 to 5.0 volts, and a valid logical 0 would be 0.0 to 0.4 volt.

*For a very complete discussion of semiconductor memory operation refer to James Coffron, *Getting Started in Digital Troubleshooting*. Reston, VA. Reston Publishing Co., 1979.

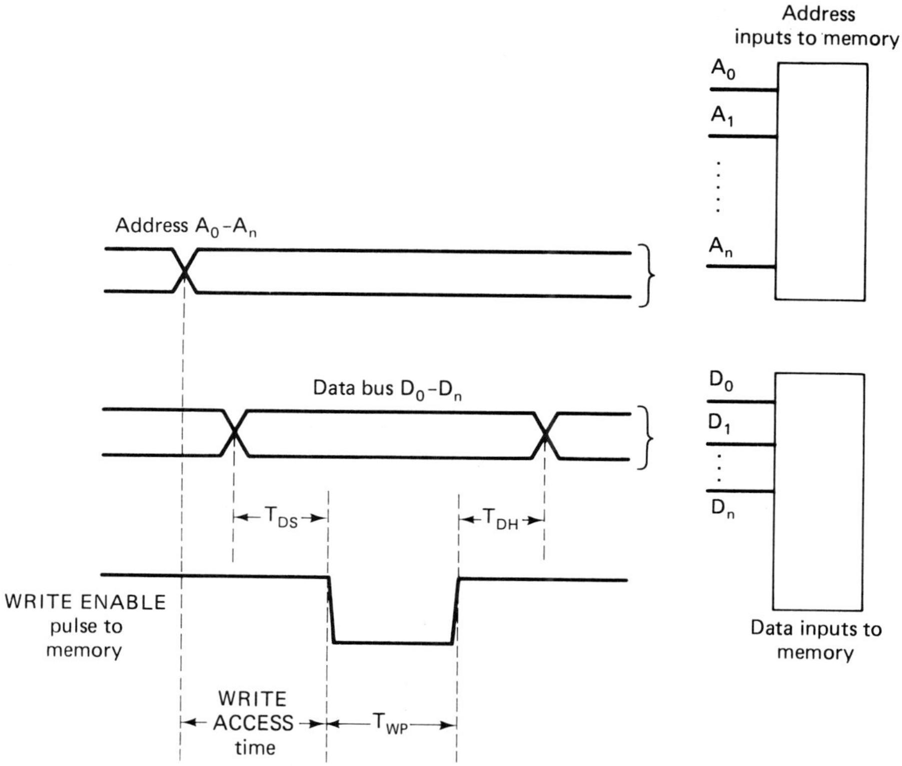

Figure 1-3 Simplified timing diagram of the three signals that are required to perform a MEMORY WRITE cycle to a semiconductor memory.

The amount of time that the address and data inputs to the memory must be valid prior to the write enable signal being asserted varies from memory device to memory device. For example, an MOS (Metal Oxide Semiconductor) type memory may require that these signals be valid at 200 nanoseconds prior to the write enable signal being asserted to memory, while a TTL memory device may require the valid inputs to be stable for only 30 nanoseconds prior to the write enable being asserted to memory. We should refer to the manufacture's data sheets for the memory in question to find exactly what the timing requirements are.

An important point to be emphasized in considering Figure 1-3 is that no matter what the timing is for a particular memory device, the microprocessor system must satisfy all of the timing requirements for that specific memory. If these timing relationships are not observed, reliable communication is not likely to be obtained between the microprocessor and the system memory.

For a memory write signal to be implemented successfully in 3-bus system architecture, the following events must be performed electrically on the system busses:

1. The address bus A_0–A_{15} must provide a valid memory address. [This is the point of destination in memory for data (on the data bus) being generated by the microprocessor.]
2. The data bus D_0–D_7 must provide valid data from the microprocessor. (This is data to be received by the destination in memory pointed to by the address bus.)
3. After events 1 and 2 have occurred, the control bus must "assert" the memory write line to the system memory by presenting a properly timed write enable pulse of the proper voltage level. This action actually performs the data transfer. In effect, the control bus is the system qualifier by means of properly timed pulses for all system activity.

There are other details that must be given attention, to be sure. We will show these details when we realize the 3-bus system architecture with actual microprocessors. For the present, we are striving to develop an insight as to what we can expect the microprocessor system to do. When we have a grasp of "what we expect to find" in a system, then it will be easy to identify quickly the hardware within a system that realizes these expected functions.

We are intentionally staying away from the exact details at this point in the discussion. This is to insure that we understand in general terms the operation of a 3-bus architecture within a microprocessor system, prior to working with "real" systems.

From the preceding discussion of Figure 1-3, we can see how logic levels on each of the three system busses (address, data, and control) interact with one another to provide the required inputs to write data into the system memory. By providing the required signal conditioning for the memory inputs, the system busses establish a reliable communication link between the microprocessor and the system memory.

1-7 Reading Data from Memory

We will now show how the 3-bus system architecture accomplishes the task of reading data from memory. Let us briefly review the important aspects of reading data from *any* semiconductor memory. To aid us, a timing diagram of a typical memory read operation is shown in Figure 1-4. In Figure 1-4, notice that addresses A_0–A_n must be valid and stable prior to the time that data from memory is enabled onto the data bus by the control bus line signal. Remember, the data in the system must always be moved from one place to another on the system data bus. For this operation the data bus is put into a mode where the data from memory can control the logic levels on the data bus line. Finally, the control bus must place the data from memory onto the data bus at the correct instant. The events for a system memory read operation are as follows:

1. the address bus A_0–A_n are stable,
2. the data bus is prepared to receive data. (The data bus is in a receive data *to* the microprocessor mode.)
3. after events 1 and 2 have occurred, the control bus asserts the memory read control line. This action places the data from memory onto the system data bus. The data is now in a mode to be received by the microprocessor.

We can see from this discussion for a system memory read that logic levels on the three busses interact with one another to perform the desired overall function.

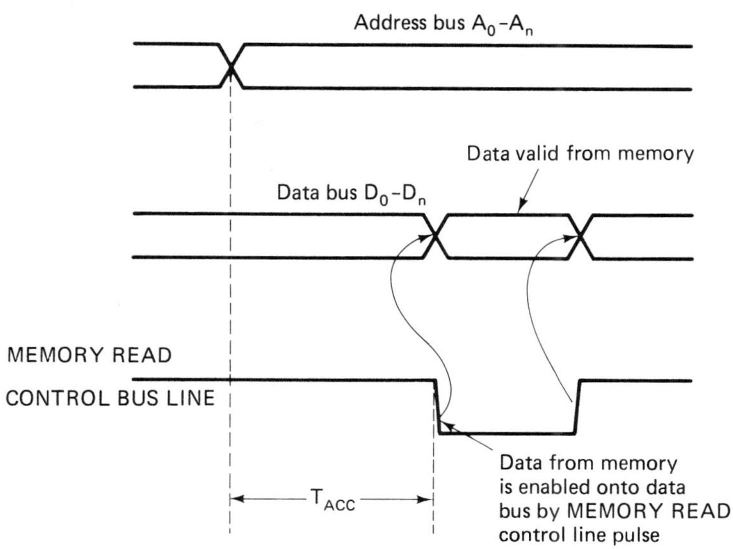

Figure 1-4 Typical timing diagram for a MEMORY READ cycle in a memory.

1-8 Writing Data to an Output Device

In a microprocessor system the use of the word *memory* has a very specific meaning. That is, it evokes a particular picture or set of images. It is easy to visualize the functions of reading and writing to a semiconductor memory. On the other hand, the term output device is not so cleary defined. An *output device* can be a line printer, a light emitting diode (LED) display, a cathode ray tube (CRT), tape cassette, floppy disc, or any number of other items in a microprocessor system. For our discussion we will define an output device in the following way:

"An output device is any destination other than memory for the communication of data between the microprocessor and the system."

Another way of viewing this is to think of an output device as a destination in a system that is capable of receiving 1 to 8 bits of data in a parallel fashion. The data will be received by the output device when the control bus asserts the *output write control line*.

We can visualize an output device acting electrically in the same way as system memory. The difference is that the output device itself is programmed to respond to a control signal that is *different* from that of the system memory. In fact, the 6800 microprocessor does not distinguish between the events of writing data into the memory and writing data to the output devices. Many microprocessors are capable of interacting electrically with the output devices in exactly the same way as a system memory. There is a special name given to a system that treats output devices in this fashion, and it is called *memory mapped*

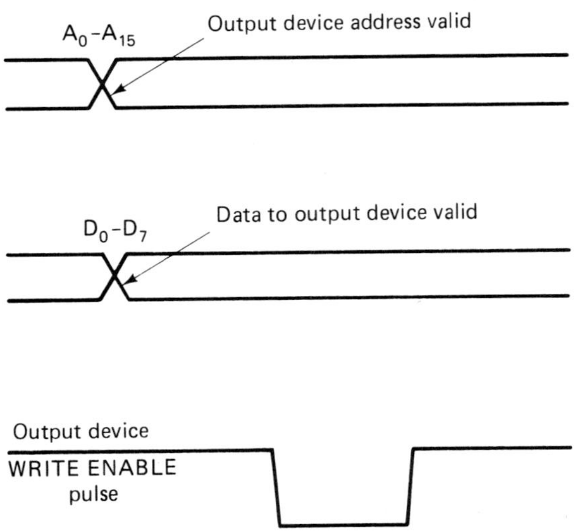

Figure 1-5 Simplified timing diagram of an OUTPUT WRITE operation within a 3-bus system architecture.

input and output. We mention this so that beginners will understand that there is little difference between the communication link for the memory and the link for the output devices in a microprocessor system.

Any output device has an address associated with it. This is similar to a system memory address. The timing for an output device write is shown in simplified form in Figure 1-5. The important point of Figure 1-5 is the understanding that the output device address and the data for the output device are both valid prior to the output write enable pulse being asserted by the system control bus. The sequence of events for the system busses performing an output device write operation is:

1. Addresses A_0–A_{15} are stable with the valid output device address. In some systems not all 16 address bits are used when addressing the output devices within a microprocessor system. This information is shown in greater detail later when we fully realize the 3-bus system with a real microprocessor.
2. The data bus D_0–D_7 is stable with the valid data to be written to the output device.
3. After events 1 and 2 are finished, the control bus asserts the output write enable signal. With the assertion of the output write enable signal the system transfers the data from the microprocessor to the output device addressed.

From this discussion of writing data to an output device we can see the function of each bus in the system. The three busses all operate in conjunction with one another to perform an overall function of writing data to an output device. The system sets up reliable communication between the microprocessor and the output terminal by utilizing all three system busses.

1-9 Reading Data from an Input Device

An *input device* in a microprocessor system can be thought of as any source, other than system memory, that is capable of sending data to the microprocessor. The data from an input device is sent to the microprocessor upon request by the microprocessor. An example of an input device could be a keyboard on a CRT terminal. The keyboard sends data to the microprocessor when the microprocessor requests the data.

In some systems the microprocessor does not distinguish between reading an input device and reading the system memory. This is similiar to the statement we made concerning the system and the output device. When a microprocessor system does not distinguish between reading data from memory and reading data from an input device, we say that the system is using *Memory Mapped Input*. This is the same type of mapped system architecture we mentioned for writing data to an output device.

The best example of a microprocessor that uses memory-mapped input and output is the 6800 microprocessor. We will discuss this in detail when we realize the 3-bus architecture with the 6800 device in later chapters.

A timing diagram displaying the relationship between the system busses is shown in Figure 1-6. Referring to this figure, notice that the input device address is valid on the address bus prior to the input read control signal being asserted on the control bus. During the time when the input read signal is active on the control bus, data from the input device is placed on the data bus. While this is happening the microprocessor "samples" or receives the data that is on the data bus.

On examination of the timing diagrams presented thus far, we note the similarities between the timing for a memory read and the timing for an input device read. The memory write and the output device write timing diagrams are also similiar. As mentioned earlier, most microprocessors can be designed into a system where no difference will exist between the writing of data to memory and the writing of data to an output device. Further, the reading of data from an input device and the reading of data from system memory will also not be any different.

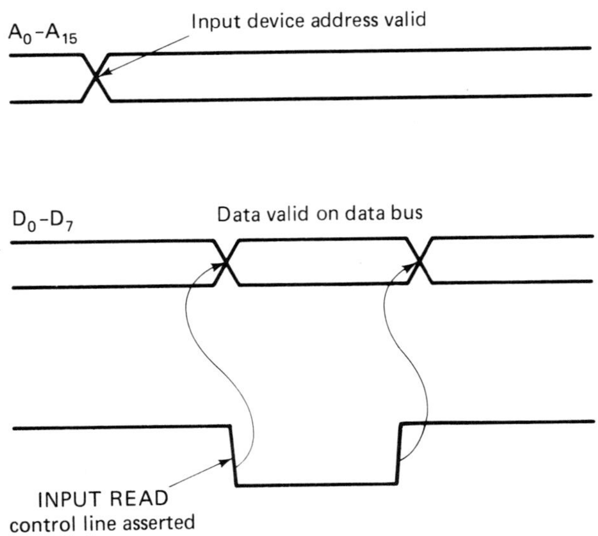

Figure 1-6 Timing diagram of an INPUT READ cycle, showing important bus signals.

1-10 Internal Register Manipulation

The fifth major function that the microprocessor system will perform is internal register manipulation. An example of this function would be an ADD operation. This is where the content of an internal register of the microprocessor is added to the content of the accumulator. The result of this addition is stored in the accumulator. Details of this operation may vary from microprocessor to microprocessor; however, all activity for this function is contained within the "single chip" of the microprocessor. No external system busses are used to perform this type of system operation.

At the onset of this discussion we stated that the five major jobs listed would allow a beginner to describe adequately most activity within a microprocessor system. We will discuss additional activities for the system later in this text. For the present, these five jobs will be the main focus for our understanding of the microprocessor system. No matter how complex the software that a system may be executing, these five major jobs are performed over and over again. As an example, let us discuss in general terms how instructions are executed in a microprocessor system. From this discussion it can be clearly seen how these five major jobs are repeated time after time.

1-11 Instruction Execution in a 3-Bus System

The basic sequence of events for all instruction execution follows:

1. The microprocessor issues an address to memory where the instruction op-code resides.
2. The instruction op-code is read from the memory and input into the microprocessor. (Job 2)
3. The instruction is decoded by the microprocessor.
4. The microprocessor is "set up" to perform one of the five major jobs. The job to be executed is based on the decoding of the op-code input to the microprocessor.
5. Let us suppose the instruction was an "immediate" instruction. This is the type of instruction where we would load a constant into one of the microprocessor's internal registers. The microprocessor would set up to read a second byte of data from memory.
6. The second byte of data from memory would be stored in an internal microprocessor register. (Job 5)

The idea is that no matter what the instruction op-code is, the microprocessor will set up to perform one of the five major jobs we discussed previously.

Again, we emphasize that there are other jobs, such as interrupts, Direct Memory Access (DMA), and wait, that are performed by the system. These are discussed in subsequent chapters. But it is possible to design a microprocessor controlled system that does not use any additional functions except the five we discussed. In fact, many real systems now in use do not use any additional capability of the microprocessor. We will be designing such systems in this text. This point is mentioned so that readers are not led to believe that the five-major-job approach to the microprocessor is totally academic. It is not. This approach is very valid and quite useful in troubleshooting, designing, and debugging many microprocessor controlled systems.

1-12 System Timing Control

Upon studying the various timing relationships required to accomplish the five major jobs, this question naturally arises: How do all of these signals get timed properly? How much of a problem is it to get all of the busses interacting correctly? Herein lies part of the fundamental elegance of using a microprocessor in system design: **the microprocessor chip itself will time all of the signals within the system.**

When the software directs the microprocessor to perform a memory read, the microprocessor generates all of the address, data, and control signal timing within the system.

As users of a microprocessor, we must know the timing of each individual signal from the microprocessor. Knowing this, we then design our memory and input and output devices to use that timing. This may seem a rather simplistic view of the complex microprocessor chip, but it accurately describes one way to view the majority of the microprocessor chips available today.

We will show exactly how this approach can be used when designing microprocessor systems with the 8080, 8085, Z80, and the 6800.

1-13 Summary

In this chapter we have presented a typical 3-bus microprocessor system architecture. The three busses include: (1) the system address bus; (2) the system data bus; and (3) the system control bus.

We have also shown how logic levels on each of these busses interact with one another to perform all overall system functions. The five major system functions we have discussed are:

1. writing data to system memory,
2. reading data from system memory,
3. writing data to system output devices,
4. reading data from system input devices, and
5. performing internal register manipulation.

We further showed how each of these five major functions were accomplished via a 3-bus architecture.

The concepts presented in this chapter apply generally to a wide number of microprocessor systems. In following chapters we use these general concepts in realizing actual microprocessor systems. In Chapter 2 we form 3-bus system architecture with actual hardware for the 8080, 8085, Z80, and 6800 microprocessors. The circuits we discuss and design carry out the concepts presented in this chapter in practical hardware.

2

REALIZING 3-BUS SYSTEM ARCHITECTURE USING THE 8080, 8085, Z80, AND 6800

In this chapter we will show how the 3-bus microprocessor system architecture can be realized with actual microprocessors. We will discuss the 8080, 8085, Z80, and 6800 microprocessors one at a time. We will design the address bus, the data bus, and the control bus for each of these four microprocessors.

As we design these busses we will discuss different electrical aspects relating to each microprocessor. The circuits shown here are real. They can be used as a general central processor unit (CPU) for the microprocessor under discussion. After forming these busses we will show how to integrate memory, input, and output devices into the total microprocessor system in this and following chapters.

2-1 Comments on the System Address Bus

In designing the address bus we first approximate how much of a current load each address line must drive satisfactorily. The address lines are bussed to many address inputs in a microprocessor system. All of these address inputs are in parallel, as shown in Figure 2-1. If the total current the address line must supply is greater than the rated current of the microprocessor output, the address line must be *buffered*.

By *buffering* we mean that the address line from the microprocessor must be provided with the means for "sinking" and "sourcing" additional current. For example, suppose that the address lines in a microprocessor system must drive the address inputs of four memories and two input and output ports. This is shown in Figure 2-2. Do not be concerned if you do not understand why the address and Input and Output (I/O) ports are connected in the way they are. We will discuss the method of connection in Chapter 3. For now, let us assume that the connection is valid.

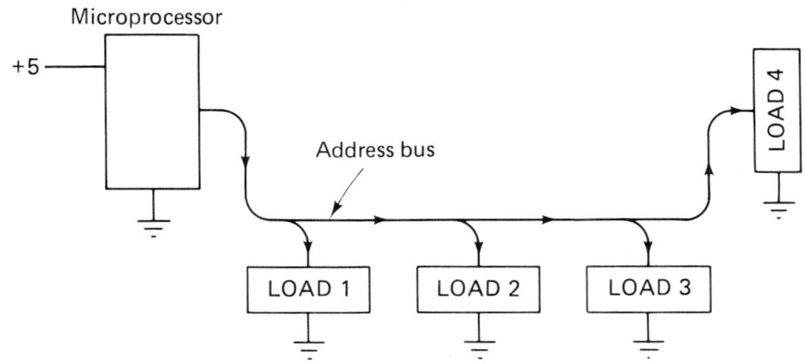

Figure 2-1 The microprocessor system address bus is connected to many loads in parallel. Here the address bus is required to drive four loads.

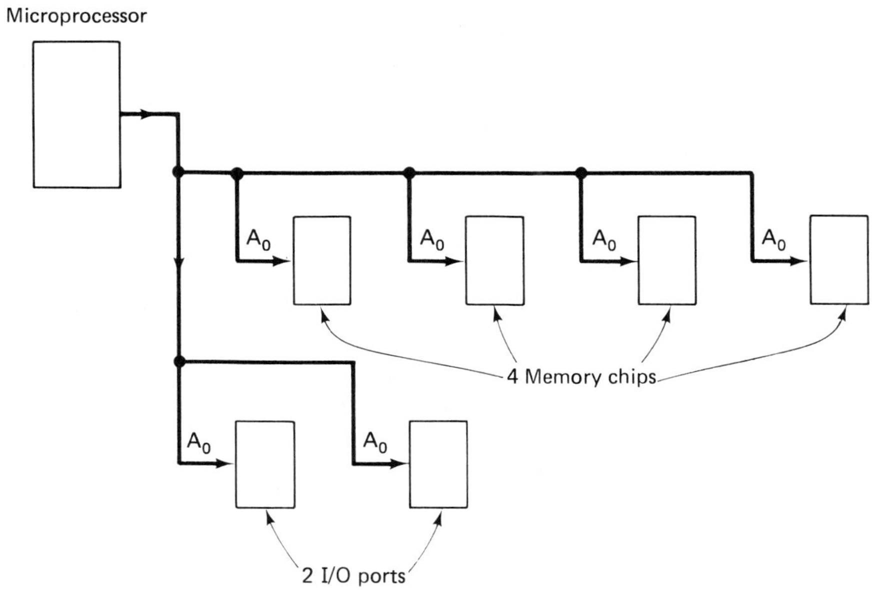

Figure 2-2 The address line A_0 originating from the microprocessor will be required to drive the inputs of four memory address lines and the inputs of two I/O ports. (Note: Grounds are not customarily shown; it is simply "understood" that they are present to complete the circuits to each load.)

The total current the address line must supply to drive the memories and I/O ports is equal to the sum of the input currents of all four memories, plus the input currents of the two I/O ports. As a practical example assume that the memories used are the 2114, 1024 × 4 bit Random Access Memory (RAM).

From the data sheet for the 2114 memory, note that each input load is equal to 10 microamperes. The 10 μA is the same load regardless of the logical state of the address input line. This means that the total load on the address line from the microprocessor due to the memory is equal to 4 × 10, or 40 μA.

We further assume that a 74LS (Low power Schotky) type device is used to realize the input ports of Figure 2-2. This means that each output device on the system will put one 74LS load on the address bus line. From the data sheet we find that each output device will load the address bus with 20 microamperes in the logical 1 level and 0.4 milliampere in the logical 0 input level.

Using these total figures for loading, we can calculate the address line loading in the logical 1 state and in the logical 0 state. The summary of address line loading for the system of Figure 2-2 is shown in Table 2-1. From Table 2-1 we see that the maximum load for a logical 1 state on the address line is 80 μA and the maximum load in the logical 0 is 840 μA.

After we have made a rough approximation of the maximum address load we then compare this loading with the "allowable" load specified by the data sheets for the microprocessor being used. As an example, the maximum allowable load in logical 0 state for an address line on the 8080 microprocessor is 1.9 mA and the maximum load in the logical 1 state is 150 μA. In comparing the actual load with the maximum allowable load on the 8080 we see that in both the logical 1 and in logical 0 states the computed load is less than the allowable load.

TABLE 2-1

The Approximate Address Line Loading for the A0 Line Shown in Figure 2-2.

MEMORY TYPE	LOAD (μA) EACH MEMORY	TOTAL MEMORY LOAD
2114	10 μA LOGICAL 1 10 μA LOGICAL 0	40 μA LOGICAL 1 40 μA LOGICAL 0
I/O DEVICE TYPE	**LOAD EACH I/O DEVICE**	**TOTAL I/O DEVICE LOAD**
74LS XX	400 μA LOGICAL 0 20 μA LOGICAL 1	800 μA LOGICAL 0 40 μA LOGICAL 1
	TOTAL LOAD	
	40 μA + 800 μA = 840 μA LOGICAL 0 40 μA + 40 μA = 80 μA LOGICAL 1	

In this instance the microprocessor can drive the memory and output devices directly. In larger systems the microprocessor would be unable to do this. When the current load on the address lines exceeds the drive capabilities of the microprocessor, address buffers need to be installed in the system; however, there are other factors that we must also consider when this is contemplated.

For example, if the address lines were designed to drive a large capacitive load, then address buffers may also need to be installed. An example of a capacitive load could be a very long cable; that is, an output device connected to the system via a long cable. This condition could exist as shown in Figure 2-3. In order to maintain the electrical integrity of the signal, we would want to buffer the address lines before the signals traverse the length of the cable. The reason for this is that a cable is usually very capacitive in nature. With limited current drive, a signal at the sending end of the cable can be distorted when it finally reaches the receiving end of the cable. This is illustrated in Figure 2-4.

Another instance where address buffering may be needed is a system in which the address lines go to other circuit boards within the same system. That is, the microprocessor is located on one circuit board and the address lines go to an edge connector and finally connect to another circuit board within the same system. This situation is illustrated in block diagram form in Figure 2-5. A system such as this has very capacitive loading on the single lines that are routed through the edge connectors and a back plane of a mother board.

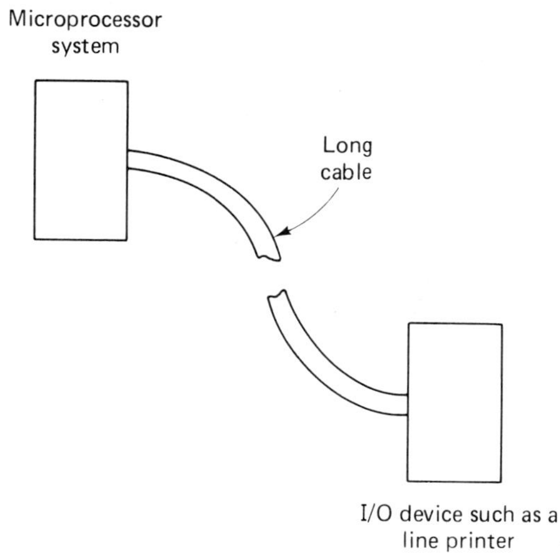

Figure 2-3 The microprocessor system could be required to drive an output device such as a line printer. The line printer may be connected to the system via a long cable. Such a cable is very capacitive, and special circuits are needed usually to drive the digital signal from one end of the cable to the other.

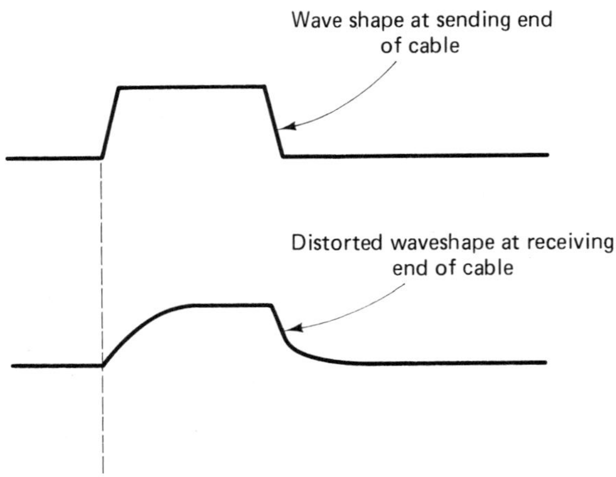

Figure 2-4 A signal that is unbuffered and sent through a long cable may become distorted. The distortion may be severe enough to give false digital levels at the receiving end of the cable.

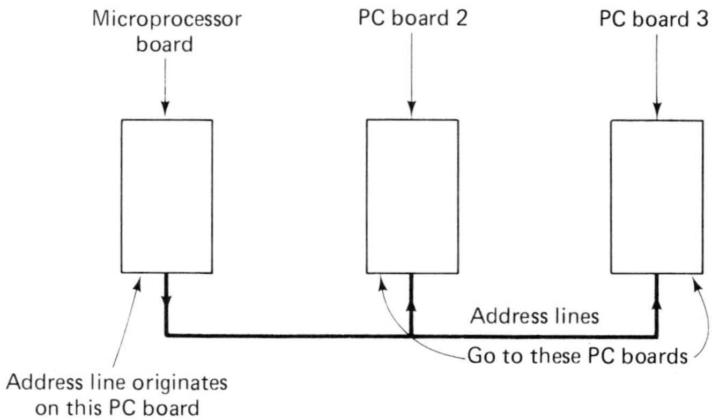

Figure 2-5 Block diagram of a typical system where the address lines are generated on one printed circuit (PC) board and are routed to other circuit boards in the same system. In such a situation we would need to use address buffers on the circuit board where the address lines originate.

As a general rule, if in doubt as to whether address buffering is required or not, these two simple rules can be of value:

1. If the current load on any address line is approximately equal to or greater than the rated capacity of the microprocessor in use, use address buffers.
2. If the address lines go to any circuit located *off* the circuit board where they are generated, use address buffers.

2-2 Selecting the Correct Address Buffers

If we have determined that address buffers are required, how do we decide which buffers to use? There are many factors to consider in determining which particular device should be used. In fact, many people have a favorite that they use again and again. A few guidelines for choosing address buffers are:

1. Use a buffer that is noninverting. This may seem rather obvious, however, a beginner in microprocessor systems may not realize that a particular buffer is inverting until it is designed or connected into the circuit. (Some microprocessor systems are designed to use inverting address buffers, so we cannot specify a hard and fast rule.) In general, the beginner will have an easier time if a noninverting buffer is used.
2. Use a buffer that (if possible) provides all the output drive capacity the system requires. This means that if your system requires 18 milliamperes of output drive from an address line, the buffer used should be capable of supplying the 18 mA or more. This will help to reduce the can or package count. If we use a buffer that can supply only a portion of the required current, then an additional buffer must be used to supply the remaining current.
3. Be sure that the buffer chosen does not have input loading in excess of the output drive capacity of the microprocessor address line. For example, if the address buffer has an input current of 2.0 mA in logical 0 state, then the microprocessor will not be electrically capable of driving the address buffer if its output drive current capability is not at least 2.0 mA or more.

We will expand this general set of rules later. Some possible candidates for address buffers are:

1. 7407 (open collector output)
2. 74LS367 Hex Buffer Tri-State
3. 74LS125 Quad Buffer Tri-State

Many microprocessor chips have special integrated circuits designed especially for address buffering.

In the design example that follows, the 74LS367 device will be used as an address buffer. The reason for this choice is arbitrary. All address busses that follow will be shown with address buffering. It should be noted, though, that we are showing address buffering in each case, but address buffering may or may not be required for a specific system in use.

D.C. CHARACTERISTICS

$T_A = 0°C$ to $70°C$, $V_{DD} = +12V \pm 5\%$, $V_{CC} = +5V \pm 5\%$, $V_{BB} = -5V \pm 5\%$, $V_{SS} = 0V$, Unless Otherwise Noted.

Symbol	Parameter	Min.	Typ.	Max.	Unit	Test Condition
V_{ILC}	Clock Input Low Voltage	$V_{SS}-1$		$V_{SS}+0.8$	V	
V_{IHC}	Clock Input High Voltage	9.0		$V_{DD}+1$	V	
V_{IL}	Input Low Voltage	$V_{SS}-1$		$V_{SS}+0.8$	V	
V_{IH}	Input High Voltage	3.3		$V_{CC}+1$	V	
V_{OL}	Output Low Voltage			0.45	V	$I_{OL} = 1.9mA$ on all outputs,
V_{OH}	Output High Voltage	3.7			V	$I_{OH} = 150\mu A$.
$I_{DD\,(AV)}$	Avg. Power Supply Current (V_{DD})		40	70	mA	Operation
$I_{CC\,(AV)}$	Avg. Power Supply Current (V_{CC})		60	80	mA	$T_{CY} = .32\mu sec$
$I_{BB\,(AV)}$	Avg. Power Supply Current (V_{BB})		.01	1	mA	
I_{IL}	Input Leakage			±10	μA	$V_{SS} \leq V_{IN} \leq V_{CC}$
I_{CL}	Clock Leakage			±10	μA	$V_{SS} \leq V_{CLOCK} \leq V_{DD}$
I_{DL} [2]	Data Bus Leakage in Input Mode			-100 -2.0	μA mA	$V_{SS} \leq V_{IN} \leq V_{SS}+0.8V$ $V_{SS}+0.8V \leq V_{IN} \leq V_{CC}$
I_{FL}	Address and Data Bus Leakage During HOLD			+10 -100	μA	$V_{ADDR/DATA} = V_{CC}$ $V_{ADDR/DATA} = V_{SS} + 0.45V$

Figure 2-6 Excerpted specifications for the 8080 address outputs. The specifications that are enclosed in heavy lines are the important ones for the address output lines for the 8080.

2-3 The 8080 Address Bus

We will now discuss the design of the address bus specifically for the 8080 microprocessor. We will show pin designations and exact devices used to form the address buffers. (The assumption is made that the system requires the address buffers.) This will allow us to see exactly how the address buffers are used in a real system.

Specifications for the address outputs on the 8080 microprocessor are shown in Figure 2-6. We see from Figure 2-6 that the address outputs sink 1.9 mA in logical 0 state and source 150 μA in logical 1 state. Let us assume that the driven system requires the address outputs to sink 3.0 mA in logical 0 state and source 200 μA in the logical 1 state. These requirements are all arbitrary. We are simply specifying conditions under which the address outputs of the microprocessor must be buffered.

2-4 Using the Address Buffers

The address buffers chosen for use are the 74LS367. Specifications for these devices should be looked up in a data book. Figure 2-7 shows a partial specification for the 74LS367 device. We see from Figure 2-7 that the input current required by the 74LS367 is 0.3 mA in the logical 0 state and 20 μA in the logical 1 state. This input current must be supplied or sunk by the address output of the 8080 microprocessor. This is illustrated in Figure 2-8.

From the specification of the 74 LS367 shown in Figure 2-8, we see that the output of the 74LS367 can provide 2 mA to the system in a logical 1 state and 12 mA in a logical 0 state. This is more than enough current for our address bus requirements. Figure 2-9 shows the complete 8080 address bus with the 74LS367 address buffers connected.

In Figure 2-9 we see that pin 15 and pin 1 of the 74LS367 are connected directly to the ground. This type of connection is made in many microprocessor systems. This always enables the tri-state buffers. However, under certain conditions we may wish to disable the tri-state buffers for direct memory access. We have not indicated yet what direct memory access implies, but we will discuss this aspect of address control later. For now it is sufficient to understand that when pin 15 and pin 1 of the 74LS367 are connected to ground or logical 0, the tri-state buffers are enabled.

Notice further in Figure 2-9 that the signal name changes after the address lines have gone through the buffer. It is very important in drawing systems that we *never* give two different signals the same name. In this example the address lines from the microprocessor are labeled (A_0–A_{15}). The address lines at the output of 74LS367 address buffers are labeled (BA_0–BA_{15}), respectively. The BA_0–BA_{15} label was chosen to mean *Buffered*, A_0–A_{15}. The label chosen is not as

HEX BUS DRIVERS

367 NONINVERTED DATA OUTPUTS
4-LINE AND 2-LINE ENABLE INPUTS
3-STATE OUTPUTS

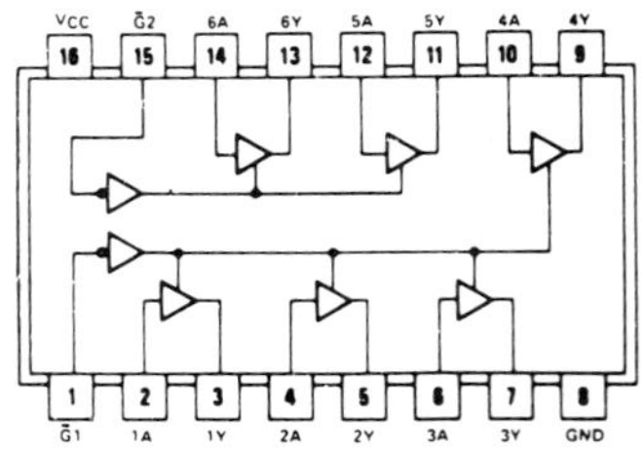

SN54367A (J, W) SN74367A (J, N)
SN54LS367A (J, W) SN74LS367A (J, N)

electrical characteristics over recommended operating free-air temperature range (unless otherwise noted)

PARAMETER		TEST FIGURE	TEST CONDITIONS†		SERIES 54 SERIES 74 '365A, '366A '367A, '368A MIN	TYP‡	MAX	SERIES 54LS SERIES 74LS 'LS365A, 'LS366A 'LS367A, 'LS368A MIN	TYP‡	MAX	UNIT
V_{IH}	High-level input voltage	1, 2			2			2			V
V_{IL}	Low-level input voltage	1, 2		54 Family			0.8			0.7	V
				74 Family			0.8			0.8	
V_{IK}	Input clamp voltage	3	V_{CC} = MIN, I_I = §				−1.5			−1.5	V
V_{OH}	High-level output voltage	1	V_{CC} = MIN, V_{IH} = 2 V, V_{IL} = V_{IL} max, I_{OH} = MAX	54 Family	2.4	3.3		2.4	3.3		V
				74 Family	2.4	3.1		2.4	3.1		
V_{OL}	Low-level output voltage	2	V_{CC} = MIN, V_{IH} = 2 V, V_{IL} = V_{IL} max, I_{OL} = MAX	54 Family			0.4		0.25	0.4	V
				74 Family			0.4		0.35	0.5	
			I_{OL} = 12 mA	Series 74LS					0.25	0.4	
I_{OZ}	Off-state (high-impedance state) output current	19	V_{CC} = MAX, V_{IH} = 2 V, V_{IL} = V_{IL} max	V_O = 2.4 V			40			20	μA
				V_O = 0.4 V			−40			−20	
I_I	Input current at maximum input voltage	4	V_{CC} = MAX	V_I = 5.5 V			1				mA
				V_I = 7 V						0.1	
I_{IH}	High-level input current	4	V_{CC} = MAX	V_{IH} = 2.4 V			40				μA
				V_{IH} = 2.7 V						20	
I_{IL}	Low-level input current, A inputs		V_{CC} = MAX, V_I = 0.5 V, Either $\overline{G}$ input at 2 V				−40			−20	μA
			V_{CC} = MAX, V_I = 0.4 V, Both $\overline{G}$ inputs at 0.4 V				−1.6			−0.4	mA
	$\overline{G}$ inputs		V_{CC} = MAX, V_I = 0.4 V,				−1.6			−0.4	mA
I_{OS}	Short-circuit output current♦	6	V_{CC} = MAX		−40		−130	−40		−225	mA
I_{CC}	Supply current	7	V_{CC} = MAX		See table on next page						mA

†For conditions shown as MIN or MAX, use the appropriate value specified under recommended operating conditions.
‡All typical values are at V_{CC} = 5 V, T_A = 25°C.
§I_I = −12 mA for SN54'/SN74' and −18 mA for SN54LS'/SN74LS', SN54S/SN74S'.
♦Not more than one output should be shorted at a time, and for SN54LS'/SN74LS' and SN54S'/SN74S', duration of output short-circuit should not exceed one second.

Figure 2-7 Partial specification for the 74LS367 bus drivers. The pinouts I_{in} 1, I_{in} 0, V_{out} 1, V_{out} 0, I_{out} 1, and I_{out} 0 are the important specifications for this device. © Texas Instruments Incorporated, 1979.

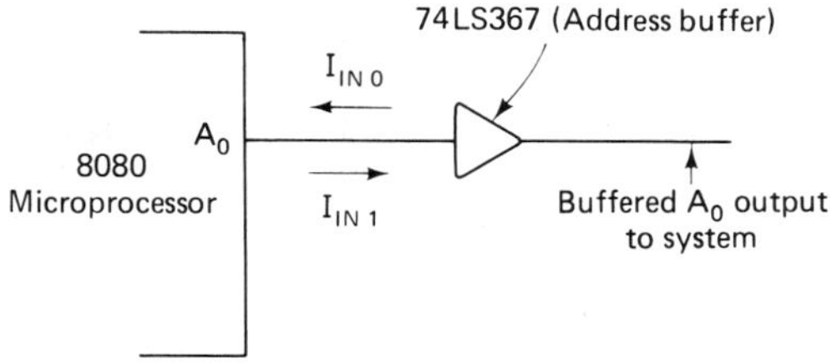

Figure 2-8 The 8080 microprocessor address output must sink and source the input required by the address buffer. In this case it will be equal to 0.4 milliampere in the logical 0 ($I_{IN\,0}$). The input current is equal to 20 microamperes in the logical 1 state ($I_{IN\,1}$). The arrows show the current direction into and out of the 8080.

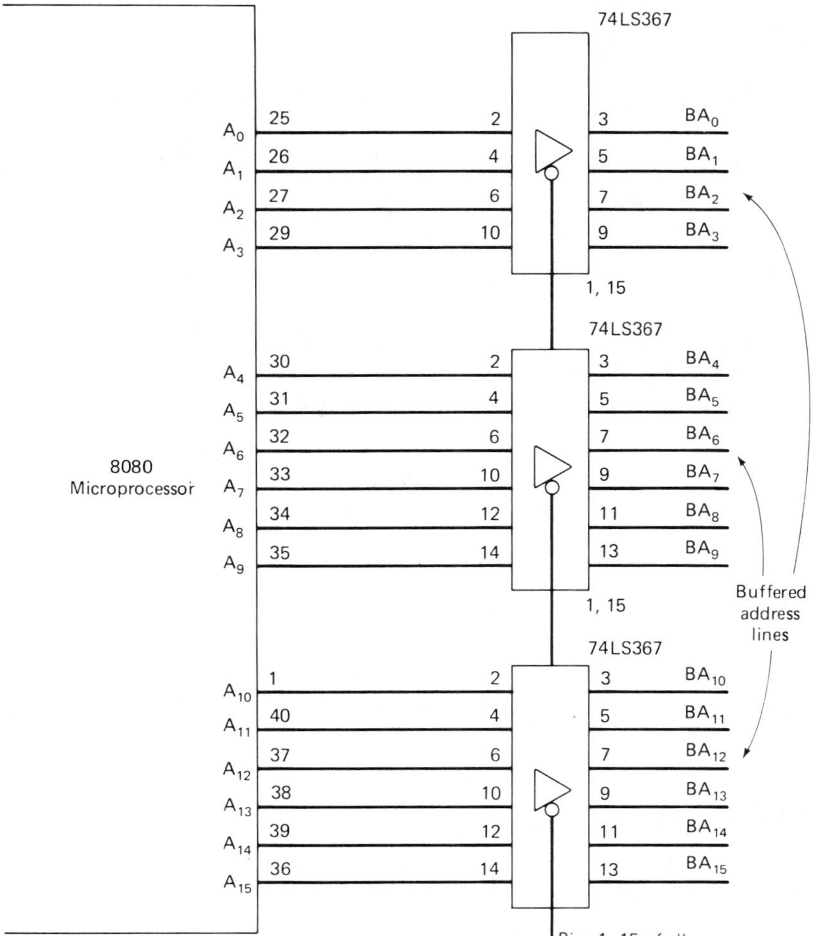

Figure 2-9 Complete schematic showing the 8080 address bus with the 74LS367 as an address line buffer.

important as the selection of a unique label for each different signal line within a system.

The importance of good documentation cannot be overemphasized. It is vital. The reason for choosing unique, unambiguous labels in a system becomes very clear the moment a person other than the designer tries to wire up or troubleshoot a system. It is frustrating, and often futile, to try to wire up a system when the schematic does not show which signal is actually meant to be connected to a certain point. A small amount of time spent at the beginning to assign unambiguous labels to system signals will save the designer and all persons who work with the design an uncounted amount of time and frustration later.

2-5 The Z80 Address Bus

We will now show how a buffered address bus could be constructed for the Z80 microprocessor. The specifications for the Z80 address inputs are shown in Figure 2-10. From this figure we see that the Z80 address outputs will source 150 μA in logical 1 state and sink 2 mA in logical 0 state. For our discussion we will require the system address bus to source 200 μA in logical 1 state and sink 3 mA in logical 0 state. In this case, we see that the Z80 will not be able to drive the address bus adequately. These conditions, again, are all chosen such that we would need to install address buffers within the system.

The address buffers chosen are 74LS367s. The complete schematic for the buffered address bus to be used with the Z80 is shown in Figure 2-11. We need not spend further time discussing the Z80 address bus because of the simplicity of interfacing the Z80 to a microprocessor system. We see that the Z80 address bus is 16 bits wide, as was the 8080 address bus (Figure 2-9).

2-6 The 6800 Address Bus

The specifications for the 6800 microprocessor address output lines are given in Figure 2-12. In Figure 2-12, note that the address output lines for the 6800 microprocessor can sink 2 mA in logical 0 state and source 150 μA in logical 1 state. Assume that the current requirements for the address bus in our system will exceed the drive capability for the 6800 address output lines. This indicates that we must buffer the address outputs of the 6800 microprocessor. For address buffers we again use the 74LS367.

The complete schematic for the 6800 buffered address bus is shown in Figure 2-13. We note from this Figure that the 6800 address bus, like that of the 8080 and the Z80, is 16 bits wide.

Z80-CPU D.C. Characteristics

T_A = 0°C to 70°C, V_{cc} = 5V ± 5% unless otherwise specified

Symbol	Parameter	Min.	Typ.	Max.	Unit	Test Condition
V_{ILC}	Clock Input Low Voltage	-0.3		0.45	V	
V_{IHC}	Clock Input High Voltage	V_{cc} −.6		V_{cc}+.3	V	
V_{IL}	Input Low Voltage	-0.3		0.8	V	
V_{IH}	Input High Voltage	2.0		V_{cc}	V	
V_{OL}	Output Low Voltage			0.4	V	I_{OL}=1.8mA
V_{OH}	Output High Voltage	2.4			V	I_{OH} = −250μA
I_{CC}	Power Supply Current			150	mA	
I_{LI}	Input Leakage Current			10	μA	V_{IN}=0 to V_{cc}
I_{LOH}	Tri-State Output Leakage Current in Float			10	μA	V_{OUT}=2.4 to V_{cc}
I_{LOL}	Tri-State Output Leakage Current in Float			-10	μA	V_{OUT}=0.4V
I_{LD}	Data Bus Leakage Current in Input Mode			±10	μA	$0 \leq V_{IN} \leq V_{cc}$

Z80A-CPU D.C. Characteristics

T_A = 0°C to 70°C, V_{cc} = 5V ± 5% unless otherwise specified

Symbol	Parameter	Min.	Typ.	Max.	Unit	Test Condition
V_{ILC}	Clock Input Low Voltage	-0.3		0.45	V	
V_{IHC}	Clock Input High Voltage	V_{cc} −.6		V_{cc}+.3	V	
V_{IL}	Input Low Voltage	-0.3		0.8	V	
V_{IH}	Input High Voltage	2.0		V_{cc}	V	
V_{OL}	Output Low Voltage			0.4	V	I_{OL}=1.8mA
V_{OH}	Output High Voltage	2.4			V	I_{OH} = −250μA
I_{CC}	Power Supply Current		90	200	mA	
I_{LI}	Input Leakage Current			10	μA	V_{IN}=0 to V_{cc}
I_{LOH}	Tri-State Output Leakage Current in Float			10	μA	V_{OUT}=2.4 to V_{cc}
I_{LOL}	Tri-State Output Leakage Current in Float			-10	μA	V_{OUT}=0.4V
I_{LD}	Data Bus Leakage Current in Input Mode			±10	μA	$0 \leq V_{IN} \leq V_{cc}$

Figure 2-10 Specifications for Z80 microprocessor address outputs and other important DC specifications. The address outputs are specified under the heading of V_{OL} and V_{OH}. (Courtesy Zilog Corporation)

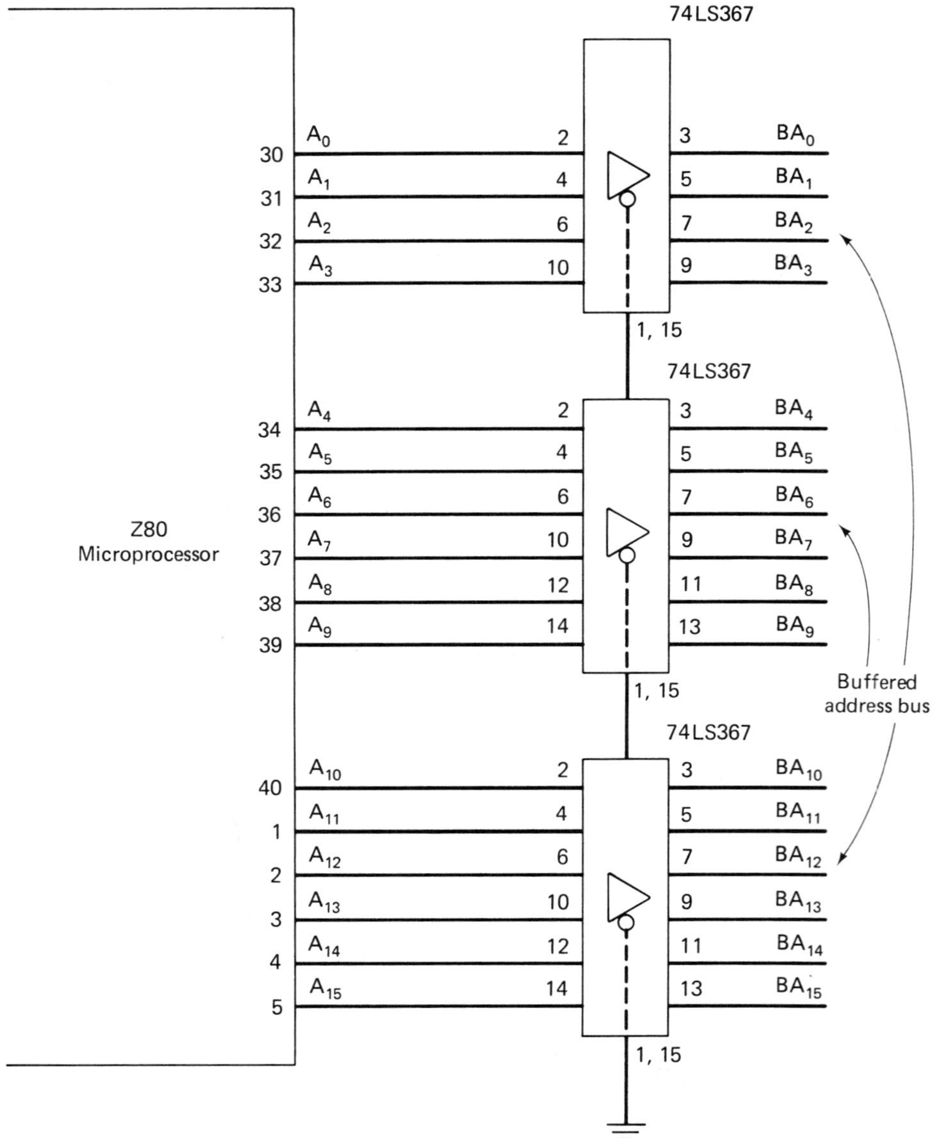

Figure 2-11 Complete schematic showing the Z80 address bus using 74LS367s as address buffers.

ELECTRICAL CHARACTERISTICS (V_{CC} = 5.0 V ± 5%, V_{SS} = 0, T_A = 0 to 70°C unless otherwise noted.)

Characteristic		Symbol	Min	Typ	Max	Unit
Input High Voltage	Logic φ1,φ2	V_{IH} V_{IHC}	V_{SS} + 2.0 V_{CC} − 0.3	– –	V_{CC} V_{CC} + 0.1	Vdc
Input Low Voltage	Logic φ1,φ2	V_{IL} V_{ILC}	V_{SS} − 0.3 V_{SS} − 0.1	– –	V_{SS} + 0.8 V_{SS} + 0.3	Vdc
Clock Overshoot/Undershoot – Input High Level – Input Low Level		V_{OS}	V_{CC} − 0.5 V_{SS} − 0.5	– –	V_{CC} + 0.5 V_{SS} + 0.5	Vdc
Input Leakage Current (V_{in} = 0 to 5.25 V, V_{CC} = max) (V_{in} = 0 to 5.25 V, V_{CC} = 0.0 V)	 Logic* φ1,φ2	I_{in}	 – –	 1.0 –	 2.5 100	μAdc
Three-State (Off State) Input Current (V_{in} 0.4 to 2.4 V, V_{CC} = max)	D0-D7 A0-A15,R/W	I_{TSI}	– –	2.0 –	10 100	μAdc
Output High Voltage (I_{Load} = −205 μAdc, V_{CC} = min) (I_{Load} = −145 μAdc, V_{CC} = min) (I_{Load} = −100 μAdc, V_{CC} = min)	 D0-D7 A0-A15,R/W,VMA BA	V_{OH}	 V_{SS} + 2.4 V_{SS} + 2.4 V_{SS} + 2.4	 – – –	 – – –	Vdc
Output Low Voltage (I_{Load} = 1.6 mAdc, V_{CC} = min)		V_{OL}	–	–	V_{SS} + 0.4	Vdc
Power Dissipation		P_D	–	0.600	1.2	W
Capacitance ⁼ (V_{in} = 0, T_A = 25°C, f = 1.0 MHz)	φ1,φ2 TSC DBE D0-D7 Logic Inputs	C_{in}	80 – – – –	120 – 7.0 10 6.5	160 15 10 12.5 8.5	pF
	A0-A15,R/W,VMA	C_{out}	–	–	12	pF
Frequency of Operation		f	0.1	–	1.0	MHz
Clock Timing (Figure 1) Cycle Time		t_{cyc}	1.0	–	10	μs
Clock Pulse Width (Measured at V_{CC} − 0.3 V)	 φ1 φ2	$PW_{\phi H}$	 430 450	 – –	 4500 4500	ns
Total φ1 and φ2 Up Time		t_{ut}	940	–	–	ns
Rise and Fall Times (Measured between V_{SS} + 0.3 V and V_{CC} − 0.3 V)	φ1,φ2	$t_{\phi r}$, $t_{\phi f}$	5.0	–	50	ns
Delay Time or Clock Separation (Measured at V_{OV} = V_{SS} + 0.5 V)		t_d	0	–	9100	ns
Overshoot Duration		t_{OS}	0	–	40	ns

*Except $\overline{IRQ}$ and $\overline{NMI}$, which require 3 kΩ pullup load resistors for wire-OR capability at optimum operation.
⁼Capacitances are periodically sampled rather than 100% tested.

Figure 2-12 Specifications for the 6800 address outputs. The address outputs are specified under the headings of Output High Voltage and Output Low Voltage. (Courtesy Motorola Semiconductor Products, Inc.)

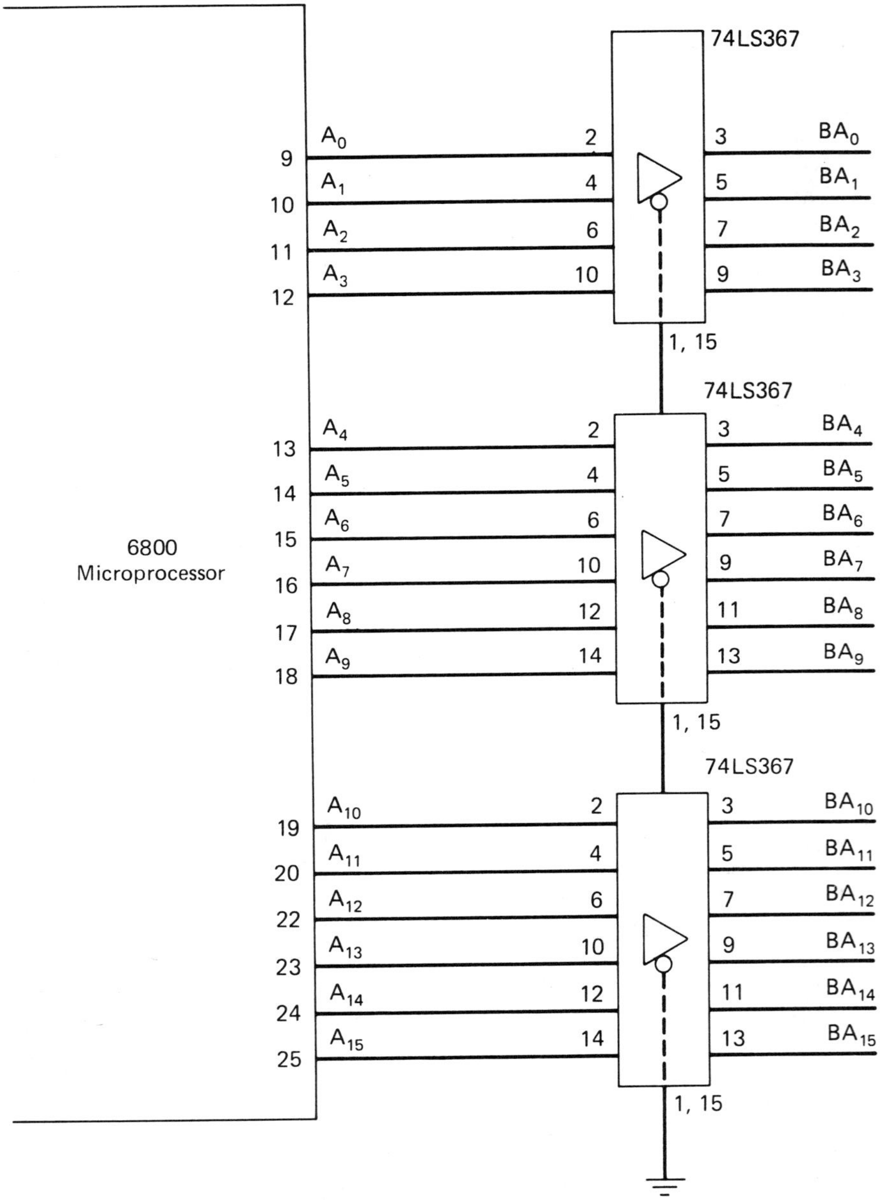

Figure 2-13 Complete schematic showing the 6800 address bus using 74LS367s as address buffers.

2-7 The 8085 Address Bus

We have kept the discussion of the 8085 address bus until last because the formation of a complete address bus for the 8085 is different from that of the three busses we have already discussed. In the address busses for the Z80, 8080, and 6800 devices a specific pin on those microprocessors is dedicated to the function of each address line output. This means that no matter what state the microprocessor is executing in, the pin labeled A0 is always functionally A_0. This makes the formation of the 16-bit address bus quite simple. We merely group the 16 bits on the microprocessor together and designate that group of pins as the system address bus.

The 8085, however, does not utilize this technique. The 8085 uses the method of "time multiplexed" pin functions, which means that the pins on the microprocessor represent different functions at different points in time. This technique allows more "different" pins in a 40-pin package than would normally be available if the pins were not time multiplexed.

The eight pins of the 8085 that are multiplexed take on the function of either the data bus or the lower bits of the address bus. Sometimes these eight physical pins are an address output. At other times the same eight pins are carrying data in or out of the 8085 microprocessor. As shown in Figure 2-14, these pins are labeled AD_0–AD_7 on the 8085 microprocessor.

Referring to Figure 2-14 we note that the upper eight bits of the system address bus A_8–A_{15} are exactly the same as the previous microprocessor address pins. That is, they have a specified physical pin on the 8085 microprocessor that is designated for use as an address output only.

Because the 8085 uses multiplex pins for address and data, it makes forming the lower byte (8 bits) of the address bus A_0–A_7 slightly more complex than the previous microprocessors we have discussed. The main idea is that we must "latch" the logical state of the AD_0–AD_7 pins of the 8085 microprocessor when they are functionally representing address bits A_0–A_7. To do this we must know exactly when the information on these pins represents address information. Fortunately, the designers of the 8085 microprocessor made this information easy to know. There is a special pin (#30) on the 8085 that is labeled ALE (Address Latch Enable). The ALE, address latch enable signal, is normally in logical 0 state. The signal goes into logical 1 state when the information on the 8085 AD_0–AD_7 pins represents address information A_0–A_7. When ALE goes from a logical 1 to a logical 0 the information on the AD_0–AD_7 pins should be latched. This is shown in the timing diagram of Figure 2-15.

Figure 2-16 shows how this data may be latched with hardware. Further, Figure 2-16 shows the information of the complete 16-bit address bus using the 8085 microprocessor. Notice that we need to buffer only the upper address bits A_8–A_{15} with the 74LS367 tri-state buffers, because the latch 74LS374 will buffer the address lines A_0–A_7. The 74LS374 is a latch and buffer in a single IC package.

In Figure 2-16 the ALE signal is inverted because of the edge triggered latch. The specifications for the 8085 calls for the address data to be latched on the *falling* edge of the ALE signal. On the other hand, specifications for the 74LS374 octal (8 bit) latch show that this device will latch data on the *rising* edge of the clock input. Therefore, we must invert the ALE signal from the 8085 microprocessor. This will allow us physically to latch the information AD_0–AD_7 into the 74LS374 octal latches on the falling edge of the ALE signal.

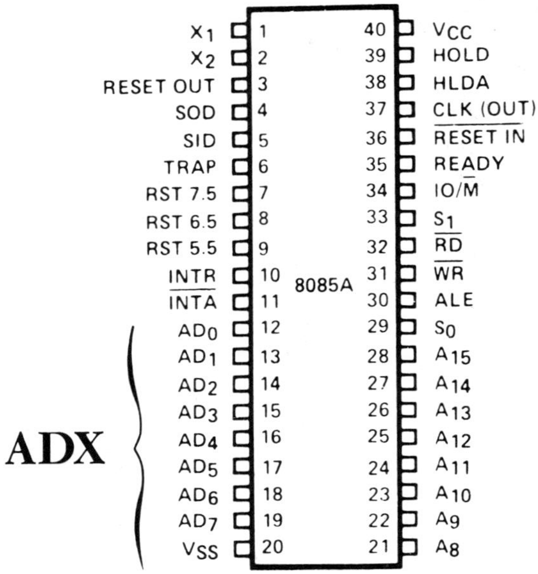

Figure 2-14 Pin designations for the 8085 microprocessor. Notice that there are pins labeled AD_0–AD_7. These pins are the time multiplexed data bus and the lower byte of the microprocessor address lines. © Intel, 1979.

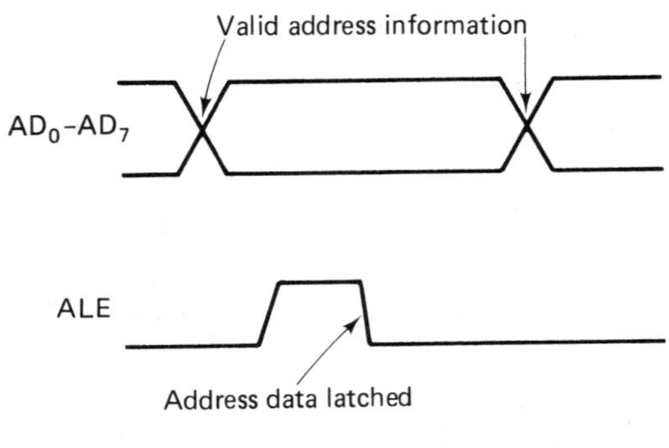

Figure 2-15 Timing diagram showing the time relationship between the ALE signal and the address information on the 8085 pins labeled AD_0–AD_7.

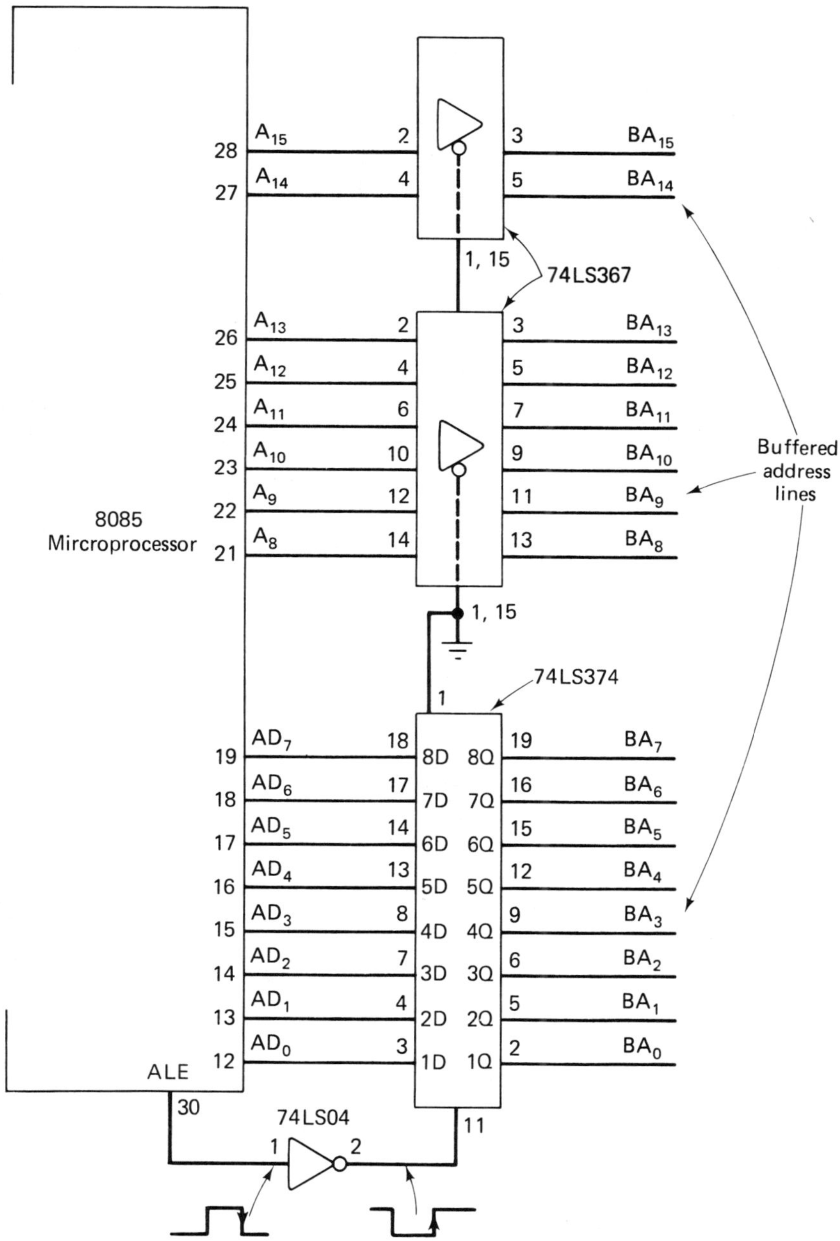

Figure 2-16 Complete schematic for the 8085 address bus. Notice the use of the 74LS374 octal latch to output the lower byte of the system address.

Another type of latch sometimes used for this function allows the data to pass through to the Q outputs when the clock is at logical 1 level. When the clock goes to a logical 0 level the data on the device output is held fixed. The 74LS373 is an example. This type of latch lets the addresses A_0–A_7 become valid as soon as the 8085 generates them. The difference in timing for the 74LS374 and the 74LS373 types of address latches is shown in Figure 2-17.

Note that any type of latch may be used to strobe address information from the 8085 microprocessor. The only precaution we must take when using a different type of latch is to be certain that input currents for the latch being used can be sunk and sourced adequately by the address pins AD_0–AD_7 of the 8085 microprocessor without overloading them. That is, we must check to see that the input currents of the latch being used do not constitute an excessive load for the 8085 microprocessor.

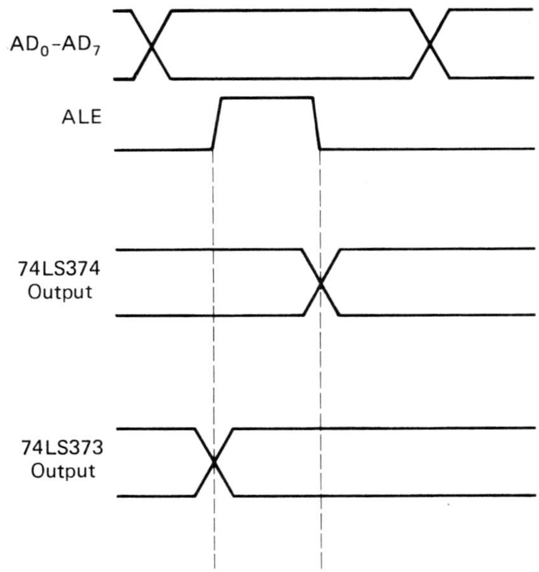

Figure 2-17 Timing diagram showing the relationship of the address output if the 74LS373 latch is used instead of the 74LS374.

2-8 Comments on the System Data Bus

As shown previously, the data bus is bi-directional. This means that information on the data bus is sometimes entering the microprocessor (when the microprocessor is in the input mode), and at other times the information is generated by the microprocessor and is then output to the system (when the microprocessor is in the output mode). The data bus is often connected to many inputs in parallel when the microprocessor system is in the output mode. This creates the possibility that all of these inputs together may load the data bus excessively. This type of loading is similar to the condition we discussed concerning the loading of an address bus. To prevent the data bus from becoming loaded excessively we can provide buffering, just as we did for the address bus.

However, for the data bus an additional factor must be considered. That is, a data bus is not uni-directional like an address bus. The data bus is *bi-directional*. This fact indicates that we cannot use the same techniques for data bus buffering as we did for address bus buffering. This new requirement is graphically illustrated in Figure 2-18(a).

Referring to Figure 2-18(a) we see that the buffering can work if the data bus is outputting data to be used by the system. However, if data from the system is being sent to the microprocessor, it will be "blocked" from reaching the

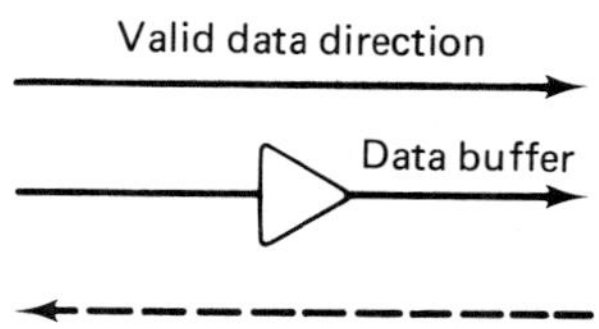

(a)

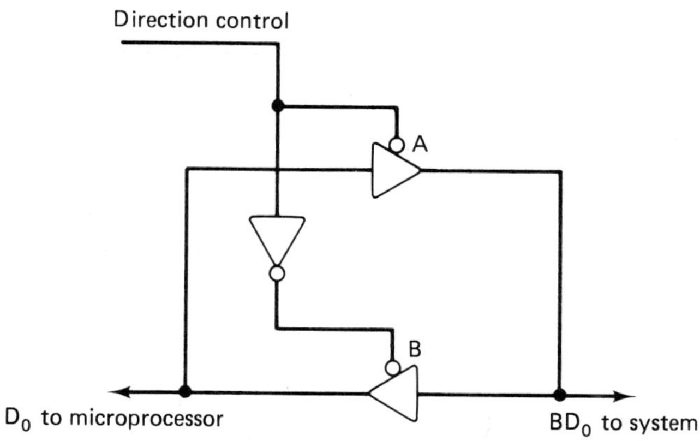

(b)

Figure 2-18 (a) Uni-directional data buffer. Data can flow in only one direction with this technique. (b) Bi-directional data buffer. Data can now flow in either direction. The logic state of the direction control determines which direction the data will travel: Direction = 0, data flows through buffer A. Direction = 1, data flows through buffer B.

microprocessor inputs. In Figure 2-18(b) we see a bi-directional buffering technique. This technique uses tri-state logic to accomplish the bi-directional buffering. Note the addition of a control signal. The logical state of this control signal will dictate the direction in which data will be buffered. For example, if the control signal is logical 1, then data is enabled from the system to the microprocessor input pins. If the control signal in Figure 2-18(b) is logical 0, then data is enabled from the microprocessor to the system through buffer A. When one tri-state buffer is enabled the other is disabled.

The circuit of Figure 2-18(b) illustrates a general bi-directional buffering concept that can be applied to the microprocessor data bus. We next discuss each of the four microprocessors in detail to show how this buffering technique can be realized. Keep in mind that bi-directional buffering requires a control signal to indicate data direction. We will further show how this control signal can be generated when using the different microprocessors. In summary, Figure 2-18(b) presents a solution to the problem of how to buffer a *bi-directional* bus.

2-9 The 8080 Buffered Data Bus

When we are thinking of using an 8080 microprocessor, the buffering of the data bus need not be a concern. The 8080 is designed to be used with a special integrated circuit called the 8228 system controller and bus driver.

In brief, the 8228 buffers the data bus and automatically controls the direction of data flow within the system. If we wish to use an 8080 microprocessor, it would be wise also to plan to use an 8228 system controller and bus driver within the system. Figure 2-19 shows the 8228 and the 8080 connected together to form the system data bus.

We will now discuss how we might implement the buffered data bus without the use of the 8228. This discussion will reinforce the understanding of the different control signals in an 8080 microprocessor system. However, when using an 8080 microprocessor we should seriously consider using the 8228 system controller and bus driver as the simplest solution. We undertake this discussion only to reinforce understanding of how the 8080 microprocessor controls system hardware.

The bi-directional buffers for the data bus are contained in two integrated circuits. These devices are 8216s. The pinout for this device is shown in Figure 2-20. In Figure 2-20 notice that the device is constructed of tri-state drivers similar to the circuits shown in Figure 2-18(b). The CS pin (#1) will allow the device to operate in a bi-directional manner when the signal on this pin is in logical 0.

For our present discussion this CS (Enable) pin will always remain in a logical 0 level; however, there are other instances where we would want the data bus disabled (tri-stated). We will discuss these instances in later chapters.

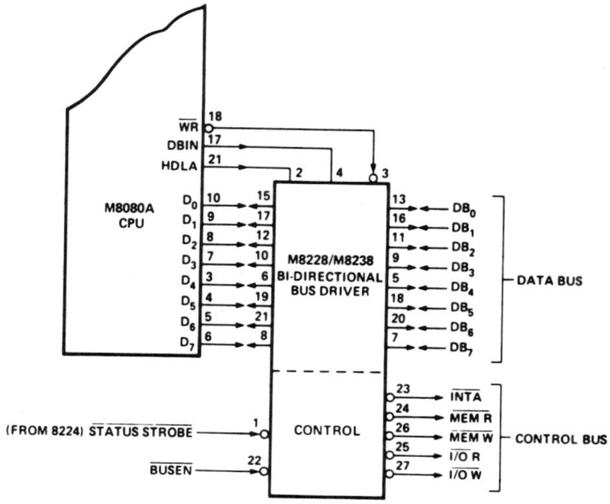

Figure 2-19 Schematic showing how the 8228 system controller connects to the 8080 microprocessor. (The 8228 does all of the data bus buffering and direction control.) © Intel, 1979.

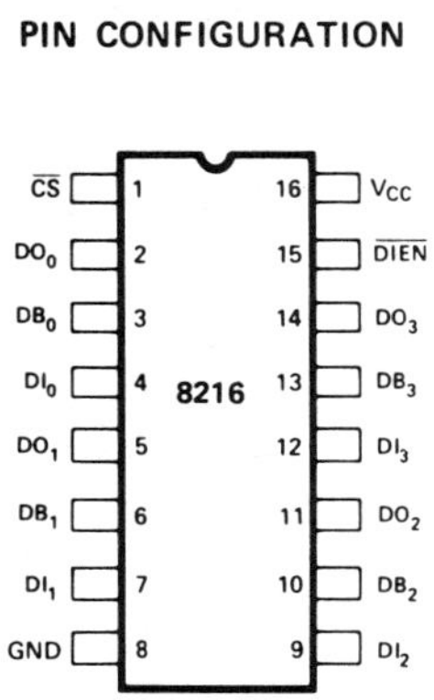

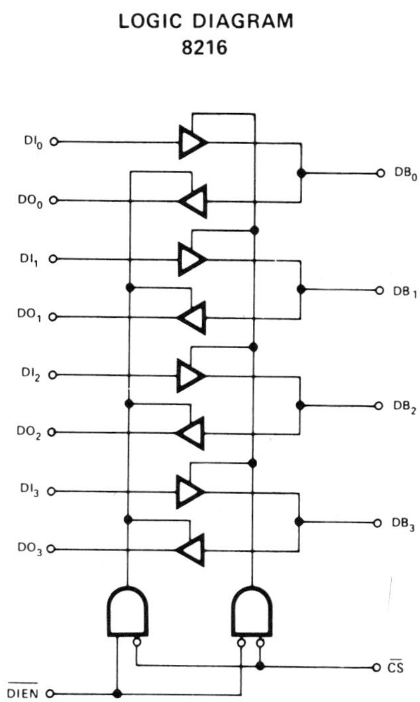

PIN NAMES

DB_0-DB_3	DATA BUS BI-DIRECTIONAL
DI_0-DI_3	DATA INPUT
DO_0-DO_3	DATA OUTPUT
$\overline{DIEN}$	DATA IN ENABLE DIRECTION CONTROL
$\overline{CS}$	CHIP SELECT

Figure 2-20 Pinout and block diagram of the 8216 device. © Intel, 1979.

Also note in Figure 2-20, the DIEN #15. This is the "direction" pin for the device. This pin signal is equivalent to the direction control signal discussed in Figure 2-18. When this pin is at logical 0, the data path is from the DI to the DB side of the device. When the DIEN pin is in logical 1, the data path is from the DB side to the DO side of the device. The DI and DO pins are physically connected together.

Let us now connect the device to the 8080 microprocessor, as shown in Figure 2-21. Here we see that we must connect the DIEN pin of the 8216 to some control signal generated by the microprocessor. Now, in the 8080 microprocessor when the DBIN signal, pin 17, is a logical 1, the 8080 is always inputting data. Therefore, we can use the DBIN signal on the DIEN line for the 8216 device. However, we must insure that the output drive capability of the DBIN signal is not exceeded. The 8216 device requires a maximum of 0.5 mA in logical 0 state and 80 μA in logical 1 state. The 8080 DBIN output signal is capable of supplying 1.9 mA in logical 0 state and 150 μA in logical 1 state. We conclude from these specifications that the DBIN output line is capable of adequately driving the DIEN input to the 8216 device. We keep stressing the importance of not exceeding the drive capability of the microprocessor because it is easy for a beginner to fall into this trap. Always be aware of the maximum permissible loading on any signal line in the system at any given time, and whether or not that limit is being exceeded.

The DBIN signal will be in logical 1 when the data is directed into the 8080 microprocessor pins. This indicates that the DI, DO side of the 8216 device must be connected to the 8080 data bus lines. This is consistent with the explanation that we presented earlier of how data flows in the 8216. Figure 2-21 shows the complete connection for the buffering of the 8080 data bus without the use of the 8228 system controller.

Again we emphasize that the 8228 is a very easy device to use and should be considered first when using the 8080 microprocessor. Use of the 8228 device greatly reduces the package count, increases the reliability, and reduces frustration.

2-10 The Z80 Buffered Data Bus

To provide data bus buffering for the Z80 microprocessor we will use a technique similar to that used for the 8080 microprocessor. The Z80 does not have a special system controller similar to the 8228, nor is one required. We will use the 74LS245 device to provide the data bus buffering required for the Z80 microprocessor. The 74LS245 will be enabled (for the present time) by connect-

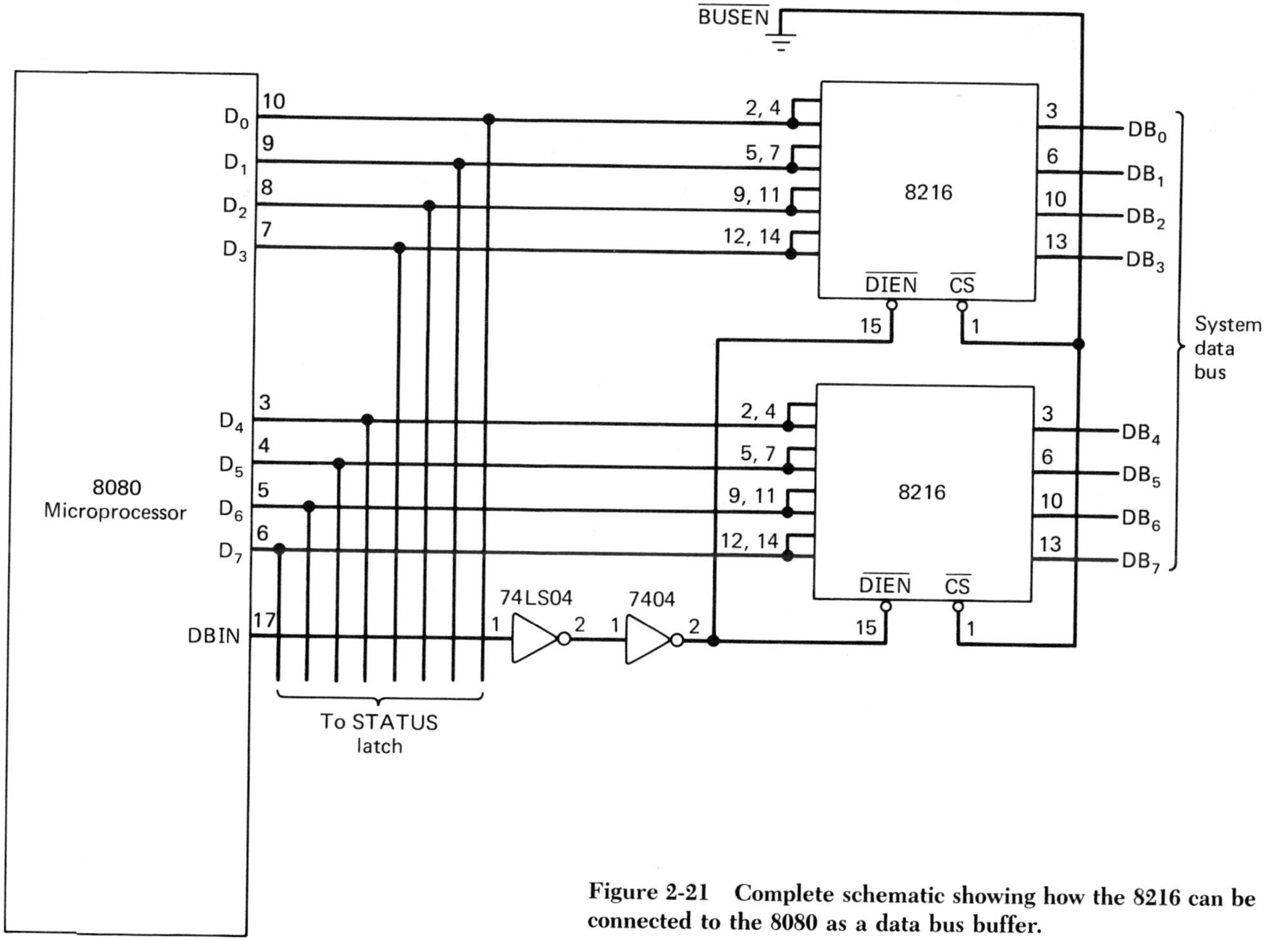

Figure 2-21 Complete schematic showing how the 8216 can be connected to the 8080 as a data bus buffer.

ing pin 19 to a logical 0. The direction DIR pin 1 on the 74LS245 device will be connected to the control signal of the Z80 microprocessor labeled $\overline{RD}$ pin 21 on the Z80 microprocessor. This is shown in Figure 2-22.

When $\overline{RD}$ is in logical 0, this indicates that the Z80 is in a mode to receive data. Therefore, the 74LS245 must be in a mode to enable data from the system to the Z80 data bus. We recall that the 8080 system used the DBIN signal (active logical 1) to control the direction of the data path. That is, the signal from the Z80 to receive data is active low, but with the 8080 the same signal is active high.

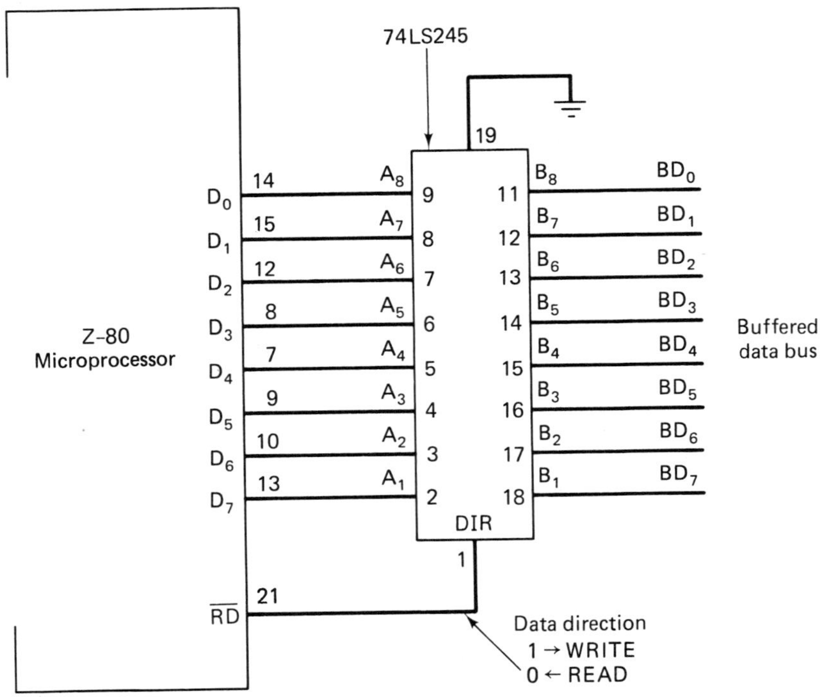

Figure 2-22 Complete schematic for the Z80 data bus buffer using the 74LS245 device.

2-11 The 6800 Buffered Data Bus

To buffer the 6800 data bus we again use the 74LS245 device. (Note that we can use any bi-directional buffering technique available.) We are using the 74LS245 because it reduces package count, but do not think that this is the only device that can be used.

The 74LS245 enable pin 19 is connected to a logical 0 or system ground for the present time. This is the condition for the 74LS245 to be enabled.

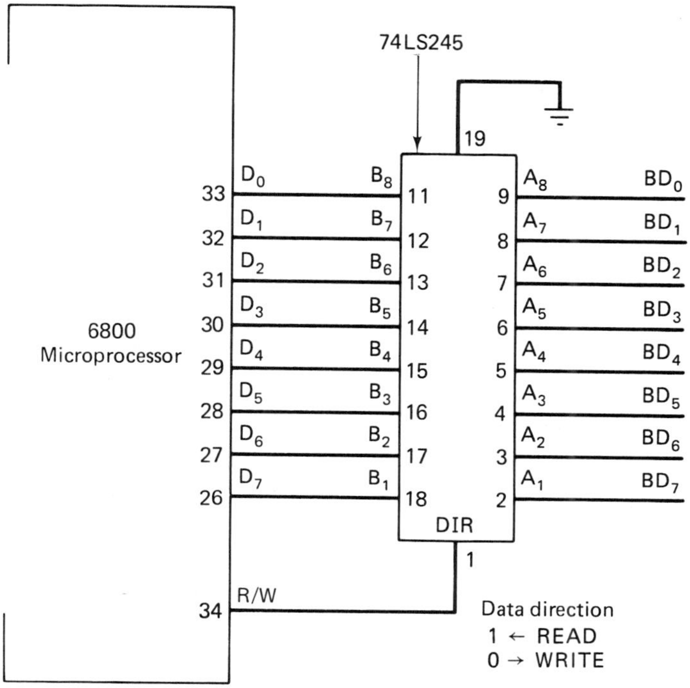

Figure 2-23 Complete schematic for the buffered data bus on the 6800. Notice that the 74LS245 device is also used here, as in Figure 2-22 with the Z80.

The direction control for the 74LS245 is connected to the R/W pin 34 of the 6800 as shown in Figure 2-23. The R/W pin will be logical 1 when the 6800 is in the mode to receive data from the system. Note that we are showing all microprocessors with the data bus in a buffered mode. If the systems we plan to build do not require data bus buffering, then simply leave out this circuitry. It is being discussed here so that we can better understand how the loading in a system is viewed, how to solve problems of overloading, and how data flows within a microprocessor system. But do not think we must always use a data bus buffer; in most small systems applications data bus buffering and address buffering may not be required at all.

2-12 The 8085 Buffered Data Bus

As discussed earlier, the 8085 has a multiplexed data and address bus. However, this point need not be stressed when dealing with the buffering of the data bus. We will again make use of the 74LS245 as the data bus buffer. The $\overline{\text{RD}}$

signal pin 32 of the 8085 is active low when the 8085 microprocessor is in the mode to receive data from the system. This signal will be the DIR signal input to the 74LS245. The complete circuit is shown in Figure 2-24 for the buffering of the 8085 data bus.

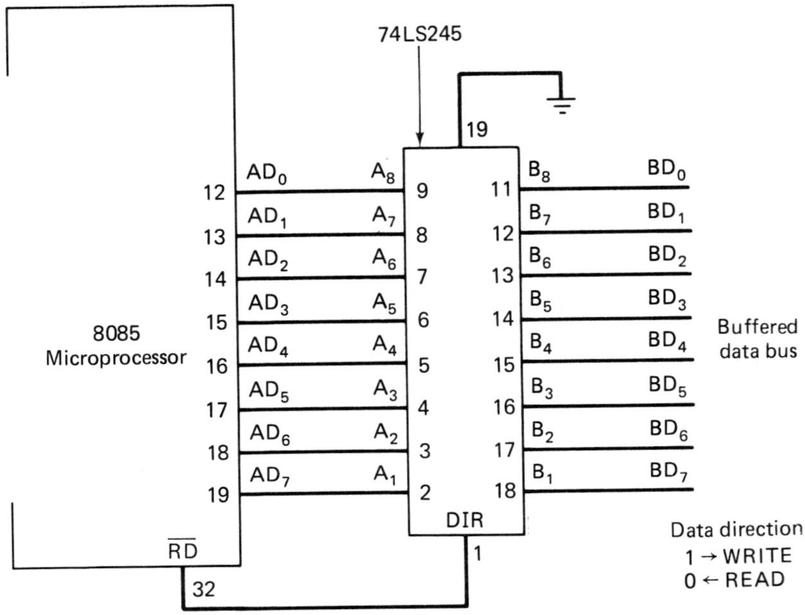

Figure 2-24 Complete schematic for the buffered data bus on the 8085 microprocessor.

2-13 Comments on the System Control Bus

Thus far we have covered two of the three major busses required in 3-bus system architecture. These have been the data bus and the address bus. We will now discuss the third bus, the system control bus.

We recall that the system control bus is comprised (for now) of four signals. These are:

1. MEMORY READ
2. MEMORY WRITE
3. INPUT DEVICE READ
4. OUTPUT DEVICE WRITE

We will now show how to realize these four control signals with each individual microprocessor.

2-14 The 8080 System Control Bus

When we discussed the 8080 data bus we found that a special device, an 8228 system controller and bus driver, provided all of the data bus buffering and direction control required for that system. This same device also generates the four basic system control signals mentioned above at the correct time. This is shown in Figure 2-25, where we see that these four control signals are labeled $\overline{\text{MEMW}}$, $\overline{\text{MEMR}}$, $\overline{\text{IOR}}$, and $\overline{\text{IOW}}$. These signals are all active logical 0 and are also mutually exclusive. That is, no two of these signals will ever be active logical 0 at the same instant.

If we use an 8080 microprocessor for a system controller, then the 8228 device can make system design much easier. However, to appreciate some alternatives we will discuss how the four control signals can be generated by using discrete digital devices. This discussion will enhance our understanding of how an 8080 microprocessor controls the hardware in the system.

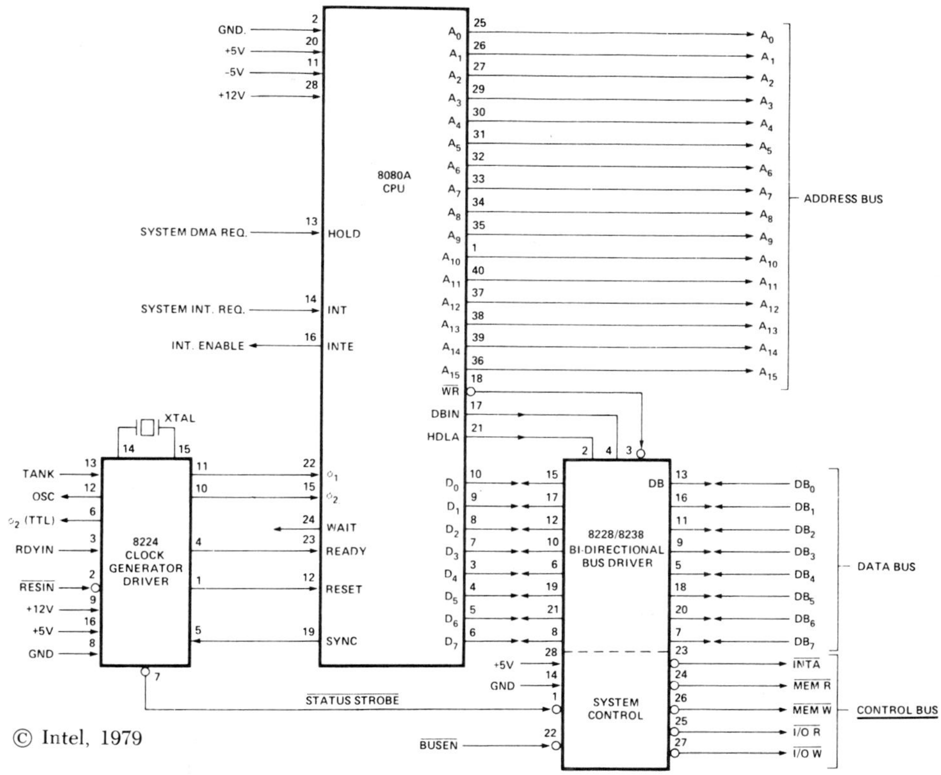

Figure 2-25 Schematic showing how the control bus is an output of the 8228 system controller. © Intel, 1979.

2-15 The 8080 Status Latch

The 8080 CPU generates a byte on the data bus pins called a *status word*. The status word is generated to let the system hardware know the microprocessor's intentions. The status word is generated during the first T-Cycle of an M-Cycle.* If the 8080 is setting up to read data from memory, the 8080 first generates the status word to indicate this. The system uses the status word to enable the correct hardware logic path for the 8080 to use.

When the status word is present on the data bus, the 8080 informs the system by forcing the sync signal pin 19 of the 8080 to logical 1. The system then uses the sync signal to enable a strobe to move the data on the data bus into a latch called the *status latch*. This is shown in Figure 2-26.

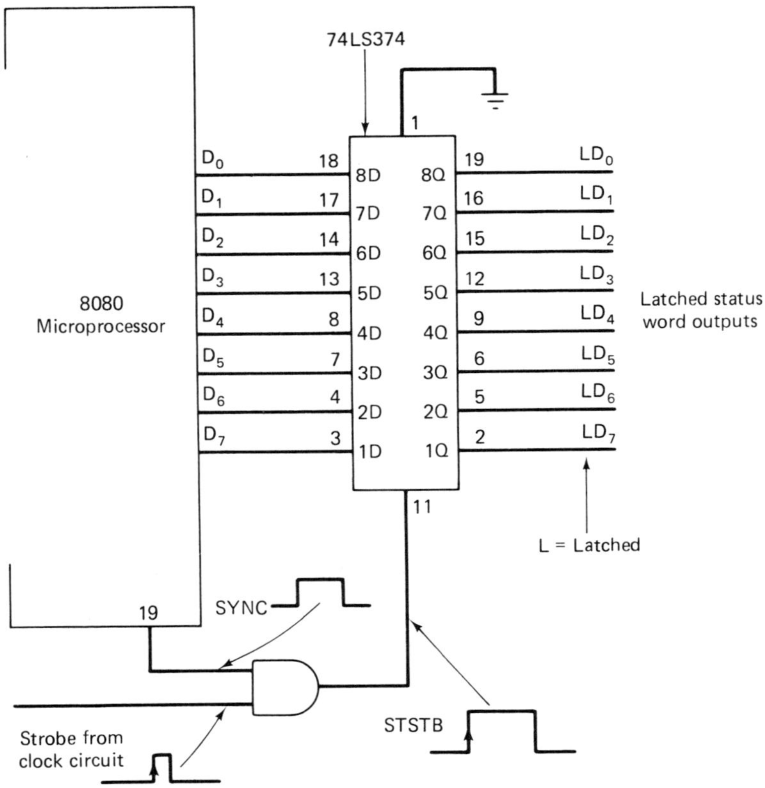

Figure 2-26 Schematic showing how the status word could be latched by using discrete logic. The sync pulse going to logical 1 level enables the status word to be latched into the 74LS374.

*Refer to James W. Coffron, *Understanding and Troubleshooting the Microprocessor*. Englewood Cliffs, NJ, Prentice-Hall, 1980.

After the status word is latched, certain bits of the status information are combined logically with the DBIN and $\overline{WR}$ signals to form the four control bus signals. This is shown in the schematic of Figure 2-27.

We have now realized the system control bus for the 8080 with discrete digital logic. One point to be stressed is that the control bus must be capable of driving all inputs connected to it. Therefore, we should provide buffering for the control bus, and the 8228 controller is a good choice. If the control bus is formed by using the discrete digital logic of Figure 2-27, a 7400 standard device can provide buffering for the control bus.

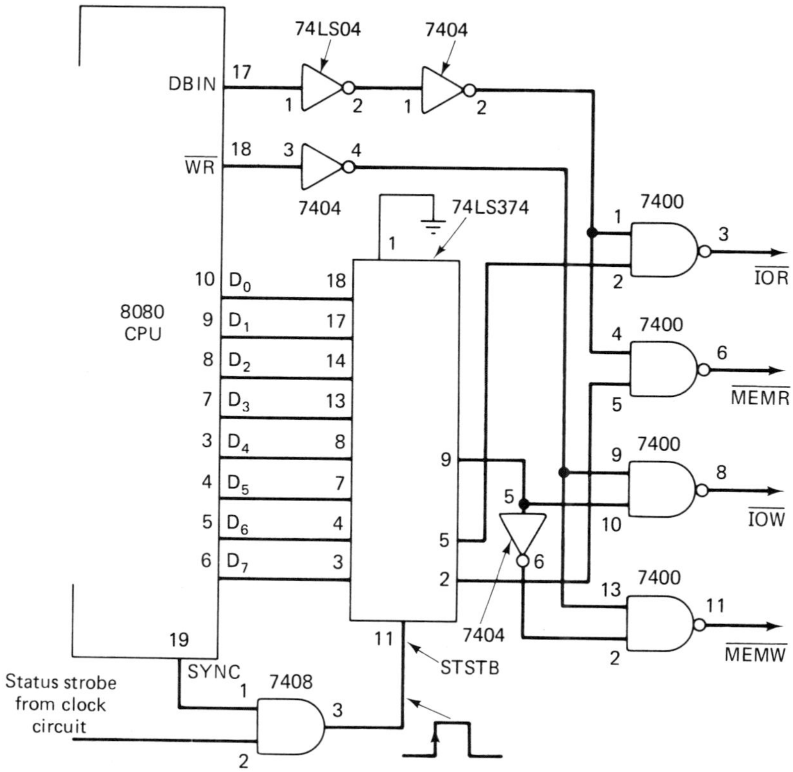

Figure 2-27 Schematic showing how the system control bus for the 8080 could be realized by using discrete logic.

2-16 The Z80 System Control Bus

Upon examining the Z80 system control we see signals labeled $\overline{MREQ}$, $\overline{IORQ}$, $\overline{RD}$, and $\overline{WR}$. A logical combination of these four signals will provide the total system control bus. This logical combination is summed up in Table 2-2. We can realize these four system control bus signals as shown in the schematic of Figure 2-28.

TABLE 2-2
Table 2-2 Logical Conditions for the Control Signal Outputs of the Z-80 Microprocessor for the System Functions Listed

#19 $\overline{MREQ}$	#20 $\overline{IORQ}$	#21 $\overline{RD}$	#22 $\overline{WR}$		
1	0	0	1	IOR	These are the system functions that the four codes designate
1	0	1	0	IOW	
0	1	0	1	MEMR	
0	1	1	0	MEMW	

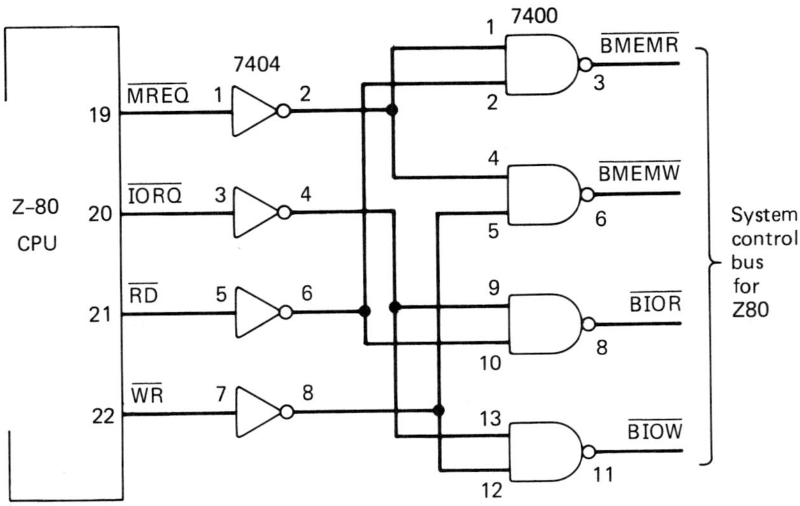

Figure 2-28 Complete schematic showing how the system control bus can be realized with discrete logic for the Z80 microprocessor.

2-17 The 8085 System Control Bus

To form the 8085 control bus we use the microprocessor control pins labeled IO/$\overline{\text{M}}$ pin 34, $\overline{\text{RD}}$ pin 32 and $\overline{\text{WR}}$ pin 31. Table 2-3 shows the logical state of each of these signals listed for the conditions of the control bus functions.

Note from Table 2-3 that the IO/$\overline{\text{M}}$ pin 34 is logical 1 whenever the system is performing input device read (IOR) or input device write (IOW) operations. This same pin is a logical 0 whenever the system is performing a memory read ($\overline{\text{MEMR}}$) or memory write ($\overline{\text{MEMW}}$) operation.

The $\overline{\text{RD}}$ and the $\overline{\text{WR}}$ pins 32 and 31, respectively, are active logical 0 whenever the function designated by the pin label is taking place within the system. That is, when the system is performing a memory read or an input device read, the $\overline{RD}$ signal is a logical 0. When the system is performing a memory write or an output device write operation the $\overline{WR}$ signal is a logical 0. Figure 2-29 shows the logic required to realize the 8085 system control data.

TABLE 2-3

TABLE 2-3 Logical Conditions for the Control Signal Output Pins of the 8085 Microprocessor for the System Functions Listed

#32 $\overline{RD}$	#31 $\overline{WR}$	#34 IO/$\overline{M}$		
0	1	1	IOR	System functions these four codes designate
1	0	1	IOW	
0	1	0	MEMR	
1	0	0	MEMW	

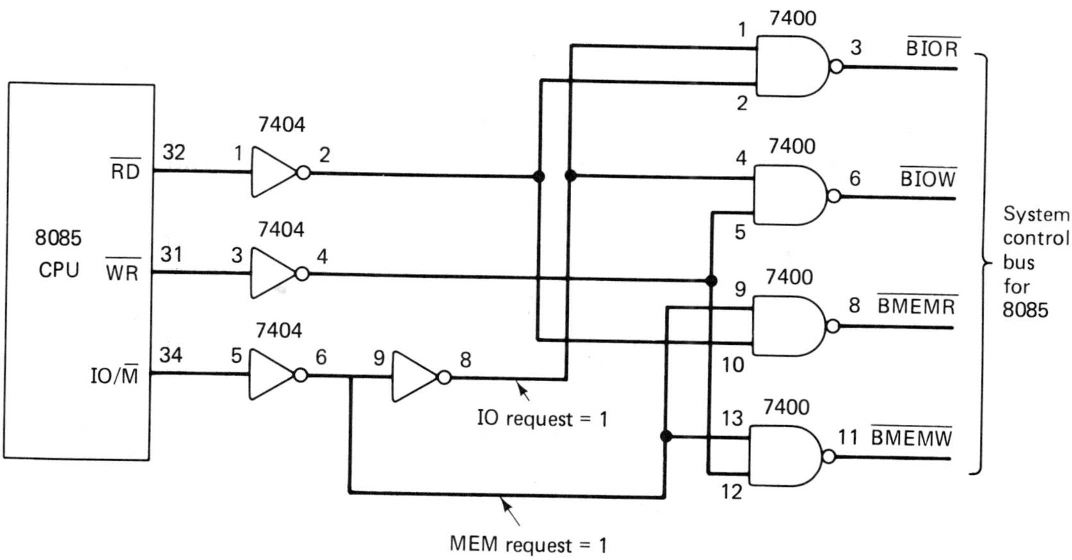

Figure 2-29 Complete schematic showing how the system control bus can be realized with discrete logic for the 8085 microprocessor.

2-18 The 6800 System Control Bus

The three microprocessors 8080, 8085, and Z80 are all designed with the functions of memory access and input/output device access being separate. These three microprocessors have special software instructions for communicating electrically with either system memory or system input and output devices. This fact made generations of the system control busses quite simple. We assumed that all three microprocessors were using standard I/O mapped I/O architecture.

The 6800 microprocessor does not have special software for electrical communication with memory or with an input or output device. The 6800 microprocessor treats memory and input/output devices in the same way. This means that the 6800 is not aware of the type of hardware that is receiving the data or that is generating the data. All system transfers are treated as memory transfers. These facts concerning the 6800 microprocessor result in only one type of input/output architecture called memory mapped input/output. To accomplish the memory mapped input/output structure with the 6800, we designate a section of memory address space for use by the input and output devices.

There are 64K (2^{16}) possible memory address spaces available with the 6800 microprocessor. We will assign part of this 64K address space for use with input and output devices. When we are assigning precise locations in the 64K possible locations where we wish to put the input and output devices, it is helpful to use a chart called a memory mapping chart. When we have gained experience in designing microprocessor systems, memory mapping can be done quite easily. However, we will cover the 6800 memory mapping in detail for the purpose of this discussion.

2-19 Memory Mapping

Memory mapping is the act of allocating the available memory space within the system for different functions. This is done with all microprocessors. Many factors influence the memory map. A few are: (1) the input/output architecture chosen (Linear Select, Memory Mapped, Standard Input/Output); (2) types of read-only memory (ROM) and random-access memory (RAM) used in the system; (3) pertinent details of the microprocessor operation. We will go through the exercise of doing a system memory map in detail when we discuss the design of a small microprocessor-controlled system.

First we must discuss some details of the 6800 microprocessor to show why certain memory space is allocated as it is. The first detail we must discuss is how the 6800 resets. When power is first applied to the 6800, the microprocessor is forced into a power-on reset mode. This action forces the 6800 to begin program execution at a specified memory location. The specific memory addresses used are FFFE and FFFF. The 6800 reads the data in these memory locations and forms a jump instruction to the address contained there. The 6800 then executes the program code located at this jump address.

For example, assume that the following data are at memory location FFFE and FFFF: FFFE = 08, FFFF = 00. After reading these, 6800 will then jump to location 0800 and start executing software code. Because the high order addresses are being used for reset we will not put our input/output memory space within the upper section of memory.

For this discussion we will assign the memory space from 0400 to 07FF for use as input and output addresses. This means we must decode this address space and generate our own I/O and memory signal. We can then combine this new signal with the R/W signal of the 6800 to form a system control bus. This concept is shown in block diagram form in Figure 2-30.

Figure 2-31 shows the complete schematic for generating the system control bus for the 6800. The selection of the address space 0400 to 07FF for input and output is certainly not a fixed location. We chose it here only to illustrate the concept.

Also shown in Figure 2-31 is a signal called VMA, which is used to form the system control bus. The VMA signal generated from the 6800 microprocessor is called a Valid Memory Address. When executing some of its software instructions, the 6800 may not always have a valid memory address on the address lines. When the VMA signal is logical 1, then the address from the 6800 address line is valid to either RAM or ROM. To avoid false writing to system memory we must use the VMA signal generated by the 6800 microprocessor to qualify all of the control signals on the control bus. That is why the VMA signal is used in the generation of the system control bus.

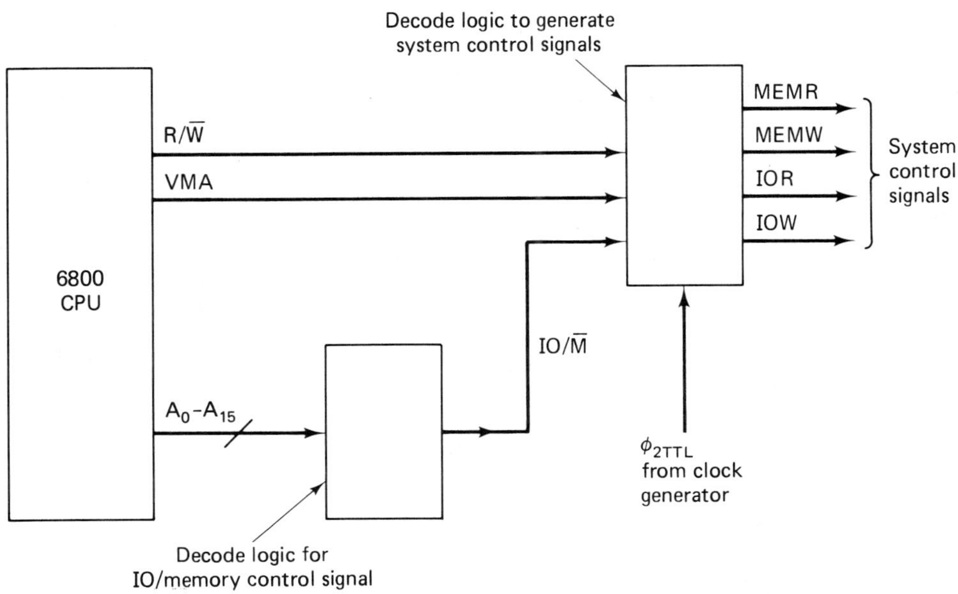

Figure 2-30 Block diagram, showing how the 6800 system must generate on IO/M signal with decoding logic. This is due to the fact that the 6800 must use memory mapped I/O architecture.

Also note the use of the phase 2 (ϕ2) clock signal in the generation of the system control bus. In timing diagrams of the 6800 microprocessor we notice that activity within the system takes place on the falling edge of the ϕ 2 clock. That is, data transfers from the 6800 to the memory on the falling edge of ϕ 2, and data transfers into the 6800 microprocessor from system memory on the falling edge of ϕ. That is why we use ϕ 2 as another qualifier for the control bus as shown in Figure 2-31. Any of the microprocessors shown can be designed to use memory mapped input and output architecture. However, the 6800 microprocessor *must* use memory-mapped architecture.

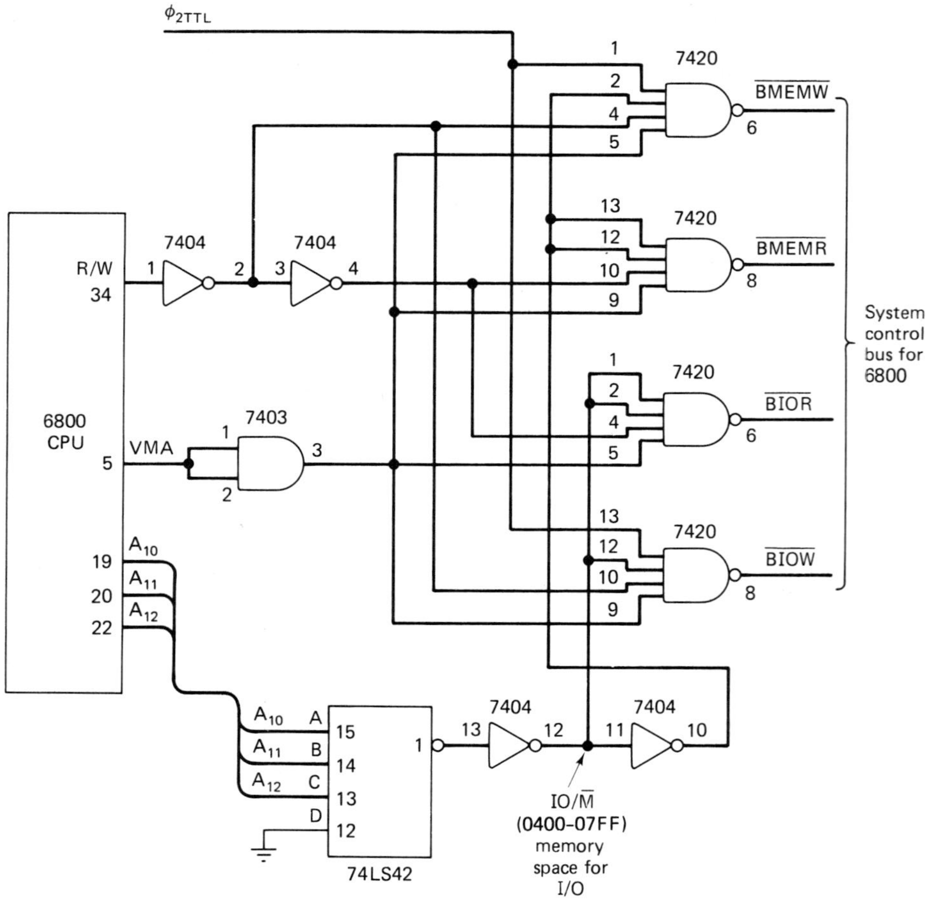

Figure 2-31 Complete schematic, showing how the system control bus can be realized by using discrete logic for the 6800 microprocessor. This schematic realizes the block diagram given in Figure 2-30.

2-20 Summary

We have shown how the 6800, the Z80, the 8085, and the 8080 microprocessors can be designed into 3-bus system architecture. We made use of the microprocessor control signals for generation of the system control bus and directing data flow on the data bus. The nice part of this is that we need not concern ourselves with the timing of the microprocessor control signals. The microprocessor itself controls the logic level and timing of the signals such as RD, WR, DBIN, and R/W.

From this discussion we can see that it is not a difficult or complex job to design 3-bus architecture with the microprocessors discussed here. We have not discussed all of the details yet, such as adding memory to the system, or how the system clocks are generated. These topics are covered in the next chapter.

As a final review of information presented in this chapter, we will show all four microprocessors realized in the 3-bus system architecture. These complete schematics are displayed in Figures 2-32(a), 2-32(b), 2-32(c), 2-32(d). In these figures notice the three busses generated: the address bus, the control bus, and the data bus. Also note the similarities in the generation of the three busses on each of the microprocessors used.

It should further be stressed that the control bus may or may not be formed in the way we have described. The formation of a control bus depends a great deal upon the type of memory and other ICs used in the system. We present the control bus in this manner only to illustrate similarities between the four common microprocessors. However, this technique for control bus formation is certainly a valid one. Further, it promotes very easy understanding of the 3-bus architecture.

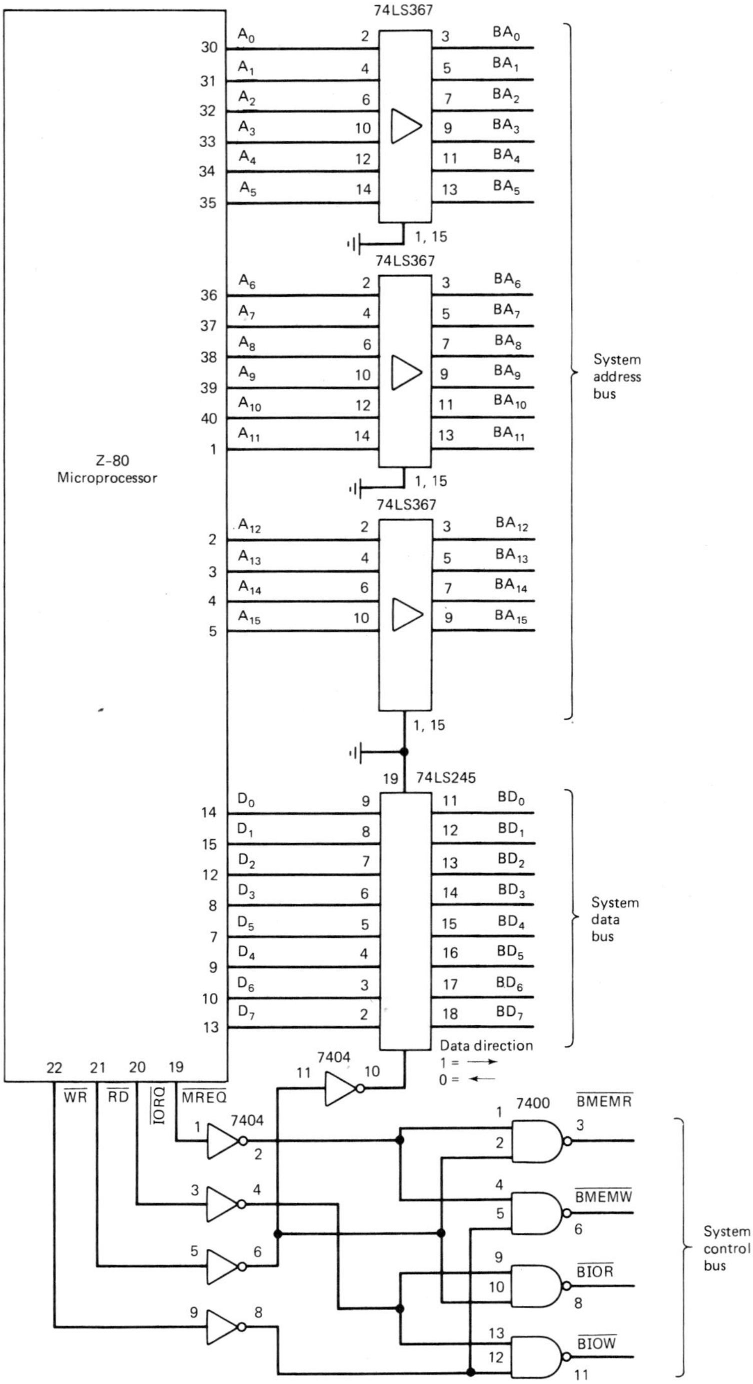

Figure 2-32(a) Schematic showing the address, data, and control busses for the Z80 microprocessor.

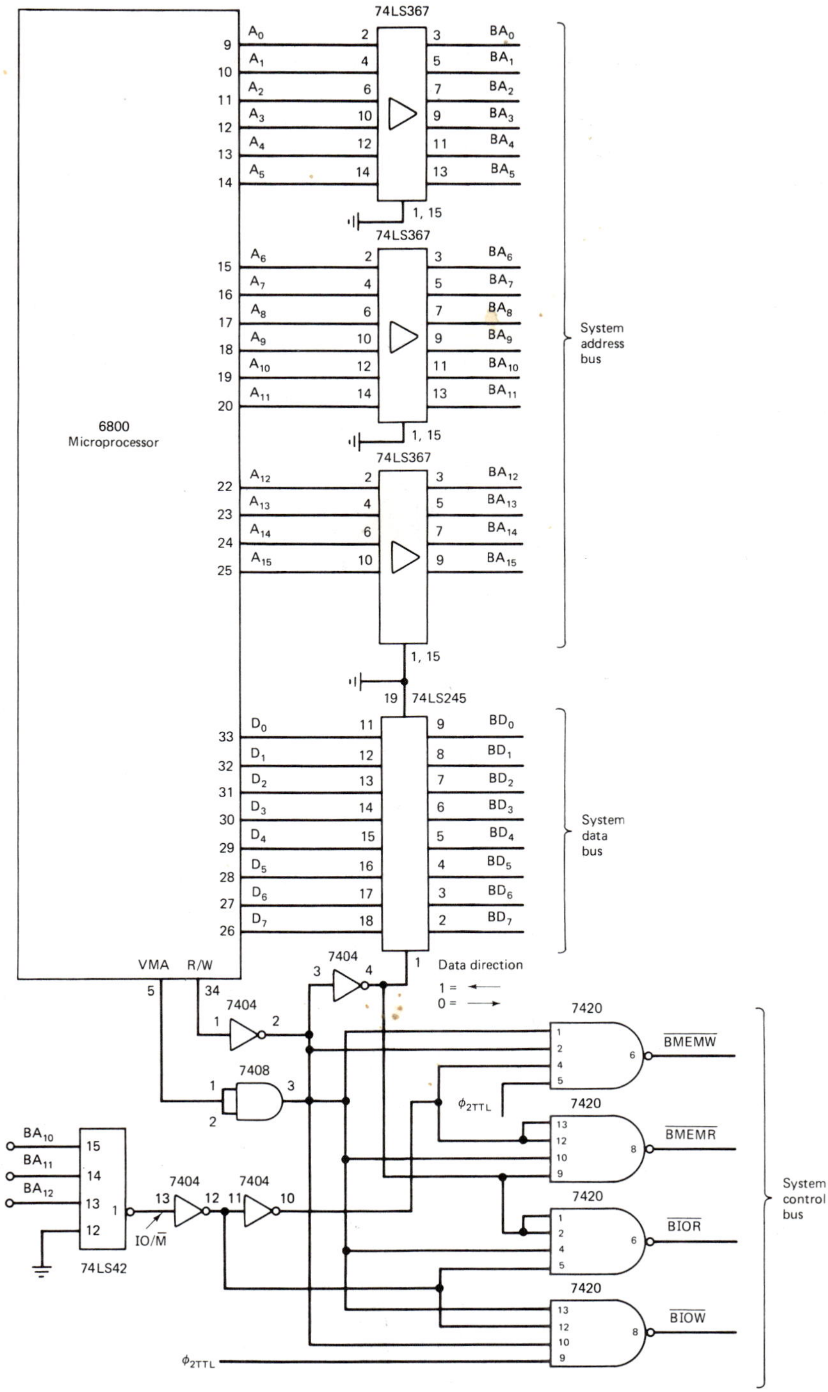

Figure 2-32(b) Schematic showing the address, data, and control busses for the 6800 microprocessor.

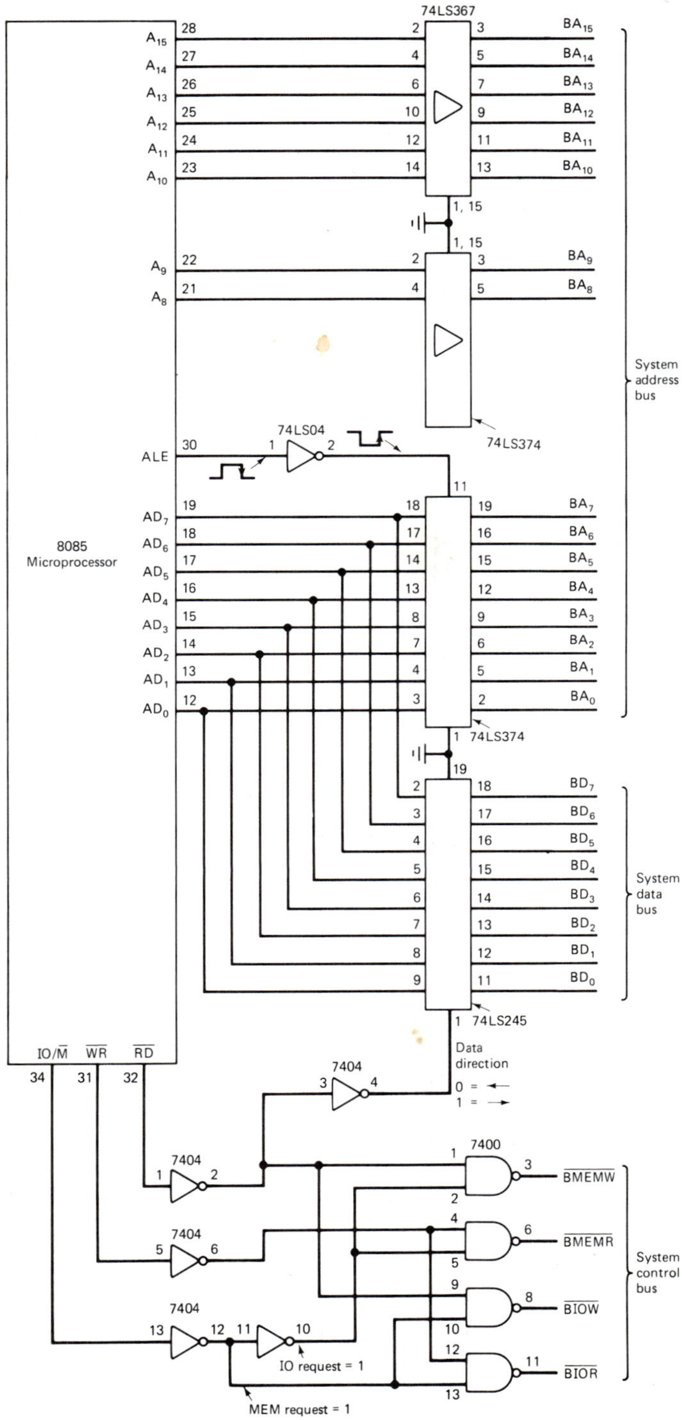

Figure 2-32(c) Complete schematic showing the data, address, and control busses for the 8085 microprocessor.

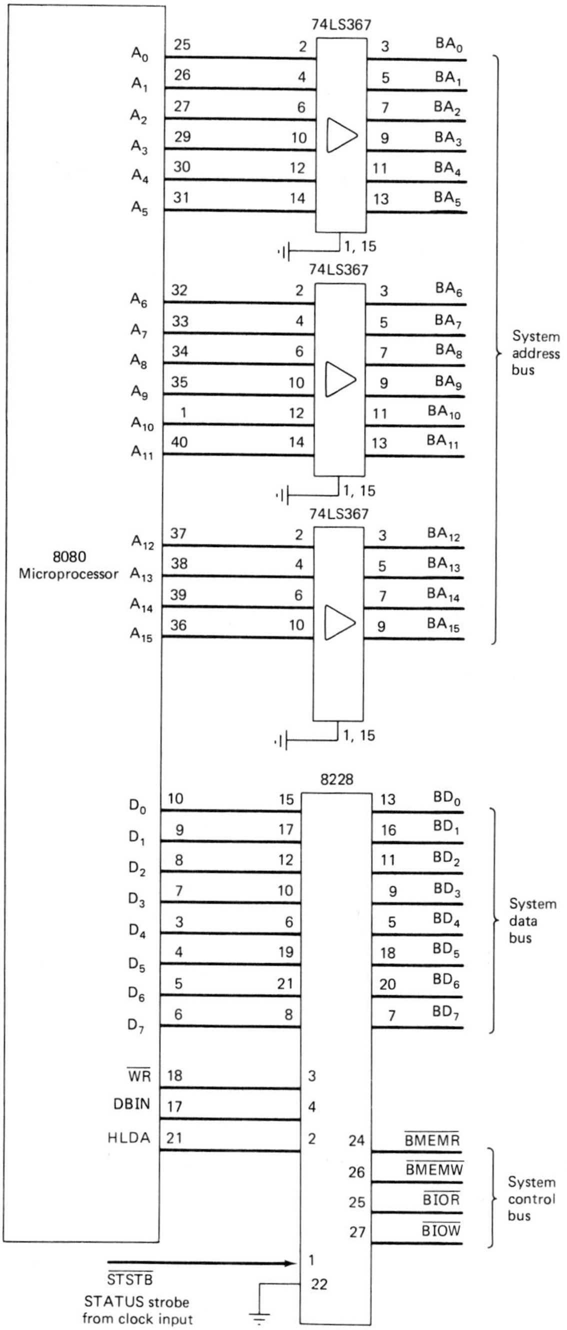

Figure 2-32(d) Complete schematic showing the data, address, and control busses for the 8080 microprocessor.

3

GENERATING SYSTEM CLOCKS AND INTERFACING SYSTEM MEMORY TO 3-BUS ARCHITECTURE

In Chapter 2 we discussed the formation of the three system busses: the address bus, the data bus, and the control bus. Each microprocessor discussed requires a system clock, and all timing of the microprocessor system will be derived from this clock. In this chapter we will discuss the generation of the system clock. That is, we will show how we can provide the system with the correct clock for the microprocessor being used.

We will also discuss the hardware aspects of adding memory to the 3-bus system architecture, including how to use different RAMs and ROMs electrically with each microprocessor. The technique of interfacing common input and output RAMs and *separate* input and output RAMs to a microprocessor system will also be shown.

3-1 The 8080 System Clocks

Let us begin by discussing the clock inputs for the 8080 microprocessor. The 8080 microprocessor requires two high-voltage (12 volts) clock inputs. These clock inputs are called phase 1 ($Ø_1$) and phase 2 ($Ø_2$). The timing relationship of the clock inputs to one another is shown in the timing diagram of Figure 3-1. This includes the specifications and limits for all appropriate clock levels.

As can be seen from the timing diagram and specifications listed in Figure 3-1, the generation of these clock wave forms is a significant hardware task. Fortunately, a special integrated circuit has been designed to provide the 8080 with properly timed and voltage limited phase 1 and phase 2 clock inputs. This device is called an 8224 clock generator. In addition to providing the 8080 with $Ø_1$ and $Ø_2$ clocks, the 8224 provides certain other functions that make its use very convenient for the 8080 microprocessor. We will discuss some of these other features of the 8224 clock generator in later chapters.

It is not worth the extra effort for a designer using an 8080-based system to design a clock generator circuit for the 8080. If we are using an 8080 as a system controller, then we should plan on using an 8224 clock generator also. Package count reduction and system reliability will most certainly be enhanced by using the 8224 device.

The block diagram and partial specification for the 8224 clock generator is shown in Figure 3-2. Basically, all that is needed to operate the 8224 device is a satisfactory DC power supply and an external crystal. The required frequency of oscillation for the external crystal is nine times greater than the t_{cy} that we

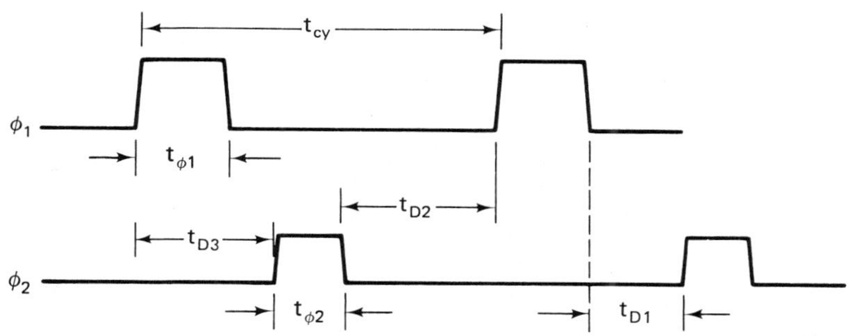

AC Characteristics

T_A = 0°C to 70°C, V_{DD} = +12 V ± 5%, V_{CC} = +5 V ± 5%, V_{BB} = −5 V ± 5%, V_{SS} = 0V, unless otherwise noted

Symbol	Parameter	Min.	Max.	Unit
t_{CY} (3)	Clock period	0.48	2.0	μ sec
t_r, t_f	Clock rise and fall time	0	50	n sec
$t_{\phi 1}$	ϕ_1 Pulse width	60		n sec
$t_{\phi 2}$	ϕ_2 Pulse width	220		n sec
t_{D1}	Delay ϕ_1 to ϕ_2	0		n sec
t_{D2}	Delay ϕ_2 to ϕ_1	70		n sec
t_{D3}	Delay ϕ_1 to ϕ_2 leading edges	80		n sec

Figure 3-1 Timing diagram of phase 1 and phase 2 clocks for the 8080. Below is the excerpted clock specification for the 8080 clocks. © Intel, 1979.

want at $Ø_1$ and $Ø_2$ clock inputs to the 8080. For example, suppose we want a t_{cy} of 1 microsecond, which corresponds to a frequency of 1 megahertz. The crystal frequency will be equal to 9 MHz, or nine times the desired t_{cy}.

Figure 3-3 shows how the 8224 device interfaces to the 8080 microprocessor. Notice the output signal from the 8224 called $\overline{\text{STSTB}}$. This is the status strobe signal we mentioned in Chapter 2 for strobing the status word into the status latches. This signal is active when status information is present on the data bus. If you are uncertain about the function of the status strobe in the system, refer to Section 2-13 in Chapter 2 dealing with the 8080 system control bus. We can see that by using an 8224 clock generator there is little difficulty in providing the correct $Ø_1$ and $Ø_2$ clock inputs to the 8080 microprocessor. It is highly recommended that this device be used for system control when designated with an 8080 microprocessor.

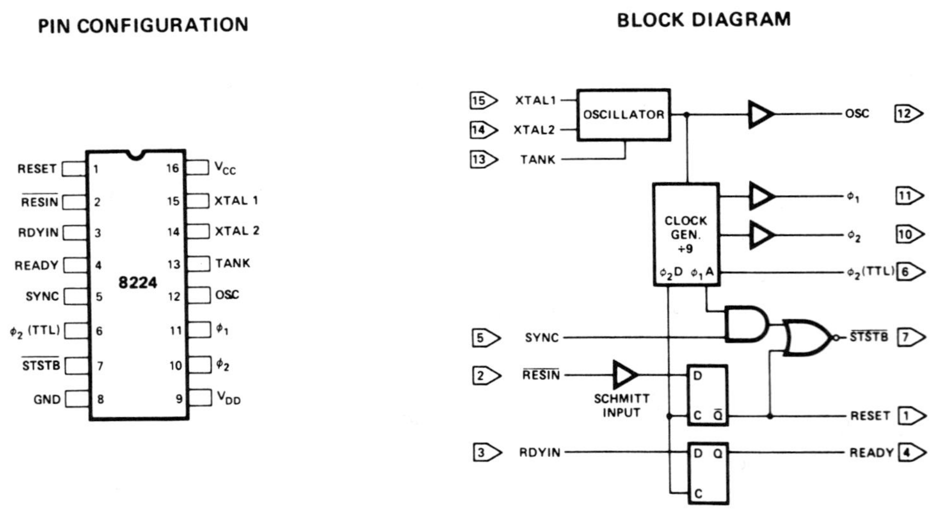

PIN NAMES

$\overline{\text{RESIN}}$	RESET INPUT
RESET	RESET OUTPUT
RDYIN	READY INPUT
READY	READY OUTPUT
SYNC	SYNC INPUT
$\overline{\text{STSTB}}$	STATUS STB (ACTIVE LOW)
φ1	8080 CLOCKS
φ2	

XTAL 1	CONNECTIONS FOR CRYSTAL
XTAL 2	
TANK	USED WITH OVERTONE XTAL
OSC	OSCILLATOR OUTPUT
φ2 (TTL)	φ2 CLK (TTL LEVEL)
V_{CC}	+5V
V_{DD}	+12V
GND	0V

Figure 3-2(a) Block diagram and pinout for the 8224 clock generator for use with the 8080 microprocessor. © Intel, 1979.

D.C. Characteristics

T_A = 0°C to 70°C; V_{CC} = +5.0V ±5%; V_{DD} = +12V ±5%.

Symbol	Parameter	Limits Min.	Limits Typ.	Limits Max.	Units	Test Conditions
I_F	Input Current Loading			-.25	mA	V_F = .45V
I_R	Input Leakage Current			10	μA	V_R = 5.25V
V_C	Input Forward Clamp Voltage			1.0	V	I_C = -5mA
V_{IL}	Input "Low" Voltage			.8	V	V_{CC} = 5.0V
V_{IH}	Input "High" Voltage	2.6 2.0			V	Reset Input All Other Inputs
V_{IH}-V_{IL}	REDIN Input Hysteresis	.25			mV	V_{CC} = 5.0V
V_{OL}	Output "Low" Voltage			.45 .45	V V	(ϕ_1,ϕ_2), Ready, Reset, $\overline{STSTB}$ I_{OL} =2.5mA All Other Outputs I_{OL} = 15mA
V_{OH}	Output "High" Voltage ϕ_1 , ϕ_2 READY, RESET All Other Outputs	 9.4 3.6 2.4			 V V V	 I_{OH} = -100μA I_{OH} = -100μA I_{OH} = -1mA
I_{SC}[1]	Output Short Circuit Current (All Low Voltage Outputs Only)	-10		-60	mA	V_O = 0V V_{CC} = 5.0V
I_{CC}	Power Supply Current			115	mA	
I_{DD}	Power Supply Current			12	mA	

Note: 1. Caution, ϕ_1 and ϕ_2 output drivers do not have short circuit protection

CRYSTAL REQUIREMENTS

Tolerance: .005% at 0°C -70°C
Resonance: Series (Fundamental)*
Load Capacitance: 20-35pF
Equivalent Resistance: 75-20 ohms
Power Dissipation (Min): 4mW

*With tank circuit use 3rd overtone mode.

Figure 3-2(b) Specifications for the 8224 clock generator.
© Intel, 1979.

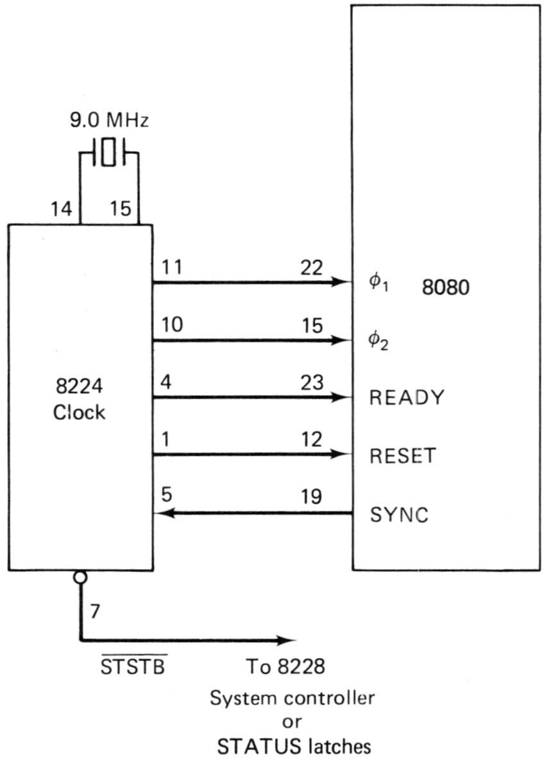

Figure 3-3 Schematic showing how the 8224 clock generator is connected to the 8080 microprocessor.

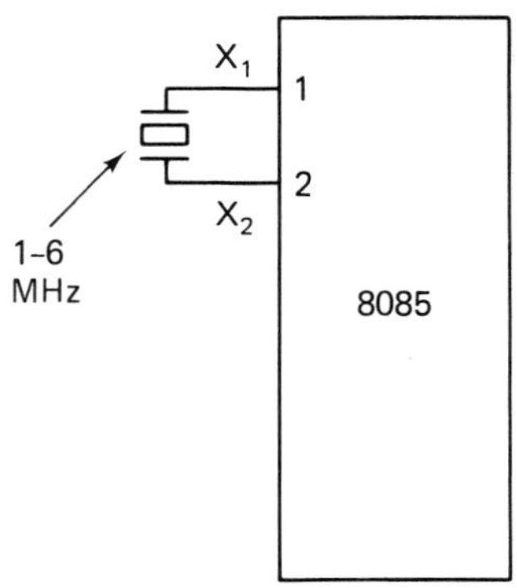

Figure 3-4 Schematic showing how the crystal is connected to the 8085 for proper operation. Note that the 8085 will operate at one-half the crystal frequency.

3-2 The 8085 System Clock

The 8085 clock generator circuit is contained entirely within the 8085 microprocessor. We simply connect a crystal between pins labeled X_1 (pin 1) and X_2 (pin 2) of the 8085 microprocessor. The crystal frequency can be any value between 1 and 6 MHz. This frequency is then divided by 2 and used as the t_{cy} of the 8085 microprocessor. Figure 3-4 shows how simple it is to provide correct timing for the 8085 microprocessor.

3-3 The Z80 System Clocks

The Z80 microprocessor requires a single clock input to function correctly. This clock input may be generated in several ways. One method of providing a free-running clock input to the Z80 microprocessor is shown in Figure 3-5. Here we see that the frequency of oscillation is set by the crystal X1. However, in order for the circuit to work, the R_1C_1 product must be greater than the period of oscillation. For example, assume that we want a frequency of 1 megahertz. This represents a period of 1×10^{-6} seconds. This means that the R_1C_1 product must be greater than 1×10^{-6}. R_1 should remain constant at approximately 330 ohms. This gives a value of C_1, which is greater than or equal to $1 \times 10^{-6}/330$ (farads). This is approximately equal to 3000 picofarads. This RC product allows enough phase shift at the frequency of oscillation for the circuit to oscillate. Specifications for the Z80 clock are given in Figure 3-6.

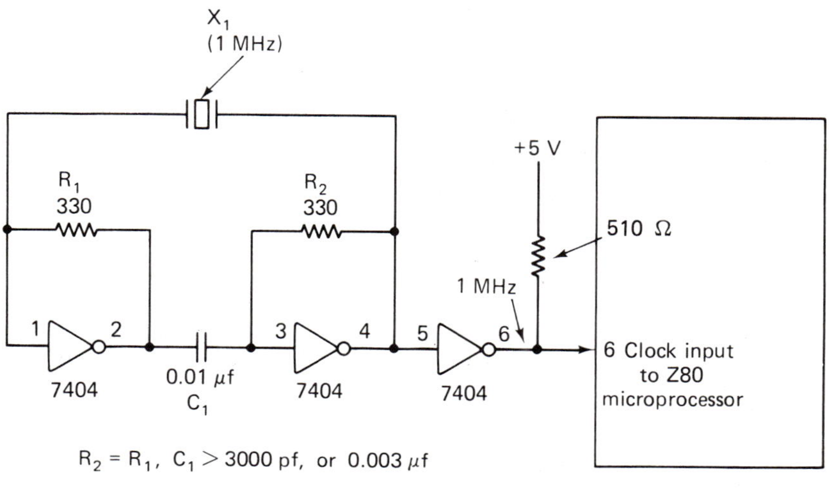

Figure 3-5 Schematic for a possible clock generator that can be used with the Z80 microprocessor. The clock output is not TTL. The 510 pull-up resistor will increase the clock output voltage level to near +5 volts. Refer to Figure 3-6 for clock specifications.

Timing measurements are made at the following voltages, unless otherwise specified:

	"1"	"0"
CLOCK	V_{cc} -.6V	.45V
OUTPUT	2.0 V	.8 V
INPUT	2.0 V	.8 V
FLOAT	Δ V	± 0.5 V

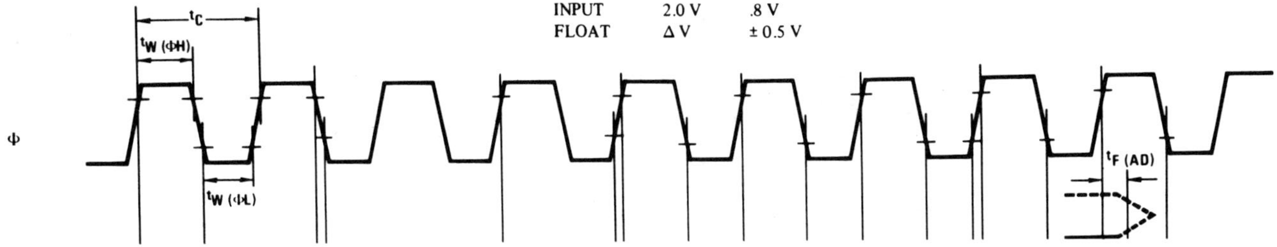

T_A = 0°C to 70°C, V_{CC} = +5V ± 5%, Unless Otherwise Noted.

Signal	Symbol	Parameter	Min	Max	Unit	Test Condition
Φ	t_c	Clock Period	.4	[12]	μsec	
	t_w (ΦH)	Clock Pulse Width, Clock High	180	[E]	nsec	
	t_w (ΦL)	Clock Pulse Width, Clock Low	180	2000	nsec	
	$t_{r,f}$	Clock Rise and Fall Time		30	nsec	

[12] $t_c = t_{w(\Phi H)} + t_{w(\Phi L)} + t_r + t_f$

Figure 3-6 Excerpted specifications for the Z80 microprocessor clock input. (Courtesy Zilog Corporation)

3-4 The 6800 System Clocks

The 6800 microprocessor, like the 8080 microprocessor, requires two non-TTL clock inputs for proper operation. These clock inputs are labeled phase 1 and phase 2. Figure 3-7 shows the clock input wave forms and partial specification for the 6800 microprocessor clock inputs. Here again, like the 8080, we see that the generation of these clock wave forms is not a trivial hardware task. Fortunately, Motorola Inc. has designed a clock module to be used in conjunction with the 6800 microprocessor. The use of this clock module, labeled 6870A or 6871A, is recommended for use with the 6800 microprocessor as a basis for the control system. This clocking device is shown in Figure 3-8.

Note also that the 6800 microprocessor uses the following edge of phase 2 clock pulses for the 6800 control bus signals. (Refer to the Chapter 2 section on the 6800 control bus if you are unclear on this point.) This means that the phase 2 clock must be input to TTL logic devices. The 6800 uses a non-TTL logic level input. Therefore, we cannot input the same Ø2 to the 6800 that we input to the TTL logic within the system, because the voltage levels of the two clocks must be different. However, the 6870A and 6871A clock modules provide a special TTL level for the Ø2 clock output that is buffered and used for TTL devices within the 6800 microprocessor system.

3-5 System Clock Summary

For proper operation of the microprocessors we have presented, except the 8085, we are required to input at least one phase, and for the 8080 and 6800 microprocessors we need two phases of clock inputs. These clock inputs are free running. And, regardless of the state of the microprocessor, the proper clock input to the microprocessor must be present. A simple and wise thing to do when troubleshooting a microprocessor control system is first to insure that all power supply levels are valid, and then make certain that all input clocks are timed correctly and are valid at the correct voltage level. The microprocessor will have no chance to operate correctly if the system clocks are not valid. Checking the system clocks should be one of the first things we do when troubleshooting a microprocessor controlled system.

3-6 Interfacing Memory to 3-Bus Architecture

In this section we will discuss how we can interface ROM and RAM to a microprocessor system. We will assume a 3-bus system architecture throughout. The first topic we will examine will be the generation of memory enable lines or

Frequency of Operation	f	0.1	—	1.0	MHz
Clock Timing (Figure 1) Cycle Time	t_{cyc}	1.0	—	10	μs
Clock Pulse Width (Measured at $V_{CC} - 0.3$ V) $\phi 1$ $\phi 2$	$PW_{\phi H}$	430 450	— —	4500 4500	ns
Total $\phi 1$ and $\phi 2$ Up Time	t_{ut}	940	—	—	ns
Rise and Fall Times $\phi 1, \phi 2$ (Measured between $V_{SS} + 0.3$ V and $V_{CC} - 0.3$ V)	$t_{\phi r}$, $t_{\phi f}$	5.0	—	50	ns
Delay Time or Clock Separation (Measured at $V_{OV} = V_{SS} + 0.5$ V)	t_d	0	—	9100	ns
Overshoot Duration	t_{OS}	0	—	40	ns

*Except $\overline{IRQ}$ and $\overline{NMI}$, which require 3 kΩ pullup load resistors for wire-OR capability at optimum operation.

#Capacitances are periodically sampled rather than 100% tested.

FIGURE 7 — MICROPROCESSOR $\phi 1$ AND $\phi 2$ CLOCKS

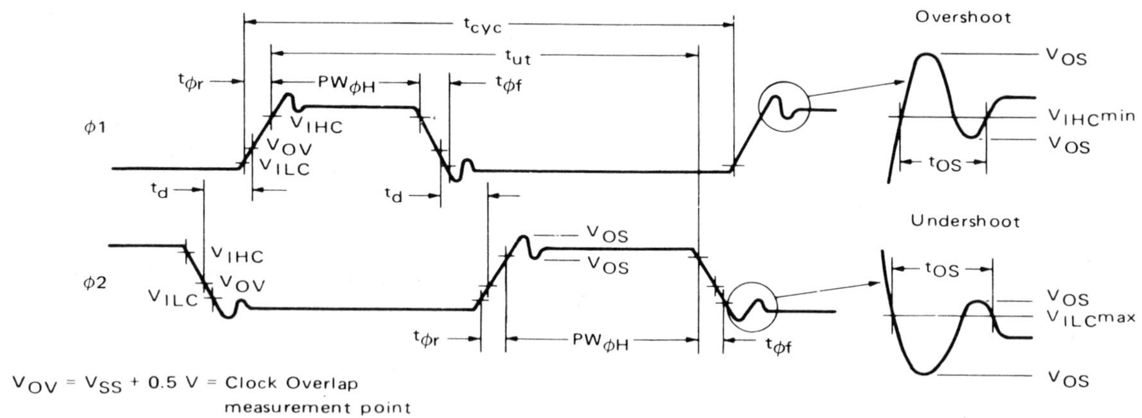

Figure 3-7 Excerpted specifications for the clock input for the 6800 microprocessor. (Courtesy Motorola Semiconductor Products, Inc.)

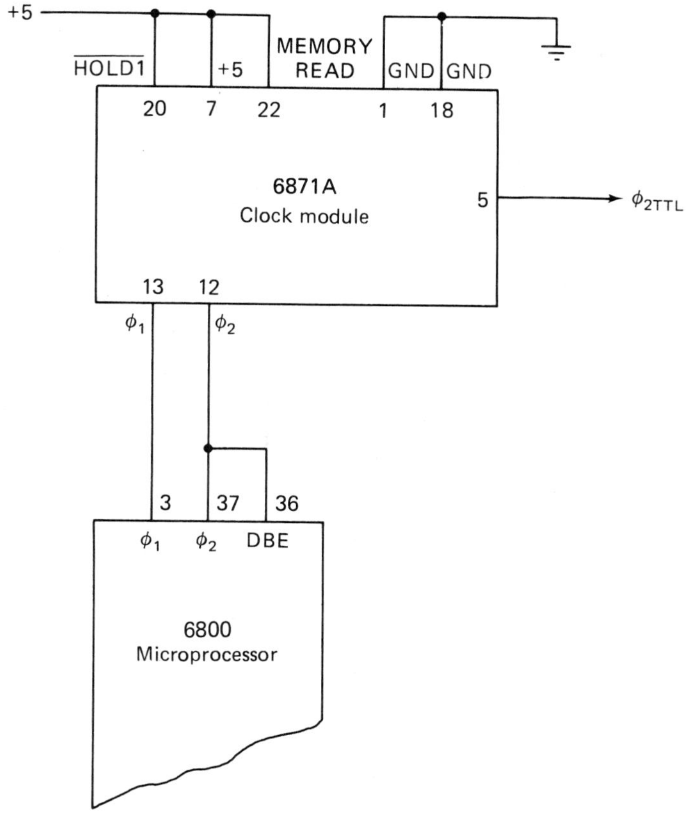

Figure 3-8 Schematic showing how the 6871A clock generator is connected for use with the 6800 microprocessor.

memory select lines. We will then show how to interface a typical ROM and some typical RAMs to a microprocessor system. The ROM we have chosen is a 2708, and the RAMs are a 2102 and a 2114. We have selected these memory devices for interfacing because they are in wide general use today. If we understand how these types of devices interface to a microprocessor control system, then understanding how to use other similar devices will be fairly straightforward.

After deciding which memory devices will be used in the system, a memory map must be drawn. We mentioned the memory map earlier when discussing the 6800 microprocessor in Chapter 2. Now we will discuss in detail what is meant by a memory map. The *memory map* is the assignment of physically available memory space for specific functions. For example, we may use memory addresses 0000-03FF for system ROM. We could use memory addresses 0400-07FF for system RAM. There are factors that influence the formation of the memory map such as the type of input and output architecture and also the type of devices used for RAM and ROM in a particular system. For this discussion we will assume that we are not using memory mapped input/output architecture.

We have decided to use the 2708 as our system ROM and the 2102 as our system RAM. Our system memory map is shown in Figure 3-9.

In Figure 3-9 we see that we have partitioned the available memory space 0000-FFFF into 1K blocks of RAM and ROM. We used 1K blocks because our memories were organized physically as 1K × 8 ROMs and 1K × 1 RAM. We will put 8 RAMs in parallel to get a 1K by 8 RAM. This will be shown later in this chapter.

If we had used 2716s as our system ROM, the ROM memory blocks would have been 2K partitions. This is because the 2716 is a 2K × 8 Erasable Programmable Read Only Memory (EPROM). As we can see, the memory map is used as a guide to allow us to visualize how the available memory space is used by the microprocessor system.

We have reserved a total of 4096 bytes, or 4K, of memory for system ROM. We need not use all of the space. However, if we had reserved too little space and needed more, it would be a major effort and not much fun to reorganize the memory map after the system was in use. So if memory space permits, be liberal in your allotment of memory for different functions. That is, always give yourself room for expansion.

0000	–	03FF	ROM_1
0400	–	07FF	ROM_2
0800	–	0BFF	ROM_3
0C00	–	0FFF	ROM_4
1000	–	13FF	RAM
1400	–	FFFF	NOT USED

Figure 3-9 Memory map of the system under discussion.

3-7 System ROM

Now let us show how the microprocessor communicates electrically with the system ROM. From the memory map, we know that when the microprocessor issues an address on the address bus between 0000–03FF, the ROM labeled ROM_0 will be exclusively enabled to communicate with the microprocessor. This same type of reasoning must be applied to ROMs labeled ROM_1, ROM_2, ROM_3. From this we conclude that somehow a unique selection process must take place within the address scheme of the system. What we do is use the address lines labeled BA_{10}–BA_{13} to provide a unique select code or memory enable signal to an individual memory or set of memories. For example, if the microprocessor were communicating with ROM_2, the binary condition of address lines BA_{10}–BA_{13}

would be 1000, respectively. Figure 3-10 shows the binary condition of address lines BA_{10}–BA_{13} for several specific address limits.

Using Figure 3-10, we can design combinational logic circuits that will provide an active signal when the memory address is within certain limits. That is, when the memory address is within a 1K partition of one of the memory functions, then a line will indicate this to the system.

BA_{13}	BA_{12}	BA_{11}	BA_{10}	MEMORY Space	
0	0	0	0	0000 – 03FF	ROM_0
0	0	0	1	0400 – 07FF	ROM_1
0	0	1	0	0800 – 0BFF	ROM_2
0	0	1	1	0C00 – 0FFF	ROM_3
0	1	0	0	1000 – 13FF	RAM

Figure 3-10 Binary values of selected address outputs for the memory space shown.

Fortunately, this is a classic problem and simple solutions have been devised. One easy method is to use an MSI, TTL device known as a *decoder*. An example of a decoder is a 7442 BCD binary to decimal decoder.*

Figure 3-11 shows how a 7442 BCD can be used to provide memory select decoding in the microprocessor control system. Manufacturers of semiconductor

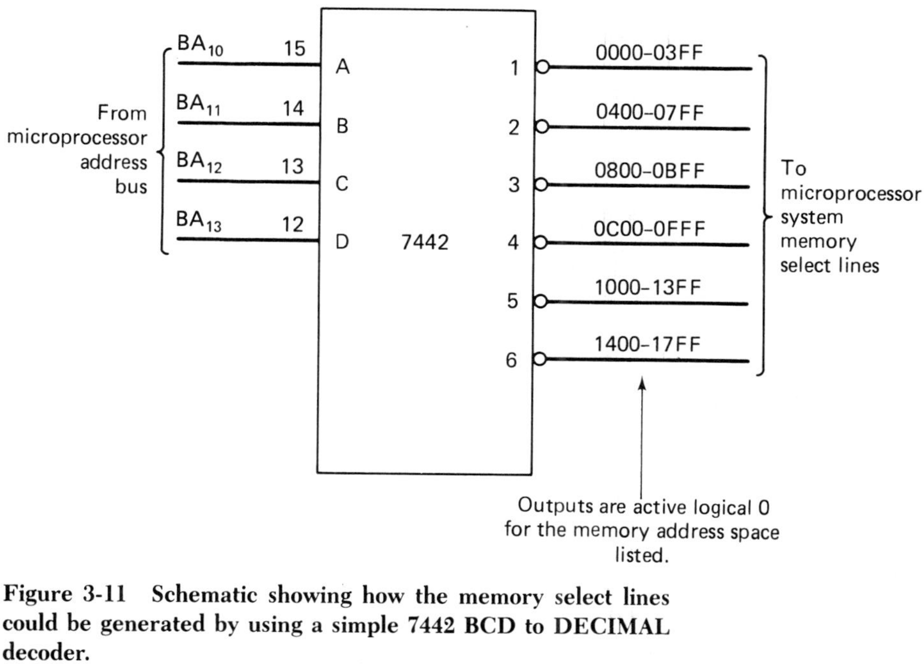

Figure 3-11 Schematic showing how the memory select lines could be generated by using a simple 7442 BCD to DECIMAL decoder.

*James W. Coffron, *Getting Started in Digital Troubleshooting*. Reston Publishing Co., 1979.

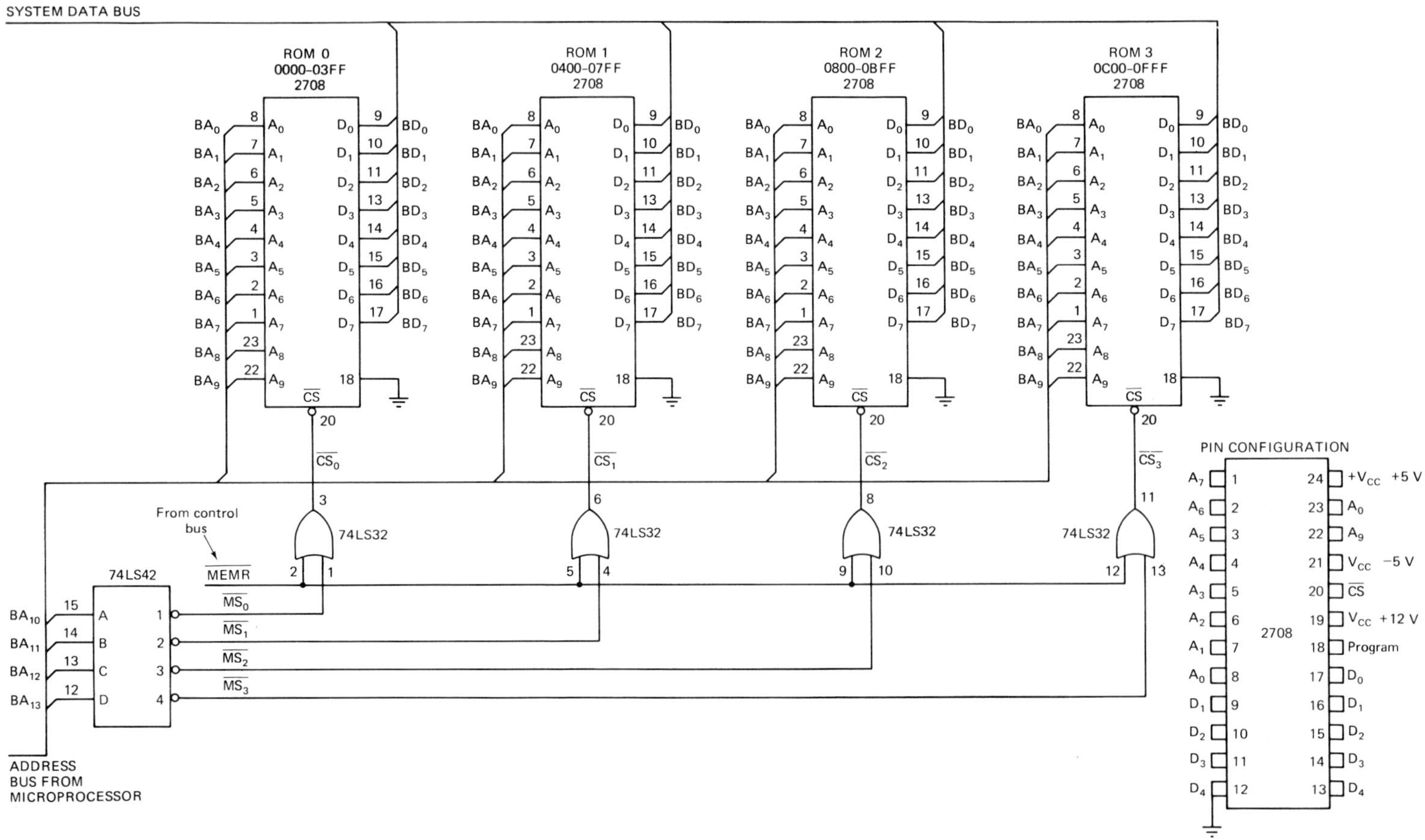

Figure 3-12 Schematic showing how the address, data, and control busses are used to interface to four 2708 EPROMs. The total ROM space is 4096 × 8.

memories often design their own digital decoders for use with specific memories. Intel Corp., for example, offers a one-of-eight decoder called an 8205 digital decoder. This device may be used to generate different memory select lines.

We will now show how to use the memory select lines and the memory address bus, data bus, and control bus to communicate electrically between the microprocessor and the system ROM. The schematic diagram of the ROM_0–ROM_3 interface to the busses is shown in Figure 3-12. The following discussion explains how the system of Figure 3-12 operates.

Notice in Figure 3-12 that the system address lines BA_0–BA_9 are connected to the respective address pins A_0–A_9 on the four 2708 EPROMs. Pins that are connected in this fashion are said to be "daisy chained." We also note in Figure 3-12 that all data out pins on the four ROMs are "daisy chained" to the respective lines on the buffered data bus pins.

Because the data output pins on the ROMs are daisy chained, if the output of more than one ROM were enabled onto the data bus at the same time a disaster would result. This type of problem is known as a "data bus conflict." A *data bus conflict* exists when more than one set of outputs tries to gain control over the data bus line at any given time. In effect, two outputs of different active devices are being shorted together. This is never a valid condition within a system.

To prevent data bus conflicts between the four ROMs, the system enables only one ROM at any given moment. This is the function of the memory select lines discussed previously. The memory select lines are active in the logical 0 state for this particular system. However, this is not always the case, but differs from system to system.

The memory select lines are labeled MS_0–MS_3. These memory select line outputs are inputs to the two input OR gates 74LS32 shown in Figure 3-12. When the control bus signal MEMR is active logical 0, then the outputs of the OR gate that have the memory select line input at a logical 0 state will generate a logical 0 output.

The logical 0 at the output of the OR gate then provides a valid CS or chip select input to the selected ROM. When the CS input signal to the ROM is logical 0, the outputs of the ROM are active and will control the data bus. The outputs of the other ROMs that have their CS signal inputs at logical 1 level (nonactive) are in a tri-state mode. When an output is in a tri-state mode it will not interfere electrically with any other output connected to it.

By using the chip select pin on a memory device we are able to connect memory device outputs in a daisy chain fashion. For example, let us propose that the microprocessor system were performing a memory read operation from memory address 0409_{16}. The address bus would be decoded as selecting ROM_1. The MS_1 select line, pin 2 of the 74LS42 device in Figure 3-12 would be an active logical 0. This would set a logical 0 at pin 4 of the 74LS32. The OR gate with pin 4 as an input is the only OR gate, out of the four, with a logical 0 at this input. This OR gate is now the only one that has a chance of being enabled.

We use the phrase "has a chance of being enabled" because the control bus must generate the proper control signals for this to occur. The control bus must generate a memory read control signal for the proper OR gate to be totally enabled. At the proper time after the memory has had time to access data, the microprocessor will generate the memory read control signal on the system control bus. The CS input to ROM $_1$, pin 20, of the 2708 will be in active logical 0 at this time. When this action occurs within the system the data outputs of ROM $_1$ are enabled onto the data bus via the internal logic of the 2708 EPROM.

When the microprocessor has had adequate time to input the data from the 2708 ROM$_1$, it will force the control bus to "un-assert," to go to logical 1 on the memory read control bus signal. This same activity occurs over and over every time the microprocessor reads data from the system ROMs. When we contemplate this occurrence of reading data from the ROMs in the fashion shown, some striking realities begin to make themselves visible. Let us review. Because the microprocessor itself controls the timing of generating address and generating control signals, we do not have to deal with the problem of generating all timing pulses. The biggest problem we have when using the 3-bus architecture is insuring that all decoding circuits are operating correctly.

Our combinatorial logic for decoding signals generated by the microprocessor should prevent any bus conflicts from occurring. It is true that we may have the problem of interfacing the microprocessor to a memory that is slower in accessing data than the time allotted by the microprocessor. We can solve this problem. However, in a majority of the cases we will be using ROMs that are far quicker in accessing data than the time alloted by the microprocessor. If this is the case, our design problem becomes a simple static combinatorial logic decoding problem. In Chapter 6 we discuss how to interface the four microprocessors to memories that require more than the allotted time given for accessing data.

When we become familiar with interfacing ROMs to a microprocessor control system, certain personal favorite techniques for solving the decoding problems will be developed. We will then be able to do simple microprocessor system designs more rapidly and with greater confidence, simply because we are using a tried and proven technique. Do not think that the decoding techniques given in this text are the final answer. The techniques presented here are calculated to promote conceptual understanding. These techniques *do* work. However, if we are willing to give some thought to the problem, other clever techniques may be developed to reduce system package count even further.

3-8 Interfacing to System RAM

Microprocessor systems use some amount of random access memory (RAM) in the execution of system functions. The system RAM is used for temporary storage of data and temporary storage of return address when the microprocessor is using subroutines in the execution of the software. In the following discussion we will show the techniques for interfacing three common types of static RAMs to a 3-bus system microprocessor architecture.

Two categories of static RAMs are called separate input and output, and common input and output. The separate I/O RAM has one device pin for inputting and one for outputting data. The common I/O RAM uses the same pin for inputting and outputting data. We will first discuss interfacing the microprocessor to separate I/O memories. Then we will discuss interfacing to common I/O memories.

The concept of interfacing a RAM to the 3-bus system architecture is described in the following manner. First, we remind ourselves that the microprocessor must be electrically able to write data to memory and electrically able to read data from memory. The data that is written into the memory is placed on the system data bus *by the microprocessor*. The data that is read from the memory is placed on the system data bus *by the RAM*.

This means that the data bus must have an electrical path for both the data input to the RAM and for the data output from the RAM. This is shown in Figure 3-13. During a write cycle to the memory, the RAM data inputs are connected to the data bus, and during a write cycle from the memory, the RAM data

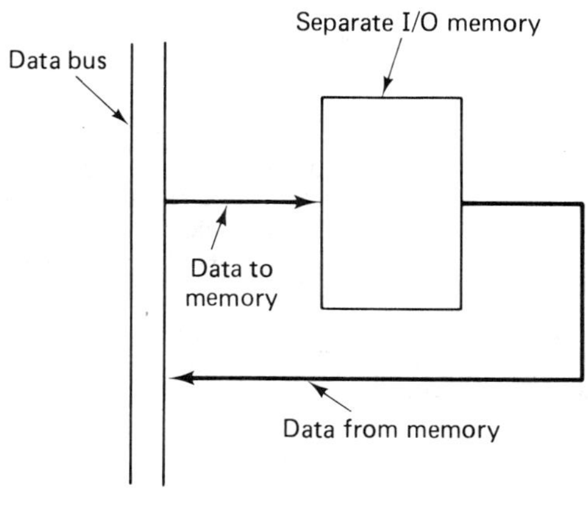

Figure 3-13 Block diagram showing that the data bus must supply the data in for the memory, and that the data bus must accept the data out from the memory.

outputs are connected to the system data bus. The reason we are stressing this fact is that if an improper path for data is enabled, we may have a possible bus conflict situation. This can happen because the RAM outputs will be connected to the data bus, with the possibility of control, and the microprocessor may have a conflict when it wishes to write data to the RAM data inputs. This is shown in conceptual form in the block diagram of Figure 3-14.

When using separate I/O memories the following technique may be used to prevent possible bus conflicts from occurring. Note, however, that this technique may not always be required on separate I/O memory devices. Some memory devices have already been designed with internal circuitry to handle the problem of interfacing separate I/O devices to a 3-bus system architecture. If we understand how to interface a 2102 separate I/O RAM to a 3-bus system architecture, then the interfacing of other separate I/O memory devices will be an easy matter.

On memory devices such as the 2102, we must disconnect the RAM outputs from the system data bus when we are writing data to the memory. To do this we will use a device called a tri-state buffer. The memory outputs are connected to the tri-state buffer inputs, the tri-state buffer outputs are then connected to the system data bus. This is shown in block diagram of Figure 3-15.

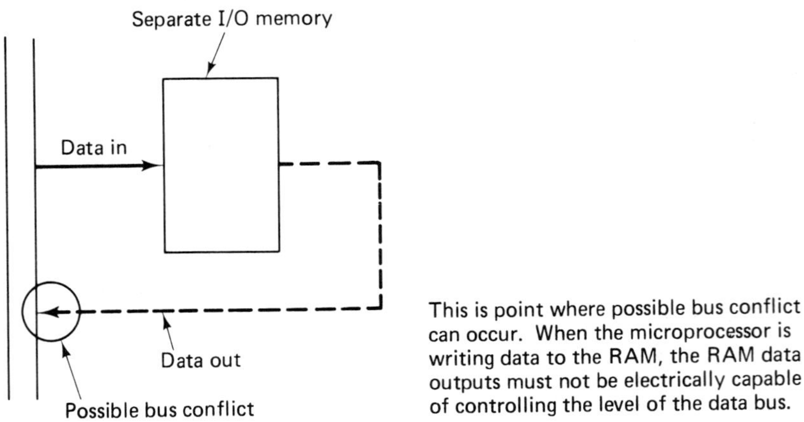

Figure 3-14 Block diagram showing how a possible bus conflict can occur when interfacing the microprocessor to a RAM memory.

The tri-state buffers that we are using for this discussion are 74LS367. Referring to Figure 3-16, the 74LS367 is disabled (in the tri-state mode) when pin 1 and pin 15 are in a logical 1 state. When the system microprocessor is writing data to the 2102 RAM, the enable pins 1 and 15 of the 74LS367 tri-state buffers is in logical 1 state. It is the job of the external hardware to insure that these pins are logical 1 whenever the microprocessor is writing data to the 2102 memory.

During the write operation, the microprocessor will place data on the system data bus. Then the microprocessor will assert the memory write enable line via the system control bus. During this entire operation the output of the 2102 is disabled or not connected to the system data bus via the tri-state buffers. The important point to note is that to eliminate the possibility of a bus conflict we must insert into the system a device that will electrically isolate the RAM output from the system data bus during a write operation to memory. The device we chose for doing this was the 74LS367 tri-state buffer. However, this is not the only device that may be used. We may choose any device that is capable of performing this same function. Again, we stress the fact that some semiconductor memories that use separate I/O have the buffering circuitry internal to the memory device for isolating its output pin from the system data bus during a memory write operation. For these types of memories all that is required is to connect the device output pin to the device input pin and then connect these two pins to the system data bus.

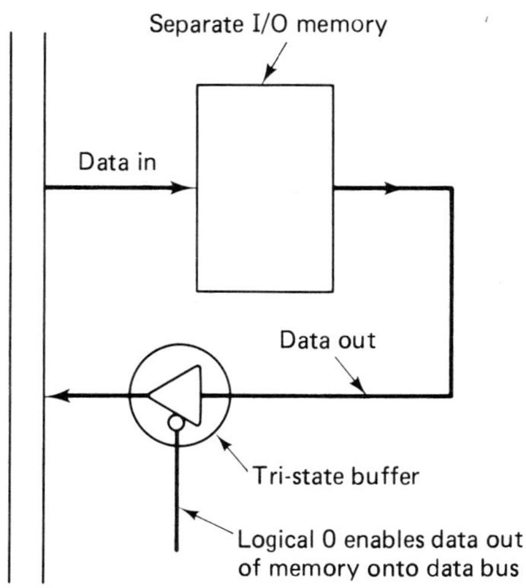

Figure 3-15 The tri-state buffers are inserted in series with the RAM data output. When the data bus is controlled by the microprocessor (write data to RAM), the RAM data outputs are effectively disconnected from the system data bus. This eliminates the possibility of a bus conflict.

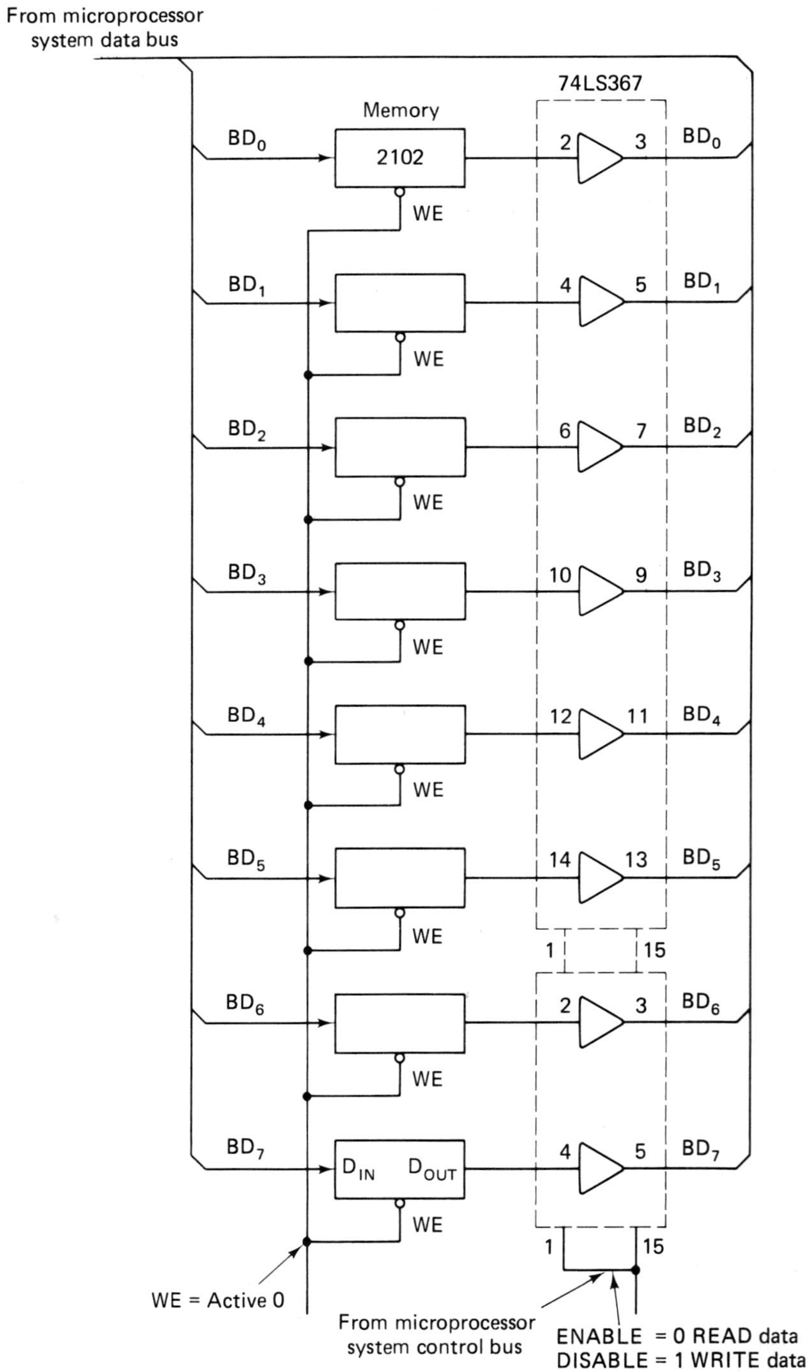

Figure 3-16 Partial schematic showing how the outputs of the 2102 RAMs are disconnected by using the 74LS367 device.

3-9 Reading Data from System RAM

When the system wishes to electrically read data from the RAM, the output of the RAM must control the system data bus. The microprocessor data lines will be in an input mode. The data input pin of the RAM will not affect or control the data on the data bus. The data input pin does not affect the data on the data bus because the input pin is meant to be driven by some other source. In this mode we treat the RAM just like the ROM we discussed earlier.

The memory select line and the system control bus line are combined to form a chip select signal to the system RAM. This is shown in Figure 3-17. During the RAM read operation the write enable input line to the 2102 pin 3 is a logical 1. When the 2102 has been selected by the address bus and the system control bus asserts the memory read line, the 74LS367 tri-state buffers are enabled via pin 15 and pin 1. When the tri-state buffers are enabled, the data output from the 2102 is electrically placed on the data bus. At this point the 2102 output pin is in control of the data bus line to which it is connected. After the microprocessor has input the data from the 2102 RAM, the memory read line from the system control bus is then unasserted. When the memory read line is unasserted the 74LS367 tri-state buffers will be put into the tri-state mode. This action will electrically remove the data on the 2102 RAM from the data bus. We see from this discussion that reading data from the RAM is no different from the operation of reading data from the system ROM.

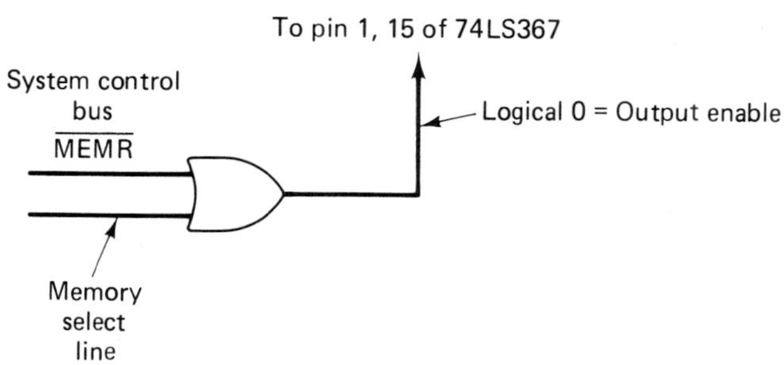

Figure 3-17 Schematic showing how the data outputs of the 2102 RAMs are enabled by the signal connected to pins 1 and 15 of the 74LS367 devices.

3-10 Writing Data to the System RAM

Let us now discuss the overall system operation of writing data to the memory. To write data to the 2102 device we must:

1. apply the correct memory address,

2. apply the correct data to the data input lines of the RAM,
3. assert the right enable input line to the memory by going from high to low.

Now, the address will be applied via the address bus of the microprocessor system; the memory select line will become asserted via the address bus; the data bus will be controlled by the microprocessor. This is how data is made ready to input to the memory.

At this point the RAM has not been enabled. That is, the chip select line has not become asserted. However, we must enable the memory in order to write data to it. But when we enable the memory we also enable the output of the memory. This is the action that could cause a conflict between the microprocessor output data to be written to RAM and the data output of the RAM. It is to prevent this possible conflict that we have inserted the 74LS367 tri-state device between the memory output lines and the system data bus. Now, when we apply the write enable pulse and enable the memory, the output of the memory is disabled by the 74LS367 from conflicting with the input data to the system RAM provided by the microprocessor. This sequence is shown in the timing diagram of Figure 3-18.

It is clear that we must enable the RAM whether we are reading *or* writing data to it. But the write enable line for memory is asserted only when we are writing data to the RAM. The logic for performing this particular operation is shown in Figure 3-19.

We have discussed how a single memory device may be written to and read from in a 3-bus system architecture. The microprocessors we are examining in this text use an 8-bit data bus. This means we must read and write 8 bits at a time. Since we are using a memory that has a single input line and a single output line, we must write to eight individual RAMs and read from eight individual RAMs at the same time. This is achieved by treating all control functions of the RAMs, that is, address, write enable, and chip select, as a single unit. We daisy-chained all control pins of the eight individual RAMs. We then connected the data input to the individual data lines. The data output from the RAM will go through a 74LS367 tri-state buffer. The output of the 74LS367 will then be connected to the data input of that same RAM. We have effectively constructed a single memory organized as a 1K × 8 static RAM. This memory system is shown in Figure 3-20.

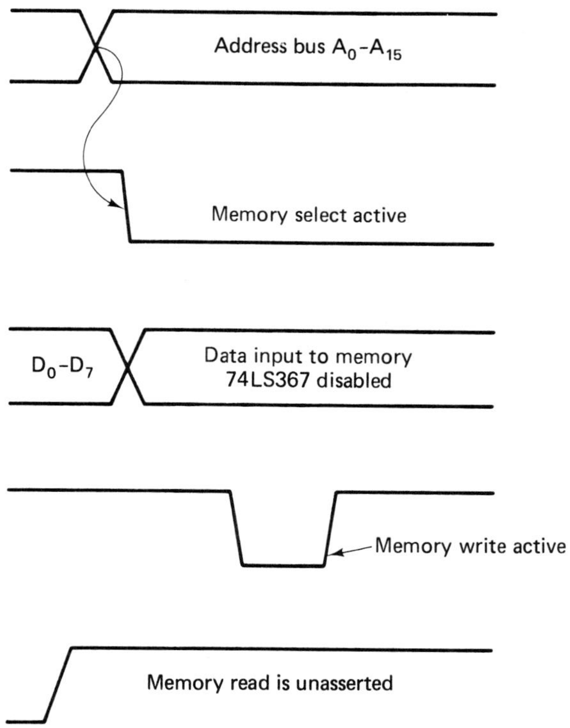

Figure 3-18 Logical state of system signals during a memory write operation.

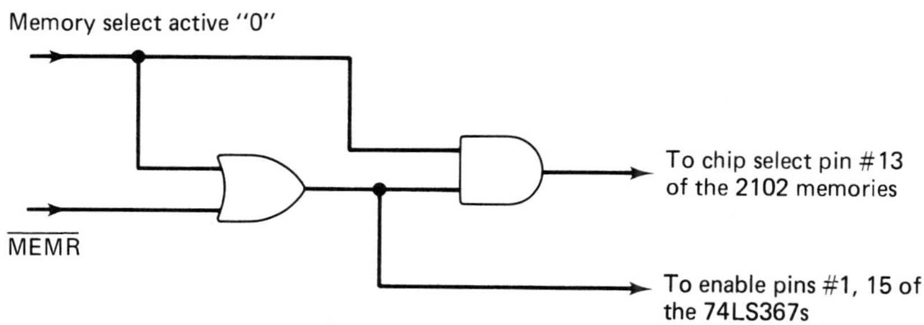

Figure 3-19 Schematic showing how RAM control signals are generated by using the system control bus and memory select lines.

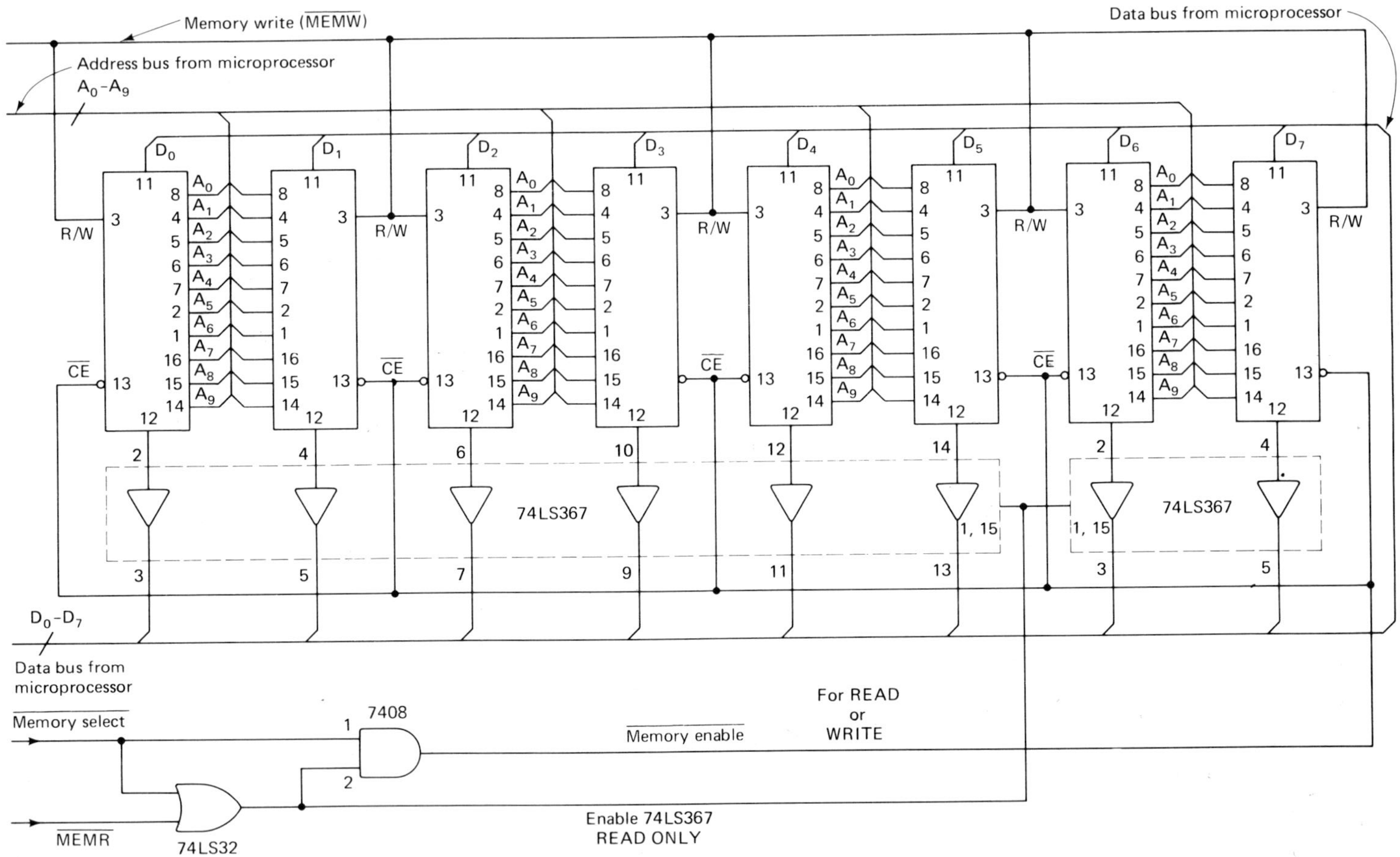

Figure 3-20 Complete schematic showing how a 1024 × 8-bit memory is designed by using eight 2102 memory chips.

3-11 Interfacing to Common I/O RAMs

Interfacing to common I/O RAMs is very similar to the technique we discussed for interfacing to the separate I/O 2102 RAM. However, in the common I/O RAMs there is to the memory a single input pin that represents data input and data output. This will not cause confusion within the memory chip because we realize that the memory can either be having data read from it or be having data written into it, but can never be performing these two functions at the same instant in time. The common I/O RAM we have chosen to discuss is the 2114 1K × 4 static RAM. When we are writing data to the 2114 RAM the I/O pins represent data inputs. During this time, the data output of the 2114 RAM will be disabled via the internal RAM circuitry. Figure 3-21 shows a partial data sheet for the 2114 RAM.

PIN CONFIGURATION

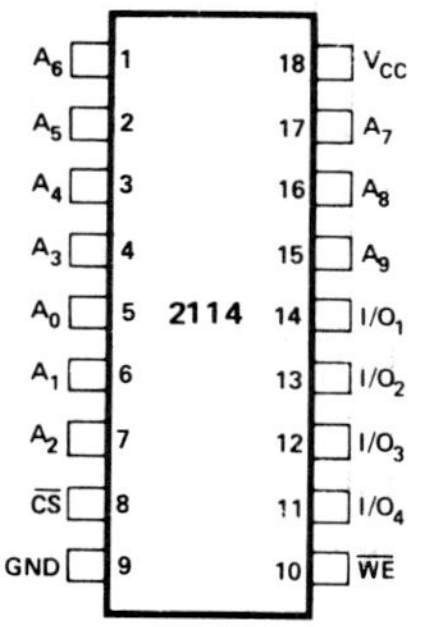

PIN NAMES

A_0–A_9	ADDRESS INPUTS	V_{CC} POWER (+5V)
$\overline{WE}$	WRITE ENABLE	GND GROUND
$\overline{CS}$	CHIP SELECT	
I/O_1–I/O_4	DATA INPUT/OUTPUT	

LOGIC SYMBOL

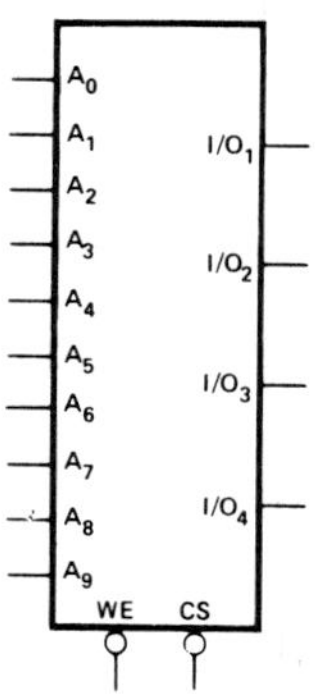

BLOCK DIAGRAM

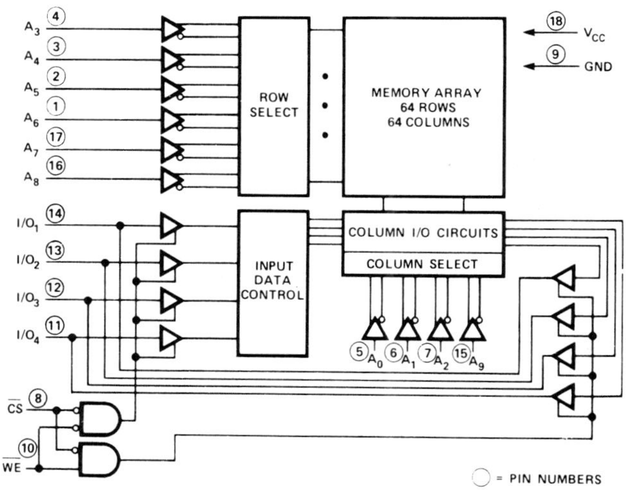

Figure 3-21 Partial data sheet for the 2114, 1024 × 4 static RAM. © Intel, 1979.

When the microprocessor applies data to the I/O input pins the RAM chip must be selected in order to accept it. To insure that the internal memory output lines do not conflict with the microprocessor data being input to the RAM when the write enable line to the 2114 goes to a logical 0, the internal outputs of the RAM are disabled via internal circuitry. That is, they are put into a tri-state mode that prevents them from causing any bus conflict. This means that we must take both the write enable and the chip select lines to the 2114 to a logical 0 at the same time when performing a memory write operation to a 2114 device. This is shown in the timing diagram of Figure 3-22.

When we are reading data from the 2114 static RAM the chip select line must go to a logical 0 while the write enable line is held in a logical 1 state. When the chip select line goes to a logical 0 the data from the RAM is placed on the I/O pins. (During a memory read operation the I/O pins of the 2114 become data output pins.) It is the job of external circuitry to insure that, when reading data from the 2114, the chip select line is a logical 0 and the write enable line is a logical 1. This is shown in Figure 3-23.

The 2114 RAM memory system interface to a 3-bus microprocessor architecture is shown in Figure 3-24. In this design Figure only two 2114 devices are needed to realize the 1K × 8 static memory. When using the 2102 static RAM, we recall that we needed eight memory devices to realize the same 1K × 8 static RAM. This is why the 2114 device has become very popular in small microprocessor systems.

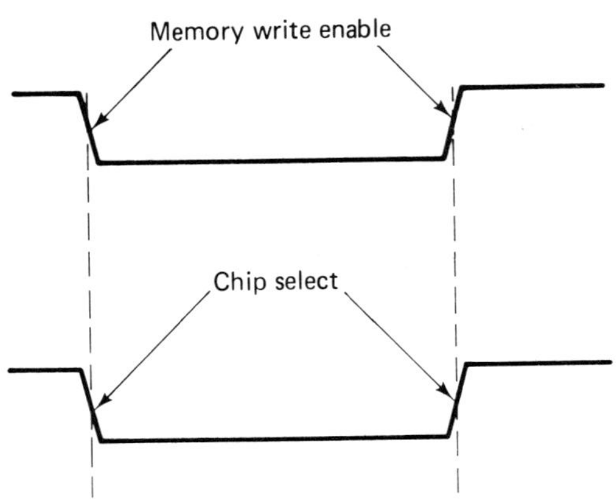

Figure 3-22 Timing diagram showing how the chip select line and the memory write enable line must go to logical 0 at the same instant to avoid data bus conflict when using a common I/O RAM.

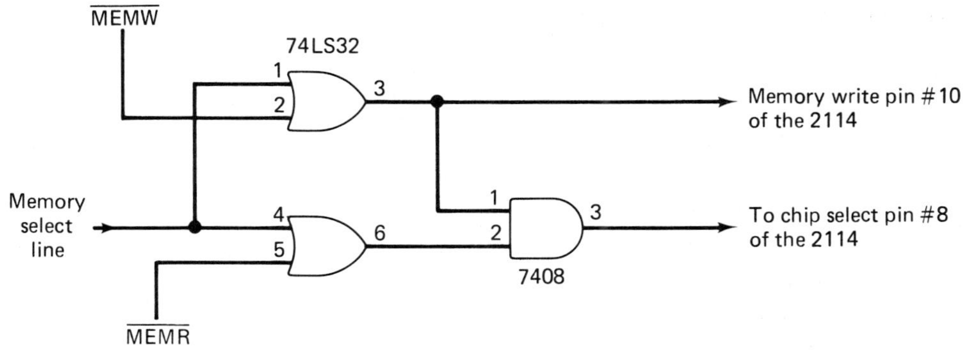

Figure 3-23 Schematic showing how memory control signals can be generated by using the system control bus and the memory select lines.

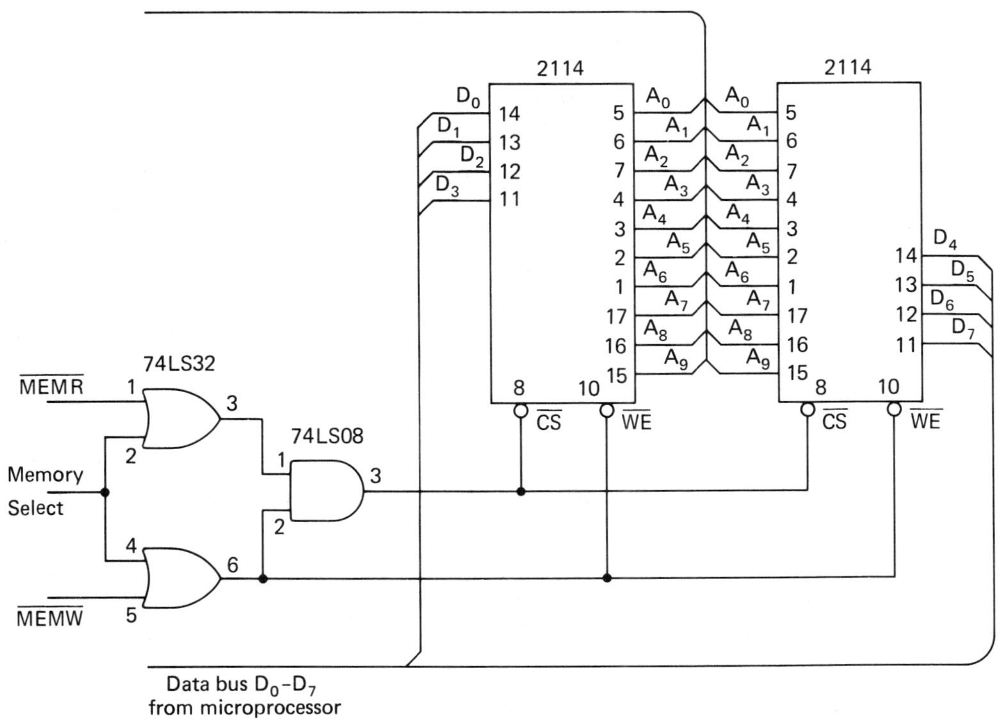

Figure 3-24 Complete schematic showing how a 1024 × 8-bit memory can be designed by using two 2114 RAM chips.

3-12 The Microprocessor as a System Controller

We have now presented the main hardware elements in a general microprocessor system. These elements are: (1) the system clock, (2) the microprocessor ROM and RAM, (3) the address bus, (4) the control bus, and (5) the data bus. Of course, we will need to add some input and output devices for the system to control. These input and output devices are really just extensions of the general system we have described. In Chapter 4 we will discuss in detail different types of input and output devices that serve as essential functional parts of typical microprocessor systems.

Let us now discuss what hardware details are still needed in order for the microprocessor to operate correctly. For this discussion we will assume:

1. there will be no system interrupts,
2. there will be no DMA (Direct Memory Access) by another source,
3. there will be no pauses or waits in the normal executive cycle of the microprocessor.

These three assumptions are not drastic. Many systems in daily operation use all three of these assumptions. When the microprocessor is operating in this mode it is truly a system controller, because it is *always* executing a program. It never stops program execution unless the power is turned off.

In the following sections of this chapter we will discuss how each of the four microprocessors must be connected to execute in this manner. As soon as we have completed this discussion we will be ready to start applying what we have learned about microprocessor controllers to a system in order to perform some useful, interesting, and challenging tasks.

3-13 8080 Details

To put the 8080 microprocessor into the mode where it will perform as a system controller we must connect the hold input pin 13 to a logical 0. This eliminates the possibility of a DMA being applied to this system. The INT input pin 14 of the 8080 must also be connected to a logical 0. This will keep the 8080 from being interrupted. We will then connect the RDYIN input pin of the 8224 clock generator to a logical 1. This will keep the 8080 from pausing during normal execution mode. In sum, what we have just done is to force the 8080 to use the assumptions of no DMA, no interrupting, and no pausing or waiting during system execution of the program. We accomplished this by connecting the pins that enable these functions to a logic level that always holds them in a disabled mode.

3-14 Resetting the 8080

When the 8080 is initially powered up there must be a way to force the central processing unit (CPU) to start executing a program at a certain address location each time, rather than at random. To accomplish this we must reset the 8080 when power is first turned on, or at any time that we wish the 8080 to return and start executing the system program from that same special location. To reset the 8080, we connect components to the RESIN input to the 8224 system clock generator pin 2 as shown in Figure 3-25. When the 8080 is reset, it will begin executing from address location 0000. This will always allow the programmer to put any initialization software at a fixed address space.

Referring to Figure 3-25 we see that the RC network will provide a power-on reset signal. That is, when V_{CC} is initially applied to the system, the capacitor will be in a discharge mode. Upon the application of power, the capacitor will charge toward V_{CC} via the resistor R_1. When the capacitor voltage reaches a certain predetermined value, the reset will be disabled and the system will start execution from address 0000.

The switch shown in Figure 3-25 will allow the system to be reset at any time. Pressing the switch will discharge the capacitor and the 8080 will again reset until the capacitor voltage charges to a specified value. The 8224 clock generator device has a Schmidt Trigger input that will monitor the voltage between the capacitor and resistor and at the same time provide very little loading of the RC network.

Figure 3-26 shows a complete 8080 system with all pinouts and wiring indicated that will permit the 8080 to act as a system controller in the manner that we have described.

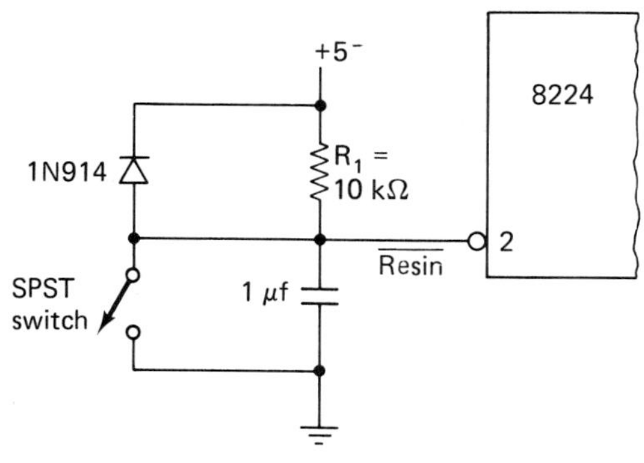

Figure 3-25 Schematic showing a power-on reset circuit for the 8080 microprocessor when using an 8224 clock generator.

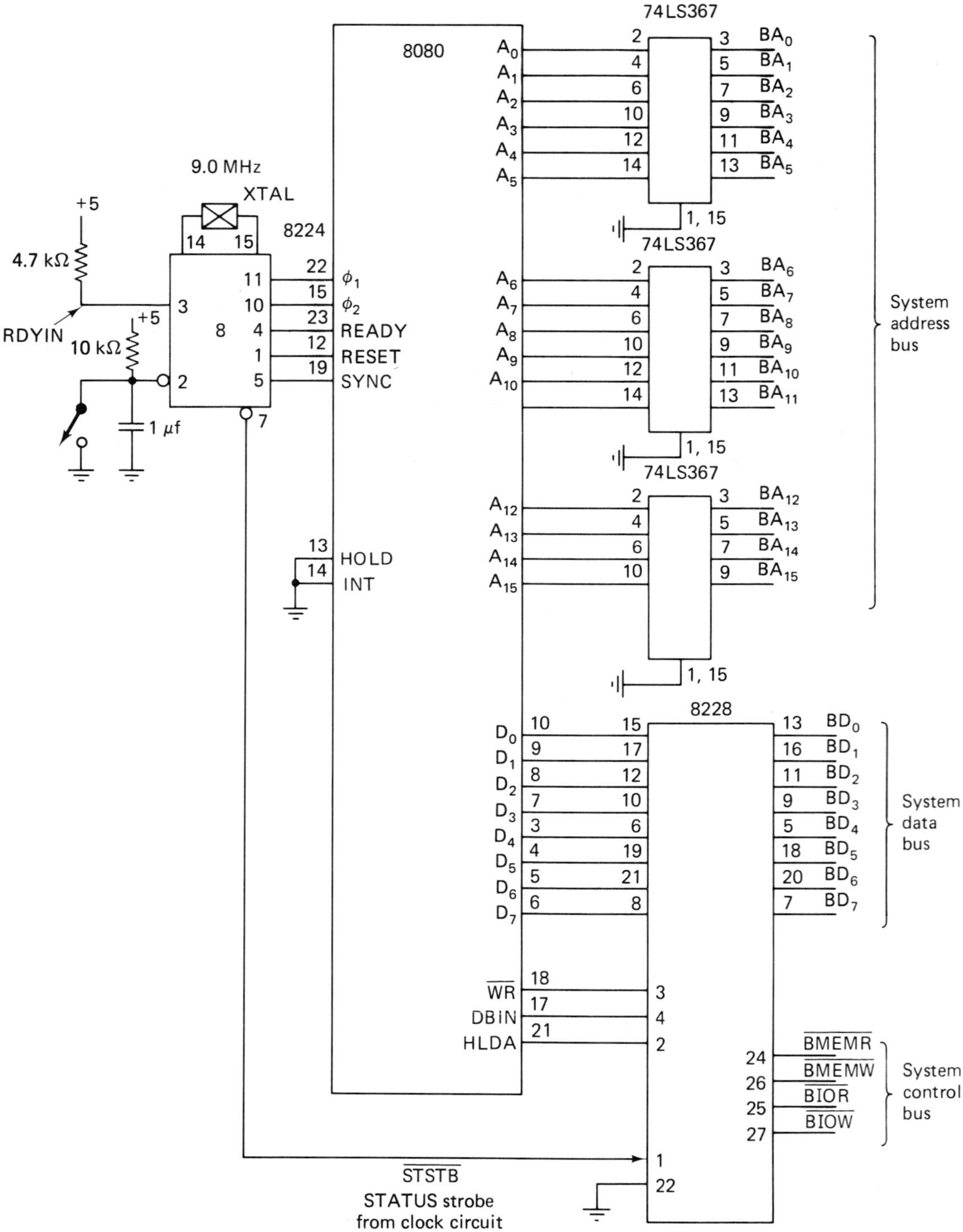

Figure 3-26 **Complete schematic for the 8080 as a system controller.**

3-15 8085 Details

We will now discuss the details of how to connect the 8085 to execute as a system controller. To accomplish this we connect the HOLD input pin 39 to zero volts. This will eliminate any DMA possibility. We next connect the READY input pin 35 to a logical 1. This will keep the 8085 from pausing during normal program execution. We then connect the TRAP pin 6, to RST 7.5 pin 7, RST 6.5 pin 8, RST 5.5 pin 9, and INTR pin 10 to a logical 0. This will keep the 8085 from being interrupted during normal program execution. Each of these functions on the 8085 will be discussed farther when we cover interrupts for the various microprocessors in Chapter 6.

To reset the 8085, we connect the reset input pin 36 to the same components we discussed for the 8224 clock generator reset input. With the 8085 connected in the fashion we have described it will execute as a system controller, immune to DMA, waits, or interrupts. The complete system schematic for the 8085 in this mode is shown in Figure 3-27.

3-16 Z80 Details

Let us now turn our attention to the Z80 microprocessor as a system controller. To eliminate the possibility of DMA, we connect the BSRQ input signal pin 25 to a logical 1. We next connect the WAIT input pin 24 to a logical 1. This will keep the Z80 from pausing during normal program execution. We then connect the INT and the NMI pins to 16 and 17, respectively, to a logical 1. This will keep the Z80 from being interrupted.

3-17 Resetting the Z80

To reset the Z80 we can use a circuit as shown in Figure 3-28. This circuit works like the reset circuit we discussed for the 8080 and the 8085. As with the others, when the Z80 is reset it begins program execution from address location 0000. Figure 3-29 shows the complete Z80 system designed to operate as a system controller.

3-18 6800 Details

We now focus our attention on the details of using the 6800 microprocessor as a system controller. We connect the HALT input pin #2 to a logical 1. This will insure no DMA operation. We also connect the IRQ pin 4 and the NMI pin 6 input signals to a logical 1 level. This will insure that the 6800 is not interrupted.

The 6800 has no provision for pausing during a normal program execution. This is accomplished in normal program execution by "stretching" the clock inputs to the 6800. We will discuss this in greater detail later in Chapter 6.

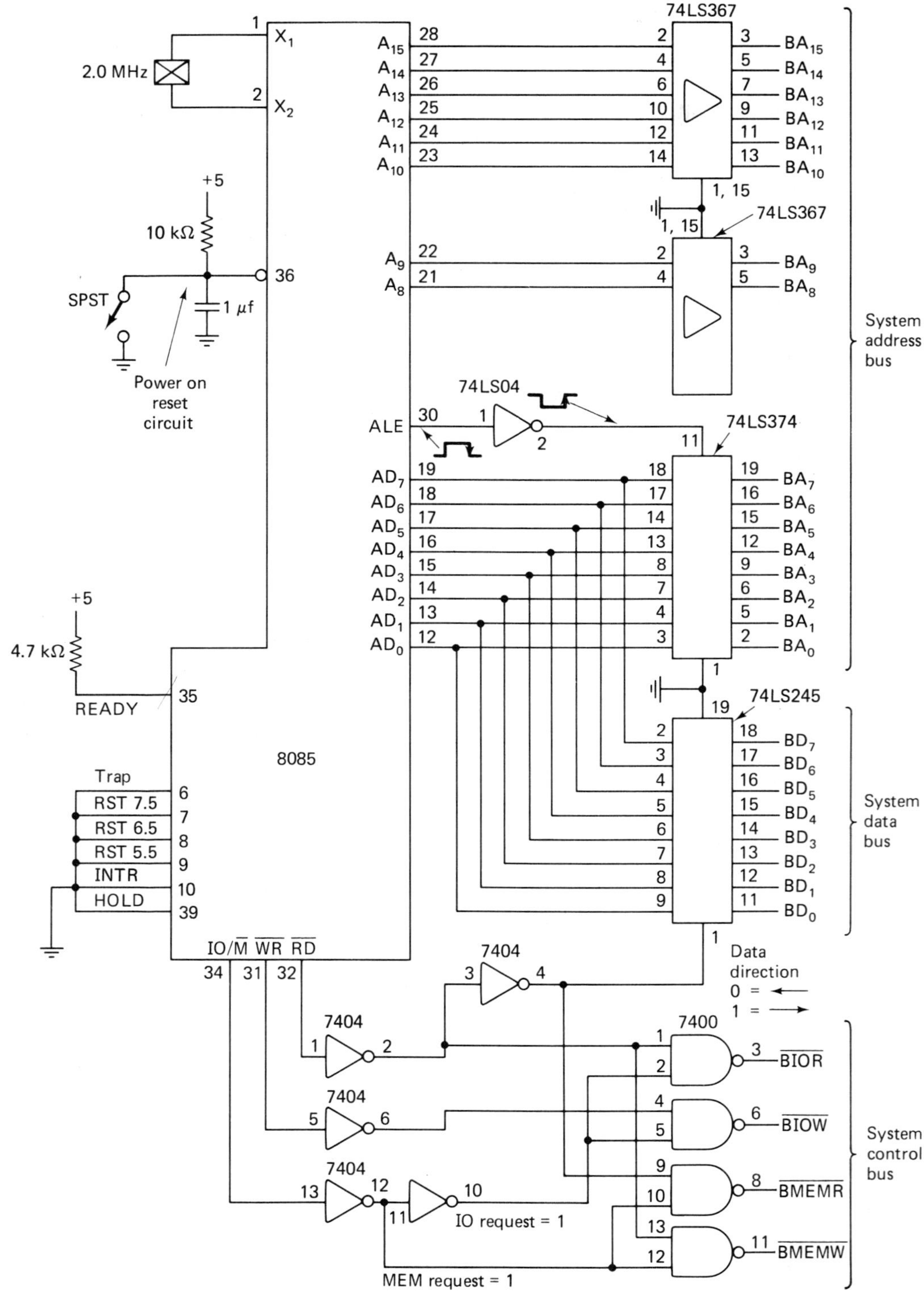

Figure 3-27 Complete schematic for using the 8085 as a system controller.

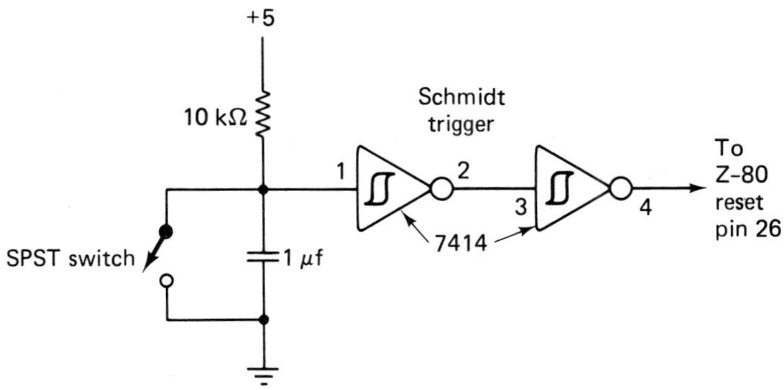

Figure 3-28 Schematic showing a power-on reset circuit for use with the Z80 microprocessor.

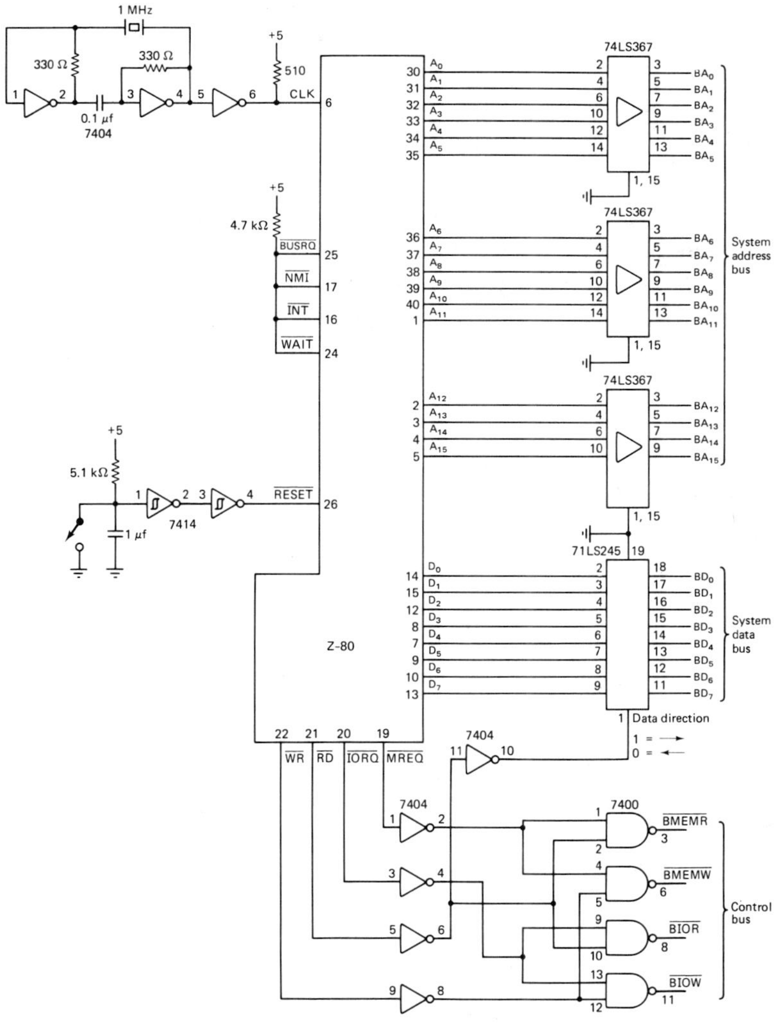

Figure 3-29 Complete schematic using the Z80 as a system controller.

We also connect the DBE (data bus enable signal) to the Phase 2 clock input. When Phase 2 is a logical 1, the data bus is enabled to receive or generate data for the microprocessor system.

3-19 Resetting the 6800

The resetting of the 6800 microprocessor can be accomplished by using the same reset circuit we discussed with the Z80. This circuit is shown in Figure 3-30. We must remember that when the 6800 microprocessor is reset, it *does not* begin executions from address location 0000.

When reset, the 6800 will output address FFFE and FFFF on the address bus. At address location FFFE the lower 8 bits of a new address is presented as data to the 6800. At address FFFF, the upper 8 bits of the address is presented as data to the microprocessor. The entire 16-bit address obtained from the data and memory locations FFFE and FFFF is the *actual* restart address for the 6800 microprocessor.

This feature of the 6800 microprocessor will usually require system ROM to be located in the upper 64K of available address space. We can now see that contained in the ROM is an address that must be placed on the data bus when the 6800 is reset. To give an example, let us suppose that in memory location FFFE the data is 63 and at memory location FFFF the data is 7F. Thus, when the 6800 microprocessor is reset, the overall effect is that its system reset software will start at memory address 7F63, whereas the other three microprocessors when reset started at address location 0000.

The complete schematic for using the 6800 as a system controller is shown in Figure 3-31.

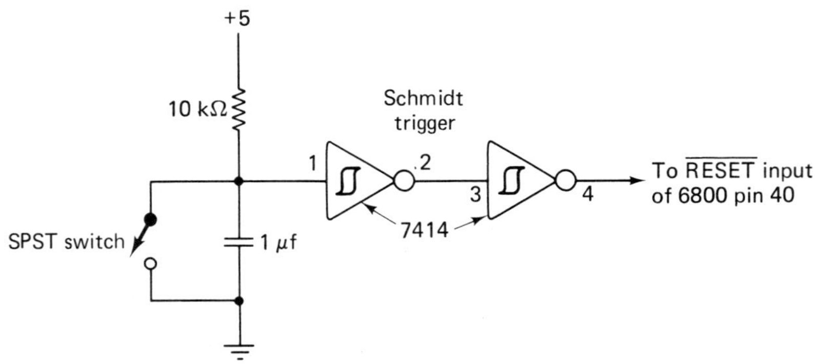

Figure 3-30 Schematic showing a power-on reset circuit for use with the 6800 microprocessor.

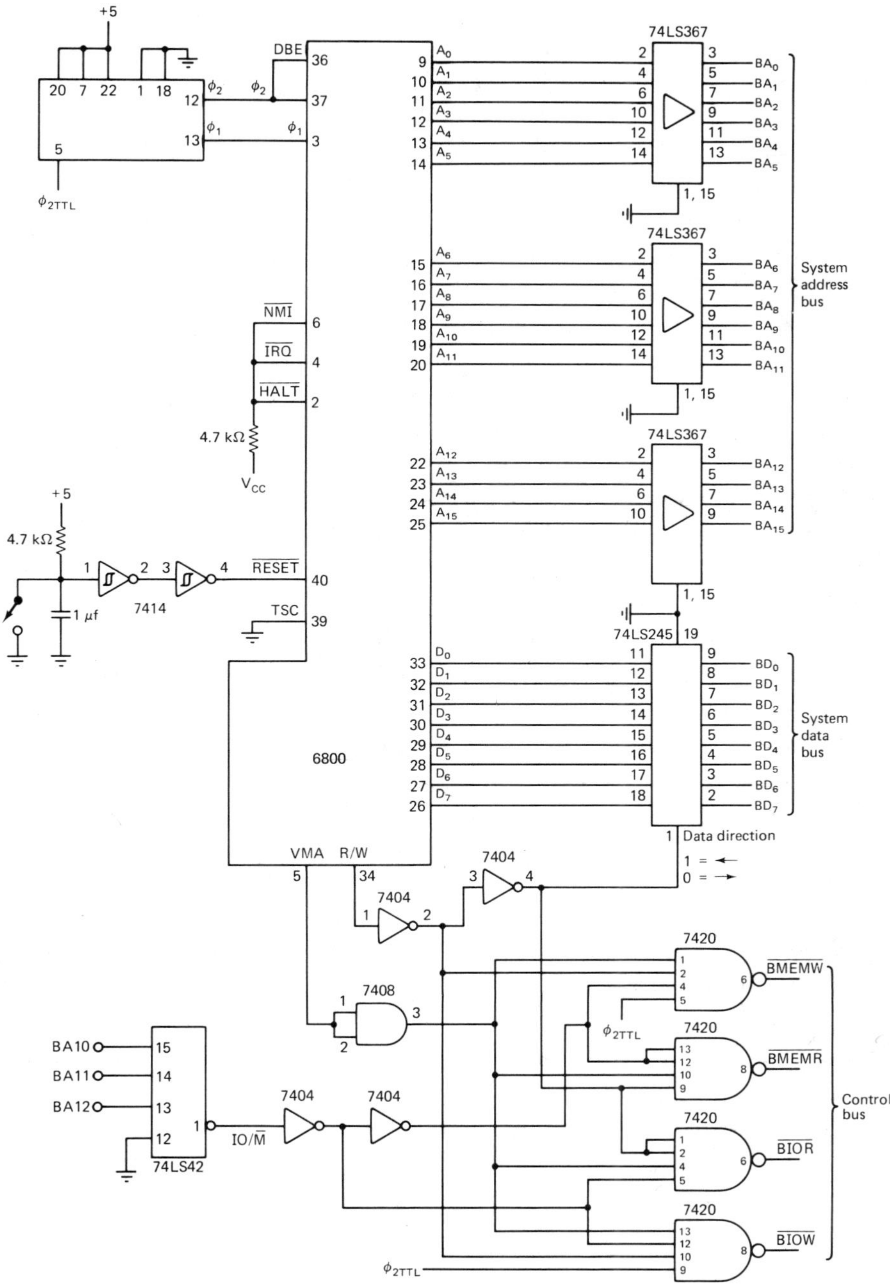

Figure 3-31 Complete schematic for using the 6800 microprocessor as a system controller.

3-20 Summary

In this chapter we have discussed details of realizing the 3-bus microprocessor system architecture with the 6800, 8080, 8085, and Z80 microprocessors. We have shown how to interface system ROM and system RAM to each microprocessor architecture. Finally, we described complete system schematics to allow the use of any of the four microprocessors as a microprocessor system controller.

In the remainder of this text we will add further details and refinements to these general microprocessor systems. However, we have already taken the first step. It is essential to understand how the system operates at this level before undertaking a study of more complex additional system circuitry and capability. In essence, what we have covered is the "bare bones" system. However, because it is bare bones, do not be misled into thinking the system is useless; quite the contrary is true.

The fact is, systems built around this bare bones concept are in use everywhere. We sometimes forget that we need not use all of the capability of a microprocessor to justify its use in a system design. We sometimes forget also that the systems in use do not need to be exotic. The microprocessor today is a very inexpensive device and makes circuit design, in most cases, quite simple. *It is not necessary to be a highly skilled system designer or design engineer to use and design microprocessor systems*. The first step is to overcome the natural anxiety we have when approaching a system design for the first time. In the following chapters we will show techniques for further developing an initial system. These techniques may be applied by persons who are in a low-cost mode and who do not have thousands of dollars to spend on development of equipment. The person working on a home computer project, for example, will find these techniques useful as well as will a person working in industry.

Our plan calls for us to discuss the design phase of a small system and actually go through all the stages of designing microprocessor control systems. Of course, to undertake such a task successfully we must first have a clear understanding of exactly how the microprocessor communicates electrically within a system environment. This chapter was the beginning. Each following chapter will reveal more details of the microprocessor system communication as our knowledge and understanding grows.

Upon understanding the information presented in this chapter, and the information and details relating to partial systems presented in the next chapter, we will have a firm grasp of the fundamentals. We show the exact information and details that we must have in hand before we can fruitfully study the actual use of the microprocessor in a real system environment. While block diagrams are used to illustrate concepts, throughout this text we include the complete schematics and leave nothing to the reader's imagination.

4

INTERFACING INPUT AND OUTPUT DEVICES TO 3-BUS ARCHITECTURE

In Chapter 3 we discussed the hardware realization of a 3-bus microprocessor system for the 8080, 8085, Z80, and 6800 microprocessors. We presented the general system with ROM and RAM. We did not show the system controlling any input or output devices.

In this chapter we will interface the 3-bus system architecture to some general input and output devices. We will discuss how each microprocessor could control the devices. We will present the actual hardware and software to allow each of the four microprocessors under study to function as a system controller. The input and output devices chosen for the interface are: (1) a keyboard, and (2) an output display. These input and output devices were chosen because they are very general types of functions, and anyone who is dealing in microprocessors will have had some contact with them.

Another important reason for choosing these input and output devices is the fact that some readers may wish to use these concepts in a small microprocessor system. That is, when constructing a microprocessor system for our own personal use the keyboard and output display devices may be designed into the system. If this is a first attempt at the actual design and use of the microprocessor as a system controller, it will be quite enlightening and fun to press a key on the keyboard and make the display react according to our own wishes.

This type of interaction between the user and the system will bring out very important concepts that may be applied over and over in a variety of microprocessor system applications. The sequence of events for this chapter follows:

1. We will discuss the general concept of a keyboard.

2. We will realize a 25-key keyboard with hardware. (This keyboard could be expanded to our own desires.)
3. We will discuss the general concept of output display.
4. We will realize a 6-digit display with hardware. (This display could be expanded to any number of digits.)
5. We will show how a keyboard and a display interface to a 3-bus microprocessor system architecture.
6. Finally, the software code for using the keyboard and display will be shown. With the actual software for the 8080, 8085, Z80, and 6800 microprocessors, we will show the schematics for each of the four microprocessor systems under study.

4-1 A Software Keyboard

We will now discuss the concept of a "software keyboard." The term "software keyboard" is used because all monitoring of the key depressions and actions taken due to the key depressions are functions solely of the system software. This type of keyboard differs from the "hardware" keyboard where digital logic devices monitor the key depressions and execute certain hardware functions based on the key that was depressed.

The place to start in a discussion is a general outline of keyboard function. In most cases a keyboard is comprised of a matrix of single pole single throw (SPST), push button, normally open (NO), momentary switches. A schematic diagram of this type of switch is shown in Figure 4-1. The switches are arranged in a matrix form that can be of any size. The keyboard matrix we will discuss is 5 × 5.

Figure 4-2 shows the arrangement of the switches in a 5 × 5 matrix. Referring to Figure 4-2, we see that each switch within the matrix can be described uniquely by an intersection of a row position and a column position. The columns are numbered C0 through C4 and the rows are numbered R0 through R4. With a software keyboard we do not assign a hardware function to any key based on position of the key within the array.

By proper use of programming the microprocessor, we can decode which switch position was pressed, and then we execute a section of software that is unique to that particular switch position. This means that we can change the

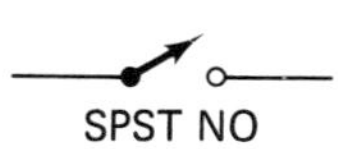

Figure 4-1 Schematic representation of a SPST NO (Single = Pole, Single = Throw, Normally Open) Switch.

function of any key by simply changing the software the microprocessor executes. This concept is shown by the flow chart in Figure 4-3.

If we understand how this general software keyboard can be implemented by using a microprocessor, then we have a very general building block for many microprocessor system applications.

The discussion of the keyboard covers the major areas:

1. Hardware required for realization
2. Software for monitoring the keyboard
3. Software for detecting a key closure
4. Software for detecting a key release

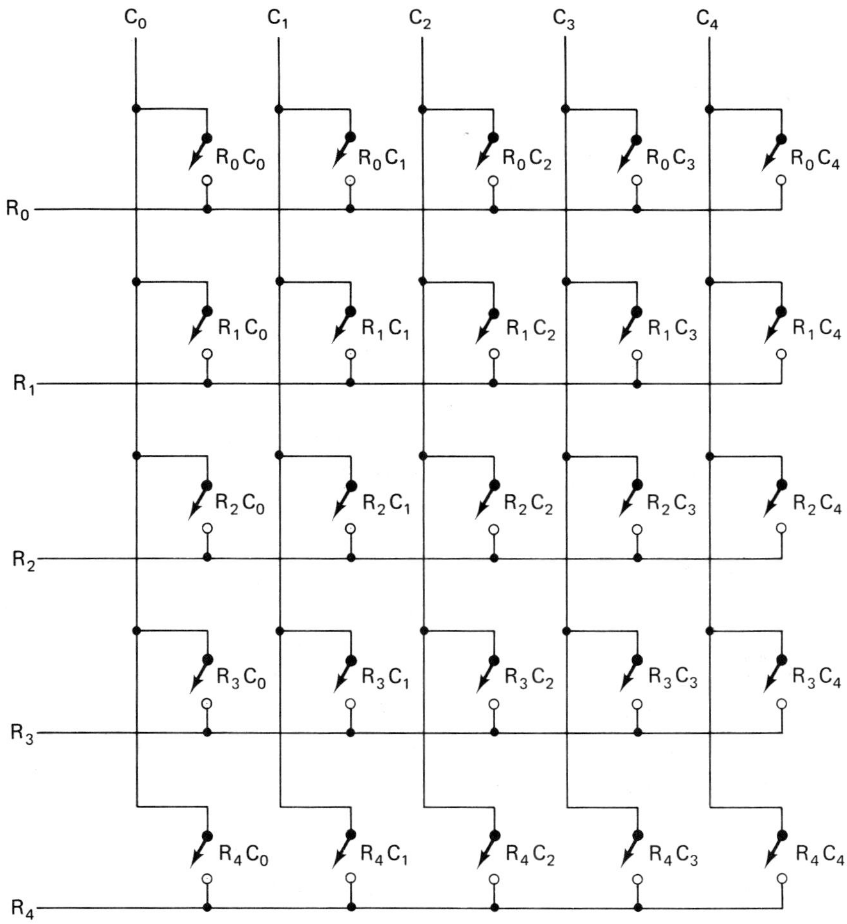

Figure 4-2 Schematic showing a 5 × 5 matrix of SPST NO switches.

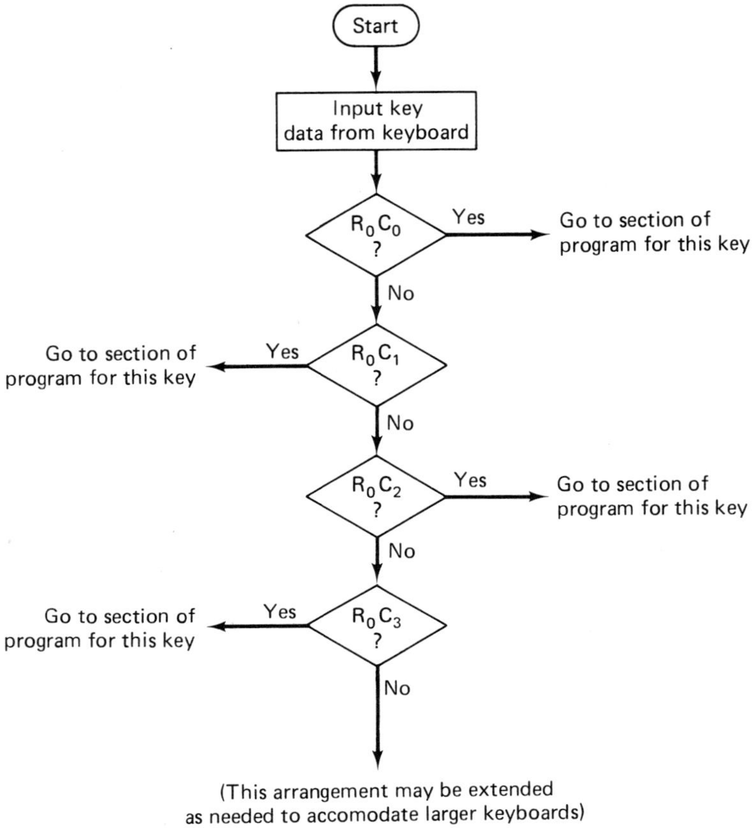

Figure 4-3 Partial flowchart showing how program flow can be directed by detecting different switch closures.

4-2 Hardware Required for Realization

The first major topic we will present is the actual hardware needed to realize a 5 × 5 keyboard matrix input device. This hardware is shown in the schematic diagram of Figure 4-4. The integrated circuits were chosen to keep package count to a minimum. However, in this and all schematics shown in this text, do not accept these techniques as the final word. The concept is the important point to be stressed. It is easier to understand a point under discussion when the actual hardware is shown. Any hardware design that will realize the same function is equally valid. Sometimes it is difficult to obtain the exact integrated circuits that are used in a textbook. Also, the ICs used in this text are those currently available, but new ICs with new functions are constantly being developed. We should monitor the literature constantly to find out about the new integrated circuits available. New ICs may help to increase system reliability and reduce the total package count. So we stress again that the important point is to understand the concept being presented. In order to transmit the concept to the reader we have shown specific hardware examples.

Referring again to Figure 4-4, let us examine the function of each hardware component within the input/output system. First, we turn our attention to the keyboard matrix. We notice that the switches are arranged in the following way. One side of each switch is connected to one of the column lines labeled C_0 through C_4. The other side of the switch is connected to one of the row lines that are labeled R_0 through R_4. The row lines R_0 through R_4 are the input lines to the keyboard switch matrix. The column lines are the output lines of the keyboard switch matrix.

The row lines R_0 through R_4 will have a logical zero input on them, one line at a time. That is, when R_0 is a logical 0, R_1, R_2, R_3, and R_4 are all logical 1. Then R_1 is set to a logical 0 and R_0, R_2, R_3, and R_4 are set to a logical 1. This is repeated as each row line is taken to a logical 0 level in a mutually exclusive fashion. The term "mutually exclusive" means that only one row line is a logical 0 at any given instant in time.

While a single row line is at logical 0 level, the column keyboard output lines are monitored by the microprocessor system. If any switch is pressed, then a single column line becomes a logical 0 level. The column output line will be a logical 0 if, and only if, the switch is closed to connect the column output to the row input that is presently being forced into a logical 0 level.

To further illustrate this point, suppose the switch that was closed is identified by the label R_3C_2. This label indicates that the switch, when closed, will connect the row 3 input line to the column 2 output line. When the keyboard is scanned by the system software, the following events will take place. (By the term "scanned," we mean the system is forcing each row input line to a logical 0 and monitoring the column outputs.)

The row line R_0 is forced to a logical 0. All other row input lines are a logical 1. While row 0 is a logical 0, the column output lines are monitored by the system software. Later in this discussion we will explain how the row lines are forced to logical 0 levels and the column lines are monitored by the system software. If the switch R_3C_2 is closed, then the column output lines will all be a logical 1 when R_0 is a logical 0. This is due to the fact that the column lines are pulled up to +5 volts via the pull-up resistors PR_1 through PR_5. Since R_0 is not physically connected to any column line via a keyboard switch, there is no path for any column line to be forced to a logical 0 voltage level.

The same type of action takes place in the keyboard as rows R_0, R_1, and R_2 are forced to a logical zero in a mutually exclusive fashion. However, when row input line R_3 is forced to a logical 0, the following will occur. The column line

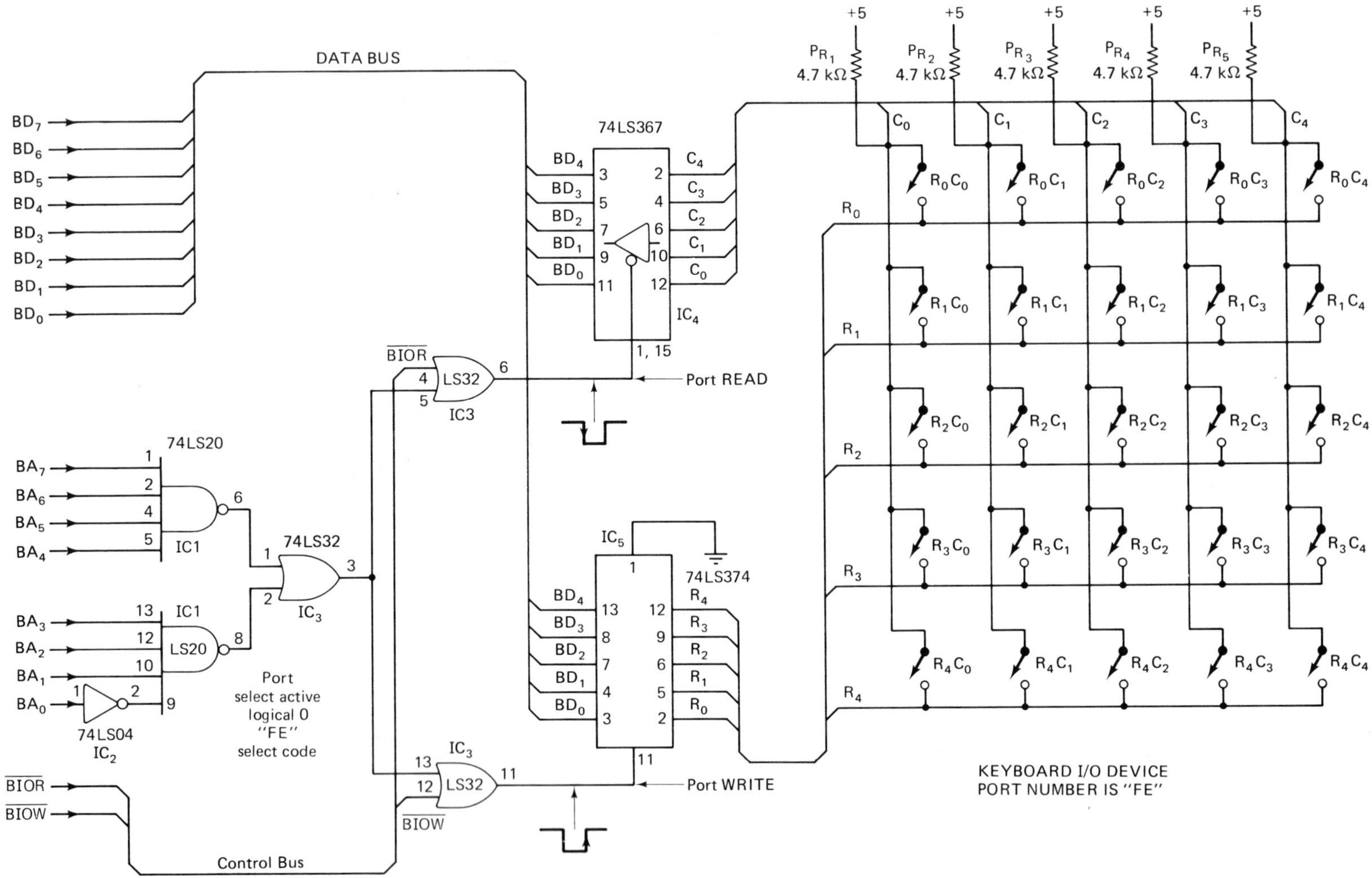

Figure 4-4 Complete schematic for interfacing the 5 × 5 keyboard matrix for a microprocessor-controlled system.

labeled C_2 will be forced to a logical 0. This will occur because there is a physical path through the switch labeled R_3C_2. This path is from the column C_2 output through the switch to a row 3 input line. When the system detects a logical 0 on any column, it indicates that a switch has been depressed.

The system determines the exact switch that was pressed by remembering (electrically) the row being forced to a logical 0 and decoding logically the column that is a logical 0. Later in this chapter we will show the actual software code needed to implement this.

4-3 Row Stimulus

We will now discuss how the row lines are forced to a logical 0 level in a mutually exclusive fashion. The 74LS374 octal latch, IC5, in Figure 4-4 is the physical connection to the keyboard that forces the logical 0 on the correct row input line. The inputs to the latch are taken from the system data bus. These inputs are labeled BD_0-BD_4. The data bus lines correspond to the keyboard row input lines in the following way. BD_0-R_0, BD_1-R_1, BD_2-R_2, BD_3-R_3, BD_4-R_4. The microprocessor forms the correct logical level to be forced at the keyboard row inputs and then writes this word to the 74LS374 latch via the system data bus.

The data on the data bus BD_0-BD_7 is written to the 74LS374 when the system performs an output write operation. We recall that when the system performs an output device write operation, the following events occur:

1. the address of the output device is placed on the address bus,
2. the output data to be written is placed on the data bus,
3. the control bus asserts the $\overline{\text{BIOW}}$ signal.

Let us examine how each of the three actions listed will be used electrically by the schematic of Figure 4-4. First, the address of the output device is designed to be "FE." The schematic for the address decode is shown in Figure 4-5, which is excerpted from Figure 4-4. Notice in Figure 4-5 that the address decode circuit is a simple realization of a combinational logic block to decode an exact 8-bit combination of the address bus. We design a combinational logic circuit to decode the word 1111 1110 (FE). The output of the 74LS32 in Figure 4-5 will be a logical 0 only when the lower 8 bits of the address bus are equal to FE.

The output pin 3 of the 74LS32, IC_3 is called the "port select line." This line is active logical 0 whenever the port select decode logic detects the correct logical combination on the lower 8 bits of the address bus. We must stress a point here that is sometimes overlooked by beginners in microprocessor systems. That point is: *the Port Select line may be active even when the system is not communicating with the output device.*

As an example of this, suppose the system were communicating or reading data from a memory location FE. The address bus would contain the correct

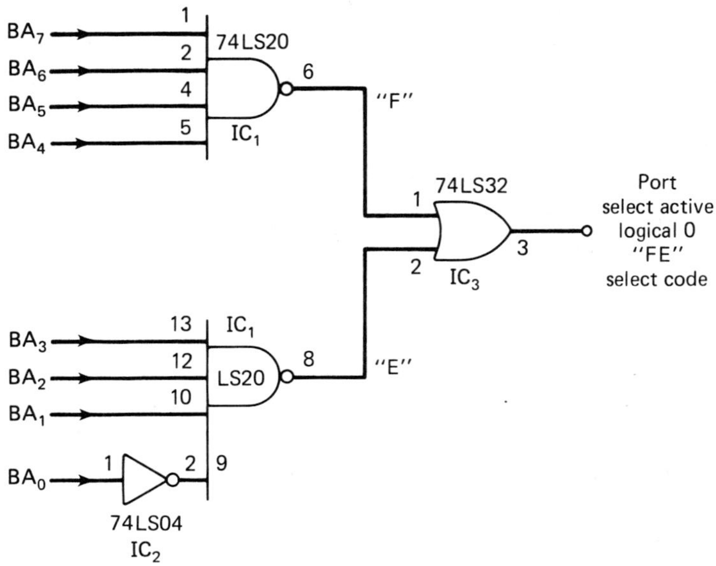

Figure 4-5 Partial schematic excerpted from Figure 4-4. This schematic shows the port decoding of FE.

logic combination to assert the port select line "FE." This is the reason the events of the microprocessor system must be "qualified" by the system control bus. If we did not use the control bus as an event qualified, then many devices could be selected that were not intended to be communicated with at a particular instant in time. It is important to bear this fact in mind when examining logic signals within a microprocessor controlled system. The port select line can be enabled when the system is electrically communicating with other devices. This situation may bring up many questions when looking at the port select line with an oscilloscope and detecting the select line being activated when the system is not supposed to be communicating with the output device.

After the port select line of Figure 4-4 is forced to a logical 0 via the address bus decoding, the OR Gate IC_3 pin 13 is enabled with a logical 0. The data on the data bus is placed at the inputs to the 74LS374 octal latch pins 3, 4, 7, 8, 13. Finally the control bus asserts the $\overline{\text{BIOW}}$ signal. When this happens the output pin 11 of IC_3 is forced to a logical 0. The $\overline{\text{BIOW}}$ then goes to a logical 1. At this point the data on the data bus is latched into the 74LS374 octal latches IC_5. This is shown by the timing diagram of Figure 4-6.

We have now discussed all electrical events that occur when the row input lines are forced to different logic levels by the microprocessor system. This is also the same event that occurs in a general output write in a microprocessor system. These events occur regardless of the microprocessor being used as a system controller. The events may appear in a different form, but the sequence of events must be constant. We have not made reference to a distinct microprocessor in this entire discussion; instead we discussed electrical events as they relate to a 3-bus microprocessor system architecture. This is part of the value of discussing general microprocessor systems with a 3-bus microprocessor architecture view. In this way we can design the general CPU to fit the 3-bus system architecture and it will then support the design for all of our input and output devices.

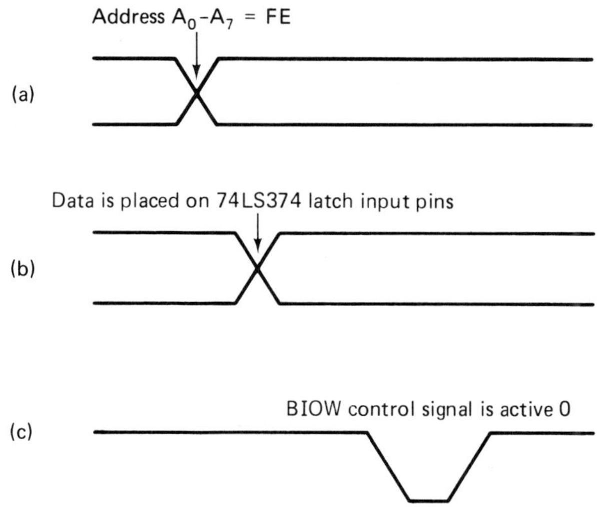

Figure 4-6 Timing diagram showing the relationships of important signals for an output write to port FE.

4-4 Keyboard Column Output Monitoring

Let us now discuss how the microprocessor electrically monitors the column output of Figure 4-4. We notice in Figure 4-4 that the port select code FE is used as a port select for the input reading function. This same port select was used for an output write port select. We have used the select code as truly an input and output select code. This is a very valid thing to do because the event of input read will never occur at the same instant in time as an output write. This means that the select code hardware can be utilized in two different capacities. These are, namely, an input select code and an output select code. This will allow us to reduce system hardware.

The basic idea behind the monitoring of the keyboard column outputs is to perform a system input device read. The system will perform an input read and the electrical state of the column outputs of the keyboard will be input to the microprocessor. We recall that the events for an input read operation in a 3-bus system architecture are:

1. input device select address is placed upon the address bus,
2. data bus is prepared for microprocessor input operation (this means that microprocessor data inputs must be put in input mode rather than output mode),
3. the control bus asserts the $\overline{\text{BIOR}}$ signal.

The input port address for the discussion is FE. The address is decoded exactly the same way as it was decoded for the output device operation we discussed previously. This is because we are using exactly same hardware for the input port select code as we used for the output port select code. When the port

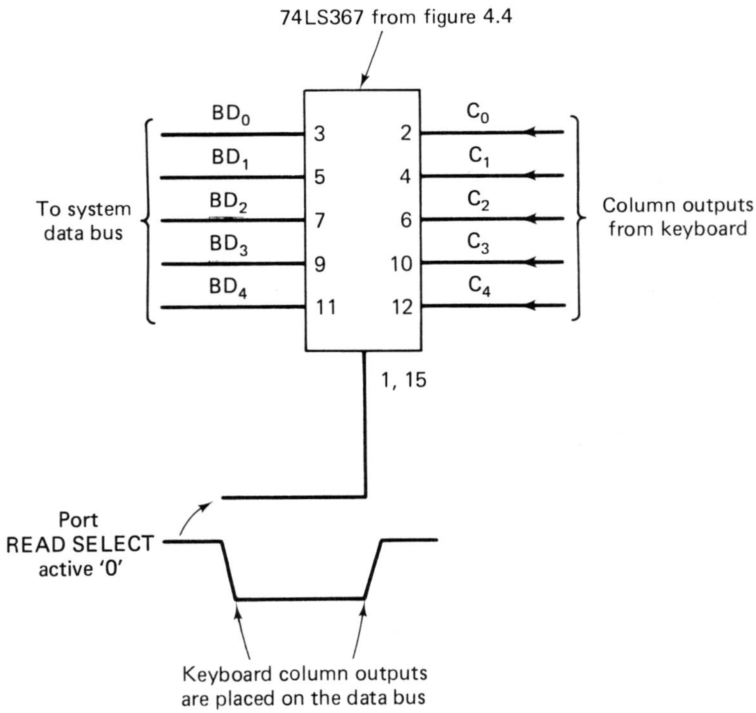

Figure 4-7 Partial schematic excerpted from Figure 4-4. This schematic shows the hardware required to read the logical condition of the column outputs.

select code is detected, the input pin 5 of IC_3 in Figure 4-4 is enabled to a logical 0 level.

The control bus will now assert the $\overline{BIOR}$ signal. When the $\overline{BIOR}$ signal is a logical 0 (the assertive mode) the output pin 6 of IC_3 is a logical zero level. When this output pin is a logical 0 it forces a logical 0 input on the 74LS367, tri-state buffer (IC_4) pins 1, 15. The input pins 1, 15 when taken to a logical 0 level enable the outputs of the 74LS367 onto the system data bus. The outputs of the 74LS367 correspond to the logical condition of the column outputs for the keyboard column lines. See Figure 4-7.

While the 74LS367 tri-state buffers are enabled onto the data bus, the microprocessor inputs the data placed on the bus. Since no other device in the system is controlling the data bus, the microprocessor will input the data that is being placed on the data bus by the 74LS367s. This data is a logical representation of the logic state of the column output lines of the keyboard matrix. In this fashion we can send data from the input device to the microprocessor. The microprocessor can then make decisions based on the data it has received.

4-5 Summary of the Keyboard Input and Output Circuits

We have shown how the hardware of the keyboard input and output circuits interfaces to the 3-bus microprocessor system architecture. We have stressed concepts in every aspect of this discussion. We also showed actual circuits that could realize the concepts presented. If we understand how this general input and output circuit interfaces to the 3-bus microprocessor system, then adapting this concept to other input and output circuits will be an easy matter. Later in this chapter we will discuss how the software will control this input and output port.

4-6 The Output Display Device

The output display that we will discuss will be 6 hexadecimal digits wide. The display digits will be Hewlett Packard P/N 5082-7340 ICs. The Hewlett Packard 5082-7340 display has all decoding internal on the display digit. This particular display also has a latch input to connect directly to a microprocessor system data bus. We will not take advantage of this attribute of the display in order to show more vividly the concept of latching data at a system output port. The output display circuit is shown by the schematic of Figure 4-8. Referring to Figure 4-8, the following is an explanation of how the circuit operates. The output display labeled DP_1 through DP_6 receive their input signals from the 74LS374 octal latches IC_1 through IC_3. The inputs to the latches are connected to the system data bus BD_0-BD_7.

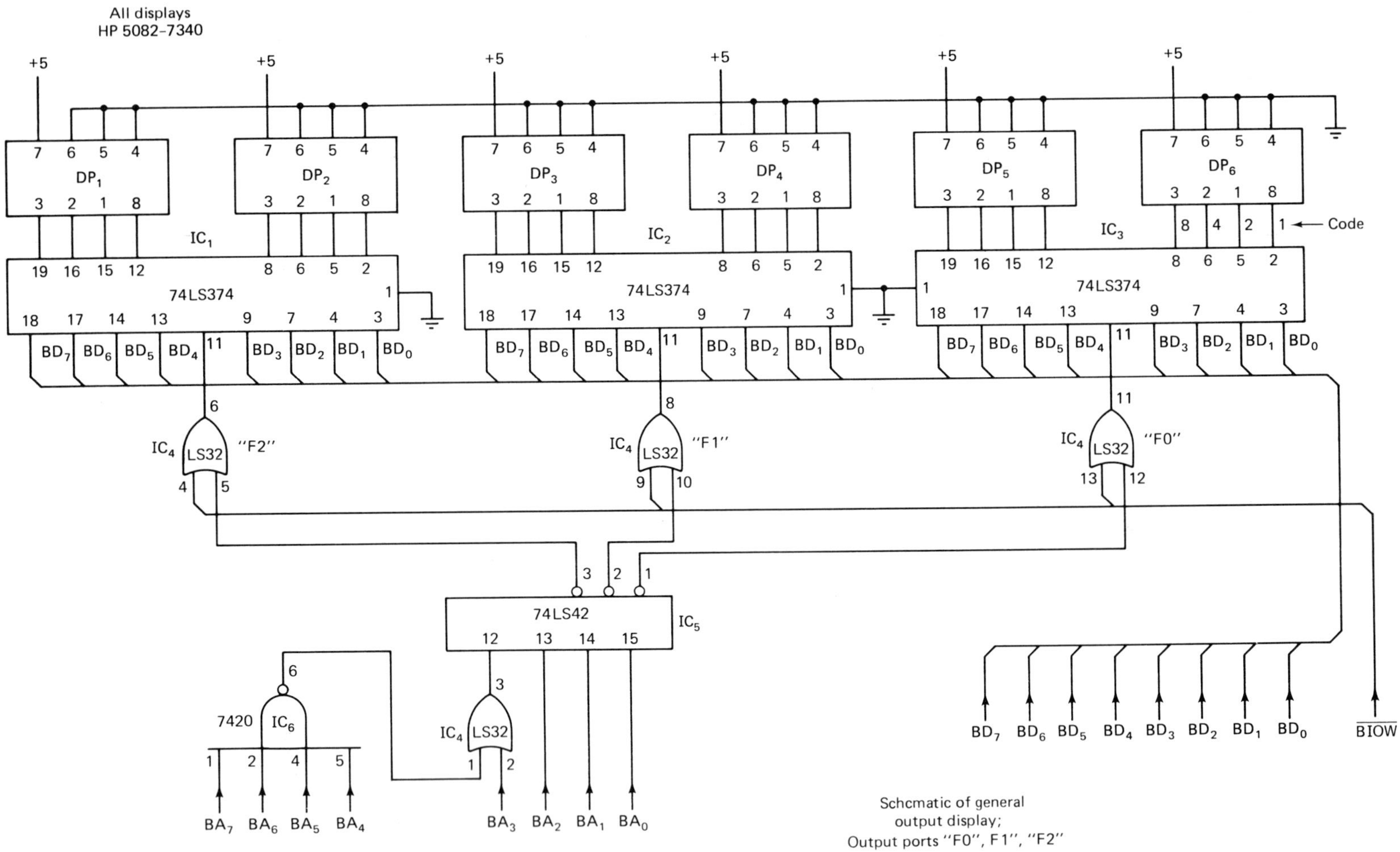

Figure 4-8 Complete schematic showing the interface for a general 6-digit output display to a microprocessor-controlled system.

Output port decoding for the octal latches are decoded as $F0_{16}$, IC_3 enabled; $F1_{16}$, IC_2 enabled; F2, IC_1 enabled. When the address lines BA_4-BA_7 are equal to 1111, the output pin 6 of the 7420 pin 6 is a logical 0. This logical 0 is applied to the pin 1 input of the 74LS32, IC_4. This action will enable the 74LS42 if the address line BA_3 is a logical 0. With the 74LS42 enabled, the output pins 1, 2, or 3 become active logical 0s via the binary state of the address lines BA_0–BA_2.

The logical outputs of the 74LS42, IC_5, are shown in Figure 4-9. This figure also shows the address select codes that will generate the logical output of the 74LS42, IC_5. We further see from Figure 4-9 that when the address lines BA_0–BA_7 equal F0, the output pin 1 of IC_5 of Figure 4-8 will be in a logical 0 state. With this output pin in the logical 0 state, the input pin to IC_4 pin 12 is forced to the logical zero state. When the $\overline{BIOW}$ signal is asserted via the system control bus, the output pin 11 of the 74LS32 IC_4 will go to logical 0 level. When output pin 11 goes to logical 1 after being logical 0, the data on the data bus is written into the 74LS374 octal latch, IC_3.

This same type of reasoning may be applied to the octal latches of IC_1 and IC_2. Octal latch IC_1 will be written into when the logical condition of the address lines equal F2. The octal latch IC_2 will be written into when the address lines equal F1.

The microprocessor system will write data to the octal latches 8 bits at a time. This indicates that two display digits will be written in parallel. It will be the function of the system software to keep track of which digits should be "updated" or written into. Later in the chapter we will show how software will control the output display.

OUTPUT OF 74LS42

Pin #1	Pin #2	Pin #3	ADDRESS Codes
0	1	1	$F0_{16}$
1	0	1	$F1_{16}$
1	1	0	$F2_{16}$

Figure 4-9 The logical output conditions of the 74LS42 of Figure 4-8 in relation to address codes.

4-7 Keyboard Software Control

In the remainder of this chapter we will discuss the software required to allow the keyboard to function. We will input a key closure from the keyboard and write a unique number to display based on the key that was closed. We will discuss useful, non-exotic and inexpensive techniques that can be used to develop software and debug it. Finally, we will show the software required to operate the system. The software will be shown for the four microprocessors we are discussing, namely, the 8080, 8085, Z80, and 6800.

The software for the 8080 and 8085 will be the same. This same software can be executed directly by the Z80 microprocessor, but we will not show the Z80 software mnemonics. We should be able to gain insight as to the interaction between the software and hardware in a microprocessor control system application. We will write the software in small pieces for each control function. At the end we will coalesce these pieces into a functional software program. The writing of the software in small pieces makes the overall job much less formidable than tackling it as a single system function. The software is also easier to debug, if we debug small pieces at a time.

4-8 Generating the Row Inputs with Software

We will now discuss the software required to control the hardware to allow the row input lines to be forced to a logical 0 in a mutually exclusive fashion. We recall from our discussion of the operation of the keyboard that the row input lines are forced to a logical zero 1 at a time. We will first show the flow chart necessary to accomplish this. Next, we will show software for the 8080, 8085, Z80, and 6800 to realize this flow chart.

We note at this time that the 8080, 8085, and Z80 can all execute software code designed for the 8080. Therefore we will present the software in the 8080 mnemonics and the 6800 mnemonics only. The Z80 microprocessor will execute the same code that we design for the 8080 microprocessor. However, the Z80 has many more possible instructions than the 8080, so the Z80 also has its own set of mnemonics. We mention this because we want the reader to understand that the software structures for different microprocessors may be different. We should refer to the user software manual for the particular microprocessor being used as a system controller. This will allow us to determine what software structure looks like for that particular microprocessor. It will also show the set of mnemonics for a particular microprocessor.

The flow chart for generating the row inputs is shown in Figure 4-10. Notice that the row input generation is a subroutine. When the microprocessor system is "initialized," starting word S1 is set. Later in this chapter we will discuss exactly what is meant when we say the system is "initialized." For now it is sufficient to understand that the start word S1 will be set in memory before the routine in Figure 4-10 is ever executed by the microprocessor. This fact is relevant because we notice from Figure 4-10 that this routine will make decisions based on this word S1. If we did not initialize the word, then when the power was turned on, the data in the memory would be random. This means the word S1 would be random data, and decisions made on it may or may not be correct.

The routine of Figure 4-10 recalls the word from memory. The routine then checks the word to see if it is equal to 10_{16}. If this is the case, then it indicates that the last row line has had a logical 0 input to it, and the next row line to have a logical 0 input should be R_0. If the present row word is not equal to 10_{16}, then the routine simply shifts the word left one place. In making this shift we must

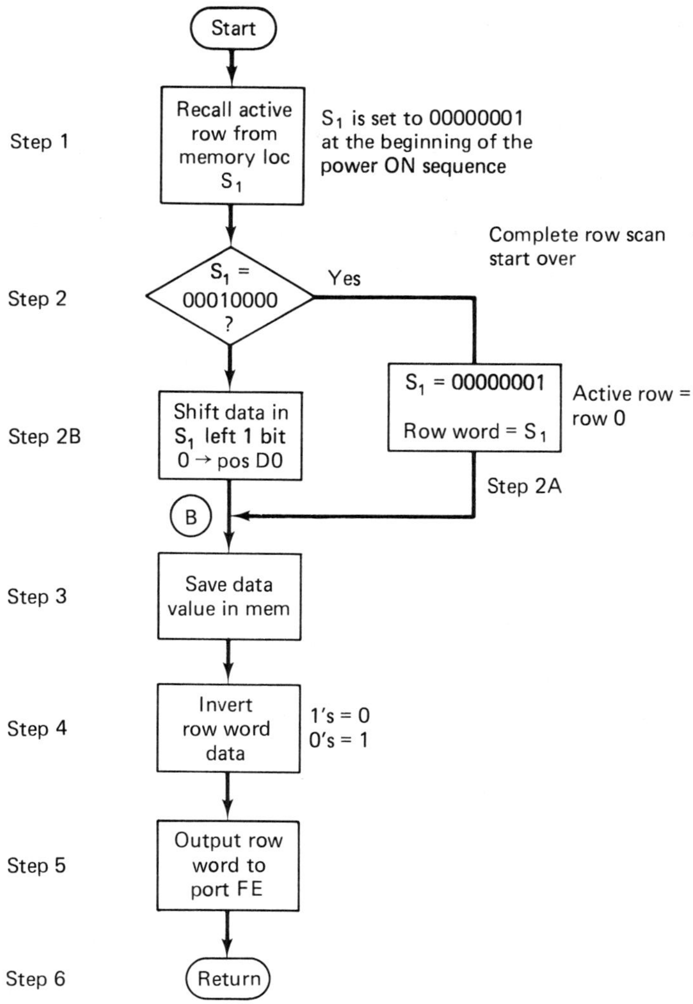

Figure 4-10 Flowchart showing major system events for generating the row inputs to the keyboard matrix.

insure that a logical 0 is shifted into the first bit position (R_0). This is mentioned because different microprocessors perform data shifts in different ways. Some microprocessors may shift a logical 1 input into the first bit position. We should refer to the software manual for the particular microprocessor being used to determine exactly how the data left shift is performed.

Referring to Figure 4-10, if the present row word is equal to $10_{(16)}$ then the routine will set the row word equal to $01_{(16)}$. When this happens, the routine will proceed to point B in the flowchart. From point B in the flowchart the routine will store the new row word into memory. This new row word will be used to make decisions the next time the routine of Figure 4-10 is executed by the system.

After storing the new row word in memory, the routine will invert or complement the row word. This action will cause all the data bits except the active row bit to go to a logical 1. The active row bit will be forced to a logical 0. (See Figure 4-11.) Finally, the routine will output the formatted row word to the hardware output port.

We recall from Figure 4-4 that the output port for the row line is FE. Figure 4-12 shows the actual 8080 mnemonics required to realize the flowchart of Figure 4-11. We should bear in mind that the mnemonics of Figure 4-12 is one way the flowchart of Figure 4-11 can be realized. There most certainly are many different ways of realizing, with software, a general flowchart. This is analogous to the many different methods of realizing different functions with hardware.

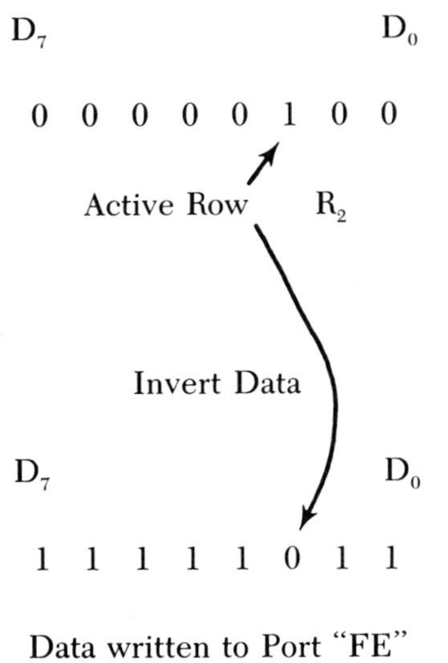

Figure 4-11 Illustrating steps 3 through 5 of Figure 4-10. The active row is stored in memory. The data is then inverted and written to the output port. Note that the active row is logical 0.

```
00EB                ************************************************************
00EB                *
00EB                * SUBROUTINE TO OUTPUT THE ACTIVE ROW TO THE KEYBOARD
00EB                *
00EB                *  OROW IS THE NAME OF THIS SUBROUTINE
00EB                *
00EB                *  THIS IS FIGURE 4-12
00EB                *
00EB                ************************************************************
00EB                ************************************************************
00EB                *
00EB                *  FIGURE  4-12     8080 MNEMONICS FOR FIGURE 4-10
00EB                *
00EB                ************************************************************
00EB                *
00EB                *
00EB 3A 04 10       OROW   LDA KROW    RECALL ACTIVE ROW
00EE                *
00EE                * STEP  2
00EE                *
00EE FE 10                 CPI  10H       COMPLETE ROW SCAN????
00F0 C2 F8 00              JNZ  OROW1     IF NOT THEN STEP 2B
00F3                *
00F3                * STEP  2A
00F3                *
00F3 3E 01                 MVI  A,01H     RESET THE ACTIVE ROW
00F5 C3 F9 00              JMP  ST3       GOTO STEP 3
00F8                *
00F8                * STEP  2B
00F8                *
00F8 07             OROW1 RLC             SHIFT DATA LEFT,0 INTO D0
00F9                *
00F9                * STEP 3
00F9                *
00F9 32 04 10       ST3    STA  KROW      SAVE ACTIVE ROW IN MEM
00FC                *
00FC                *  STEP 4
00FC                *
00FC 2F                    CMA            INVERT ROW WORD
00FD                *
00FD                * STEP 5
00FD                *
00FD D3 FE                 OUT 0FEH       OUTPUT ACTIVE ROW TO PORT FE
00FF                *
00FF                *STEP 6
00FF                *
00FF C9                    RET
0100                *
0100                *
```

Figure 4-12 Mnemonics for Figure 4-10.

Whichever way we realize the software, always document the program well. When the time comes to debug the software, or for the software to be transferred to some other person, good documentation is invaluable. In some instances it is wiser to be less clever in the software and more straightforward in the techniques

```
LF413   T=00003 IS ON CR00020 USING 00009 BLKS R=1410

1 PAGE      1  F412       TUE OCT 02, 1979    02:27:04.13



00001                          NAM    F412
00002                   *
00003                   *
00004                   *  THIS SUBROUTINE IS THE 6800 VERSION OF 4-12
00005                   *
00006 0000                     ORG    $00
00007                   *
00008                   *****(STEP 2)
00009                   *
00010 0000 81 10               CMP A  #$10      COMPLETE ROW SCAN??
00011 0002 26 05               BNE    ST2B      IF NOT THEN STEP 2B
00012                   *
00013                   *****(STEP 2A)
00014                   *
00015 0004 86 01               LDA A  #$01      RESET THE ACTIVE ROW
00016 0006 7E 000A             JMP    ST3       GOTO STEP 3
00017                   *
00018                   ******(STEP 2B)
00019                   *
00020 0009 48           ST2B    ASL A            SHIFT LEFT,0 INTO D0
00021                   *
00022                   *******(STEP 3)
00023                   *
00024 000A B7 1000 ST3         STA A  KROW
00025                   *
00026                   ********(STEP 4)
00027                   *
00028 000D 43                  COM A            INVERT THE ROW WORD
00029                   *
00030                   *********(STEP 5)
00031                   *
00032 000E 01 FE               STA A  #$00FE    OUTPUT ACTIVE ROW TO PORT FE
00033                   *
00034                   **********(STEP 6)
00035                   *
00036 0010 39                  RTS              RETURN FROM SUBROUINE
00037                   *
00038                   *
00039                   *********END OF THIS ROUTINE
00040                   *
00041                   *  NOW TO SET THE VARIABLES IN MEMORY
00042                   *
00043           1000 KROW      EQU    $1000
00044                   *
00045                          END              END STATEMENT FOR ASSMBLER
1 PAGE      2  F412       TUE OCT 02, 1979    02:27:04.13



KROW    1000 00043 00024
ST2B    0009 00020 00011
ST3     000A 00024 00016
```

Figure 4-13 The 6800 version of Figure 4-12.

used for realization of a flowchart. When someone who is less clever than you, or has not had as much exposure to software as you, cannot follow your logic you will be the one spending extra time troubleshooting and explaining your technique. Usually this extra demand on your time will come at a point when you are under pressure yourself to get another project completed. I do not know why this is usually true, but in the majority of instances it is!

Figure 4-13 shows the flowchart of Figure 4-11 realized by using the 6800 mnemonics. The 6800 system we are using employs memory mapped input and output architecture. The 6800 microprocessor does not have the equivalent of an OUT instruction for writing data to external hardware. All circuits are treated as memory space.

4-9 Examining the Column Input Lines with Software

We will next discuss a technique for the software to control the hardware for determining exactly which column line C_0, C_1, C_2, C_3, or C_4 is active, if any. The flowchart for determining the active column C_0 through C_4 is shown in Figure 4-14. There we see that the routine will first set the column flag indication in system memory to a logical 0. This flag will be used by the calling routine to determine if any columns are active. The next event to occur is for the routine to input the data from the keyboard input port. Then step 3 will set the upper 3 bits of the data word input equal to a logical 1. This is done because the input port where we read the data uses only the lower 5 bits of the data bus. We have an indeterminate case for the data input. It is best to "mask off" these data bits so they cannot cause the flow of program to be dependent upon them.

In step 4 we now examine the data that was input from the keyboard column input port. If this data is all 1s, FF, then we know that no column line was active logical 0. This condition will exist when we are asserting a row line that is not physically connected to any column line. If this is true, we return from the subroutine and the column flag is still all 0s. This indicates that there were no active column outputs.

If there was an active column output, then we will complement the data as shown in step 5 of the flowchart. We then set the column flag equal to the data obtained in step 5. The routine then returns to the calling program. Figure 4-15 and 4-16 show this software flowchart realized in the 8080 and 6800 mnemonics, respectively.

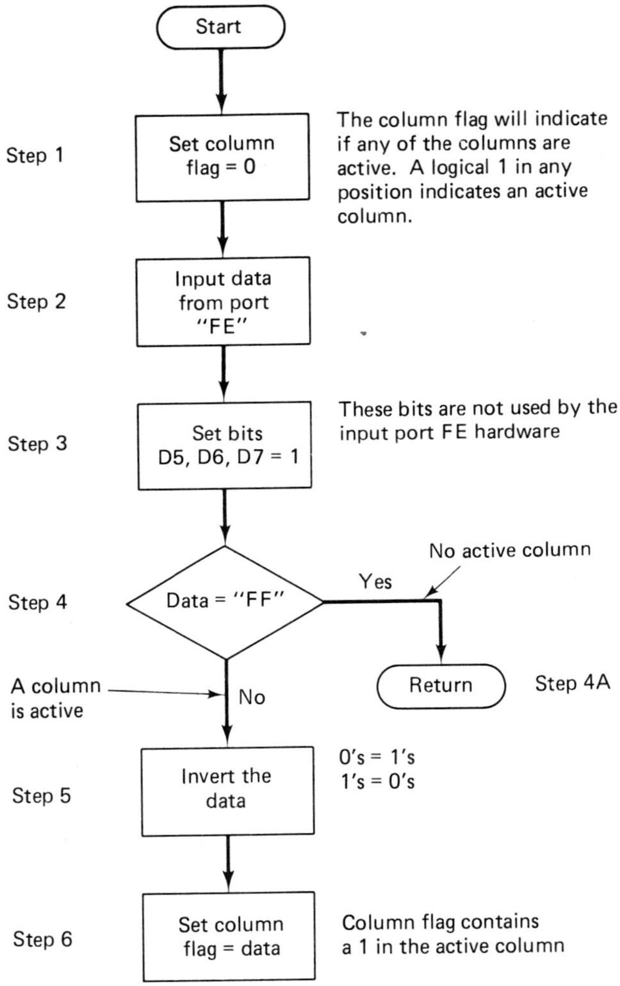

Figure 4-14 Flowchart showing major system events for electrically determining the active column, if any.

```
00DB                 *****************************************************************
00DB                 *
00DB                 *    THIS SUBROUTINE IS FIGURE 4-15
00DB                 *
00DB                 *****************************************************************
00DB                 *
00DB                 ******(STEP 1)
00DB                 *
00DB AF              COLM   XRA   A
00DC 32 01 10               STA   CFLAG       SET THE COLUMN FLAG=0
00DF                 *
00DF                 ******(STEP 2)
00DF                 *
00DF DB FE                  IN    0FEH        INPUT DATA FROM PORT FE
00E1                 *
00E1                 ******(STEP 3)
00E1                 *
00E1 F6 E0                  ORI   0E0H        SET BITS D5,D6,D7=1
00E3                 *
00E3                 *******(STEP 4)
00E3                 *
00E3 FE FF                  CPI   0FFH
00E5 C8                     RZ                STEP(4A)
00E6                 *
00E6                 *****(STEP 5)
00E6                 *
00E6 2F                     CMA               INVERT THE DATA
00E7                 *
00E7                 ******(STEP 6)
00E7                 *
00E7 32 01 10               STA   CFLAG       SET THE COLUMN FLAG
00EA C9                     RET               RETURN FROM THIS SUB
00EB                 *
```

Figure 4-15 8080 Mnemonics for realization of the flowchart in Figure 4-14.

```
LF416  T=00003 IS ON CR00020 USING 00009 BLKS R=1410

1 PAGE      1   F4          TUE OCT 02, 1979    01:59:27.45



 00001                        NAM    F4.15
 00002                 *
 00003                 *
 00004                 *  THIS IS 6800 VERSION OF FIGURE 4-15
 00005                 *
 00006                 *
 00007 0000                     ORG    00        SET THE ORGIN OF THIS ROUTINE
 00008                 *
 00009                 *  SET THE VARIABLES IN MEMORY
 00010                 *
 00011           1001 CFLAG  EQU    $1001
 00012                 *
 00013                 *  START THE PROGRAM
 00014                 *
 00015                 *
 00016                 *        (STEP 1)
 00017                 *
 00018 0000 86 00      COLM    LDA A  #$00       SET THE COLM FLAG
 00019 0002 97 00              STA A  COLM
 00020                 *
 00021                 *        (STEP 2)
 00022                 *
 00023 0004 96 FE              LDA A  $00FE      INPUT DATA FROM PORT FE
 00024                 *
 00025                 *******(STEP 3)
 00026                 *
 00027 0006 8A E0              ORA A  #$E0       SET BITS D5,D6,D7=1
 00028                 *
 00029                 ********(STEP 4)
 00030                 *
 00031 0008 81 FF              CMP A  #$00FF
 00032 000A 27 01              BEQ    NEXT       IF ZERO THEN BRANCH
 00033 000C 39                 RTS               RETURN FROM SUB IF NOT ZERO
 00034                 *
 00035                 ********(STEP 5)
 00036                 *
 00037 000D 43         NEXT    COM A             INVERT THE DATA
 00038                 *
 00039                 ********(STEP 6)
 00040                 *
 00041 000E B7 1001            STA A  CFLAG      SET THE COLUMN FLAG
 00042 0011 39                 RTS               RETURN FROM SUBROUTINE
 00043                 *
 00044                 *
 00045                 *  END OF THE SUBROUTINE
 00046                 *
 00047                         END               END STATEMENT FOR ASSEMBLER
1 PAGE      2   F4          TUE OCT 02, 1979    01:59:27.45



  CFLAG   1001 00011 00041
  COLM    0000 00018 00019
  NEXT    000D 00037 00032
```

Figure 4-16 The 6800 version of Figure 4-15.

4-10 Calculating the Key Value

Each key in the keyboard matrix is assigned a value 0-N; here key 0 is the first key labeled R_0C_0, and key N is the last key labeled R_4C_4. Figure 4-17 shows how the keys are weighted. We are *not* assigning a function to the key at this point. For example, a function could be a number 4 or a number 9. We will assign the functions later. The weight we assign to each key simply allows us to calculate mathematically which key is being pushed, based on its column and row position in the keyboard matrix.

	C_0	C_1	C_2	C_3	C_4
R_0	X 0	X 5	X 10	X 15	X 20
R_1	X 1	X 6	X 11	X 16	X 21
R_2	X 2	X 7	X 12	X 17	X 22
R_3	X 3	X 8	X 13	X 18	X 23
R_4	X 4	X 9	X 14	X 19	X 24

Figure 4-17 The decimal weight value that has been assigned to each switch position in the 5 × 5 keyboard matrix.

Figure 4-18 shows the flowchart required to calculate the key weight of the particular key that was pushed. The flowchart assumes that the column position is stored in memory at location "tagged" column flag. The row position is stored in memory at location tagged "row word." The terms "column position" and "row position" refer to the intersection in the keyboard matrix where the pushed key provides a physical path between the column line and row line.

Referring to the flowchart of Figure 4-18, let us examine exactly how this routine works. First, the routine recalls the value of the column position from memory. This is any of these five binary values:

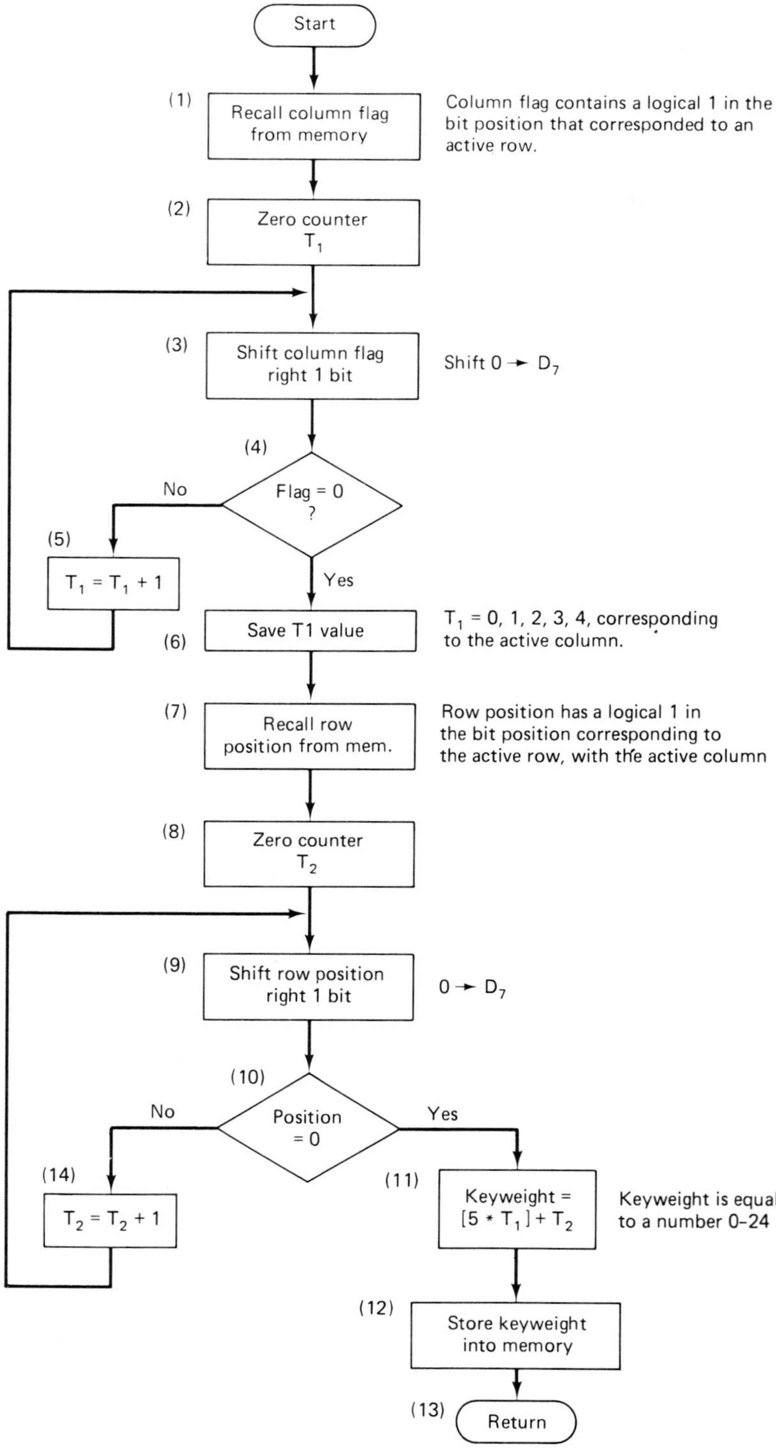

Figure 4-18 Flowchart showing the major system events for calculating the decimal "key weight" value of the switch that was pressed.

00000001 (column 0)

00000010 (column 1)

00000100 (column 2)

00001000 (column 3)

00010000 (column 4)

The flowchart of Figure 4-18 next sets a counter labeled T_1 equal to 0. T_1 eventually will contain the decimal value 0, 1, 2, 3, or 4, corresponding to the active column line. To accomplish this, the routine of Figure 4-18 shifts the data word obtained in step 1 right 1 bit. During this shift, a 0 is shifted into position D_7. (See Figure 4-19.) The routine then tests to see if the shifted data word equals 0. If the word equals 0, then the active column was column 0. The T_1 counter value is equal to 0 at this time.

If the shifted data word in step 4 of Figure 4-18 is not equal to 0, then the T_1 counter is incremented by 1. The shifting and testing of the data word, accompanied by incrementing the T_1 counter value, continues until the shifted data word does equal 0. At this point the T_1 counter value is temporarily saved in a memory location.

The routine of Figure 4-18 now performs the same type of procedure on the value of the data in the row position word. The T_2 counter is used for this function.

Finally, after both the decimal equivalent of the row position and the column position have been stored into memory locations labeled T_2 and T_1, respectively, the routine calculates the weight of the key pushed based on the following formula:

$$\text{Keyweight} = (5 \times \text{Column Position}) + \text{Row Position}$$

D_7 D_0

0 0 0 0 1 0 0 0

Data is shifted right 1bit
0 is shifted into D_7

→ 0 0 0 0 0 1 0 0 →

Figure 4-19 Diagram showing how the data is shifted right 1 bit. A logical 0 is shifted into the MSB position (D7).

After the keyweight is known, we know exactly which key out of the entire matrix was depressed. From here we can jump to a section of software that corresponds to that particular key function.

However, prior to jumping to a location in the system, we must first insure that the key we obtained was actually meant to be pushed. Also we must not perform any action until the key has been released. These two points are subject to debate and opinion. In this system we use the following criteria that a key was actually pushed and that a key was released.

We will define a key as being pushed when the microprocessor system detects the same weight key 50 consecutive times.

We will define a key as being released when the system does not detect any key closure for 50 consecutive scans of the row input line.

We repeat that the assignment of these numbers is completely arbitrary. We are eliminating the mechanical key debouncing that exists within keyboard systems. The length of time a key may bounce differs from keyboard to keyboard.

4-11 Debouncing a Keyboard with Software

We will now discuss the software necessary to realize the function of debouncing the keyboard switches. We will show the flowchart for the sequence of events. Then we will present the actual software code necessary to realize this flowchart. The problem is in two parts. The first part is the software required to detect 50 consecutive equal key closures. The second part of the problem is to detect 50 consecutive complete scans of the keyboard row input lines without detecting any active column output line. This corresponds to no key being pushed or a key release.

Figure 4-20 shows the flowchart for inputting a single key into the system. Notice that this routine makes use of the routine we discussed in Figure 4-10 for enabling the correct row input line to the keyboard. Next, the routine of Figure 4-20 makes use of the routine we discussed for detecting an active column. The column flag will be set to 0 if there is no key input. If the column flag is equal to 0, the flow of the program in Figure 4-20 returns to the row routine to enable the next row input line to logical 0 level. This is the loop the system is executing while waiting for the user to press any key on the keyboard.

If a key were detected in step 8 of Figure 4-20, this would be indicated by the column flag being set to a value other than 0. The routine of Figure 4-20 will then call the routine of Figure 4-18. This routine calculates the keyweight decimal 0 through 24. The routine then stores this number in a memory location labeled KWGT.

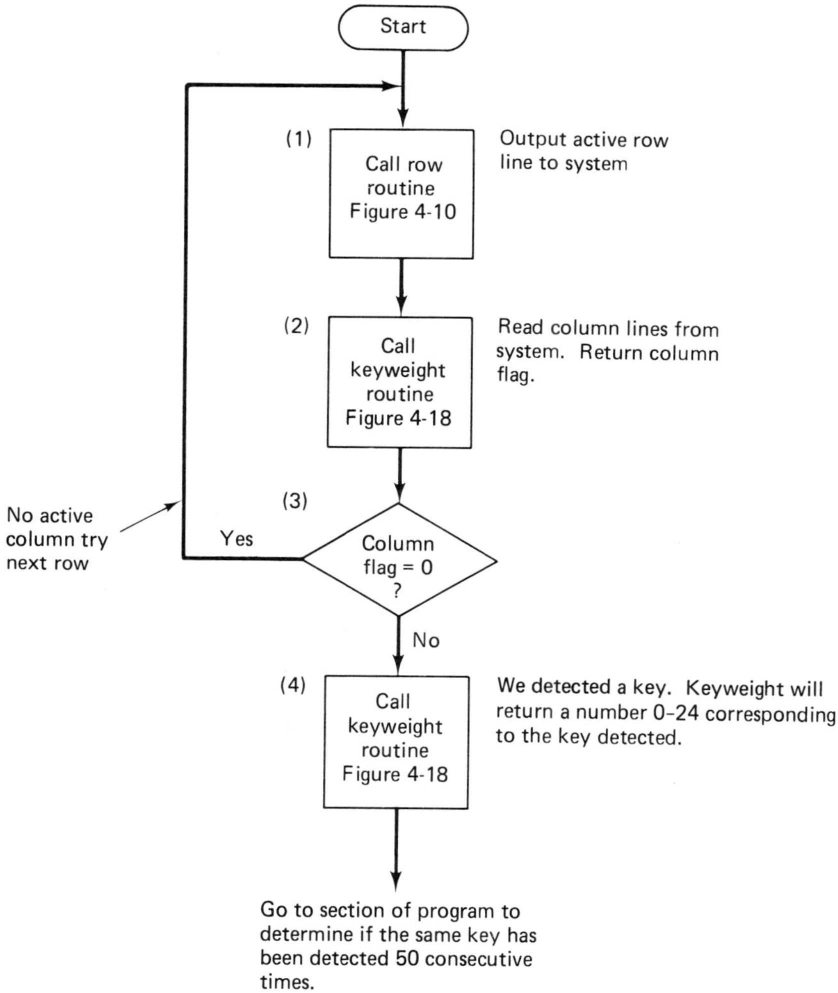

Figure 4-20 Flowchart showing major system events for inputting a single key push to the microprocessor system.

Now that the system has detected a key, the decision still must be made whether this same key has been active for 50 consecutive keyboard inputs or not. The flowchart for realizing this function is shown in Figure 4-21. To check this, the system examines a counter labeled KTIME. The KTIME counter is a software device that keeps track of how many consecutive times the same key is input to the system.

If the counter KTIME equals 0 in step 2 of Figure 4-21, it shows that this is the first time this particular key has been input to the system. Since this is the first time, the system electrically remembers what the value of the key is. The system does this by setting a variable labeled KCOMP equal to the value of the key that has been input to the system. The value of the key input is stored in a location of memory under the label of KWGT. This is shown in step 3 of the flowchart in Figure 4-21.

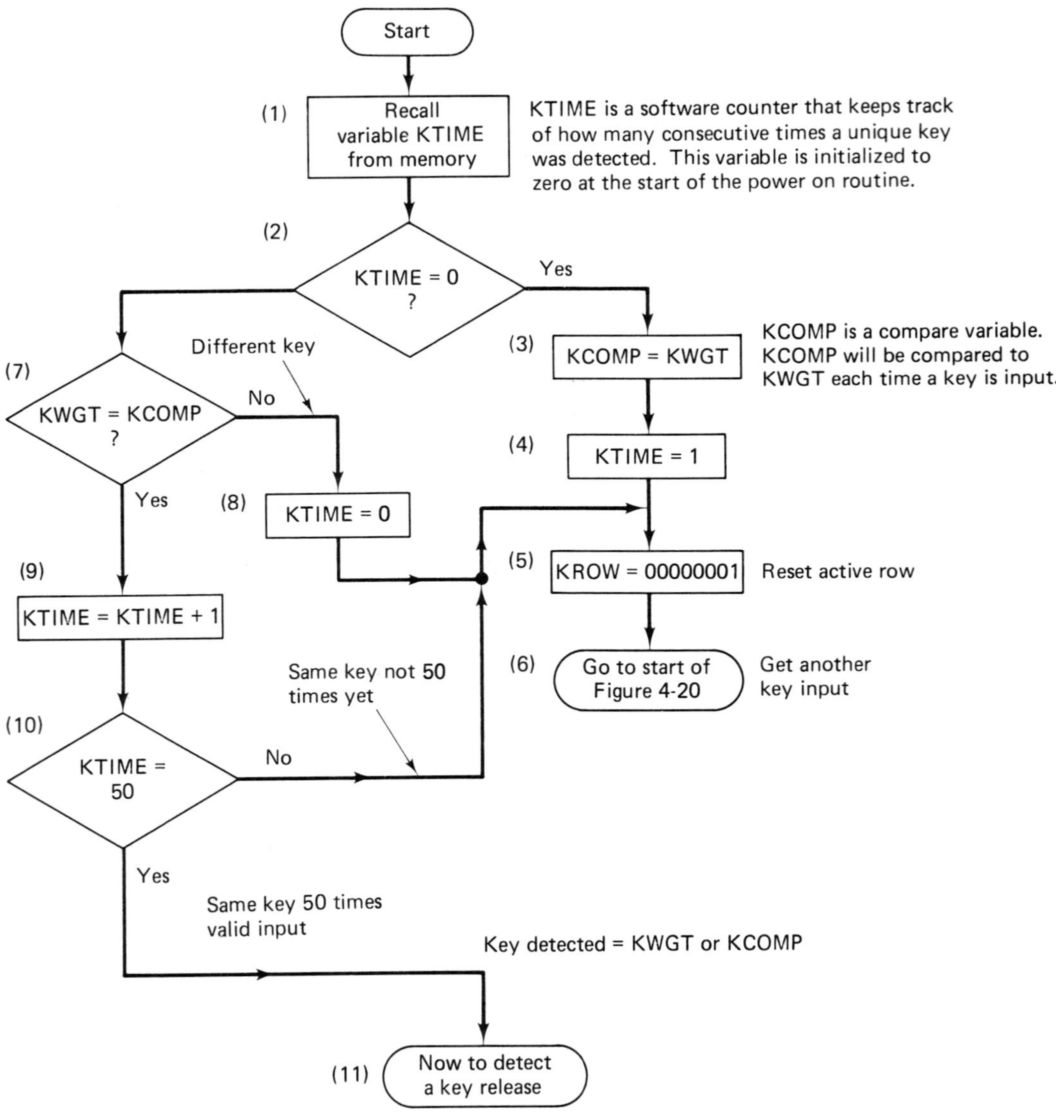

Figure 4-21 **Flowchart showing major system events for detecting the same active key push 50 consecutive times.**

After the compare-word is set (KCOMP), the system will increment the KTIME counter by 1 and then jump to the section of the program to receive another input from the keyboard. Before the system jumps to this section of software, it again resets the active row counter (KROW) to enable the first row input line to a logical 0 level. This action is shown in step 4 of the flowchart of Figure 4-21.

When the system inputs a key for the second time, the value of the counter KTIME will not be a logical 0. This means the program will flow in the path from step 2 to step 7 of Figure 4-21. At step 7 the system compares the key input (KWGT) against the first key input (KCOMP); if they do not compare the following happens. The system follows the flowchart path from step 7 to step 8. At step 8 the KTIME counter is reset to 0 and the system again tries to input 50 consecutive equal key inputs.

If the value of the present key input compares with the value of the first key input in step 7, then the system follows a path from step 7 to step 9. At step 9 the KTIME counter is incremented by 1, indicating another consecutive equal key input. The system then checks the value of the counter KTIME. This is shown in step 10 of Figure 4-21. In step 10 the system is determining if 50 consecutive equal key inputs have been received.

If the value of the KTIME counter is not equal to 50, the system jumps back to step 5 in the flowchart of Figure 4-21. At step 5 the row enable is reset such that row 0 is active and the system returns again to the software section to input another key from the keyboard.

If the value of the KTIME counter in step 10 of the flowchart in Figure 4-21 is equal to 50, the following occurs. First, this indicates to the system that a valid key has been input. The value of the key is stored in two different places. These places are KWGT and KCOMP. The system uses KWGT for the location of the valid key input weight.

Once the system has detected 50 consecutive key closures, it jumps to the section of code that will detect 50 consecutive key releases. Until the key is once again released, we must not execute any function based on the key that was closed. Otherwise, the microprocessor system could execute so fast that before we could release the key, the system would have executed the key function many times. So we must go to a section of code where we can wait for 50 key releases before any action is taken on a detected key input.

A single key release is defined by a complete scan of all rows without detecting any active column. The flowchart for realizing this function is shown in Figure 4-22. Notice that the first event to occur is the KROW value being set to enable the first input row line to the keyboard (step 1 of Figure 4-22). Next, the KTIME counter is reset to 0. In this section of code the KTIME counter will keep track of how many consecutive times no key was detected per scan of the keyboard

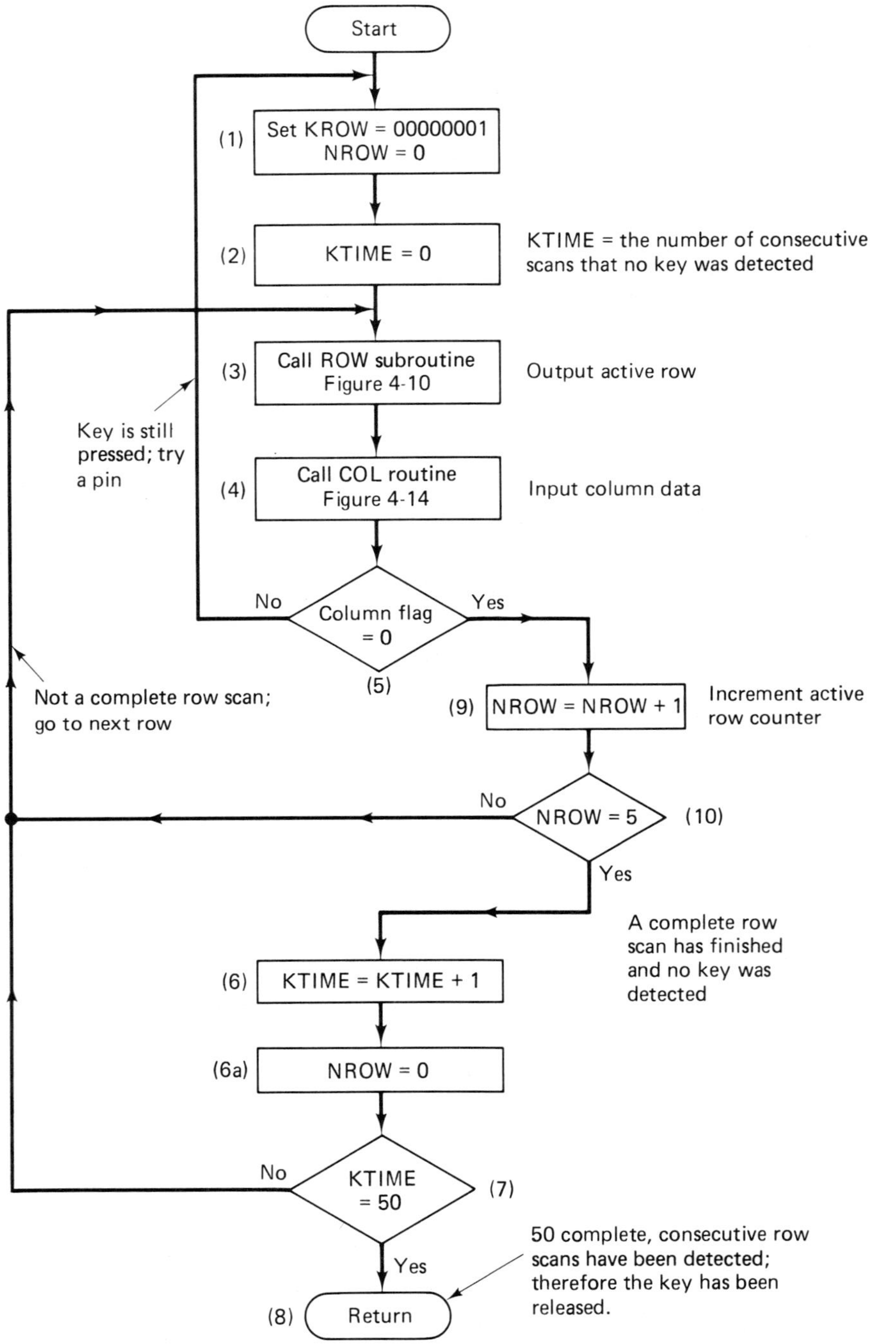

Figure 4-22 Flowchart showing major system events for detecting a valid key release.

rows (step 2 of the flowchart). The system then calls the subroutine labeled ROW (step 3 of the flowchart). This subroutine enables the correct row input to the keyboard output device. Now the system calls the subroutine labeled COL.

The COL subroutine monitors the column outputs of the keyboard. The COL subroutine will set the column flag equal to a 0 if no column line is active. If a column line were active, the system would start the subroutine over again as shown by the line from step 5 to step 1 in the flowchart.

If the column flag were equal to 0, indicating that all columns were nonactive, the routine would take the path from step 5 to step 9. In step 9 the system would increment a counter called NROW. The NROW counter keeps track of how many consecutive times the COL subroutine is executed when no key input is detected by the system. The NROW counter is actually keeping track of which row is presently active. When NROW equals 5, the fifth row has been asserted and no key has been detected by the system.

In this case, the routine of Figure 4-22 branches from step 10 to step 6. In step 6 the KTIME counter is incremented by 1. The KTIME counter keeps track of how many consecutive row scans are made without a key closure.

When KTIME equals 50, the entire key input routine for a single key closure is complete. We can see that many events occur within a system for a single key closure. When the system returns from the key release routine labeled KREL to the main program, the software checks the value of the key being entered and directs the system where to start executing the system software. This system software will then perform the function that is indicated by the key that is being depressed.

Figure 4-23 is a general flowchart that shows how the main program uses a KEYIN subroutine. A KEYIN subroutine returns to the main program only after it has input a valid key. The validity of the key input is based on the restriction of 50 consecutive key closures and 50 consecutive key releases. Therefore, the KEYIN routine does not return until after the pressed key has been released.

The main program then computes an address to jump to based on the value of KWGT that was set by the KEYIN routine. At these sections of the program the system will execute certain functions based on the key that was input. We can see how the keyboard could be used for any general purpose application. The functions of the keys are assigned to be used in the system software. This means they may be changed from one function to another easily.

For our system the function of each key will be to write a unique KWGT value to the system output display's lower 2 digits. This means that if we press key labeled R_4C_4, which corresponds to a weight of 24, the display will read 000024. With this program we can initially determine if our key input routine is working. After the input routine is working we can assign real functions to the keys within the keyboard matrix.

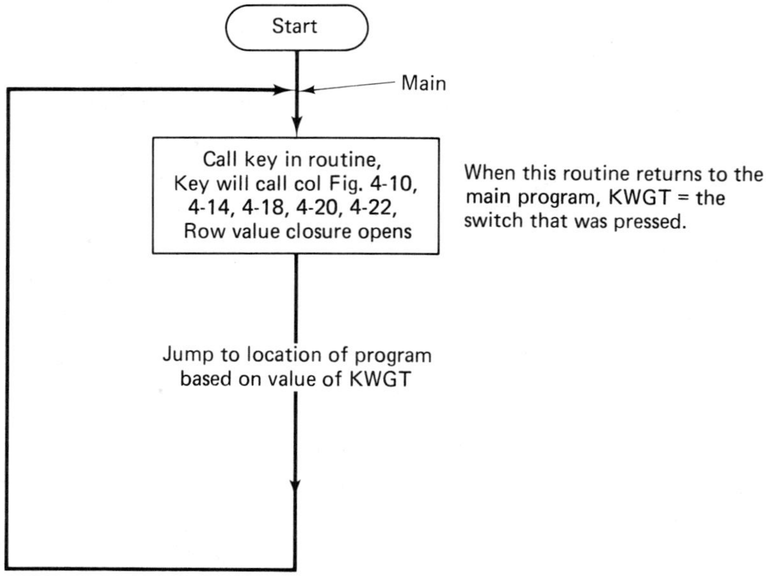

Figure 4-23 Flowchart showing how the main program calls the subroutine for inputting a key value.

4-12 Program Initialization

Before we write the program to perform the overall system functions, we must decide what the initialization section of our system software should be. Normally this section of code is executed only when power is first turned on to the system. It may also be executed when the overall system reset key is pressed by the operator. (Refer to Chapter 2 for the discussion of system reset on the microprocessors you are studying.)

In the initialization section of the program, we set all variables that must be initialized to certain values that will be required later in the program. For example, the stack pointer is initialized, and the interrupt masks are set if applicable. (We have not discussed the interrupts yet. We will do so in Chapter 6.)

For our program we need to set the following variables:

1. Stack Pointer (this is a function of the memory mapping of our system)
2. KROW = 00000001
3. NROW = 0
4. KTIME = 0

5. COLFG = 0 (Column Flag)
6. Write Display = FF0000

This will initialize our display to a known value.

The complete program for executing this overall system function is shown in Figure 4-24. Figure 4-24 shows the 8080 mnemonics, and Figure 4-25 shows the 6800 mnemonics. These figures appear on the following 14 pages.

4-13 Summary

In this chapter we have discussed a complete microprocessor system for inputting data from a general keyboard and writing data to a general system display. We may be inclined to think that this system performs a useless function because in effect it does nothing. However, if we understand how the system operates, then a universal building block for small microprocessor systems has been added to our design tools. In Chapter 8 we will show how this concept can be expanded to perform a very useful function—that of automatically programming an EPROM. We will use the same keyboard concept and the same general output display presented here. More software will be written and some hardware will be added. But this general interactive mode of keyboard and display will be used. In Chapter 5 we will discuss a technique for debugging a small prototype system and for trouble-shooting defective hardware. You should understand in detail the concepts presents in this chapter before proceeding to the next chapters because the information that follows depends on your understanding of the information presented here.

```
0000            ******************************************************************
0000            *
0000            *   8080 PROGRAM FOR INPUTTING A KEY AND WRITE TO DISPLAY
0000            *
0000            *******  PROGRAMMER: JIM COFFRON    8-28-79   ****************
0000            *
0000            *
0000                ORG  00         SET STARTING ADDRESS IN MEM
0000            *
0000            *   WE FIRST MUST INITIALIZE ALL VARIABLES
0000            *
0000 31 FF 13       LXI  SP,13FFH INITAILIZE STACK POINTER
0003 AF             XRA  A          RESET FLAGS, ZERO ACC
0004 FB             EI              ENABLE INTERRUPTS
0005 D3 F0          OUT  0F0H       ZERO OUT DISPLAY
0007 D3 F1          OUT  0F1H
0009 D3 F2          OUT  0F2H       SET DISPLAY=000000
000B 32 00 10       STA  KTIME      KTIME=0
000E 32 01 10       STA  CFLAG      CFLAG=0
0011 32 02 10       STA  KWGHT      KWGHT=0
0014 32 03 10       STA  KCOMP      KCOMP=0
0017 3C             INR  A          ACC=1
0018 32 04 10       STA  KROW       KROW=00000001
001B            *
001B            *
001B            *   NOW TO SET MEMORY ADDRESS OF VARIABLES
001B            *
001B            KTIME EQU  1000H
001B            CFLAG EQU  KTIME+1
001B            KWGHT EQU  CFLAG+1
001B            KCOMP EQU  KWGHT+1
001B            KROW  EQU  KCOMP+1
001B            NROW  EQU  KROW+1
001B            *
001B            *
001B            ******  NOW TO START THE PROGRAM  *********
001B            *
001B            *   START OF FIGURE 4-20
001B            *
001B CD EB 00 SROW  CALL  OROW      OUTPUT THE ACTIVE ROW
001E CD DB 00       CALL COLM       CALL COLUMN ROUTINE
0021 3A 01 10       LDA  CFLAG      NEED TO CHECK THE COLUMN FLAG
0024 FE 00          CPI  00H        CHECK FOR ACTIVE COLUMN
0026 CA 1B 00       JZ   SROW       NO ACTIVE COLUMN LOOP AGAIN
0029 CD B1 00       CALL  KEYW      ACTIVE COLUMN, WHICH ONE???
002C            *
002C            *   END OF FIGURE 4-20
002C            *
002C            *   START OF FIGURE 4-21
002C            *
002C            ***** WE HAVE AN ACTIVE KEY *******
002C            *
002C            *****(STEP 1)
002C            *
002C 3A 00 10       LDA  KTIME      RECALL KTIME FROM MEM
002F            *
002F            *
002F            *****(STEP 2)
002F            *
002F FE 00          CPI  00H        KTIME=0??
```

Figure 4-24 Program for inputting a key and write to display.

```
0031 CA 5B 00        JZ   KCL01     YES THIS IS FIRST TIME
0034                 *
0034                 *** NOT THE FIRST TIME *****
0034                 *
0034                 *****(STEP 7)
0034                 *
0034 3A 02 10        LDA  KWGHT     WHAT KEY VALUE WAS PUSHED???
0037 4F              MOV  C,A       C REG = KWGHT
0038 3A 03 10        LDA  KCOMP     A REG = COMPARE VALUE
003B B9              CMP  C         KCOMP=KWGHT?
003C CA 46 00        JZ   KCL02     YES THEY DO!!!!!!
003F                 *
003F                 *****(STEP 8)
003F                 *
003F AF              XRA  A         THEY ARE NOT EQUAL
0040 32 00 10        STA  KTIME     RESET THE KTIME VARIABLE
0043 C3 66 00        JMP  KCL03     GOTO RESET ACTIVE ROW
0046                 *
0046                 ****(STEP 9)
0046                 *
0046 3A 00 10  KCL02 LDA  KTIME     RECALL KTIME FROM MEM
0049 3C              INR  A         KTIME=KTIME+1
004A 32 00 10        STA  KTIME     KTIME=KTIME+1
004D                 *
004D                 *****(STEP 10)
004D                 *
004D FE 32           CPI  50        KTIME=50??
004F C2 65 00        JNZ  KCL03     NOT 50 YET
0052 CD 6F 00        CALL KOPN      CHECK FOR KEY OPEN
0055 CD A7 00        CALL KOUT      OUTPUT THE KEY
0058 C3 1B 00        JMP  SROW      BACK TO THE START
005B                 *
005B                 *****(STEP 3)
005B                 *
005B 3A 02 10  KCL01 LDA  KWGHT
005E 32 03 10        STA  KCOMP     KCOMP=KWGHT
0061                 *
0061                 *****(STEP 4)
0061                 *
0061 3E 01           MVI  A,01
0063 32 00 10        STA  KTIME     UP DATE KTIME=1
0066                 *
0066                 ****(STEP 5)
0056                 *
0066 3E 01     KCL03 MVI  A,01
0068 32 04 10        STA  KROW      RESET ACTIVE ROW=00000001
006B                 *
006B                 *****(STEP 6)
006B                 *
006B C3 1B 00        JMP  SROW      GOTO START OF PROGRAM
006E                 *
006E                 *
006E                 ***********************************************************
006E                 *
006E                 ******    START OF SUBROUTINES     ************
006E                 *
006E                 ***********************************************************
006E                 *
006E                 *
006E                 *  FIGURE 4-22
```

Figure 4-24 (Cont'd.)

```
006E               *  KEY OPEN SUBROUTINE
006E               *
006E               ***************************************************************
006E               *
006E               ******(STEP 1)
006E               *
006E 3E 01         KOPN  MVI  A,01
0070 32 04 10            STA  KROW      SET KROW=00000001
0073 3D                  DCR  A
0074 32 05 10            STA  NROW      SET NROW=00000000
0077               *
0077               *****(STEP 2)
0077               *
0077 32 00 10            STA  KTIME     KTIME=0
007A               *
007A               *****(STEP 3)
007A               *
007A CD EB 00      KOPN1 CALL OROW      OUTPUT THE ROW
007D               *
007D               *****(STEP 4)
007D               *
007D CD DB 00            CALL COLM      INPUT THE COLUMN DATA
0080               *
0080               *****(STEP 5)
0080               *
0080 3A 01 10            LDA  CFLAG     INPUT THE CFLAG DATA
0083 FE 00               CPI  00        CFLAG=0??
0085 C2 6E 00            JNZ  KOPN      KEY NOT RELEASED YET
0088               *
0088               *****(STEP 9)
0088               *
0088 3A 05 10            LDA  NROW      INPUT THE ACTIVE ROW
008B 3C                  INR  A
008C 32 05 10            STA  NROW      UPDATE THE ACTIVE ROW
008F               *
008F               *****(STEP 10)
008F               *
008F FE 05               CPI  05
0091 C2 7A 00            JNZ  KOPN1     NOT A COMPLETE SCAN
0094               *
0094               *****(STEP 6)
0094               *
0094 3A 00 10            LDA  KTIME
0097 3C                  INR  A
0098 32 00 10            STA  KTIME
009B 47                  MOV  B,A       B REG=KTIME
009C               *
009C               ******(STEP 6A)
009C               *
009C AF                  XRA  A
009D 32 05 10            STA  NROW      ROW VALUE =0
00A0               *
00A0               *****(STEP 7)
00A0               *
00A0 3E 32               MVI  A,50
00A2 B8                  CMP  B         KTIME=50???
00A3 C2 7A 00            JNZ  KOPN1     NO, TRY ANOTHER SCAN
00A6               *
00A6               ******(STEP 8)
00A6               *
```

Figure 4-24 (Cont'd.)

```
00A6 C9                RET             RETURN FROM THIS OPEN ROUTINE
00A7              *
00A7              *
00A7              ***************************************************************
00A7              *
00A7              *     SUBROUTINE KOUT
00A7              *
00A7              *  THIS SUBROUTINE WILL OUTPUT THE KEY TO THE DISPLAY
00A7              *
00A7              ***************************************************************
00A7              *
00A7 3A 02 10 KOUT   LDA   KWGHT     VALUE OF KEY IN ACC
00AA D3 F0             OUT   0F0H
00AC D3 F1             OUT 0F1H
00AE D3 F2             OUT 0F2H
00B0 C9                RET
00B1              *
00B1              ***************************************************************
00B1              *
00B1              *  SUBROUTINE KEYW
00B1              *
00B1              *  THIS SUBROUTINE WILL COMPUTE THE VALUE OF THE KEY PUSHED
00B1              *
00B1              ***************************************************************
00B1              *
00B1              ***** THIS ROUTINE IS FROM FIGURE 4-18
00B1              *
00B1              ******(STEP 1)
00B1              *
00B1 AF           KEYW   XRA   A          ZERO FLAGS AND ACC
00B2 3A 01 10          LDA   CFLAG     GET COLUMN FLAG FROM MEM
00B5              *
00B5              *****(STEP 2)
00B5              *
00B5 06 00             MVI   B,00      ZERO THE COUNTER
00B7              *
00B7              ****(STEP 3)
00B7              *
00B7 1F           KEYW1 RAR             SHIFT RIGHT 1 BIT,0 INTO D7
00B8 FE 00             CPI   00
00BA              *
00BA              ****(STEP 4)
00BA              *
00BA CA C1 00          JZ   KEYW2      BREG=0,1,2,3,4 (STEP 6)
00BD              *
00BD              *****(STEP 5)
00BD              *
00BD 04                INR   B
00BE C3 B7 00          JMP   KEYW1     INCREMENT COUNTER GO AGAIN
00C1              *
00C1              *****(STEP 7)
00C1              *
00C1 AF           KEYW2 XRA   A        ZERO THE FLAGS
00C2 3A 04 10          LDA   KROW      RECALL ACTIVE ROW
00C5              *
00C5              *****(STEP 8)
00C5              *
00C5 0E 00             MVI   C,00      ZERO THE COUNTER T2
00C7              *
00C7              ******(STEP 9)
```

Figure 4-24 (Cont'd.)

```
00C7            *
00C7 1F         KEYW3 RAR               SHIFT RIGHT 1 BIT,0 INTO D7
00C8 FE 00            CPI   00
00CA            *
00CA            *******(STEP 10)
00CA            *
00CA CA D1 00         JZ    KEYW4       IF ZERO THEN DONE
00CD            *
00CD            *****(STEP 14)
00CD            *
00CD 0C               INR   C           INCREMENT THE COUNTER
00CE C3 C7 00         JMP   KEYW3       GO AGAIN
00D1            *
00D1            *****(STEP 11)
00D1            *
00D1 AF         KEYW4 XRA   A           ZERO THE FLAGS
00D2 78               MOV   A,B         ACC=COLUMN COUNT(T1)
00D3 17               RAL               B*2
00D4 17               RAL               B*4
00D5 80               ADD B             B*5
00D6 81               ADD C             (B*5)+C=0 - 24
00D7            *
00D7            *******(STEP 12)
00D7            *
00D7 32 02 10         STA   KWGHT
00DA            *
00DA            *******(STEP 13)
00DA            *
00DA C9               RET               RETURN FROM THIS SUBROUTINE
00DB            *
00DB            ****************************************************************
00DB            *
00DB            *  COLM SUBROUTINE
00DB            *
00DB            *   THIS SUBROUTINE WILL DETERMINE THE ACTIVE COLUMN
00DB            *   IF THERE IS ONE.
00DB            *
00DB            ****************************************************************
00DB            *
00DB            *   THIS SUBROUTINE IS FIGURE 4-15
00DB            *
00DB            ****************************************************************
00DB            *
00DB            ******(STEP 1)
00DB            *
00DB AF         COLM  XRA   A
00DC 32 01 10         STA   CFLAG       SET THE COLUMN FLAG=0
00DF            *
00DF            ******(STEP 2)
00DF            *
00DF DB FE            IN    0FEH        INPUT DATA FROM PORT FE
00E1            *
00E1            ******(STEP 3)
00E1            *
00E1 F6 E0            ORI   0E0H        SET BITS D5,D6,D7=1
00E3            *
00E3            *******(STEP 4)
00E3            *
00E3 FE FF            CPI   0FFH
00E5 C8               RZ                STEP(4A)
```

Figure 4-24 (Cont'd.)

```
00E6                *
00E6                *****(STEP 5)
00E6                *
00E6 2F                  CMA              INVERT THE DATA
00E7                *
00E7                ******(STEP 6)
00E7                *
00E7 32 01 10            STA   CFLAG      SET THE COLUMN FLAG
00EA C9                  RET              RETURN FROM THIS SUB
00EB                *
00EB                *************************************************************
00EB                *
00EB                * SUBROUTINE TO OUTPUT THE ACTIVE ROW TO THE KEYBOARD
00EB                *
00EB                *  OROW IS THE NAME OF THIS SUBROUTINE
00EB                *
00EB                *  THIS IS FIGURE 4-12
00EB                *
00EB                *************************************************************
00EB                *************************************************************
00EB                *
00EB                *  FIGURE  4-12     8080 MNEMONICS FOR FIGURE 4-10
00EB                *
00EB                *************************************************************
00EB                *
00EB                *
00EB 3A 04 10 OROW   LDA KROW   RECALL ACTIVE ROW
00EE                *
00EE                * STEP  2
00EE                *
00EE FE 10               CPI   10H        COMPLETE ROW SCAN????
00F0 C2 F8 00            JNZ   OROW1      IF NOT THEN STEP 2B
00F3                *
00F3                * STEP  2A
00F3                *
00F3 3E 01               MVI   A,01H      RESET THE ACTIVE ROW
00F5 C3 F9 00            JMP   ST3        GOTO STEP 3
00F8                *
00F8                * STEP  2B
00F8                *
00F8 07             OROW1 RLC             SHIFT DATA LEFT,0 INTO D0
00F9                *
00F9                * STEP 3
00F9                *
00F9 32 04 10 ST3    STA   KROW       SAVE ACTIVE ROW IN MEM
00FC                *
00FC                *  STEP 4
00FC                *
00FC 2F                  CMA              INVERT ROW WORD
00FD                *
00FD                * STEP 5
00FD                *
00FD D3 FE               OUT 0FEH         OUTPUT ACTIVE ROW TO PORT FE
00FF                *
00FF                *STEP 6
00FF                *
00FF C9                  RET
0100                *
0100                *
0100                *************************************************************
0100                *
0100                     END              END STATEMENT FOR THE ASSEMBLER

  0 ERRORS              22 SYMBOLS
```

Figure 4-24 (Cont'd.)

```
LF426   T=00003 IS ON CR00020 USING 00071 BLKS R=1410

1 PAGE      1  F425       WED OCT 03, 1979    11:22:42.58



                      ****************************************************
                      *
                      *  6800 PROGRAM FOR INPUTTING A KEY AND WRITE TO DISP
                      *
                      *******  PROGRAMMER: JIM COFFRON    ******************
                      *
                      *
                                NAM    F425
FC00                            ORG    $FC00     SET STARTING ADDRESS IN MEM
                      *
                      *  WE FIRST MUST INITIALIZE ALL VARIABLES
                      *
FC00 8E 13FF BEGIN      LDS    #$13FF    INITAILIZE STACK POINTER
FC03 86 00              LDA A  #$00      RESET FLAGS, ZERO ACC
FC05 01 F0              STA A  #$F0      ZERO OUT DISPLAY
FC07 01 F1              STA A  #$F1
FC09 01 F2              STA A  #$F2      SET DISPLAY=000000
FC0B B7 1000            STA A  KTIME     KTIME=0
FC0E B7 1001            STA A  CFLAG     CFLAG=0
FC11 B7 1002            STA A  KWGHT     KWGHT=0
FC14 B7 1003            STA A  KCOMP     KCOMP=0
FC17 4C                 INC A            ACC=1
FC18 B7 1004            STA A  KROW      KROW=00000001
                      *
                      *
                      *  NOW TO SET MEMORY ADDRESS OF VARIABLES
                      *
             1000 KTIME EQU    $1000
             1001 CFLAG EQU    KTIME+1
             1002 KWGHT EQU    CFLAG+1
             1003 KCOMP EQU    KWGHT+1
             1004 KROW  EQU    KCOMP+1
             1005 NROW  EQU    KROW+1
                      *
                      *
                      ******  NOW TO START THE PROGRAM  *********
                      *
                      *  START OF FIGURE 4-20
                      *
FC1B BD FCF2 SROW       JSR    OROW      OUTPUT THE ACTIVE ROW
FC1E BD FCDF            JSR    COLM      CALL COLUMN ROUTINE
FC21 B6 1001            LDA A  CFLAG     NEED TO CHECK THE COLUMN FLAG
FC24 81 00              CMP A  #$00      CHECK FOR ACTIVE COLUMN
FC26 27 F3              BEQ    SROW      NO ACTIVE COLUMN LOOP AGAIN
FC28 BD FCAD            JSR    KEYW      ACTIVE COLUMN, WHICH ONE???
                      *
                      *  END OF FIGURE 4-20
                      *
                      *  START OF FIGURE 4-21
                      *
                      ***** WE HAVE AN ACTIVE KEY *******
                      *
                      *****(STEP 1)
                      *
```

Figure 4-25(a) Program for inputting a key and write to display.

```
1 PAGE      2  F425       WED OCT 03, 1979    11:22:42.58



 00055 FC2B B6 1000          LDA A   KTIME     RECALL KTIME FROM MEM
 00056                 *
 00057                 *
 00058                 *****(STEP 2)
 00059                 *
 00060 FC2E 81 00            CMP A   #$00      KTIME=0??
 00061 FC30 27 25            BEQ     KCL01     YES THIS IS FIRST TIME
 00062                 *
 00063                 *** NOT THE FIRST TIME *****
 00064                 *
 00065                 *****(STEP 7)
 00066                 *
 00067 FC32 F6 1002          LDA B   KWGHT     WHAT KEY VALUE WAS PUSHED???
 00068 FC35 B6 1003          LDA A   KCOMP     A REG = COMPARE VALUE
 00069 FC38 11               CBA               COMPARE THE TWO VALUES
 00070 FC39 27 08            BEQ     KCL02     YES THEY DO!!!!!!
 00071                 *
 00072                 *****(STEP 8)
 00073                 *
 00074 FC3B 86 00            LDA A   #$00      THEY ARE NOT EQUAL
 00075 FC3D B7 1000          STA A   KTIME     RESET THE KTIME VARIABLE
 00076 FC40 7E FC62          JMP     KCL03     GOTO RESET ACTIVE ROW
 00077                 *
 00078                 ****(STEP 9)
 00079                 *
 00080 FC43 B6 1000 KCL02    LDA A   KTIME     RECALL KTIME FROM MEM
 00081 FC46 4C               INC A             KTIME=KTIME+1
 00082 FC47 B7 1000          STA A   KTIME     KTIME=KTIME+1
 00083                 *
 00084                 *****(STEP 10)
 00085                 *
 00086 FC4A 81 32            CMP A   #50       KTIME=50??
 00087 FC4C 26 14            BNE     KCL03     NOT 50 YET
 00088 FC4E BD FC6A          JSR     KOPN      CHECK FOR KEY OPEN
 00089 FC51 BD FCA3          JSR     KOUT      OUTPUT THE KEY
 00090 FC54 7E FC1B          JMP     SROW      BACK TO THE START
 00091                 *
 00092                 *****(STEP 3)
 00093                 *
 00094 FC57 B6 1002 KCL01    LDA A   KWGHT
 00095 FC5A B7 1003          STA A   KCOMP     KCOMP=KWGHT
 00096                 *
 00097                 *****(STEP 4)
 00098                 *
 00099 FC5D 86 01            LDA A   #$01
 00100 FC5F B7 1000          STA A   KTIME     UP DATE KTIME=1
 00101                 *
 00102                 ****(STEP 5)
 00103                 *
 00104 FC62 86 01   KCL03    LDA A   #$01
 00105 FC64 B7 1004          STA A   KROW      RESET ACTIVE ROW=00000001
 00106                 *
 00107                 *****(STEP 6)
 00108                 *
 00109 FC67 7E FC1B          JMP     SROW      GOTO START OF PROGRAM
1 PAGE      3  F425       WED OCT 03, 1979    11:22:42.58
```

Figure 4-25 (Cont'd.)

```
00110                   *
00111                   *
00112                   ***************************************************************
00113                   *
00114                   ******    START OF SUBROUTINES     ************
00115                   *
00116                   ***************************************************************
00117                   *
00118                   *
00119                   *  FIGURE 4-22
00120                   *  KEY OPEN SUBROUTINE
00121                   *
00122                   ***************************************************************
00123                   *
00124                   ******(STEP 1)
00125                   *
00126 FC6A 86 01        KOPN   LDA A   #$01
00127 FC6C B7 1004             STA A   KROW     SET KROW=00000001
00128 FC6F 4A                  DEC A
00129 FC70 B7 1005             STA A   NROW     SET NROW=00000000
00130                   *
00131                   *****(STEP 2)
00132                   *
00133 FC73 B7 1000             STA A   KTIME    KTIME=0
00134                   *
00135                   *****(STEP 3)
00136                   *
00137 FC76 BD FCF2      KOPN1  JSR     OROW     OUTPUT THE ROW
00138                   *
00139                   *****(STEP 4)
00140                   *
00141 FC79 BD FCDF             JSR     COLM     INPUT THE COLUMN DATA
00142                   *
00143                   *****(STEP 5)
00144                   *
00145 FC7C B6 1001             LDA A   CFLAG    INPUT THE CFLAG DATA
00146 FC7F 81 00               CMP A   #00      CFLAG=0??
00147 FC81 26 E7               BNE     KOPN     KEY NOT RELEASED YET
00148                   *
00149                   *****(STEP 9)
00150                   *
00151 FC83 B6 1005             LDA A   NROW     INPUT THE ACTIVE ROW
00152 FC86 4C                  INC A
00153 FC87 B7 1005             STA A   NROW     UPDATE THE ACTIVE ROW
00154                   *
00155                   *****(STEP 10)
00156                   *
00157 FC8A 81 05               CMP A   #05
00158 FC8C 26 E8               BNE     KOPN1    NOT A COMPLETE SCAN
00159                   *
00160                   *****(STEP 6)
00161                   *
00162 FC8E B6 1000             LDA A   KTIME
00163 FC91 4C                  INC A
00164 FC92 B7 1000             STA A   KTIME
1 PAGE     4  F425         WED OCT 03, 1979    11:22:42.58
```

Figure 4-25 (Cont'd.)

```
FC95 F6 1000            LDA B  KTIME      B REG=KTIME
                 *
                 ******(STEP 6A)
                 *
FC98 86 00              LDA A  #00
FC9A B7 1005            STA A  NROW       ROW VALUE =0
                 *
                 *****(STEP 7)
                 *
FC9D 86 32              LDA A  #50
FC9F 11                 CBA               KTIME=50???
FCA0 26 D4              BNE    KOPN1      NO, TRY ANOTHER SCAN
                 *
                 ******(STEP 8)
                 *
FCA2 39                 RTS               RETURN FROM THIS OPEN ROUTINE
                 *
                 *
                 ************************************************************
                 *
                 *    SUBROUTINE KOUT
                 *
                 *  THIS SUBROUTINE WILL OUTPUT THE KEY TO THE DISPLAY
                 *
                 ************************************************************
                 *
FCA3 B6 1002     KOUT   LDA A  KWGHT      VALUE OF KEY IN ACC
FCA6 01 F0              STA A  #$F0
FCA8 01 F1              STA A  #$F1
FCAA 01 F2              STA A  #$F2
FCAC 39                 RTS
                 *
                 ************************************************************
                 *
                 *  SUBROUTINE KEYW
                 *
                 *  THIS SUBROUTINE WILL COMPUTE THE VALUE OF THE KEY
                 *
                 ************************************************************
                 *
                 ***** THIS ROUTINE IS FROM FIGURE 4-18
                 *
                 ******(STEP 1)
                 *
FCAD 86 00       KEYW   LDA A  #00        ZERO FLAGS AND ACC
FCAF B6 1001            LDA A  CFLAG      GET COLUMN FLAG FROM MEM
                 *
                 *****(STEP 2)
                 *
FCB2 C6 00              LDA B  #00        ZERO THE COUNTER
                 *
                 ****(STEP 3)
                 *
FCB4 47          KEYW1  ASR A             SHIFT RIGHT 1 BIT,0 INTO B7
FCB5 81 00              CMP A  #00
1 PAGE      5  F425      WED OCT 03, 1979    11:22:42.58
```

Figure 4-25 (Cont'd.)

```
00220 FCB7 37                PSH B
00221                  *
00222                  ****(STEP 4)
00223                  *
00224 FCB8 27 05             BEQ    KEYW2     BREG=0,1,2,3,4 (STEP 6)
00225                  *
00226 FCBA 33                PUL B
00227                  *****(STEP 5)
00228                  *
00229 FCBB 5C                INC B
00230 FCBC 7E FCB4           JMP    KEYW1     INCREMENT COUNTER GO AGAIN
00231                  *
00232                  *****(STEP 7)
00233                  *
00234 FCBF 86 00       KEYW2 LDA A  #00       ZERO THE FLAGS
00235 FCC1 B6 1004           LDA A  KROW      RECALL ACTIVE ROW
00236                  *
00237                  *****(STEP 8)
00238                  *
00239 FCC4 C6 00             LDA B  #00       ZERO THE COUNTER T2
00240                  *
00241                  ******(STEP 9)
00242                  *
00243 FCC6 47          KEYW3 ASR A            SHIFT RIGHT 1 BIT,0 INTO D7
00244 FCC7 81 00             CMP A  #00
00245 FCC9 37                PSH B
00246                  *
00247                  *******(STEP 10)
00248                  *
00249 FCCA 27 05             BEQ    KEYW4     IF ZERO THEN DONE
00250                  *
00251 FCCC 33                PUL B
00252                  *****(STEP 14)
00253                  *
00254 FCCD 5C                INC B            INCREMENT THE COUNTER
00255 FCCE 7E FCC6           JMP    KEYW3     GO AGAIN
00256                  *
00257                  *****(STEP 11)
00258                  *
00259 FCD1 33          KEYW4 PUL B            B REG = T2
00260 FCD2 32                PUL A            ACC=COLUMN COUNT(T1)
00261 FCD3 37                PSH B
00262 FCD4 36                PSH A
00263 FCD5 48                ASL A            T1*2
00264 FCD6 48                ASL A            T1*4
00265 FCD7 33                PUL B
00266 FCD8 1B                ABA              T1*5
00267 FCD9 33                PUL B
00268 FCDA 1B                ABA              (T1*5)+T2
00269                  *
00270                  *******(STEP 12)
00271                  *
00272 FCDB B7 1002           STA A  KWGHT
00273                  *
00274                  *******(STEP 13)
1 PAGE     6  F425      WED OCT 03, 1979    11:22:42.58
```

Figure 4-25 (Cont'd.)

```
00275                         *
00276 FCDE 39                       RTS                RETURN FROM THIS SUBROUTINE
00277                         *
00278                         ***********************************************************
00279                         *
00280                         *   COLM SUBROUTINE
00281                         *
00282                         *    THIS SUBROUTINE WILL DETERMINE THE ACTIVE COLUMN
00283                         *    IF THERE IS ONE.
00284                         *
00285                         ***********************************************************
00286                         *
00287                         *
00288                         *
00289                         ***********************************************************
00290                         *
00291                         ******(STEP 1)
00292                         *
00293 FCDF 86 00              COLM    LDA A   #00
00294 FCE1 B7 1001                    STA A   CFLAG      SET THE COLUMN FLAG=0
00295                         *
00296                         ******(STEP 2)
00297                         *
00298 FCE4 86 FE                      LDA A   #$FE       INPUT DATA FROM PORT FE
00299                         *
00300                         ******(STEP 3)
00301                         *
00302 FCE6 8A E0                      ORA A   #$E0       SET BITS D5,D6,D7=1
00303                         *
00304                         *******(STEP 4)
00305                         *
00306 FCE8 81 FF                      CMP A   #$FF
00307 FCEA 26 01                      BNE     NEXT
00308 FCEC 39                         RTS                STEP(4A)
00309                         *
00310                         *****(STEP 5)
00311                         *
00312 FCED 43                 NEXT    COM A              INVERT THE DATA
00313                         *
00314                         ******(STEP 6)
00315                         *
00316 FCEE B7 1001                    STA A   CFLAG      SET THE COLUMN FLAG
00317 FCF1 39                         RTS                RETURN FROM THIS SUB
00318                         *
00319                         ***********************************************************
00320                         *
00321                         * SUBROUTINE TO OUTPUT THE ACTIVE ROW TO THE KEYBOARD
00322                         *
00323                         *  OROW IS THE NAME OF THIS SUBROUTINE
00324                         *
00325                         *
00326                         *
00327                         ***********************************************************
00328                         ***********************************************************
00329                         *
1 PAGE      7  F425            WED OCT 03, 1979    11:22:42.58



00330                         *  FIGURE  4-12     6800 MNEMONICS FOR FIGURE 4-10
```

Figure 4-25 (Cont'd.)

```
00331                       *
00332                       ************************************************************
00333                       *
00334                       *
00335 FCF2 B6 1004 OROW     LDA A  KROW       RECALL ACTIVE ROW
00336                       *
00337                       * STEP  2
00338                       *
00339 FCF5 81 10            CMP A  #$10       COMPLETE ROW SCAN????
00340 FCF7 26 05            BNE    OROW1      IF NOT THEN STEP 2B
00341                       *
00342                       * STEP  2A
00343                       *
00344 FCF9 86 01            LDA A  #$01       RESET THE ACTIVE ROW
00345 FCFB 7E FCFF          JMP    ST3        GOTO STEP 3
00346                       *
00347                       * STEP  2B
00348                       *
00349 FCFE 48      OROW1    ASL A             SHIFT DATA LEFT,0 INTO D0
00350                       *
00351                       * STEP 3
00352                       *
00353 FCFF B7 1004 ST3      STA A  KROW       SAVE ACTIVE ROW IN MEM
00354                       *
00355                       *  STEP 4
00356                       *
00357 FD02 43               COM A             INVERT ROW WORD
00358                       *
00359                       * STEP 5
00360                       *
00361 FD03 01 FE            STA A  #$FE       OUTPUT ACTIVE ROW TO PORT FE
00362                       *
00363                       *STEP 6
00364                       *
00365 FD05 39               RTS
00366                       *
00367                       ********NOW TO SET THE RESTART VECTOR *****
00368                       *
00369 FFFE                  ORG    $FFFE
00370 FFFE    FC00          FDB    BEGIN
00371                       *
00372                       *
00373                       *
00374                       ************************************************************
00375                       *
00376                       END               END STATEMENT FOR THE ASSEMBLE
1 PAGE      8  F425      WED OCT 03, 1979   11:22:42.58



BEGIN   FC00 00013 00370
CFLAG   1001 00029 00316 00294 00210 00145 00042 00030 00019
COLM    FCDF 00293 00141 00041
KCL01   FC57 00094 00061
KCL02   FC43 00080 00070
KCL03   FC62 00104 00087 00076
KCOMP   1003 00031 00095 00068 00032 00021
KEYW    FCAD 00209 00045
KEYW1   FCB4 00218 00230
KEYW2   FCBF 00234 00224
```

Figure 4-25 (Cont'd.)

```
KEYW3  FCC6 00243 00255
KEYW4  FCD1 00259 00249
KOPN   FC6A 00126 00147 00088
KOPN1  FC76 00137 00176 00158
KOUT   FCA3 00191 00089
KROW   1004 00032 00353 00335 00235 00127 00105 00033 00023
KTIME  1000 00028 00165 00164 00162 00133 00100 00082 00080 00075 00055
                  00029 00018
KWGHT  1002 00030 00272 00191 00094 00067 00031 00020
NEXT   FCED 00312 00307
NROW   1005 00033 00170 00153 00151 00129
OROW   FCF2 00335 00137 00040
OROW1  FCFE 00349 00340
SROW   FC18 00040 00109 00090 00044
ST3    FCFF 00353 00345
```

Figure 4-25 (Cont'd.)

5

DEBUGGING THE HARDWARE USING STATIC STIMULUS TESTING

In this chapter we will present a technique for debugging the hardware of a microprocessor system. This technique will work equally well for a system that has just been constructed and has never been working (prototype system) or a system that was once working and has now become inoperative.

The technique we will use for debugging the hardware is called "Static Stimulus Testing." The technique for status stimulus testing was developed by the author. The concept was first presented in a text entitled *Understanding and Troubleshooting the Microprocessor,* published by Prentice Hall, 1980. We will show how to use static stimulus testing for finding system hardware faults.

5-1 The Concept of Static Stimulus Testing

In the first four chapters of this text we discussed many details concerning a microprocessor system. In Chapter 4 we actually designed system software for a complete microprocessor controlled system. In reviewing these chapters let us examine exactly what the hardware consisted of.

The hardware of the microprocessor consisted of these eight major blocks:

1. the microprocessor
2. the system address bus
3. the bi-directional data bus

4. the system control bus logic and buffers
5. the system ROM
6. the system RAM
7. the system input devices and
8. the system output devices

Further, we notice that each of the items 2 through 8, just listed, are controlled by the microprocessor. That is, the microprocessor generates the signals that access all ROM, RAM, or input and output devices. The bus buffers merely reflect the binary information generated at the microprocessor outputs. This is the first key to the use of a static stimulus tester as a powerful debugging tool.

Now let us examine the characteristics of the major hardware blocks. *All these hardware blocks are static by nature*. That is, these hardware blocks do not require a special clock to be input to them periodically to refresh information. The system RAM that we will use is static, not dynamic. In many small microprocessor systems, the RAM will be static.

We now have two key points concerning the hardware of a microprocessor system that are valuable to know.

1. All peripheral hardware such as ROM, RAM, and input and output devices are controlled by the microprocessor.
2. The nature of all controlled hardware blocks is static.

Let us now, in a general sense, make use of the two key points to show some of the ways that hardware can be debugged by using a Static Stimulus Tester. We will take the example of reading data from the system ROM. In review, the microprocessor will electrically perform the four major events when we read data from the system ROM; it will

1. apply an address on the Address Bus,
2. prepare the microprocessor's Data Bus to receive data.
3. assert the Memory Read and Control signals
4. unassert the Memory Read and Control signals

Let us examine each of these four major events in detail. During this examination certain points will be stressed to bring to light the value of static stimulus testing.

As stated above, when the system is reading ROM, the microprocessor will first apply an address on the system address bus. *What does this address do?* This address will select a correct system ROM and the correct location within the system ROM for the microprocessor to obtain 8 bits of data. *How is the selection process accomplished in the hardware?* Some of the address lines will be inputs to address decoders that generate the correct memory select lines. Other address lines will be connected directly to the memory address input lines of the system ROM.

We recall that selecting the correct memory chip in the system, and the correct address in the chip, is truly an exercise in decoding combinational logic. We could set a microprocessor address on the address lines, leave the address stable for a long period of time, and the address decoders would always respond correctly. *In essence, address decoding is a non-time dependent function.*

The same microprocessor control signals that prepare the data bus to receive data are also used to assert the memory read signal. Here again the control bus signals are generated through the decoding logic of certain microprocessor output signals. This is similar to the memory select lines that are generated from the decoding of certain address lines. The control bus signals are generated from the decoding of certain microprocessor control signals. Further, we can leave the microprocessor control signals in a static logic state for a long period of time and the control bus signals will still respond correctly.

Unasserting the Memory Read and Control signals, the fourth major event, is really the same as the third major event in that the control bus is responding to control signals generated from the microprocessor.

From this discussion we see that the microprocessor is in reality a controller of the system that is capable of performing static operations very rapidly. Because each static operation occurs so rapidly we tend to forget the static nature of a microprocessor controlled system. It is the static nature of the system that leads us to this very effective method of debugging system hardware known as static stimulus testing.

5-2 The Hardware of the Static Stimulus Tester

We have presented an overview in the form of "If we could do this to the system, then that would happen." If we could apply an address to the system, or if we could apply the control signal to the system, then we could debug it. Let us see exactly what type of hardware is required to perform such signal input and monitoring. The type of signal input we will be doing is similar to the signal injection techniques used to debug analog circuits.

5-3 Address Lines

First, let us discuss how we could apply the address lines to the system. If we removed the microprocessor from the system we could install a cable into the socket where the microprocessor used to reside. (See Figure 5-1.) We could

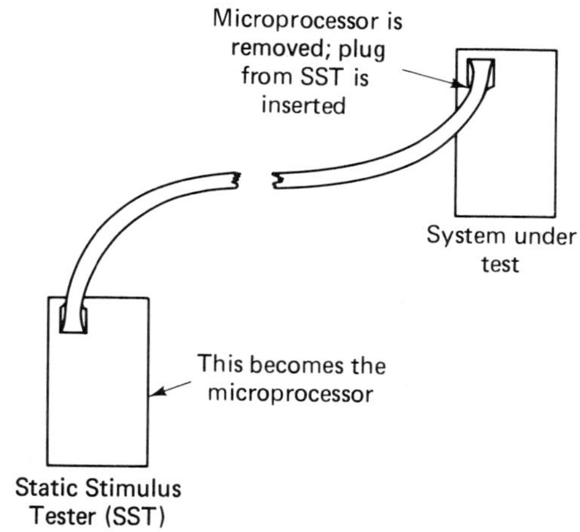

Figure 5-1 Block diagram showing how the Static Stimulus Tester is connected to the system under test.

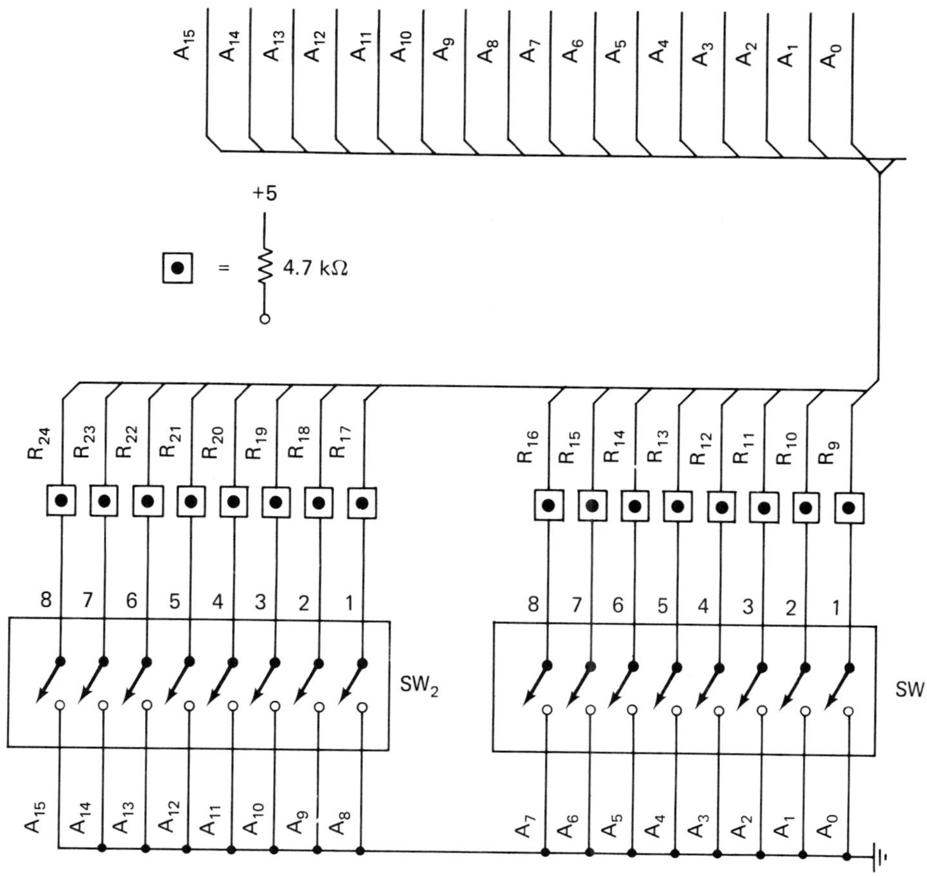

Figure 5-2 Schematic showing the hardware realization of the address switches for the Static Stimulus Tester.

then connect to the other end of this cable a group of toggle switches. Each switch would correspond to a microprocessor address line. Figure 5-2 shows the hardware realization of the switches required for all of the address lines.

5-4 Control Signals

We can set a group of switches similar to the address switches that can be designated as the microprocessor control signals. There will be as many switches in the group as there are control signal outputs on the microprocessor we are using. We will illustrate all the specifics when we design a Static Stimulus Tester for use with both the 8080 and 8085 microprocessors. The schematic for generation of the control signals is shown in Figure 5-3.

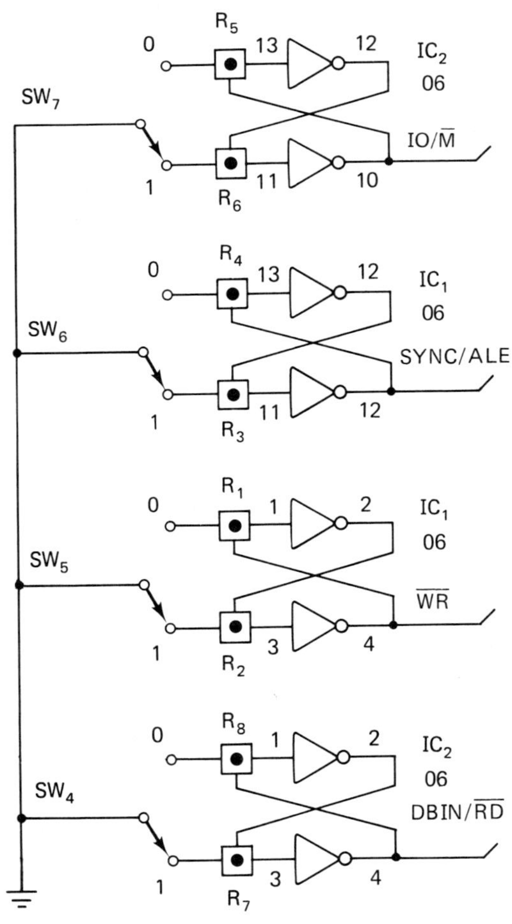

Figure 5-3 Schematic showing how control signals are generated for the Static Stimulus Tester.

5-5 Data Bus Lines

Data bus generation on a Static Stimulus Tester differs from either address bus or control bus generation, because this data bus is bi-directional, instead of uni-directional. So we must provide circuitry to generate data onto the system data bus and must provide additional circuitry for monitoring data placed on the bus by some other source. These two separate functions are exactly what a microprocessor does with the system data bus.

For each different microprocessor a different line is used to determine which mode the system is in. That is, is the system receiving data or is the system outputting data? For example, in the 8080 system when the DBIN control signal is logical 1, the system is in the read mode. In an 8085 system when the $\overline{\text{RD}}$ signal is in a logical 0 state, the system is in a read mode. Thus we must control our static stimulus test hardware differently for different microprocessors. Figure 5-4 shows the block diagram concept of two different modes the data bus must

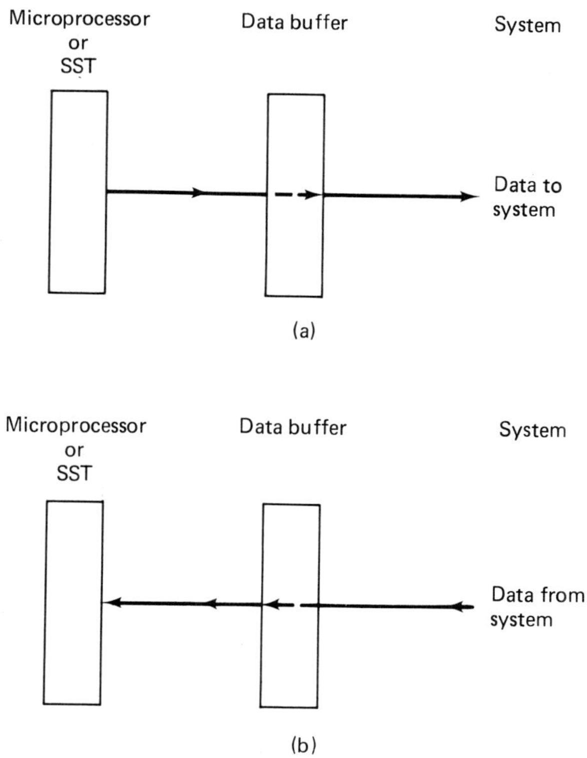

Figure 5-4 Block diagram showing the data flow into and out of the SST. These are exactly the same events that occur when the microprocessor is in control of a system and operating.

be placed in. Figure 5-5 shows the actual hardware required to realize the function of bi-directional data bus with hardware.

Referring to Figure 5-5, we note the following. When the control signal input is a logical 0, the LEDs reflect data placed on the data bus by the switches. This is the mode where a Static Stimulus Tester or the microprocessor is *outputting* data to the system on the data bus. When a control signal input is logical 1, the LEDs reflect data placed on the data bus by some other source within the system.

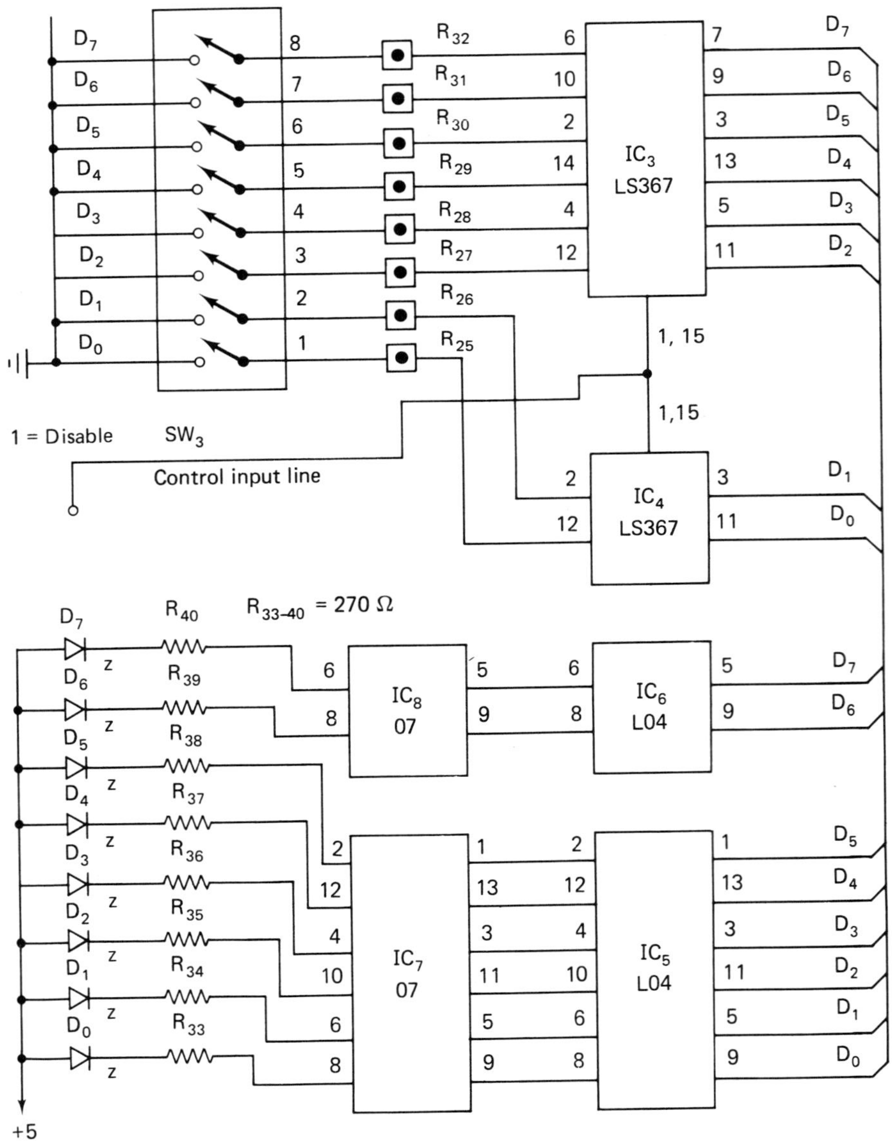

Figure 5-5 Schematic showing how the bi-directional data buffers are realized in the Static Stimulus Tester.

This is the mode where a Static Stimulus Tester or the microprocessor *is inputting data*. It is similar to the mode in which the microprocessor requests data from memory or requests data from an input device.

Figure 5-6 shows the schematic for the Static Stimulus Tester for the 8080 and 8085 microprocessors. We chose to show the schematic for these microprocessors as a real example of exactly what is required to realize static stimulus testing. In the Appendix a complete schematic is shown for the Static Stimulus Tester for each of the four microprocessors we are discussing in this text.*

5-6 Using the Static Stimulus Tester

Figure 5-7 shows how to apply the Static Stimulus Tester for a Z80 microprocessor. The Static Stimulus Tester, or SST, will be used to check or debug the system hardware described in Chapter 4. The system is diagrammed in Figure 5-8 for the reader's convenience. Using the Static Stimulus Tester and a logic probe, oscilloscope, or voltmeter, we will verify the operation of each section of system hardware in an orderly, systematic, and effective way. The techniques that are being presented have been used by the author in actual practice in industry and have proven to be effective.

These techniques are meant as guidelines to enable a beginner to have a low cost, easily understood means of debugging microprocessor hardware. A more experienced microprocessor person may wish to apply the SST in different ways. This is certainly to be encouraged. The guidelines that we will present may be modified to suit an individual system or application.

5-7 Choosing a Starting Point for Debugging

No matter what type of microprocessor system we are using, the system requires some type of power supply. The power supply is a good place to start our system checks. With a voltmeter, check to insure that all power supplies are operating correctly. When we have made certain that all power supplies are correct (within the specifications for the system) we turn our attention to the clocks. If the microprocessor uses a system clock, such as the 8080, Z80, and 6800 devices, we should monitor these clocks with an oscilloscope to determine if they are within specifications. The system specifications give a minimum and maximum limit for all clock timing and clock voltage levels. When we have verified that all voltages and free-running clocks are operating correctly, then we may proceed to the next step. Always be certain to verify that the power and clocks are valid *at the device pin*.

*Each SST described is available with instructions from CREATIVE MICROPROCESSOR SYSTEMS, P.O. Box 1538, Los Gatos, CA 95030.

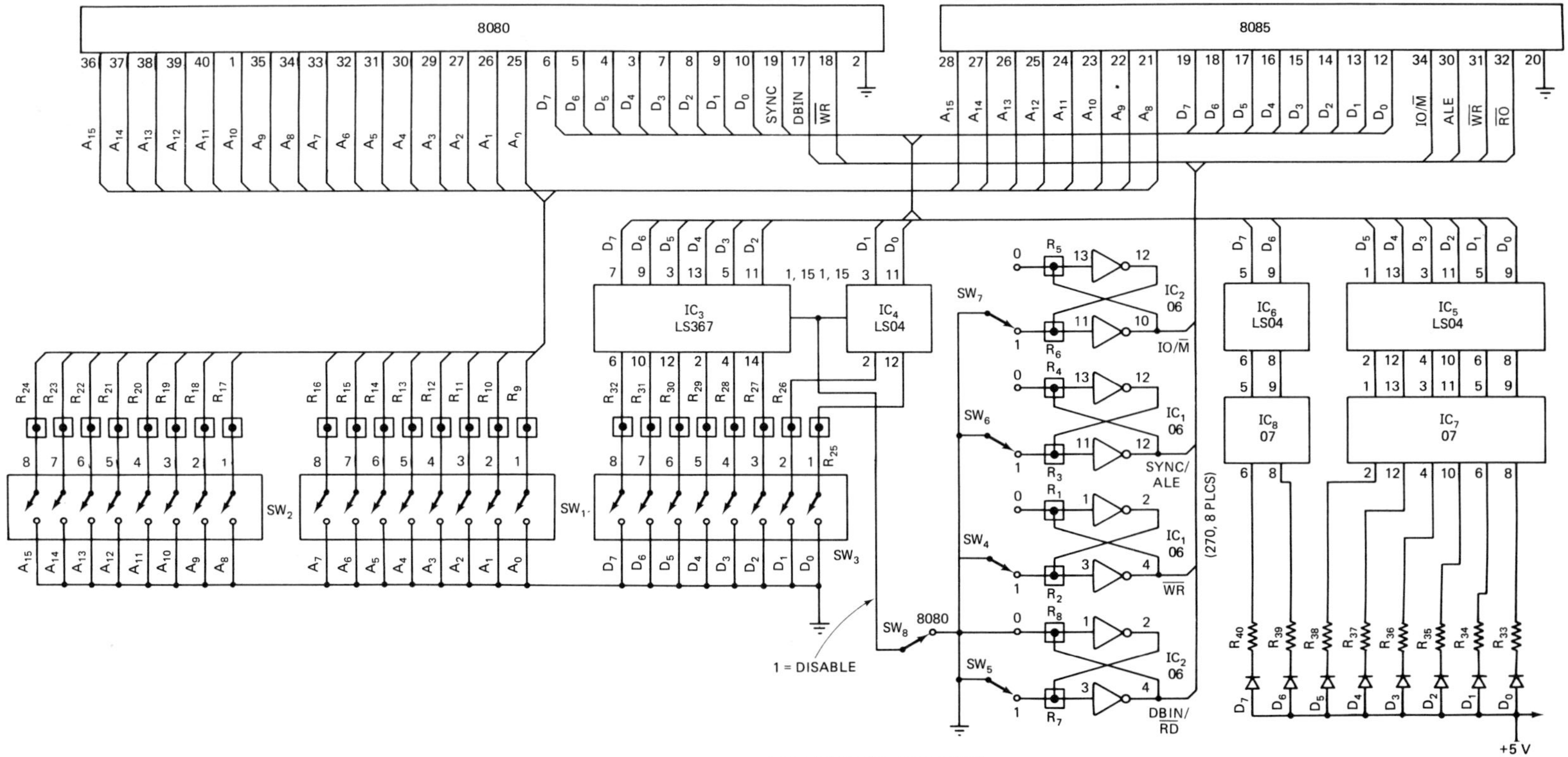

Notes: (Unless otherwise specified)

1. All resistors are in ohms, $\frac{1}{4}$ W, 5%.
2. [■] Denotes resistor to +5, 4.7 K. (R1 thru R32)
3. $R_{33\text{–}40} = 270\ \Omega$

Figure 5-6 Schematic showing the SST for the 8080 and 8085 units.

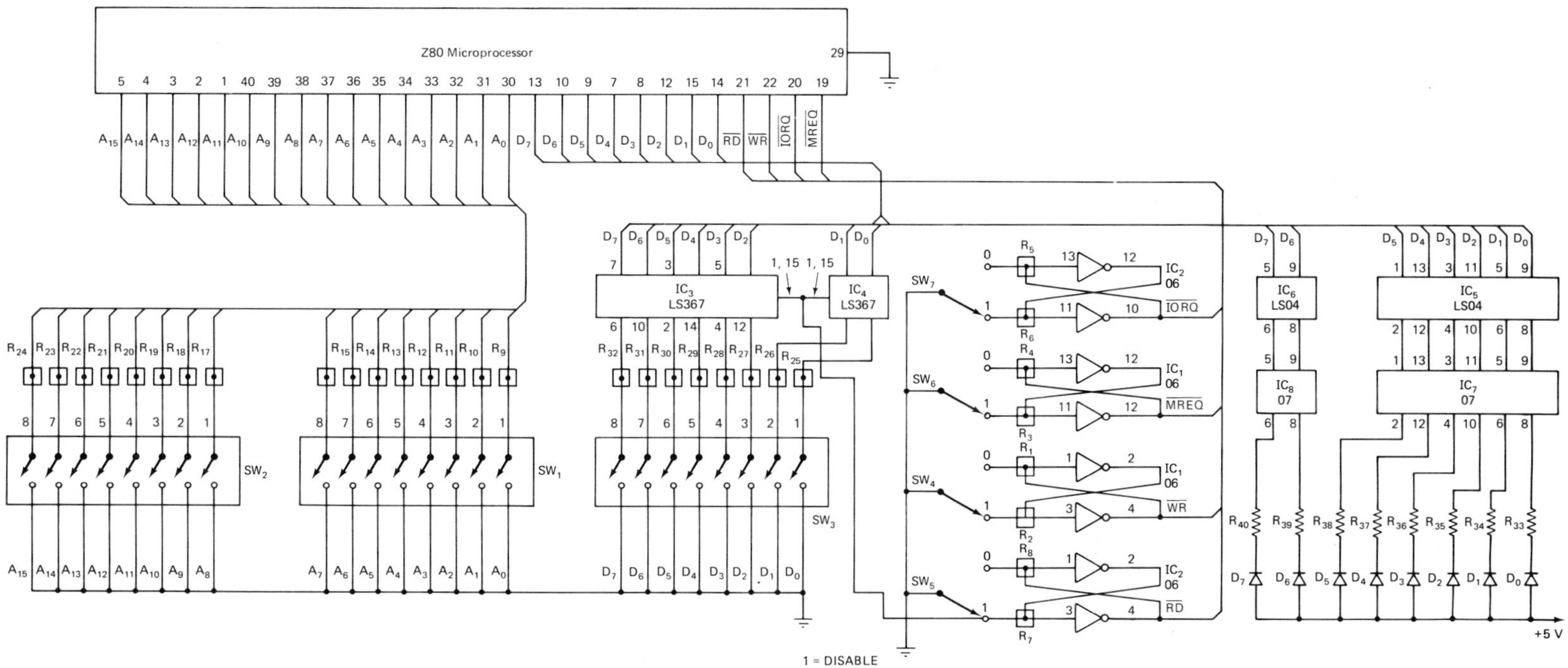

Figure 5-7 Schematic showing how to apply the SST for the Z80 unit.

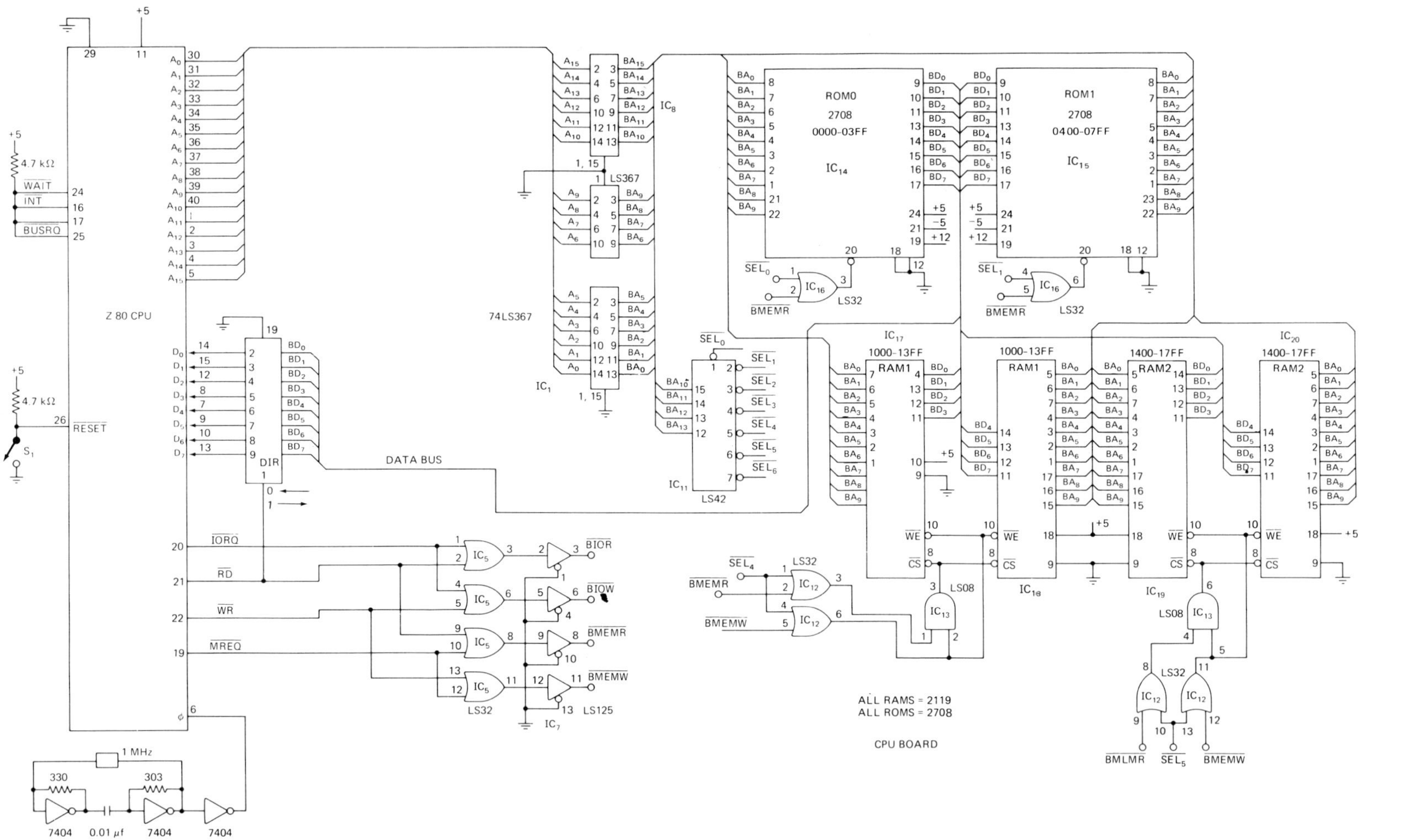

Figure 5-8(a) Complete schematic of the CPU circuit for the Z80 microprocessor.

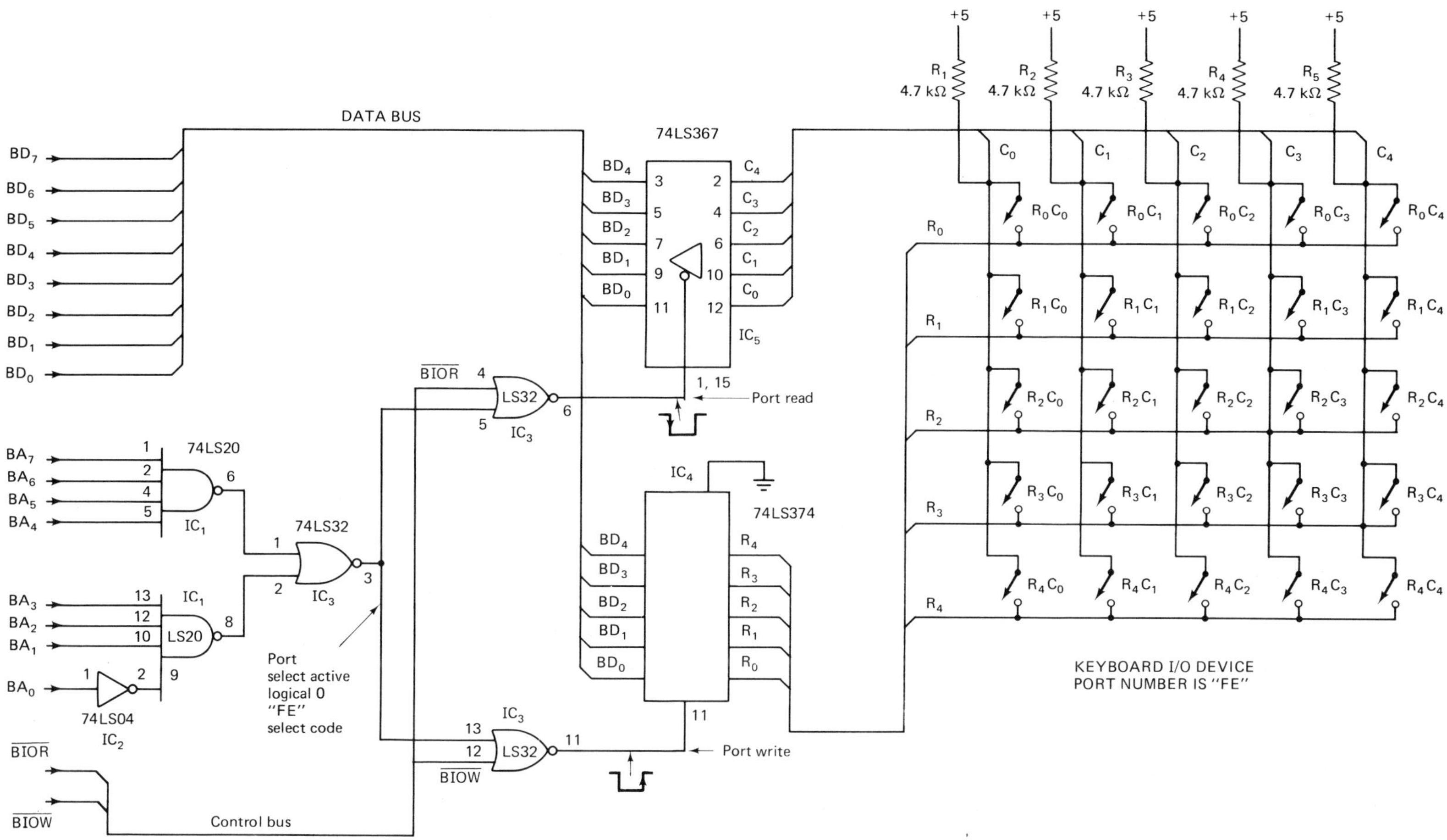

Figure 5-8(b) Complete schematic showing the keyboard interface to the microprocessor system.

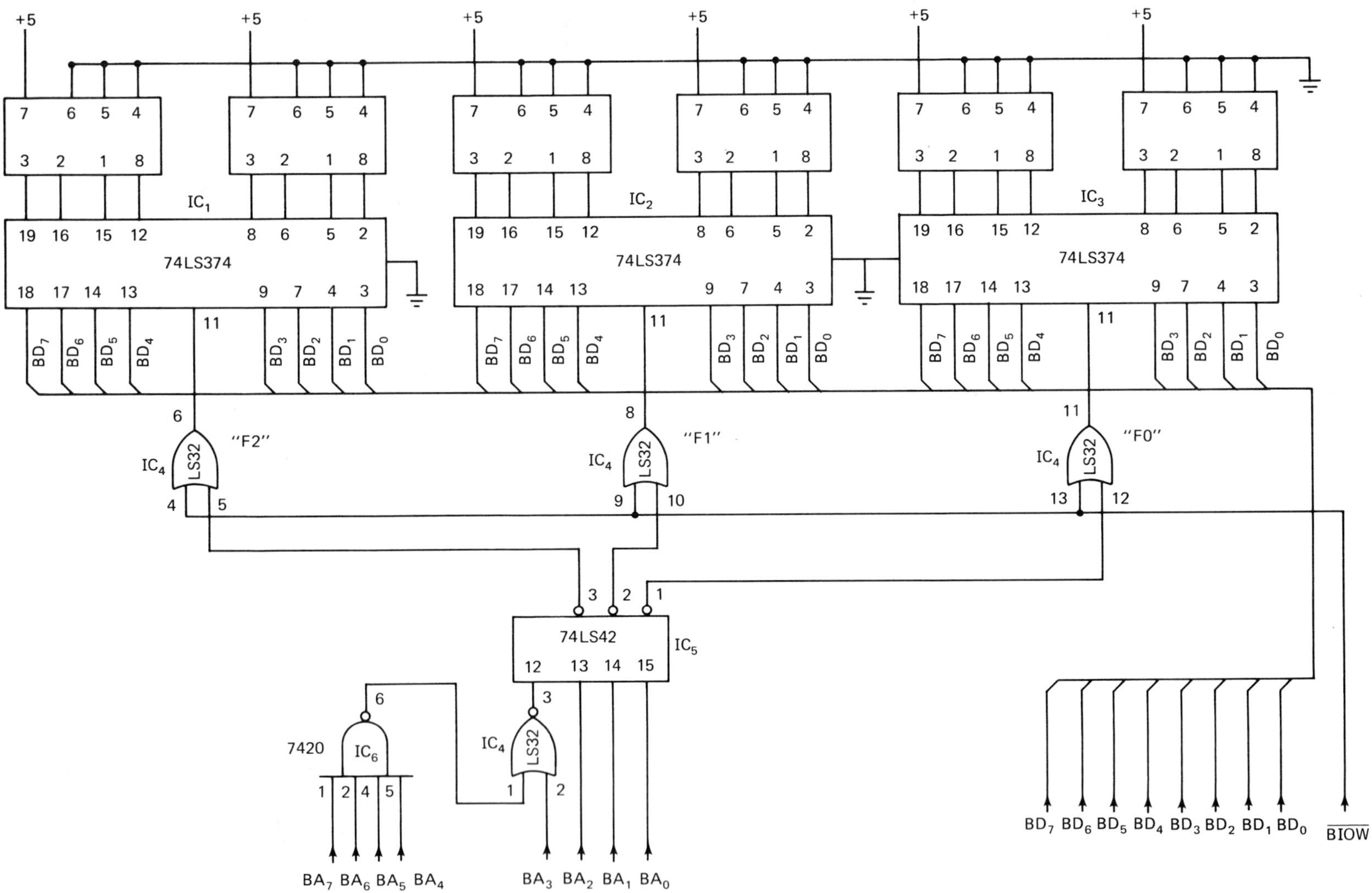

Figure 5-8(c) Complete schematic showing the interface of the general output display to the microprocessor system.

The details of the next step will vary from microprocessor to microprocessor. We will discuss the trouble-shooting details for the Z80 microprocessor. When we have been through an exact discussion of one microprocessor, it will be an easy matter to adapt the details to a different microprocessor. We have discussed the operation of the system to be debugged in detail. We know that the microprocessor will be operating as a system controller: that is, that the microprocessor will be executing a program continually. The microprocessor will not be interrupted, or put in a wait state, nor will any other device that could perform a DMA on the system. Bearing this fact in mind we notice that the input pins to the microprocessor that perform these functions are put into the nonassertive state; that is, they are disabled. These are the inputs that we should verify next in the debugging procedure. For the Z80, this means that pins 24, 16, 17, and 25 should all be held at logical 1 input level.

The reset input to the system, pin 26 of the Z80, will be set to a logical 0 when the system reset switch is active. We should make certain that the reset input on the microprocessor is capable of switching to both a logical 0 and a logical 1 state under the control of the system reset switch. For the Z80 to operate correctly, reset input pin 26 should be in logical 1 state when this microprocessor is executing a program.

The actual logic state and numbers of the input control pins vary from microprocessor to microprocessor. We should become familiar with the details of each individual microprocessor pin configuration and control logic state.

We have now determined that all signals provided by the system are in a valid state to permit the microprocessor to execute normally. If we have not already done so, the actual microprocessor is removed from the system. *Do not remove any logic device or PC board from a system without first turning off the system power.* If power is not turned off first, damage to the integrated circuits may result. The trouble-shooting or debugging procedure can hardly be termed effective if in the process we cause more hardware failures.

When the microprocessor is removed, we connect the Static Stimulus Tester to the system, as shown in Figure 5-1. We note here that to connect the SST, the microprocessor must be installed in a socket within the system. If the microprocessor is not installed in a socket, then it is worth the extra effort to put a socket in the system.

Now that we have the static stimulus test box connected to the system hardware what do we do? In the discussion that follows we show a very methodical step by step approach to checking a microprocessor controlled system.

5-8 Checking the Address Bus

The first item we will check is the address bus. We will insure that all address lines are connected to every bus point in the system. Further, we will insure that there is no decoding problem either from defective hardware or from some oversight in system design.

The address inputs to the system originate from the microprocessor address line outputs. The following procedure is meant only as a guideline for checking the address bus and is complete to the extent of being ultraconservative. However, it will accurately check the entire system address bus. As we gain experience in troubleshooting microprocessor hardware, this procedure can be shortened due to certain quick checks that you will learn to make on a particular system in question.

Procedure:

1. We set all address lines at the microprocessor output to logical 0 via the address switches on the Static Stimulus Tester.
2. Next, set address line switch A_0 on the Static Stimulus Tester to logical 1 state. This will set pin 30 on the Z80 socket to logical 1.
3. We monitor the output pin 13 of the 74LS367 IC1 of Figure 5-8(a), address buffers, to insure this output is a logical 1.
4. If the output pin 13 of the 74LS367 is a logical 1, then we set the address switch A_0 on the SST to logical 0 and recheck pin 13 for logical 0. When we do this we make certain that output pin 13 of IC1 will follow a logical state of the address switch A_0 on the SST.
5. If output pin 13 of the 74LS367 IC1 does follow a logical state of the address switch A_0, then we are sure that the 74LS367 device is operating correctly and that the connection from microprocessor to system is correct. We can go directly to step 7 now.
6. If the output pin 13 of the 74LS367 IC1 does not follow the logical state of the address switch A_0, then we are not sure whether the 74LS367 IC1 is defective or if the output is being loaded excessively. Remember, the outputs of the address bus go to many parallel points in the system. Any one of these points may be causing the output to become excessively loaded.

6(a) If output pin 13 of the 74LS367 does not respond correctly, we must make certain that input pin 14 does respond to changes in the logic level from output pin 30 of the microprocessor.

6(b) If the input to the 74LS367 pin 14 does respond correctly, but the output does not respond correctly, then the troubleshooter can use standard digital trouble-shooting techniques to determine the cause.*

*Refer to James W. Coffron, *Getting Started in Digital Troubleshooting*. Reston, VA.: Reston Publishing Co., 1979.

7. Let us assume that pin 13 of the 74LS367 IC1 does respond as it should. We next proceed to *every* parallel point in the system that this output is connected to and insure that each point can and does respond correctly. In this way we can insure that buffered address A_0 is correctly connected and bussed to every point within the system.

7(a) In the Z80 we would put our monitoring device first on the system ROM0 A_0 input. This is IC14, pin 8 of Figure 5-8(a). Next, we would check the system RAM input address A_0. This is IC17, 18, 19, 20, pin 5. At each point we would toggle the address switch A_0 on the SST to insure that each parallel point in the system is responding correctly.

7(b) Next we will check the input and output device address points. The keyboard input output device has BA_0 connected to IC2 pin 1 of Figure 5-8(b). We insure that these address inputs will respond to changes at the static stimulus tester output. The display BA_0 input is connected to IC5 pin 15 of Figure 5-8(c). Here, again, we check to insure that this point will respond correctly to changes at the static stimulus tester.

8. We repeat steps 2 through 7 for all address line outputs of the Z80.

It may become clear at this point that by using the Static Stimulus Tester we have provided a means by which standard digital trouble-shooting techniques can be employed to debug a very complicated microprocessor system. We do not have to learn a new set of trouble-shooting skills. Rather, we learn a new application of old skills.

9. Now we will check the memory select decoding lines. The memory select signals are generated by the 74LS42 IC11 of Figure 5-8(a). Input to the 74LS42 are address lines BA_{10}, BA_{11}, BA_{12}, and BA_{13}. The output of a 74LS42 provides a memory select signal for the system ROM and RAMs. In this Z80 system we are using only 2K of ROM, but we have expansion room for a maximum of 4K of ROM. We are using 2K of RAM, but have expansion room for 3K of RAM. This memory map is shown in Figure 5-9.
   Using the memory map, we can easily determine if the memory selects are operating correctly.

10. We set the address switches A_{10} to A_{13} to the different codes shown in Figure 5-9 and monitor the output pins 1, 2, 3, 4, 5, 6, 7, of the 74LS42. We check to insure that the outputs will respond correctly to changes in the address inputs. These outputs *should* correspond as shown in Figure 5-10.

ADDRESS Space	Function	
0000 – 03FF	ROM_0	
0400 – 07FF	ROM_1	
0800 – 0BFF	ROM_2	NOT USED
0C00 – 0FFF	ROM_3	NOT USED
1000 – 13FF	RAM_1	
1400 – 17FF	RAM_2	
1800 – 1BFF	RAM_3	NOT USED

Figure 5-9 The memory map for the microprocessor system under test.

IC_{11} Outputs 1	2	3	4	5	6	7		BA_{13}	BA_{12}	BA_{11}	BA_{10}
0	1	1	1	1	1	1	______	0	0	0	0
1	0	1	1	1	1	1	______	0	0	0	1
1	1	0	1	1	1	1	______	0	0	1	0
1	1	1	0	1	1	1	______	0	0	1	1
1	1	1	1	0	1	1	______	0	1	0	0
1	1	1	1	1	0	1	______	0	1	0	1
1	1	1	1	1	1	0	______	0	1	1	0

Figure 5-10 The logical state of the IC11 outputs. Address outputs BA10, BA11, BA12, and BA13 determine which will be the asserted output pin of IC11.

11(a) The outputs of memory select decoder IC11 are connected to different points within the system. For example pin 1, select ROM0, is connected to IC16 pin 1. We will monitor IC16 pin 1 to insure that it will respond correctly to output pin 1 of IC11.

11(b) We check all memory select lines and their end points for proper operation and system interconnection.

12. When step 11 is completed we have determined that the entire address bus is wired correctly and that each line is not being loaded excessively.

5-9 Checking the Control Bus

We can now start the process of determining if the control bus is operating correctly. To do this we will use the following procedure. Again, this procedure is meant only as a guideline and may be modified to suit special needs.

1. We set the control switches on the SST to logical 1.
2. With all control bits in a logical 1 state, each control line in the system should be logical 1: that is, no control line is asserted.
3. Next we set the control bit switches on the SST in the mode for each control function. There are four, as shown in Figure 5-11.
4. We set each condition of the control bit switches on the SST and verify that the control bus outputs are responding correctly. If the control bus outputs do not respond as they should, then we can easily determine if all input conditions are correct.
5. If the input conditions for the control bus are correct, but the control bus outputs fail to respond correctly, then we may be loading the outputs excessively. Again we use standard digital troubleshooting techniques to determine the cause of the malfunction.
6. The control bus outputs are connected to many parallel points within the system. We must insure that each parallel point is indeed responding to the control bus signal condition as it should.

7(a) For example, control bus signal $\overline{\text{BMEMR}}$ is connected to the inputs of several logic gates. One of these is pin 2 of IC12 of Figure 5-8(a). We set the control bits of the SST to the condition for a memory read. When this is done, we monitor pin 2 of IC12 to insure that it has responded correctly to the $\overline{\text{BMEMR}}$ signal.

7(b) We perform the same type of checking on each point within the system that is connected to a control bus output.

8. When we have checked all control bus signals in the system for proper operation, we have made certain that all control bus signals will perform as expected within the system architecture.

Control Bits of the Z80				Function
$\overline{\text{IORQ}}$	$\overline{\text{MREQ}}$	$\overline{\text{RD}}$	$\overline{\text{WR}}$	
0	1	1	0	$\overline{\text{IOW}}$
0	1	0	1	$\overline{\text{IOR}}$
1	0	1	0	$\overline{\text{MEMW}}$
1	0	0	1	$\overline{\text{MEMR}}$

Figure 5-11 Control bit signals, indicating the system function to which they correspond.

5-10 Checking Individual Chip Select and Write Enable Signals for Memory

We will now verify that the individual ROMs and RAMs are responding correctly to the address bus and control bus. First, let us verify the operation of the chip select signals for ROM0. We notice in the system schematic of Figure 5-8(a), that the CS pin 20 of the 2708 EPROM IC14 is connected to output pin 3 of the 74LS32 IC16. When output pin 3 is logical 0, the data outputs of the 2708 EPROM (ROM0) are enabled onto the system data bus.

The 2708 ROM0 will be enabled when the address bus is decoding a valid ROM0 address and the control bus is asserting the $\overline{\text{BMEMR}}$ control bus signal. From the schematic of Figure 5-8(a) we see that this condition is realized by the OR gate of IC16. When both SEL_0 memory select line IC16 pin 1 and $\overline{\text{BMEMR}}$ control signal, IC16 pin 2 are logical 0, pin 20 of ROM0 IC14 will be logical 0.

We can set these conditions on the static stimulus tester by setting the address switches labeled A_{10}–A_{13} to all logical 0. We can set the control bit switches for the condition that would set a valid memory read control signal. These are

$$\overline{\text{MREQ}} = 0,\ \overline{\text{RD}} = 0,\ \overline{\text{IORQ}} = 1,\ \overline{\text{WR}} = 1.$$

We notice also that because $\overline{\text{RD}}$ is logical 0, the LEDs located in the static stimulus tester reflect the data on the data bus.

If we had a ROM installed in this system, the LEDs would reflect the data stored in the ROM at the selected address shown by switches A_0–A_9. However, if we remove the ROM we can perform some useful checks within the system.

With the ROM removed, the LEDs in the SST should all be lit. Now one at a time we can ground the output pins of the ROM socket with a clip lead. While we do this we can verify that the LED connected to that bit of the data bus goes to logical 0, or off. In this way we can insure that all data bus bits are physically connected to the proper pin on the ROM.

For example, with both the address bus and the control bus set as described, we connect ROM_0 (socket) pin 9 to a logical 0 via a clip lead. We should see the LED on the static stimulus tester labeled D_0 go off. Repeat this procedure for all output pins 9, 10, 11, 13, 14, 15, 16, and 17. In this way we can insure that all data pins are connected correctly. We have also determined that the ROM will be selected only when the proper conditions exist on the system address and control busses.

We repeat this procedure for all ROM select codes and for all RAM select codes. The RAM also requires a CS signal when data is read from it.

The write enable signal for the system RAM can be checked for validity in a fashion similar to that just discussed for the ROM. The main difference in checking a write enable signal is that the control bus will be asserting the $\overline{\text{BMEMW}}$ signal instead of the $\overline{\text{BMEMR}}$ signal.

We have now shown how to verify that all CS signals and memory write enable signals are being decoded correctly. We have also shown a technique of determining if the data output of the RAM and ROM are physically connected through a correct logic path to the microprocessor data input lines.

A note here is that we can actually write data to any RAM location and read data back via the static stimulus tester. Here is a procedure for doing it.

1. Set the address switches to a valid RAM address.
2. Set the data switches to the data we went to write to the memory address selected.
3. Set the control bit $\overline{MREQ}$ to a logical 0.
4. Set the control bit $\overline{WR}$ to a logical 0. This asserts the write enable signal to memory.
5. Set the control bit $\overline{WR}$ to logical 1. This unasserts the write enable to the memory.

The data is now stored in the RAM. This memory write operation is performed in exactly the same way that the Z80 would perform it under software control. We will now read the data back from that memory location selected to verify if the write operation was valid.

6. Set all the data switches to logical 0.
7. Set the control bit $\overline{RD}$ to logical 0. This will assert the chip select to the RAM.
8. The LEDs will reflect the data that was just written into the memory in steps 1 through 5. Note that the RAM is read in exactly the same way that the Z80 would read data.

This technique of writing and reading data from a RAM can be very helpful if we suspect that a particular RAM location or RAM chip may be defective. If we can set the unique RAM address on the address bus and actually perform a system RAM write and read, this will verify or disprove the suspect RAM.

5-11 Writing and Reading Data from I/O Devices

Similar to the function of writing and reading data to memory, we can perform this same operation to *any* input or output device. To illustrate this point, let us write data to our system output display that was shown in Figure 5-8(c).

The output ports for our system are F0, F1, F2. These correspond to the least significant digits, next significant two digits, and finally the most significant two digits, respectively. In Chapter 4 we explained details of exactly how the display works. By using the technique of writing data to the display we can verify if the system display is operating correctly. If the display does not respond correctly, then we can step through the output write sequence and "freeze" the system under any conditions. While the system is in static mode we can easily verify which decoding circuitry in the output device is malfunctioning.

We will write the following numbers to the system display: 1,2,3,4,5,6. This means that the most significant digit will display a 1 and the least significant digit will display a 6. The following procedure allows us to do this:

1. Set the address switches for the proper address of the most significant two digits. This is $00F2_{16}$.
2. Set the data switch to numbers 12_{16}. Recall that the two digits will be written at the same time for our output display. The data bus bits D_0–D_3 are input to one digit, and data bus bits D_4–D_7 are inputs to the other digit.
3. Set the control bit switch labeled IORQ to logical 0 position. This will set the system in the I/O request mode.
4. Set the control bit switch labeled $\overline{WR}$ to logical 0. This will set the system to do an output write.
5. Set the control bit switch $\overline{WR}$ to logical 1. This will unassert the I/O write control signal. When the WR signal goes to logical 1, the data on the data switches will be written into the output display at the most significant digits.

If the data failed to be written to the display, we could easily step through the sequence given and at each step verify whether the system was responding as it should. For example, we could set the address to $00F2_{16}$ and verify that the F2 select line on the output device does in fact get asserted. When the $\overline{WR}$ signal goes to logical 0 we can verify that the clock input pin 1 to the 74LS374 IC1 of Figure 5-8(c) is at logical 0 input level.

In short, we can verify all conditions in the system for any type of system data tranfer that can occur by using the Static Stimulus Tester. We can repeat this procedure given in steps 1 through 5 for the data to be written to the other four display digits. By performing this check on the output display with the SST we have insured that all logic in the system is working and all system wiring is correct for this particular device.

5-12 Verifying Keyboard Circuit Operation With the SST

We will now discuss a technique for quickly determining whether the keyboard is operating correctly. This procedure will insure that all logic is operating and that all key switches are functional.

We will perform an output device WRITE operation to set a single row line input R_0–R_4 active logical 0. We will then perform an input device READ operation, leaving the system in READ mode. Then, one at a time, we will press the keys along the active row. While pressing the keys we will watch the LEDs on our SST. As each key is pressed, the LED corresponding to that column position should go off. That outlines the procedure; here is the complete procedure:

1. Set address switches to 00FE. This is the input device and output device address.
2. Set the control bit switch labeled $\overline{IORQ}$ to logical 0.
3. Set the data switches to FE. This will be the condition row R_0 to be active.
4. Set the control bit switch $\overline{WR}$ to logical 0 position.
5. Set the control bit switch $\overline{WR}$ to logical 1 position. The row input latch should now have the correct data at the latch outputs.
6. Set the $\overline{RD}$ control bit switch to logical 0.

6(a) The LEDs on the SST should be on, because no key is being depressed at this time. We should ignore the LEDs for D_5, D_6 and D_7 because the keyboard does not control these data bits. In our program of Chapter 4 we masked off these data bits.

7(a) Press the switches labeled R_0C_0, R_0C_1, R_0C_2, R_0C_3, R_0C_4 on the keyboard, one at a time. While each key is pushed, insure that the corresponding LED in the SST goes off. For example, if the key R_0C_0 were pushed, the LED labeled D_0 should go off.

7(b) If the LED does not go off, then we apply standard digital troubleshooting techniques to isolate the malfunction.

8. The sequence of steps 3 through 7 may be repeated for each row input line. Each time, the new data is written to enable another row input line.
9. After each row enable is checked, be certain to set the $\overline{RD}$ control bit switch to logical 1 level.

This procedure for checking the keyboard is very effective. It gives us a method to verify that the entire keyboard is working correctly. If at any point the keyboard does not work correctly, then we can troubleshoot it statically within the system.

5-13 Summary

We have presented a technique for a complete hardware checkout of a Z80 microprocessor control system. The technique is called *STATIC STIMULUS TESTING*. We have shown how to verify, with the use of the static stimulus tester, all system buses, memory, and input and output devices.

The use of an SST is not limited to new systems that have never worked (prototypes). It can be used effectively on systems that once worked, but are now malfunctioning. The SST can also be used to debug new input and output device interfaces that we may be designing to add to an already existing system.

We may be inclined to believe that, since static stimulus testing checks the system only in a static mode, we have no guarantee of this system working at regular operational speed. Through experience it has been found that if the system hardware operates correctly in static mode, the probability is very high that it will operate at regular system speed. That is especially true for systems that were once working and now for some reason have malfunctioned.

In a new design too many delays may have been generated for right conditions to exist, or perhaps noise interference on power lines occurs. In such cases, the SST will not help much in finding the problem. Other trouble-shooting techniques can be employed in those instances.

We may safely say that if the microprocessor system does not operate by using the static stimulus tester, then it will certainly not operate at system speed. The static stimulus tester is of extreme value in determining if all logic in a system is operating correctly. It also enables us to exercise the system in a static mode to freeze the system conditions at any instant in time. We ask the beginner to try the static stimulus tester for debugging the microprocessor hardware problems. As experience is gained, the use of the static stimulus tester will become a valuable tool in the solution of many microprocessor hardware troubleshooting problems.

6

INTERRUPT, WAIT, AND DMA OPERATIONS WITH 8080, 8085, 6800, AND Z80 MICROPROCESSORS

In this chapter we will discuss the topics of interrupting, waiting, and direct memory access (DMA) operations with the 8080, 8085, 6800, and Z80 microprocessors. We will first introduce each of the three concepts, and then show a technique for realizing these concepts with hardware for each of the microprocessors under discussion. We will also discuss certain software instructions and software concepts necessary in performing these three operations.

Depth of the software and the hardware will be such that we will be able to interrupt, wait, and perform DMA operations with microprocessors on a very basic level. Once we understand the basic level of performing these operations, adapting these concepts to a much higher-level system architecture will be an easier matter.

For each of the three operations to be discussed in this chapter the following sequence of events will be given. We will introduce the concept and show how the concept would appear for a generalized microprocessor system. We will then realize this general form with each of the four microprocessors; with the realization of the form, we will compare the concept between microprocessors. This will allow us to use a system with one or all three of the operations listed as part of the architecture.

6-1 Comments on Interrupts

Let us begin by discussing the concept of the interrupt. First, what is an interrupt? In the systems discussed thus far, the microprocessor was acting as a system controller. That is, it was always executing software instructions in the order that the instructions were presented in the memory. This meant that once the processor started executing the instructions, it could not change the flow of its program by any sort of user intervention.

An interrupt allows us to change the flow of the program based on external signals applied to the microprocessor. This is shown pictorially in Figure 6-1. You will notice in Figure 6-1(a) that this program is continually executing step 1, step 2, step 3, step 4 down through step n of the program. In Figure 6-1(b) the program begins executing step 1, step 2 of the same program. However, an interrupt is then input to the microprocessor. When the interrupt is input to the microprocessor the flow of the program is changed such that a new section of program will be executed, after which the program returns to normal execution.

From Figure 6-1(b) we see that the normal flow of program execution is changed via an interrupt input. The interrupt is shown to occur between step 2

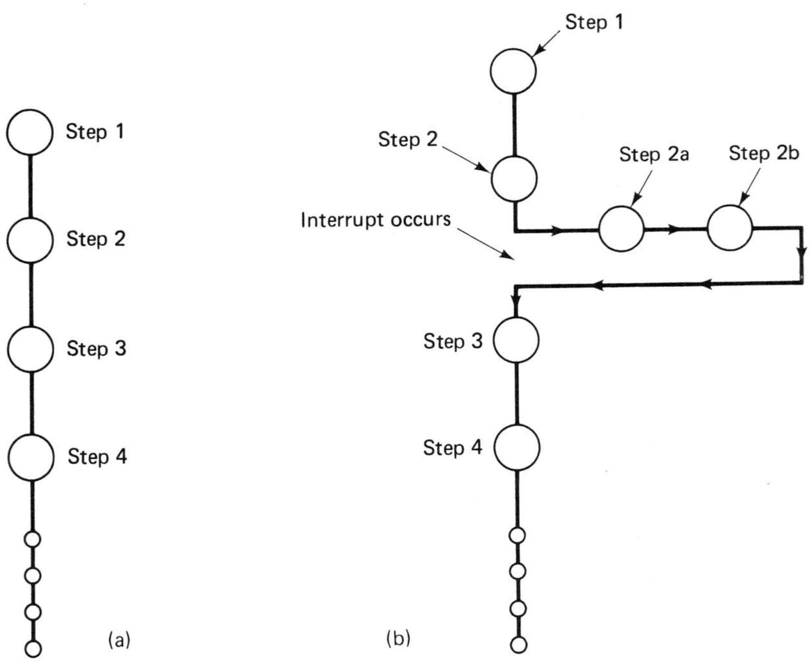

Figure 6-1(a) This type of program sequentially executes step 1, step 2, step 3, step 4, until the program is completed. (b) This type of program executes step 1 and step 2. Then an external interrupt signal is input, which stops sequential execution while steps 2a, 2b, and so on, are executed, after which the microprocessor returns to the main program.

and step 3 of the program. However, this need not be the case. Generally, an interrupt input to the microprocessor is asynchronous. *Asynchronous* means that the input can be applied at any point during program execution. That is, the interrupt input shown in Figure 6-1(b) could be moved down between step 3 and step 4. It does not matter when the interrupt occurs in program execution; the results of the interrupt will be consistent. In most microprocessor literature a term called *vector interrupts* is used.

The term *vector* means a pointer. This vector shows the microprocessor which memory address to use to start the interrupt program from the point in time that an interrupt signal is input. So the term vector here is really nothing more than an address in memory. The term "vectored interrupt," means that interrupts will be occurring within a microprocessor system, and a memory address, or vector, will be the starting address for the interrupt routine.

It would not be out of line for us to define an interrupt as forcing the microprocessor to execute a certain subroutine at any given time the interrupt signal occurs. This means that no matter what a microprocessor is doing, or what section of code it is executing in memory, when the interrupt occurs the microprocessor is forced to execute another code routine. After executing that code the microprocessor returns to the task it was doing before the interrupt input occurred.

On some microprocessors, and we will show on which of the four, there are two types of interrupts: (1) nonmaskable interrupts and (2) maskable interrupts. A *nonmaskable interrupt* means that when an interrupt signal is applied, the microprocessor will always respond to that interrupt input. The microprocessor must respond to a nonmaskable interrupt whenever that occurs during a program.

A *maskable interrupt* means that the software can enable or disable that particular input from ever being recognized by the microprocessor. Maskable interrupts can be effectively turned off with software. We will not discuss all of the applications for maskable and nonmaskable interrupts in a microprocessor system. What we will do is show how these two functions can be realized with each of the four microprocessors under discussion. We will start our discussion of interrupts with the 8080 microprocessor.

6-2 Interrupting the 8080 Microprocessor

To perform the hardware function of interrupting microprocessors, we will use the circuit of Figure 6-2. This circuit will apply the hardware interrupt signal to each of the four microprocessors. By doing this, we may be able to understand how each of the processors responds to an interrupt request being applied by external hardware. The microprocessor will then communicate with the circuit of Figure 6-2 in some fashion. This is depicted by the arrow at bottom right coming from the microprocessor to the clear input of the 74LS74 flip flop.

Let us discuss briefly how the circuit shown in Figure 6-2 operates. The first section at the left shows the switch debounce circuit which is comprised of two 7406 open collector inverters and a single-pole double-throw, momentary push-button switch.

When switch S_1 is in the resting position (NC), the center terminal of the switch is connected to the normally closed pole. The normally closed pole is connected to pin 3 of IC_1. Pin 3 of IC_1 will be logical 0. Pin 4 of IC_1 will be logical 1. This will force a logical 1 on the clock input pin of the 74LS74. The 74LS74 is an edge-triggered flip flop. When the clock input of the 74LS74 goes from a logical 0 level to a logical 1 level, data at the D input of the 74LS74 will be transferred to the Q and $\overline{Q}$ outputs. In Figure 6-2 we see that when the circuit is in the normally closed position, the clock input to the 74LS74 is logical 1.

When we press switch S_1, the center terminal of S_1 is connected to the normally open pin of the switch. This forces a logical 0 on pin 1 of IC_1 and a logical 1 at output pin 2 of IC_1. The result is that the clock input of the 74LS74 goes to logical 0 when the single-pole double-throw switch S_1 is pressed. This action will have no effect on the flip flop.

When we again release switch S_1 to its normally closed position, the clock input to the 74LS74 goes to logical 1 level from logical 0 level. It is this action

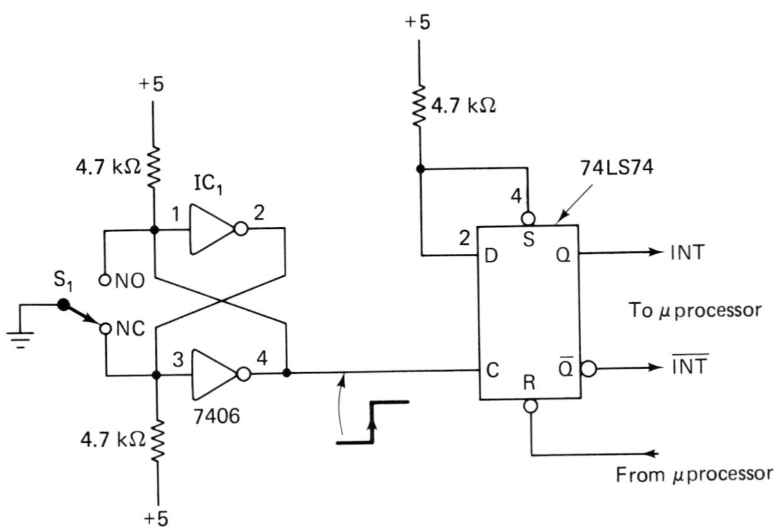

Figure 6-2 Schematic of hardware used to implement or force the interrupt input to a microprocessor.

of switch S_1 that will transfer the data at the D input of the 74LS74 to the Q and $\overline{Q}$ outputs. This is shown by the timing diagram of Figure 6-3.

The D input and the set input pins 2 and 4 of the 74LS74 flip flop are connected to +5 volts via the 4.7 kilohm resistor. There is always a logical 1 applied to the set input and a logical 1 applied to the D input of the 74LS74. When data is transferred on the rising edge of the clock input pin, the Q output always goes to logical 1 and the $\overline{Q}$ output will always go to logical 0. This is the condition for forcing the interrupt to the microprocessor under discussion.

The microprocessor must then respond by applying a logical 0 input to the clear pin of the 74LS74. In this way the Q output will go to a logical 0 and the $\overline{Q}$ output will go to a logical 1. It is by applying this clear input to the 74LS74 that the microprocessor effectively resets the interrupt request from the external hardware.

By using the circuit of Figure 6-2 we may indeed apply an interrupt input to the microprocessor in a totally asynchronous fashion. The microprocessor can be executing a program and we may push switch S_1 at any time to force an interrupt to occur. When we have discussed the specifics of how interrupts are handled with the microprocessor, we will again refer to Figure 6-2 with more details of why we must use a flip flop to generate the interrupt request. (It is premature to

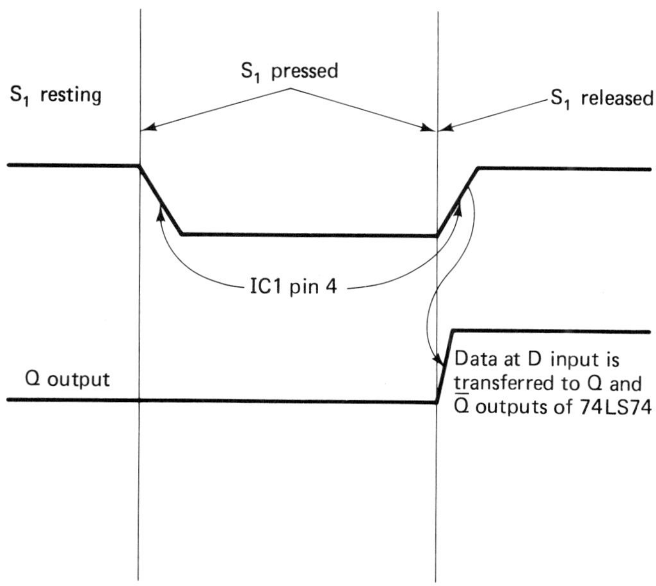

Figure 6-3 Timing diagram showing the relationship between Q output and the switch position. When the switch is released, the Q output is forced to logical 1 and the $\overline{Q}$ output is forced to logical 0.

discuss this point at this time. After we have discussed interrupting of the 8080 in detail it will be easier to understand.)

Figure 6-4 shows how to interface the hardware shown in Figure 6-2 to an 8080 microprocessor. In Figure 6-4 we see that the interface is very simple. The interrupt request line for the 8080 is labeled INT (interrupt). The INT is pin 14 on the 8080 device. The 8080 has a special output pin labeled INTE (Interrupt Enabled), pin 16, that will be used to reset the 74LS74. To explain how these two pins interact with the 8080, a general sequence for an interrupt handling with the 8080 will be given. We assume that an interrupt request is input:

1. INT pin 14 of the 8080 is forced to logical 1. This indicates that an interrupt is being requested from external hardware.
2. When the 8080 internally acknowledges the receipt of the interrupt request on pin 14, the INTE pin 16 goes to logical 0.

These are the two major events that occur for the interrupt interface we have shown. However, there is other hardware that we must discuss for interrupting the 8080. At this point we are discussing only the generation of an interrupt request and the resetting of the interrupt request. When pin 16 of an 8080 is in logical 1 state, the 8080 is in a mode to receive interrupt requests from external hardware. When INTE pin 16 is logical 0, the 8080 is in a mode to ignore all interrupt requests applied to INT pin 14. The 8080 has only maskable interrupts.

There are two software instructions for the 8080 called DI (Disable Interrupt), and EI (Enable Interrupts). These two software instructions can be used to manipulate the logical condition of the INTE pin. For example, when the 8080 is initially reset, the INTE pin is forced to a logical 0 level. This means the 8080 is in a mode to ignore all interrupt input requests from external hardware.

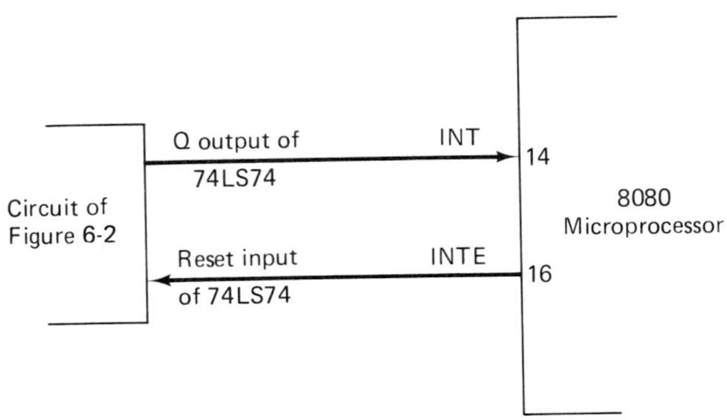

Figure 6-4 Block diagram showing how the circuit of Figure 6-2 interfaces to an 8080 microprocessor.

Effectively the 8080 is in the disable interrupt mode. The only way to force the INTE pin to a logical 1 state is for the 8080 to execute a software instruction EI, or enable interrupt. When the enable interrupt instruction is executed, the INTE pin will go to a logical 1 condition.

With the INTE pin in a logical 1 condition, the clear input to the 74LS74 is in logical 1. This allows the interrupt request to be transferred from input D to output Q of the 74LS74. Now suppose that an interrupt has been requested via external hardware. When the interrupt is accepted, the INTE pin is again forced low (to zero) via the hardware internal to the 8080 microprocessor.

What has happened is that the 8080 has again been put into a disable interrupt mode. The only way to reenable the interrupts is for the 8080 to execute an EI (Enable Interrupt) software command. So the INTE pin may be forced to a logical 0 state by either the hardware or software for the 8080 microprocessor, but the INTE pin may be set to logical 1 level only by the execution of software.

What does this particular fact mean to the user of the 8080 when interrupts are designed into the system architecture? It means that the 8080 microprocessor software must contain the proper code to enable interrupts at the correct time. That is, the interrupt is requested by the external hardware and then, during the interrupt routine, the software must again reenable the interrupts. This is logical because during the execution of the interrupt code we may not want the 8080 to receive further interrupts until a section of program has been completed. This particular aspect of interrupts is shown in Figure 6-5.

Referring to Figure 6-5, the interrupt request is issued via pin 14, then INTE pin 16 goes to logical 0. At this point the system is forced to execute a specific software program in memory. We have not discussed how the system gets to this particular memory location, but we will later. Let us assume now that the system will get to this location in memory. During the execution of this interrupt routine, the INTE pin will be logical 0. When the INTE pin is logical 0, no interrupts can be accepted by the 8080. After execution of the interrupt routine, the EI instruction is executed and the INTE pin once again goes to logical 1. The program also resumes normal execution. We have not shown how the program resumes normal execution: this, too, is discussed in detail later.

We can modify Figure 6-5 to appear as shown in Figure 6-6. In Figure 6-6 we see that after the INTE pin is forced to logical 0 via the hardware accepting the interrupt request, the enable interrupt command is executed. When an EI command is executed the INTE pin goes to logical 1. Now the 8080 is free to accept new interrupt requests.

We see that the system will start to execute the specific software and memory for the interrupt routine requested. But, this routine may again be interrupted from external hardware if another request is generated. It is the function of the software to determine whether the interrupt routine in progress can be further interrupted, or whether it should be completed before further interruptions are accepted. This particular aspect of interrupts is common to most microprocessors.

We have now discussed how an interrupt is input to the 8080 and how the 8080 responds to this request with the INTE pin. What we must show next is how the 8080 system will be forced to execute a specific software location within memory when an interrupt occurs. It is a job of the external system hardware to input to the 8080, at a specific time, the address or vector for the memory location to be executed when an interrupt occurs.

A signal on the system control bus must now be added. Up to this point we have had a system control bus comprised of four control signals. These are MEMORY WRITE, MEMORY READ, I/O WRITE, I/O READ. The new signal we must add is an interrupt acknowledge signal. We will label this signal INTA.

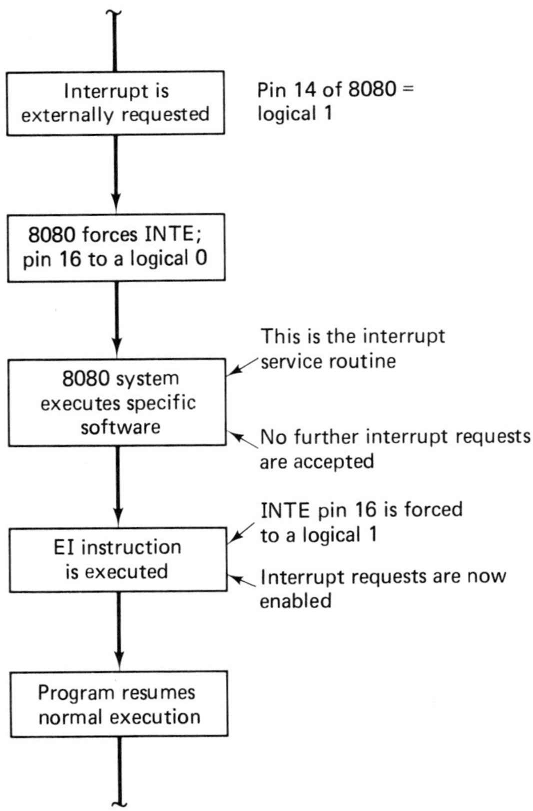

Figure 6-5 Flowchart showing the sequence of events for an 8080 microprocessor to enable interrupts within the service routine.

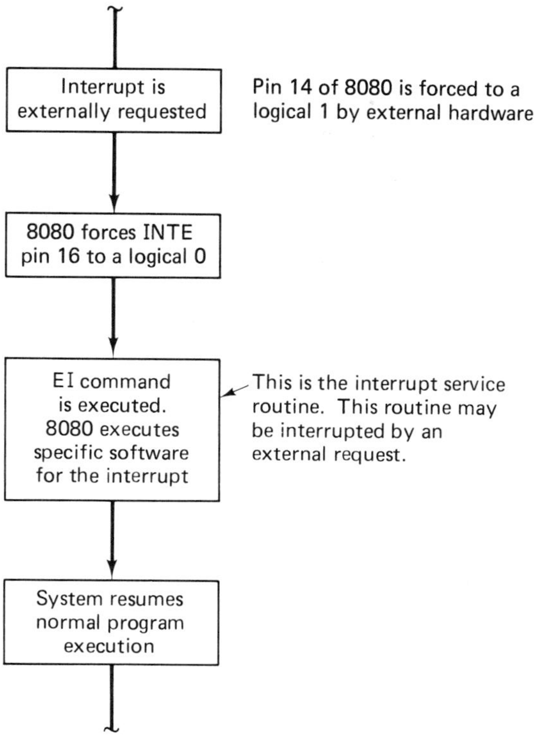

Figure 6-6 Flowchart showing the sequence of events for an 8080 to enable interrupts within the service routine.

When the INTA control signal is asserted, logical 0 level, the external hardware of the system must place certain data on the 8080 data bus to handle the interrupt vector. This sequence is shown by the flowchart of Figure 6-7.

In Figure 6-7 we see that the interrupt request will occur, the INTE pin will go to logical 0, and now the INTA will go to logical 0. Now certain hardware in the system must be enabled to allow the 8080 to input an interrupt vector. The 8080 has eight interrupt vectors—it can force the system to start executing code from eight specific memory locations. The vectors, and the memory address they correspond to are listed in Figure 6-8.

The interrupt vectors for the 8080 are given a special name, *restart vectors*. Restart is abbreviated RST. The interrupt vectors are further labeled as RST_0, RST_1, RST_2, RST_3, RST_4, RST_5, RST_6, RST_7. RST_0 corresponds to the interrupt vector with address 0. RST_1 corresponds to the interrupt vector with address 8, and so on. If we apply an RST_3 restart vector, we will be forcing data bits D_0–D_7 of the system data bus to the conditions or logical states, for the RST_3 vector.

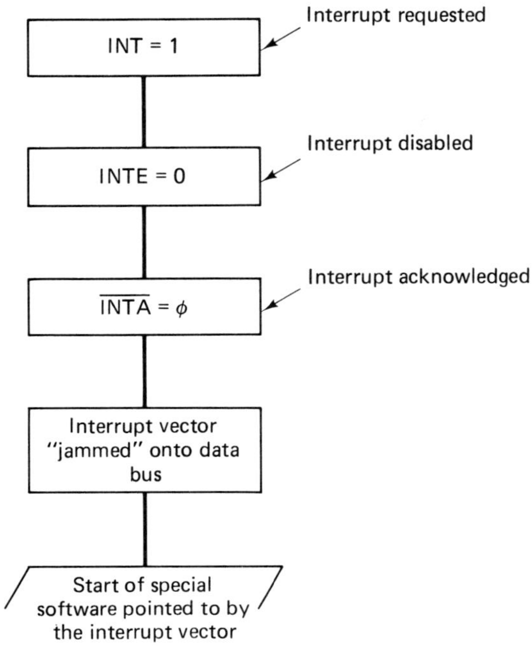

Figure 6-7 Flowchart showing the sequence of events for external hardware of the 8080 when an external interrupt is input.

RESTART Vector Name	Data Bits D_7							D_0	MEMORY Address
0	1	1	0	0	0	1	1	1	0_{16}
1	1	1	0	0	1	1	1	1	8_{16}
2	1	1	0	1	0	1	1	1	10_{16}
3	1	1	0	1	1	1	1	1	18_{16}
4	1	1	1	0	0	1	1	1	20_{16}
5	1	1	1	0	1	1	1	1	28_{16}
6	1	1	1	1	0	1	1	1	30_{16}
7	1	1	1	1	1	1	1	1	38_{16}

Figure 6-8 The relationship between the restart vector name, the "jammed" data bits, and memory address of the restart vector.

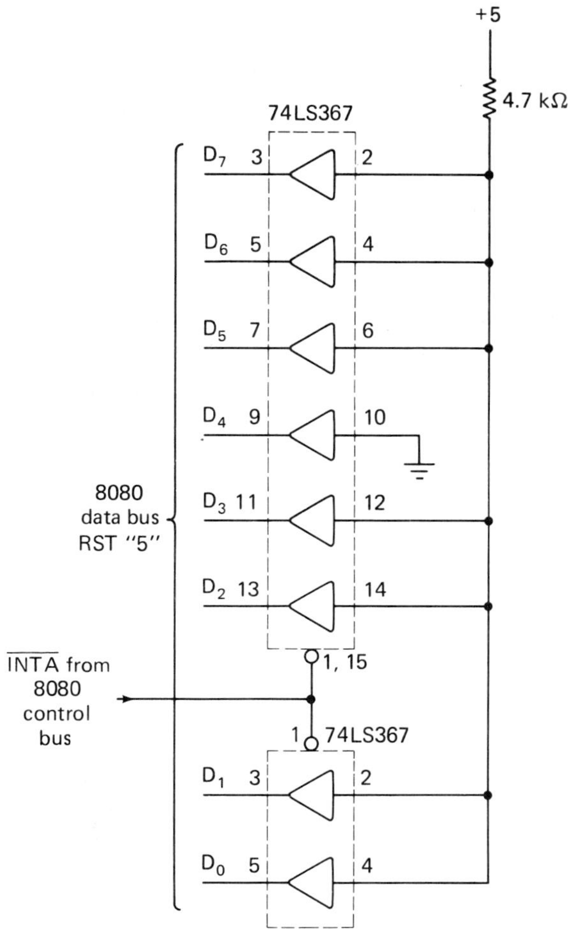

Figure 6-9 Schematic showing one way of "jamming" a restart vector onto the data bus at the correct time. The restart vector shown is an RST 5.

Figure 6-9 shows one way of forcing a restart vector onto the data bus. Forcing the restart vector is also called "jamming" a restart vector on the data bus. We see in Figure 6-9 that this operation is very similar to reading data from memory or reading from I/O. The only difference is that the function of the data input to the 8080 takes on a new meaning.

The hardware implementation of an interrupt is not difficult to accomplish, but it is still one of the five major jobs we listed. That is, the CPU is reading data from the system data bus. The timing of the data onto the data bus is controlled by the microprocessor. The microprocessor frees us from having to consider all the timing constraints for using interrupts. We simply decode correct data at the correct time and place it on the data bus.

We have now discussed how we may input an interrupt request and how we may force or "jam" the 8080 to execute certain codes within the microprocessor when an interrupt occurs. What we must discuss next is how to resume normal program execution after completion of the interrupt routine. To do this we must discuss a portion of the 8080 software and how the 8080 software handles an interrupt request.

Figure 6-10 shows a sequence of internal events that the 8080 follows when an interrupt has been requested from the external hardware. In Figure 6-10 we see that when the external interrupt request is issued the INTE pin goes to logical 0 as discussed. The INTA control bus signal goes to logical 0, and the restart vector is input to the 8080 microprocessor at this time. The 8080 will now push a return address onto the system stack.

This is similar to the sequence of events used when a subroutine is called in a program. When a subroutine is called with the 8080, the 8080 will push a return address onto the system stack. When we want to come back to the main

↓

INTERRUPT REQUEST is issued

↓

INTE is forced to logical 0

↓

INTA is issued to system

↓

RESTART vector is jammed on 8080 Data Bus

↓

RETURN address is placed on the system memory stack

↓

8080 executes software pointed to by the RESTART vector

↓

Figure 6-10 Sequence of internal events that the 8080 follows when an external interrupt is requested from external hardware.

program after the subroutine is executed, we simply execute a return (RET) instruction. The execution of an RET pops the return address off the stack so it can be used as the next address for program execution.

This time sequence of events also occurs in the handling of interrupts. The 8080 pushes a return address onto the system stack. When one wishes to return to the main program after handling the interrupt, an RET instruction will be executed in the interrupt routine. When the RET instruction is executed, the address that was put onto the stack prior to entering the interrupt routine is popped from the stack. The address popped from the stack now allows the 8080 to resume execution of the program being run prior to the interrupt request.

Another point to be made concerning the internal 8080 microprocessor action during an interrupt follows. When an interrupt occurs, the 8080 is forced to a certain memory address to execute a specific section of code. You will recall that the interrupt request may occur at any time in the program. This means the 8080 may be just getting ready to make a decision based on the condition of some internal flags. When the interrupt occurs, the 8080 switches to execute the interrupt location of code and in doing so may affect the system flags. We need to "save" the condition of any registers or flags that may be destroyed during the execution of the interrupt routine. This can be done by pushing the particular register in question onto the stack just *after* entering the interrupt routine. We can then pop the same register from the stack just before exiting the interrupt routine. This idea is demonstrated by the partial program shown in Figure 6-11.

```
   |
PUSH PSW
PUSH H     } SAVE SYSTEM STATUS
PUSH D
PUSH B
   |
INTERRUPT SOFTWARE
   |
POP B
POP D
POP H      } RESTORE SYSTEM
POP PSW        STATUS
EI
RET
```

Figure 6-11 Partial program showing how the system status is saved and later restored by pushing and popping the system stack.

To summarize the interruption of the 8080, we may describe it as follows. The external hardware provides the interrupt request. The 8080 either enables or disables further interrupt requests via the software. The control bus signal INTA is the means by which the interrupt vector is jammed onto the data bus. The interrupt vector is an address or pointer that indicates to the 8080 where to go to get and execute a particular set of instructions. Prior to the 8080 executing the interrupt code at the appropriate address, a return address is placed on the system stack similar to the return address used to call a subroutine. To exit an interrupt routine and return to normal programming, a simple RET instruction is entered by the 8080 software.

6-3 Interrupting the 8085 Microprocessor

The 8085 may be interrupted in several ways. One way is exactly the same as the 8080 that was described previously. For interrupting the 8085 in the same way as the 8080, pin 10 of the 8085 is used for the interrupt request (INTR). The interrupt acknowledge (INTA) signal pin 11 of the 8085 is an output that enables the restart vector to be placed onto the data bus. This is shown in Figure 6-12. Notice in this figure that when the INTA signal goes low to acknowledge an interrupt, the restart vector 0 thru 7 is jammed onto the data bus, and the 8085 begins executing the interrupt service routine based on the restart vector. The restart vectors are exactly the same address locations as they were for the 8080 previously discussed. These were shown in Figure 6-8. One difference between

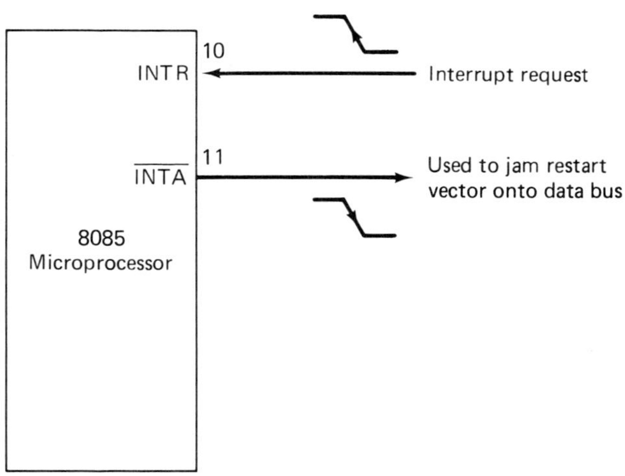

Figure 6-12 Block diagram showing the two physical pins that input and acknowledge the interrupt request of an 8085 microprocessor.

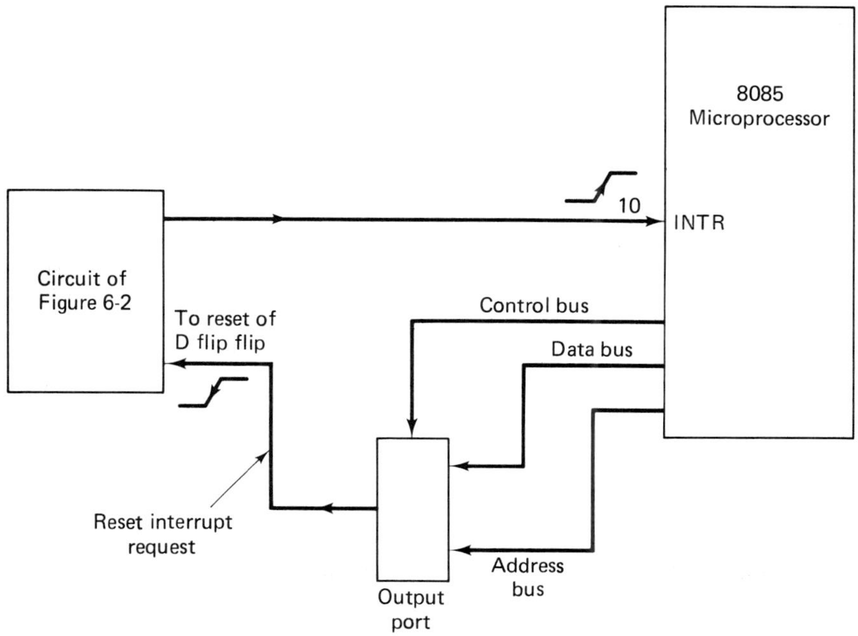

Figure 6-13 Block diagram showing an output port that will be used to reset external interrupt request hardware.

the 8085 and the 8080 is that there is no INTE signal available on the 8085. This means that we must provide an output port to reset the interrupt request. In Figure 6-13 we see that after an interrupt request is issued from the D flip flop circuit of Figure 6-2, the only way to reset the interrupt request is by resetting the D flip flop. The reset line is generated by the output port shown in Figure 6-13. To electrically remove the interrupt request, the 8085 must write a word to the output port.

The 8085 also provides an interrupt pin 6 called TRAP. The TRAP input is a nonmaskable interrupt—that is, a TRAP interrupt cannot be disabled via the software. The TRAP interrupt is assigned the highest priority of any interrupt. If two or more interrupts are issued at the same instant in time, the TRAP interrupt will take precedence over any of the other interrupt requests. When using a TRAP interrupt, we do not need to jam a restart vector onto the data bus. A restart vector is automatically issued internally on the 8085. The restart address for a TRAP interrupt is 2416. To issue a TRAP interrupt, the hardware shown in Figure 6-14 can be used. Referring to this figure, note that we have eliminated the D flip flop from the interrupt request hardware. The TRAP interrupt is both *edge and level sensitive*. The TRAP interrupt must remain high (logical 1) long enough to be electrically input to the 8085. However, the TRAP input

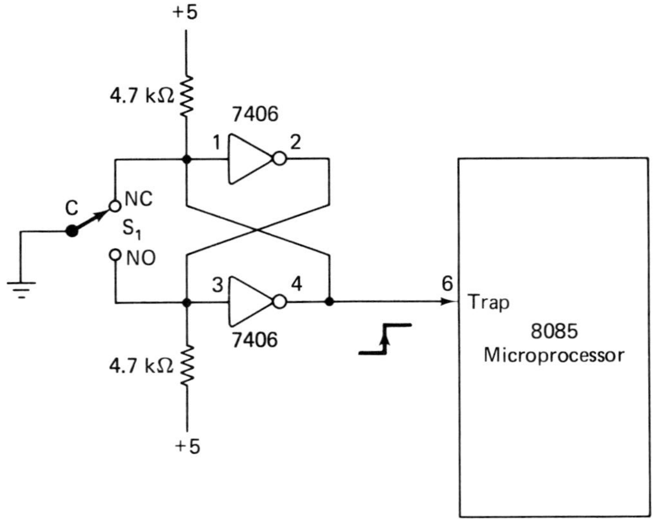

Figure 6-14 Schematic showing how a trap interrupt can be issued for an 8085 microprocessor.

line will not be electrically recognized by the 8085 until the signal goes to a logical 0 and back to a logical 1 again. For this to occur, the switch S_1 of Figure 6-14 must be released and pressed a second time.

There are three other interrupt inputs for the 8085. These interrupts are labeled RST 7.5, RST 6.5, and RST 5.5. The input pins for these are respectively, 7, 8, and 9 of the 8085. These inputs are provided so we do not need to "jam" a restart address onto the data bus. When these interrupt requests are active, the 8085 automatically inserts an internal restart vector. The address for each restart vector 5.5, 6.5, and 7.5 is given in Figure 6-15. Notice in this figure that the addresses of the 5.5, 6.5, and 7.5 interrupt vectors are physically between the restart vectors that may be jammed onto the data bus—that is a restart 5 is between restart 5 and restart 6.

On the 8085 microprocessor the restart input 5.5 and 6.5 have the same timing as the INTR interrupt input. The RST 7.5 is input differently. Restart vector 7.5 is on active, rising, edge-sensitive interrupt request. Further, only a pulse is required to set the interrupt request on the 8085 microprocessor. This means that an interrupt request can be issued on the RST 7.5 simply by inputting a pulse to the RST 7.5 pin. The pulse input will be "remembered" until the request is either serviced or reset by the software. This particular feature of the RST 7.5 is shown in the timing of diagram of Figure 6-16.

Along with these hardware differences between the 8080 interrupts and the 8085 interrupts there are software differences also. The major software difference

INTERRUPT Input	RESTART Vector Address
5.5	$2C_{16}$
6.5	34_{16}
7.5	$3C_{16}$

RESTART Vector	MEMORY Address
5	28_{16}
6	30_{16}
7	38_{16}

Figure 6-15 The memory addresses of the RST 0.5 interrupt vectors. Notice that the RST 6.5 is physically between the EST 6.0 and RST 7.0 locations.

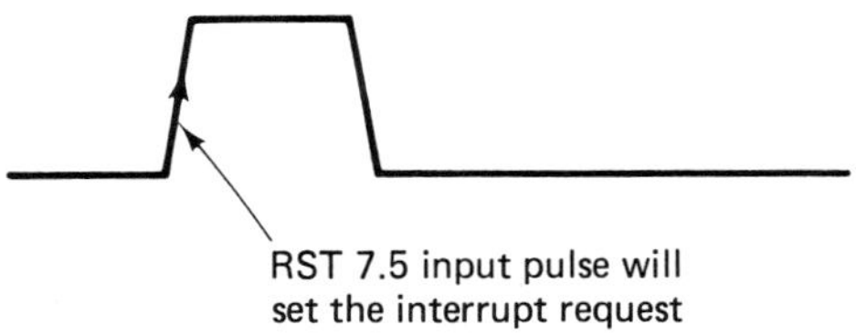

Figure 6-16 Timing diagram showing the pulse input for an RST 7.5 request.

is that the 8085 has an instruction called *set interrupt mask* (SIM). The interrupt mask for the 8085 allows a programmer to enable only certain interrupt request lines. That is, RST 5.5, 6.5, and 7.5 can be disabled as well as the INTR interrupt request. The only interrupt request that cannot be disabled by using software is the TRAP interrupt request. The TRAP interrupt is nonmaskable and will *always* be serviced.

Figure 6-17 shows a small 8085 program that uses the SIM instruction to set interrupt masks. This code is usually entered at the start of a program and also when servicing an interrupt request. Refer to an 8085 software manual for all of the bit definitions for setting the interrupt mask.

```
MVI  A, 18H
SIM
EI
```

Figure 6-17 A partial 8085 program to set the interrupt mask. Note that 18 hexadecimal will set bits 4 and 3 of the 8085 interrupt mask.

6-4 Interrupting the Z80 Microprocessor

The Z80 CPU has two interrupt request lines: the *interrupt request* (INT) pin 16, and the *nonmaskable interrupt request* NMI pin 17. INT Interrupt Request is a maskable interrupt that can be enabled or disabled via the Z80 software. A nonmaskable interrupt will be accepted by the Z80 CPU at all times. The restart vector for a nonmaskable interrupt is 66_{16}. That is, when a nonmaskable interrupt occurs, the CPU program will start executing an interrupt service routine at location 66_{16} in the system memory address space.

The Z80 has three separate modes for handling interrupt requests from the maskable interrupt input pin 16. The first mode is indentical to the interrupt handling that the 8080 performs. When the interrupt occurs a restart vector RST_0 through RST_7 is jammed onto the system data bus. This is shown in Figure 6-18. Note in this figure that the INTA signal is a combination of the M_1 signal and the the $\overline{IORQ}$ signal from the Z80 CPU. Further, there is no INTE signal as there was on the 8080. The interrupt request is reset the same way we did on the 8085. A specific output port may be used to reset the interrupt request. When the Z80 CPU is reset with reset input pin 16, the interrupt response assumes the mode we have just discussed.

A second way that the Z80 CPU responds to interrupt requests follows. Under program control we can set the Z80 device such that when an interrupt request is initiated by the system hardware, the restart vector will automatically be 38 16. This type of service for the interrupt request is identical to that of the 8085 device for an RST 6.5 or 5.5, except that the Z80 CPU goes to a different memory location. Again we stress that this mode must be selected by the programmer through software before any interrupts being requested or issued to the Z80 unit by external hardware.

The third mode in which a Z80 microprocessor responds to interrupts follows. A table of 16-bit addresses or pointers that correspond to addresses of service routines may be stored in system memory. When an interrupt occurs, the external hardware must jam the lower 8 bits of this table pointer onto the system data bus. The upper byte of 8 bits of this pointer is stored in an internal register in the Z80 CPU. The CPU then concatenates the upper order bytes inserted by the hardware. Next, the Z80 uses this word as a memory address to obtain a pointer to the service routine stored in memory. This is shown by the flowchart of Figure 6-19.

In Figure 6-19 we assume that the internal register of the Z80 was set to $3F_{16}$ prior to any interrupts being issued by external hardware. Depending on the lower byte entered when the INTA signal goes to logical 0, the system will point to some location in memory 3FXX. If we assume that the byte of 8 bits jammed onto the data bus was $B6_{16}$, then the pointer in memory for the new address would be 3FB6. The CPU would go to location 3FB6 which would be used as a 16-bit address pointing to the location of the interrupt service routine.

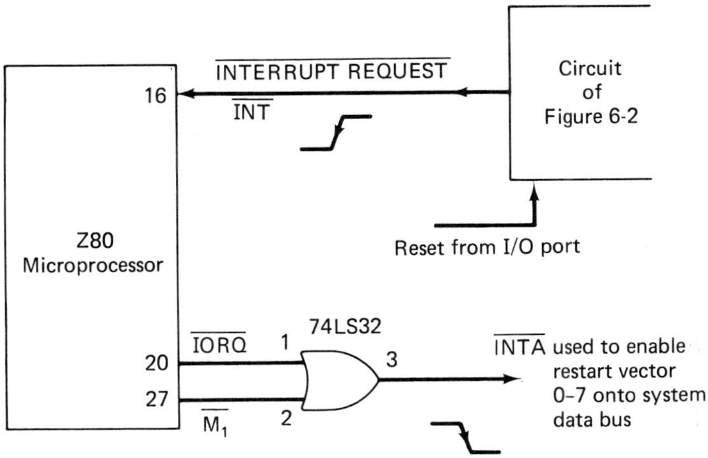

Figure 6-18 Block diagram showing how the external interrupt is input and acknowledged by the Z80 microprocessor.

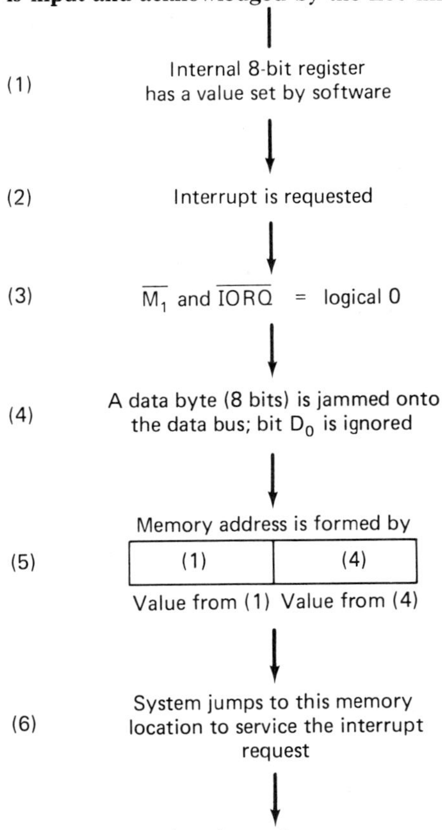

Figure 6-19 Flowchart showing one way the Z80 can respond to an external interrupt request. Eight bits are "jammed" onto the data bus. These 8 bits are concatenated with 8 bits set in an internal register. The 16 bits are then used as an address.

6-5 Interrupting the 6800 Microprocessor

The 6800 microprocessor has two interrupt inputs. These are labeled IRQ pin 4, and NMI pin 6. IRQ is a maskable interrupt request; NMI is a nonmaskable interrupt request. The NMI interrupt cannot be disabled by software. When an interrupt request is issued by external hardware and accepted by the 6800, the device goes to specific memory locations to get the address of the restart vector for handling the interrupt service routine. These restart addresses are given in Figure 6-20.

The 6800 hardware for issuing a nonmaskable interrupt or an interrupt request to the 6800 is shown in block diagram form in Figure 6-21. This hardware is again similar to that used to issue an interrupt request to the 8085 and the Z80 devices. There is no INTE output line on the 6800 that can be used to reset interrupts issued by external hardware. We must write to an output port from the 6800 to reset an interrupt request. Using the information from Figure 6-20, let us assume that at memory locations FFF8 and FFF9 the following data bytes were stored. FFF8 equals 00_{16} and FFF9 equals 35_{16}. When an interrupt request is issued by external hardware the restart vector or address is 0035_{16}.

We have shown how interrupts may be issued through external hardware for each of the four microprocessors under discussion. Here, for clarity, the same technique for issuing this hardware request was used for the four devices so the similarities and the differences in the handling of interrupts can be understood

MEMORY MAP for INTERRUPT vectors

Address		Description
FFFF	RESTART	Lower 8 bits of address (LA)
FFFE		Upper 8 bits of address (UA)
FFFD	NMI	LA
FFFC		UA
FFFB	SOFTWARE INT	LA
FFFA		UA
FFF9	INT	LA
FFF8		UA

Figure 6-20 Memory map showing the locations of the interrupt vectors for the 6800 microprocessor.

easier. In actual systems the hardware interrupt request can be issued in a variety of ways. However, when the interrupt does occur, we must know what to look for within the microprocessor hardware that enables and executes the interrupt.

On the 8080 system we must be aware that a restart vector will be jammed onto the data bus, and that this is also possible on a Z80 system. The exact timing that each microprocessor goes through during interrupt execution is given in those manufacturers' data sheets and specifications. The intent in this discussion has been to show what external hardware is required for the servicing and requesting of interrupts.

When we have an idea of what to expect as an interrupt occurs, then the timing diagrams presented in the specifications are much easier to understand.

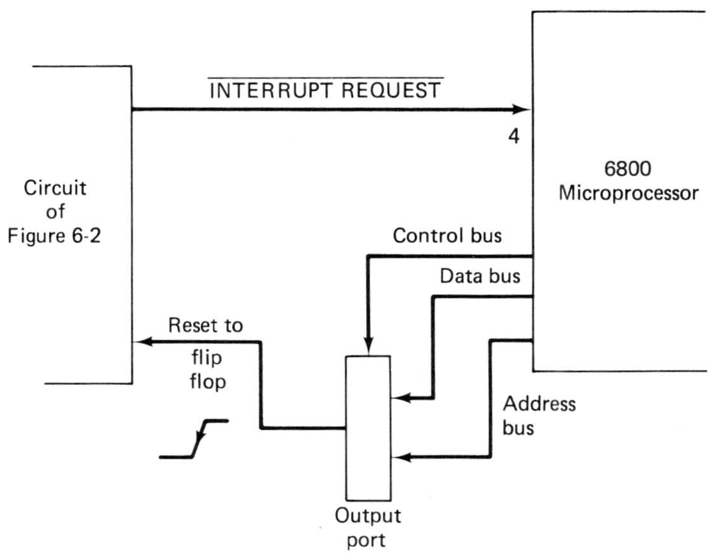

Figure 6-21 Block diagram showing how the nonmaskable interrupt is requested by the hardware shown in Figure 6-2.

6-6 Comments on WAIT Techniques

Now we will discuss different techniques for performing WAIT operations in a microprocessor system environment. We will use the term *wait* to mean any period of time needed to extend the read and write access time for memory or I/O devices. That is, when the memory or the I/O devices take longer to respond than the time allotted for the instruction cycle, the instruction cycle must be slowed down. This wait period must allow enough time for memory and I/O devices to respond. This is shown in the general timing diagram of Figure 6-22. The following section discusses the hardware details used to generate wait time for each of the four microprocessors we are discussing.

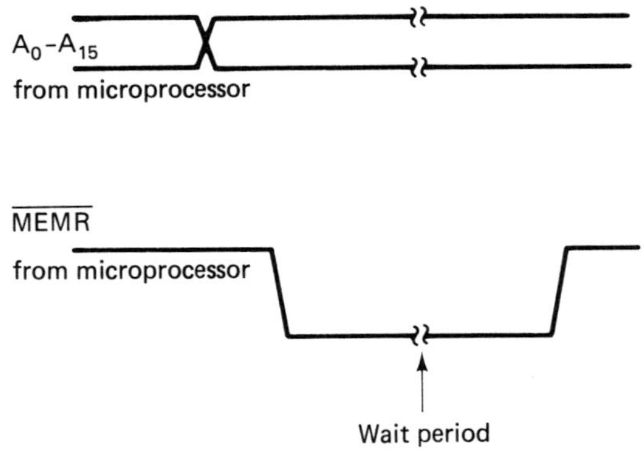

Figure 6-22 Timing diagram showing the concept of generating a wait period for a microprocessor. The memory request is asserted during the wait period.

6-7 Generating a WAIT State with the 8080, 8085, and Z80 Microprocessors

The hardware required to generate a wait state for the 8080, 8085, and Z80 microprocessors is very similar. The circuit we will show can be used with all three microprocessors; the difference is in the physical connections made to the microprocessors' input pins. We will first explain how the wait state is generated and then discuss the interface to each microprocessor.

A WAIT request (WAITREQ) may be initiated by the system memory or I/O devices. In this example we will assume that the system memory has an access time that is too slow to respond to the normal execution speed of the microprocessor. That is, when the microprocessor must read or write data from memory, the cycle time of the CPU must be slowed down. This will accommodate the access time of slow memories. Further, there may be a section of memory that is slow, but another section of memory quick enough to handle the system's speed. In this case we may wish to slow down the microprocessor only when accessing a particular section of memory.

To request a WAIT from the microprocessor we will decode the upper address bits of the address bus. When these address bits correspond to a section of memory that must be slowed down, we will output the signal called WAITREQ.

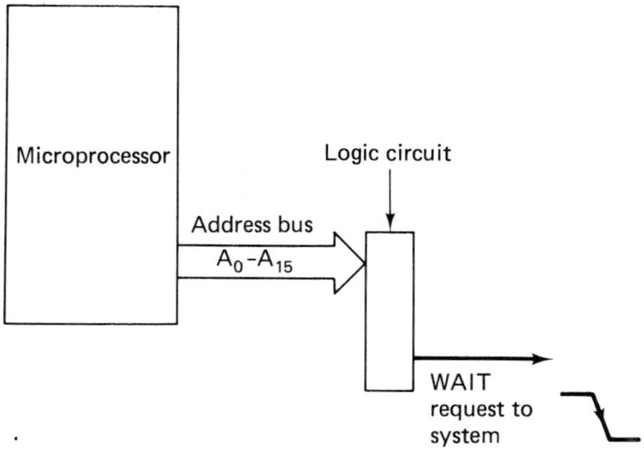

Figure 6-23 Block diagram showing how a wait request may be generated by the microprocessor. When the logical combination of address outputs is correct, the wait request is asserted.

This signal originates from a combinational logic decoding of the upper address bits. This concept is shown in block diagram form in Figure 6-23. There we see that the address inputs go to a combinational logic block that decodes the address combination that is the slower part of memory space. This circuit then outputs the WAITREQ signal. This signal is active low when the correct combination of address inputs is applied to the combination logic circuit.

The wait request signal is then used by another circuit to generate the actual input line to the microprocessor that causes the CPU to enter the WAIT mode.

The circuit we will use to generate the actual wait request input to the microprocessor is shown in Figure 6-24. This is a generalized circuit that can be expanded to accommodate a wait request of any length we desire. The circuit shown will delay system execution for two WAIT periods. We will discuss this circuit in general terms and then show which signals will be required to interface Figure 6-24 to a particular microprocessor. Note that Figure 6-24 can be used to interface to the 8080, 8085, or the Z80 microprocessor. Later in this chapter we will show a circuit to interface to the 6800 microprocessor.

The timing diagram of Figure 6-25 shows the circuit operation of Figure 6-24. First, we see the clock input. All action in Figure 6-24 takes place on the rising edge of the clock input. The clock inputs of the 7474 D flip flops are connected together. The next line in Figure 6-24 shows the actual wait request input line. The wait request input line is the output of Figure 6-23. The wait request is input to the first D flip flop of Figure 6-24. We assume that all flip flops are logical 1 level on each Q output when the circuit begins operations. We ask the reader to make this assumption; we will verify it later in the discussion.

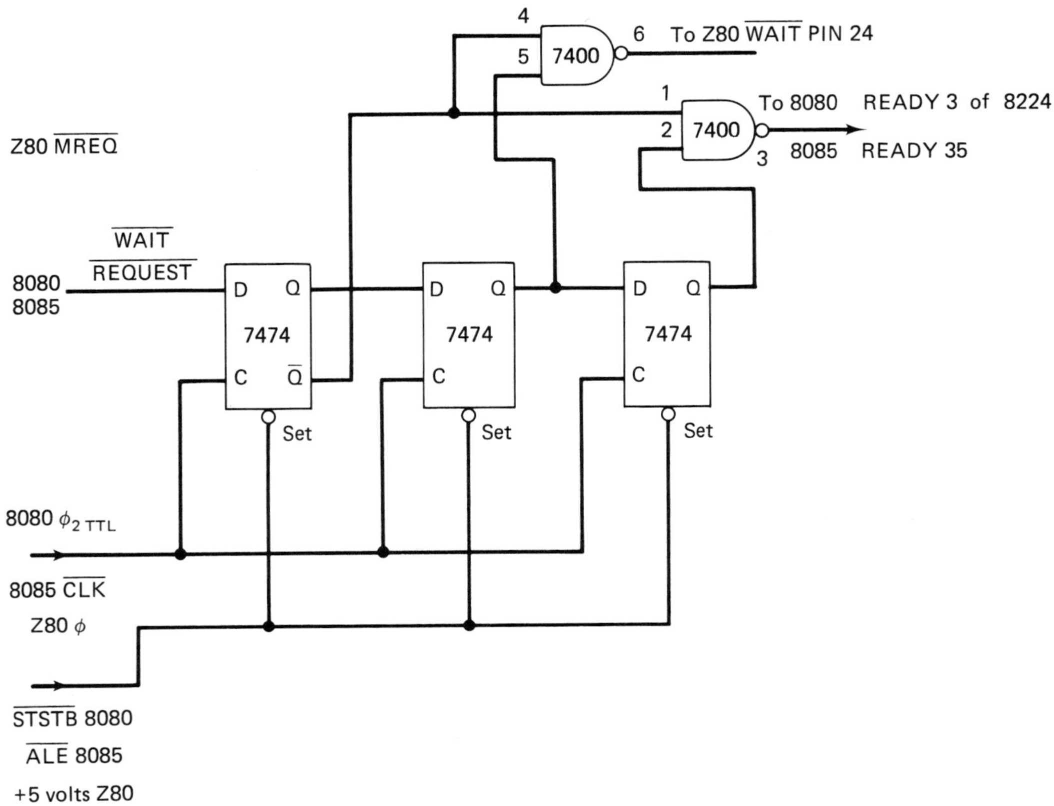

Figure 6-24 Schematic of the circuit used to generate a wait state for the 8080, 8085, and Z80 microprocessors.

In Figure 6-25 we see that the wait request to the D input of the first flip flop goes to logical 0 prior to the clock input going to logical 1. This occurs in each of the three microprocessors we are discussing, and is based on the timing of the microprocessor. When the first clock transition from logical 0 to logical 1 occurs, the Q output of the first D flip flop goes to logical 0 and the $\overline{Q}$ output goes to logical 1. Under these conditions the 7400 NAND gate pins 1 and 2 both have a logical 1 at the input. This produces a logical 0 at pin 3 output of the 7400. This is shown in the timing diagram of Figure 6-25. Notice that these conditions remain stable during the second transition of the clock.

During the third transition of the clock, when the clock input goes from logical 0 to logical 1, the following happens. The third D flip flop has a logical 0 transfer from the D input to the Q_3 output. This applies a logical 0 to 7400 input pin 2. With input pin 2 going to logical 0, output pin 3 goes to logical 1. When output pin 3 goes to logical 1, the wait request has been removed from the microprocessor input. When the request is removed from the microprocessor input, the microprocessor resumes execution at normal system speed.

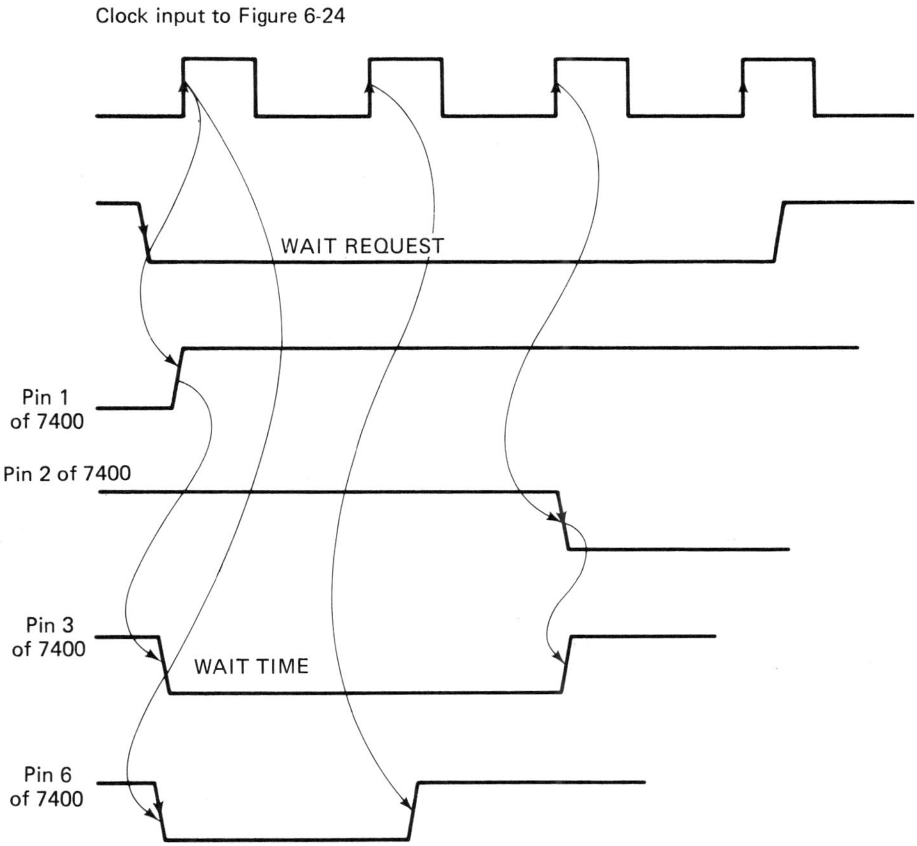

Figure 6-25 Timing diagram showing the relationship of different signals of Figure 6-24.

As the microprocessor resumes execution at the normal system speed, the three flip flops are set to logical 1 level via an active low signal that is applied to the set input. The active low signal is applied to the set input at the start of each new machine cycle on the 8080 or the 8085 microprocessors. When this has happened, all three flip flops are set to logical 1, and the circuit then responds to the wait request of logical 0 or a logical 1, depending on the address applied at the address outputs on the system address bus.

Let us now interface the circuit in Figure 6-24 to an 8080 and an 8085. This is shown in Figures 6-26 and 6-27. To do this we connect pin 3 of the 7400 of Figure 6-25 to the RDYIN input of the 8224 for the 8080 or the READY input for the 8085. The clock to the circuit of Figure 6-24 is phase 2 TTL for the 8080 and is the inverted clock output to the 8085. The set pulse to the three flip flops of Figure 6-24 is the status strobe, $\overline{\text{STSTB}}$, for the 8080, and the address latch enable, $\overline{\text{ALE}}$, from the 8085. Using these signals, we can interface this particular

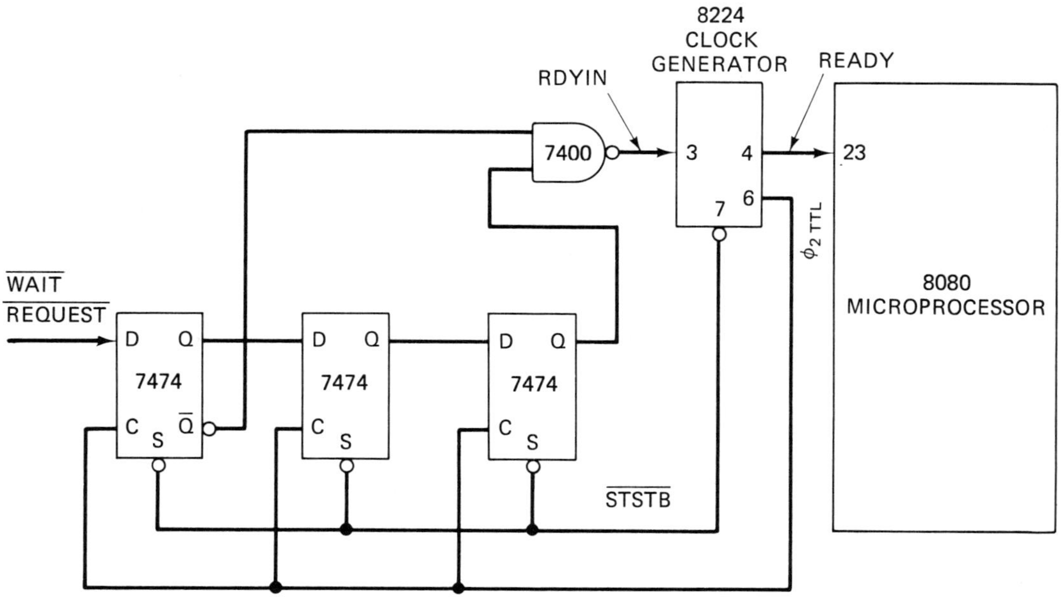

Figure 6-26 Schematic showing the actual connection of the circuit of Figure 6-24 to an 8080 microprocessor.

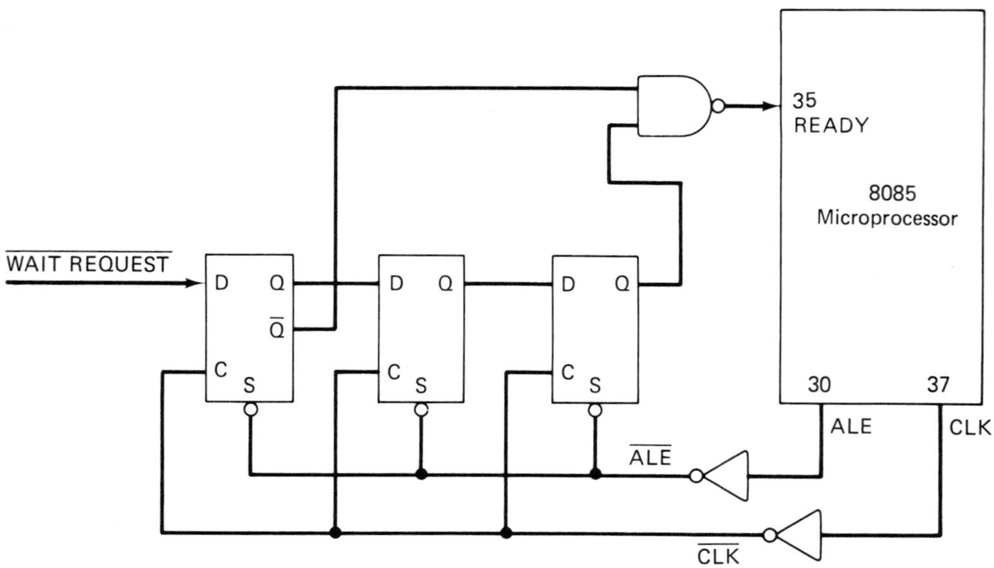

Figure 6-27 Schematic showing the actual interface of the circuit of Figure 6-24 to an 8085 microprocessor.

circuit either to an 8080 or to an 8085 microprocessor to generate one or any number of wait states.

The technique for generating a wait request for the Z80 is shown in Figure 6-28. Notice that the circuit shown here works exactly the same as described previously. The output of the second flip flop is connected to pin 4 of the NAND gate. This provides to the Z80 a wait request that is only one clock cycle wide. The wait request input to the D flip flop is the MREQ output of the Z80 microprocessor. The clock line is the same clock line that goes to the Z80 clock input pin 6.

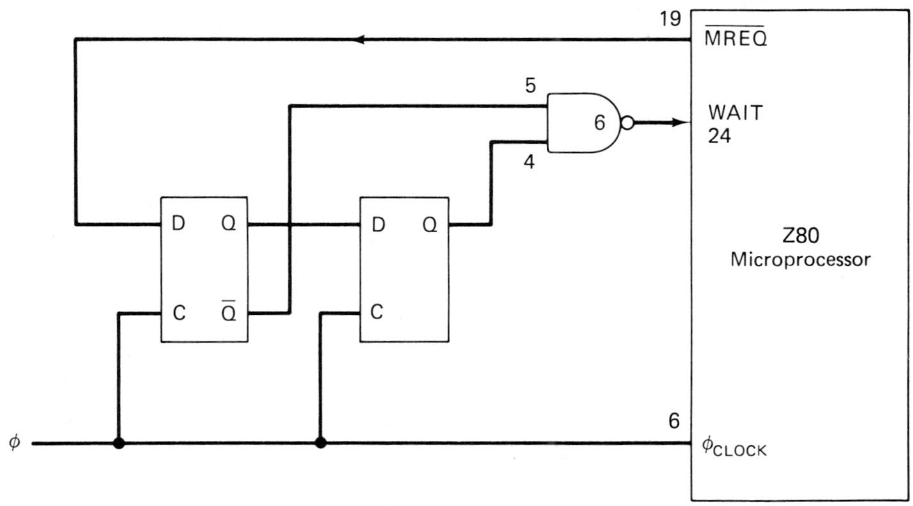

Figure 6-28 Schematic showing the actual interface of the circuit of Figure 6-24 to the Z80 microprocessor.

6-8 Generating a WAIT State for the 6800 Microprocessor

The 6800 microprocessor does not have the input pin called READY or WAIT that the 8080, 8085, and Z80 microprocessors do. The technique for slowing down the 6800 microprocessor to access memory or I/O devices follows. This technique is called "stretching the clocks." Using this technique, we can actually stretch the phase 2 ($\phi 2$) pulse width for a given length of time, based on the time it requires to access a particular memory. The specification for the 6800 $\phi 2$ pulse width indicates that this pulse may be a maximum of 4.5 microseconds wide. If the $\phi 2$ pulse width is wider, the 6800 may lose data contained within the microprocessor. What we will stretch the $\phi 2$ pulse width to must be a value that is less than 4.5 μsec.

The 6871 clock generator used with the 6800 provides an input that can slow down or stop the $\phi 2$ pulse in a given condition as long as an input pin requests it. On the 6871 the input pin that accomplishes this is called a *memory ready* line. When the memory ready line is low, the $\phi 1$ clock to the microprocessor stays in a logical 0 state and the $\phi 2$ clock stays in a logical 1 state. When the memory ready line is again taken to logical 1 level, the system resumes execution at the normal clock rate.

What we will do is to set the memory ready line to logical 0 level whenever we wish to access slower memories. The circuit for accomplishing this is shown in Figure 6-29. Note that a single shot is triggered on the negative edge of the input signal. This input signal will be generated when we have a wait request and when the $\phi 2$ signal TTL from the 6871 goes to logical 1. When these two conditions exist, a single shot will fire and its output will go to a logical 0. This is shown by the timing diagram of Figure 6-30. When the one-shot multivibrator goes to logical 0, the memory ready line to the 6871 also goes to logical 0. Under this condition the clocks to the microprocessor are frozen in a logical 0 state for $\phi 1$ and in logical 1 state for $\phi 2$. After the one shot has timed out, the memory ready line goes to logical 1 level. The 6871 now continues at normal clock speed.

We recall from the discussion of the 6800 that all activity on the data bus happens on the falling edge of $\phi 2$. This means that on the falling edge of phase $\phi 2$, data is strobed to the output devices and data is strobed into the 6800. Therefore, we are delaying the $\phi 2$ flopping to logical 0 for the length of time given by the one shot. This time must not exceed 4.5 microseconds.

Also notice in Figure 6-29 that when the $\phi 2$ input to the 6800 microprocessor goes to logical 1, the memory ready line goes to logical 0 and the $\phi 2$ stays in the

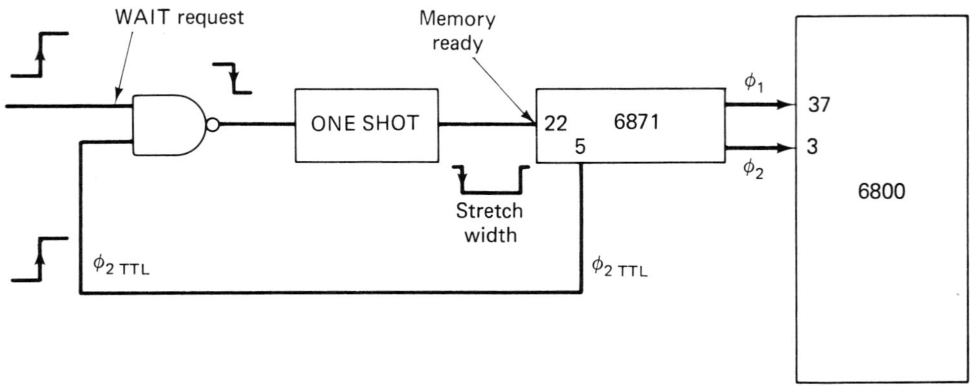

Figure 6-29 Block diagram of a type of circuit that may be used to generate a wait state for the 6800 microprocessor.

logical 1 level as long as the single shot is in the process of firing. After the one shot has timed out, the memory ready line goes to logical 1, as shown in Figure 6-30, and the ϕ2 clock output from the 6871 goes to a logical 0. When the ϕ2 goes to a logical 0, the 6800 microprocessor checks the data on the data bus or the memory accepts data into the memory input pins.

We have now shown techniques for generating WAIT states with the 8080, 8085, Z80, and 6800 microprocessors. Keep in mind that these certainly are not the only techniques that can be used. The circuits displayed here are meant only as guides to allow us to see how the timing WAIT problem can be solved with hardware. After we have a good understanding of what is needed to generate the WAIT state, it will be easier to design circuits to solve this particular problem or to understand how specific hardware within a system actually operates.

Note further that there is another solution to this problem which we may or may not wish to use. It is far easier, but may not always be the most acceptable one. This solution is to slow down the entire frequency of the microprocessor system clock. That is, if the microprocessor is running too fast to interface to standard memories, then we simply slow down the microprocessor. By slowing

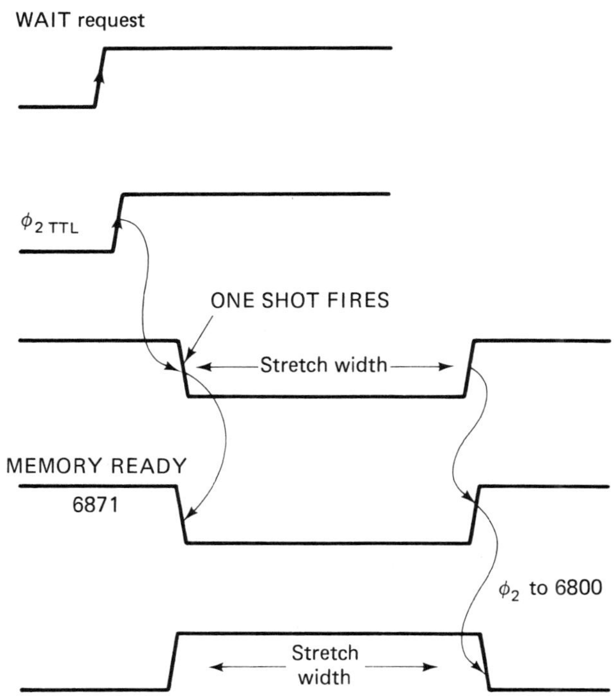

Figure 6-30 Timing diagram of the circuit action of Figure 6-29.

down the microprocessor we can allow enough time for the input to interface to slower memories without adding any hardware.

At first we may think that this solution is totally unacceptable. However, the time required to interface to slower devices is usually only a few hundred nanoseconds more than the time allowed by the microprocessor. By slowing down the clock frequency we will certainly increase the overall time of program execution, but we will also reduce system hardware. It is a trade-off we must weigh. However, we should not dismiss this solution without consideration. There are many microprocessor applications where execution speed is not critical. In such cases it may be beneficial to slow down the overall speed to obtain the reduced and smaller package hardware count that may be desired.

6-9 Direct Memory Access with the 8080, Z80, 8085, and 6800 Microprocessors

In the following discussion we will show how we may use these four microprocessors for Direct Memory Access (DMA). *Direct Memory Access* means that the microprocessor will not be addressing memory as it has done thus far in every circuit we have discussed. Some other system or processor will be addressing the memory. That is, another CPU will have access to the memory

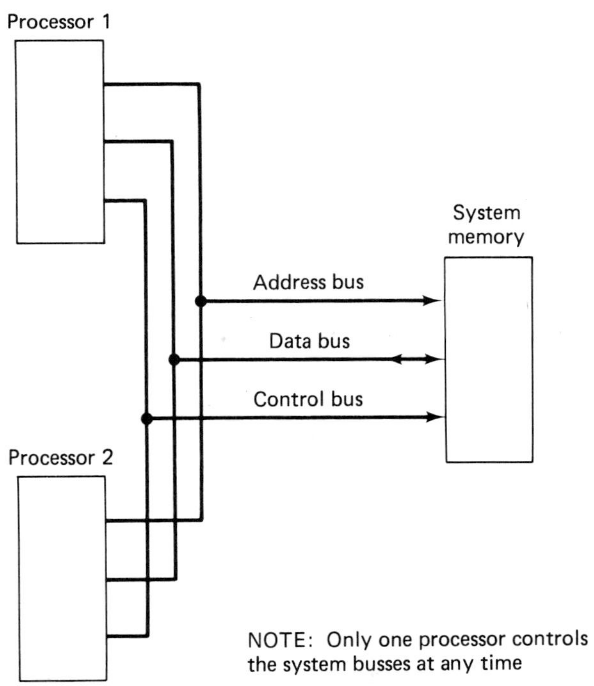

Figure 6-31 Block diagram showing how two microprocessors may need to communicate with system memory.

address lines, the data lines, and the system control bus. Under these conditions the microprocessor that would be communicating normally with the memory must relinquish control of all of these signal lines to another CPU that will be using them. This situation arises when two or more processors are included in the same system. That is, when two or more microprocessors need to use the same memory space. This concept is shown in Figure 6-31.

We will show how the microprocessors relinquish control of their address, data, and control lines to one or another microprocessor that needs to access memory. We will discuss each of the four microprocessors one at a time, and show which pins provide this control and what hardware is effective within the system.

6-10 Direct Memory Access with the 8080 Microprocessor

The 8080 has an input pin called HOLD, which allows the 8080 to use direct memory access or DMA. During normal program execution (non-DMA activity) the HOLD input pin is logical 0. Under this condition the address bus, data bus, and the control bus are all controlled by the 8080 microprocessor. When another microprocessor or system requires the use of these three busses the HOLD line to the 8080 flops to logical 1. When the HOLD line goes to a logical 1 the following sequence occurs in the 8080 device:

1. the address lines go to tri-state mode,
2. the control bit outputs go to a tri-state mode, and
3. the data bus on the 8080 goes into a tri-state mode.

These events will occur, so another processor can now take control of the address lines, data lines, and control lines. If the 8080 is used with an 8228 system controller, then the system controller responds to a HOLD request by tri-stating the output bus and the control bus. This is done by the input pin to the 8228 called HLDA.

HLDA output pin 21 of the 8080 is used as a signal to external hardware that the 8080 has responded to a HOLD request on input pin 13. This means that the external hardware must first request a DMA from the 8080 by taking pin 13 of the 8080 to logical 0 level. The external hardware then waits for HLDA to go to a logical 1 level. When HLDA goes to logical 1 it indicates that the 8080 has relinquished control of all system busses. With the HLDA in a logical 1 level the external hardware can perform the direct memory access. After the DMA is complete, the external hardware then forces the hold input pin on the 8080 to logical 0. Using the HLDA output pin and a hold input pin, the external hardware can then perform reliable direct memory accessing. (See Figure 6-32.)

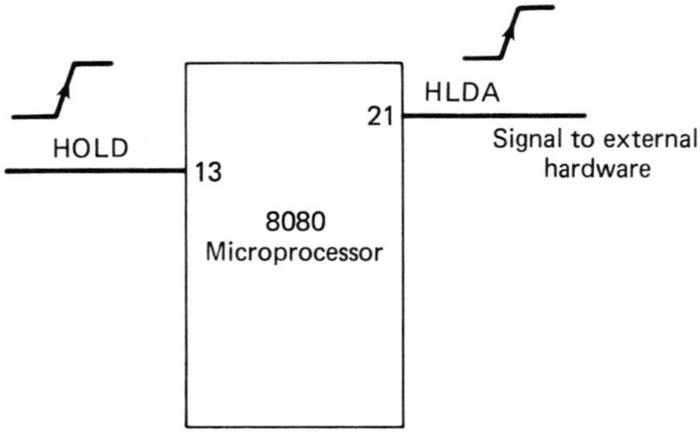

Figure 6-32 Block diagram showing how the HLDA output pin of the 8080 responds to a HOLD request.

If the 8080 device does not use an 8228 controller, then the following must be done. The address bus may or may not be buffered when using an 8080. If the 8080 address bus is buffered, then provisions must be made in the address bus buffers for tri-stating. In the hardware shown thus far we have used a 74LS367 device to buffer the address lines. The 74LS367 may be put into tri-state mode by taking pin 1 and pin 15 of this device to logical 1. The signal used to tri-state the 74LS367 in an address buffer application would be the HLDA output pin of the 8080. That is, when the HLDA output pin 21 of the 8080 goes to logical 1, the address bus must be put into the tri-state mode. This means that the address buffers must be put into a tri-state mode.

The data bus must also be put into a tri-state mode in a DMA application. In our systems we have used data buffers other than an 8228 controller. The other data bus buffers must be capable of being put into a tri-state in a DMA mode. The data bus buffers use the HLDA output signal from the 8080 as the input to indicate that they should go into a tri-state mode.

The control bus must also go into tri-state mode via the HLDA output pin on the 8080. When we are designing a system based on the 8080 microprocessor we must be aware of whether direct memory access will be needed. If DMA is needed, then provisions must be made on all busses to go tri-state and relinquish control to external hardware.

6-11 Direct Memory Access with the 8085 Microprocessor

A direct memory access operation with an 8085 microprocessor follows. The HOLD input on the 8085 microprocessor is similar to the HOLD on the 8080 device and will be taken to logical 1 level. When this input goes to logical 1 it signals the external hardware is to perform direct memory access.

When the 8085 acknowledges that the HOLD input has been applied in a similar fashion to the 8080, then the HLDA output line on the 8085 goes to logical 1 level. When the HLDA output lines goes to logical 1 it signifies that the 8085 has relinquished control of the address bus, data bus, and control bus. This activity is very similar to that described for the 8080.

In the systems we have shown, the address bus and the data bus may be buffered, and the control bus may be formed by using TTL logic. Under these conditions these three busses must be capable of being put into a tri-state mode. The signal that forces these busses into a tri-state mode is the HLDA output pin of the 8085 microprocessor. When designing with an 8085 device we must be aware of any possible DMA activity. If DMA is possible, then the system busses must be capable of being tri-stated via the HLDA output pin.

6-12 Direct Memory Access with the Z80 Microprocessor

The Z80 microprocessor has input pins similar to the 8080 and 8085 microprocessors for performing direct memory access. On the Z80 microprocessor the input pin labeled $\overline{\text{BUSRQ}}$ is the request for DMA to the busses. When this line goes to logical 0, the data bus, address bus, and control signals of the Z80 are put into tri-state mode. After these busses have been put into the tri-state mode the Z80 outputs a signal on the bus acknowledge, or $\overline{\text{BUSAK}}$, that the Z80 has relinquished control of all busses. These two pins on the Z80 are very similar to the HOLD input and the HLDA output pin of the 8080 microprocessor.

We state again that the address buffers, data buffers, and control bus may be formed by using standard TTL logic. If this is the case, the TTL logic must be capable of being put into tri-state mode if DMA activity is to be possible with this system. The signal that forces the TTL logic into tri-state mode is the $\overline{\text{BUSAK}}$ signal from the Z80 microprocessor. This is very similar to what we have previously discussed for the 8080 and 8085 microprocessors.

6-13 Direct Memory Access with the 6800 Microprocessor

In performing DMA with the 6800 microprocessor two main signals are used. The input signal requesting DMA operation from external hardware to the 6800 microprocessor is called HALT. When HALT goes to a logical 0 level the 6800 device relinquishes control of all the address bus, data bus, and the control bits. When the 6800 has released control of the address bus, data bus, and the control bits the bus acknowledge, or BA, output signal will go to logical 1. When BA goes to logical 1 it indicates to external hardware that the 6800 has relinquished control of all the system busses.

When interfacing a 6800 microprocessor to external hardware, the address bus, data bus, and control bus may be formed from standard TTL devices. If this is the case, then these TTL devices must be capable of tri-stating the system busses. The enable line for tri-stating the busses is the output signal BA from the 6800 microprocessor. When BA goes to logical 1, the address bus, data bus, and control bus are put into the tri-state mode.

In performing direct memory access with the 6800 device, the external hardware would force the HALT input line to logical 0 level. When the HALT line goes to logical 0, the external hardware waits until the BA output line of the 6800 goes to logical 1. When the BA output line goes to logical 1 it signals the external hardware that the system busses have tri-stated and are free to be used. After the external hardware has performed the DMA operation it again forces the HALT input line to logical 1. In this way DMA operations can be performed between the 6800 unit and any external hardware.

6-14 Summary

In this chapter we have discussed the concepts of interrupting, waiting, and direct memory access for the 8080, 8085, Z80 and 6800 microprocessors. We have also shown some hardware that may be used to accomplish these particular functions. The hardware was shown to allow us to see "what it would take" to perform these functions. The hardware shown does not represent the only or best solutions to the problem. Many microprocessor systems can be designed without using any of the information contained in this chapter. However, if we come across a system to be designed or repaired by using any of these interrupt, wait, or DMA functions, then the information presented here is necessary. It also helps in trouble-shooting to know what the hardware should be doing in order to perform any of these three operations. It is difficult to troubleshoot hardware if we do not know in a general sense what operations the hardware must perform. By understanding this information we will be on familiar ground when analyzing any microprocessor system. The concepts of waiting, interrupting, and DMA are constant. Details differ from one microprocessor to another. By understanding the details discussed in this chapter we can recognize the hardware realization of them in other systems.

7

PROGRAMMING AN ERASABLE PROGRAMMABLE READ-ONLY MEMORY

The microprocessor controlled system we will present in Chapter 8 will perform the function of programming an Erasable Programmable Read-Only Memory (EPROM). EPROMs are used in many microprocessor controlled systems. Anyone who is serious about designing or trouble-shooting microprocessor hardware should understand how an EPROM is programmed and erased. In this chapter we show exactly how the 2708 EPROM is programmed and erased.

The 2708 EPROM was chosen for this discussion because it is in wide general use throughout the industry today. Further, if we can understand how the 2708 is programmed, it will be a simple matter to understand how other EPROMs can be programmed. The details of programming different EPROMs vary, but the general concept remains constant.

7-1 Overview of Erasable Programmable Read-Only Memory

EPROMs are used in computing systems just as ROMs are used. The main advantage of using an EPROM lies in the fact that the information can be electrically altered. In a standard ROM, the data are permanently stored in the device when it is manufactured. The ROM comes preprogrammed with a specific pattern of 1s and 0s. In an EPROM the data are not preprogrammed by the device manufacturer. The user of the EPROM can put any data desired into the device's memory locations. Then by using special equipment the user can change the data stored in an EPROM.

The ability to alter data electrically in an EPROM is the main reason this type of device is used. When we are developing a microprocessor system for the first time, the initial software can be written and then programmed into an EPROM. The EPROM can then be installed into the system, and the microprocessor executes the program stored within the EPROM. If the program must be changed, the EPROM can be removed from the system and the information in the EPROM altered to satisfy the required changes.

Special equipment is needed to program and erase information stored within an EPROM. These problems are insignificant however, compared to the advantages these special devices provide for microprocessor system users.

7-2 Erasing an EPROM

We have stated that the information contained within an EPROM can be altered. One way in which we can alter the information in an EPROM is to electrically erase all the data that has been put into the device. After an EPROM is erased, all of the data residing within the EPROM is the same. In a 2708 EPROM the data, when erased, equals all logical 1s. This means that if we erase the 2708, and then electrically read the remaining data, all of the data in all of the memory locations would equal logical 1s.

There are various schemes for erasing the data in an EPROM. The 2708 EPROM requires an ultraviolet light source to erase the data stored within it. The 2708 device is fabricated with a window in the top of the device such that the ultraviolet light can reach the device. This is shown in Figure 7–1. To erase the 2708 device, we place it near an ultraviolet light source for a specified period of time. As an approximate erase time we assume one-half hour exposure, but this is a function of many factors.

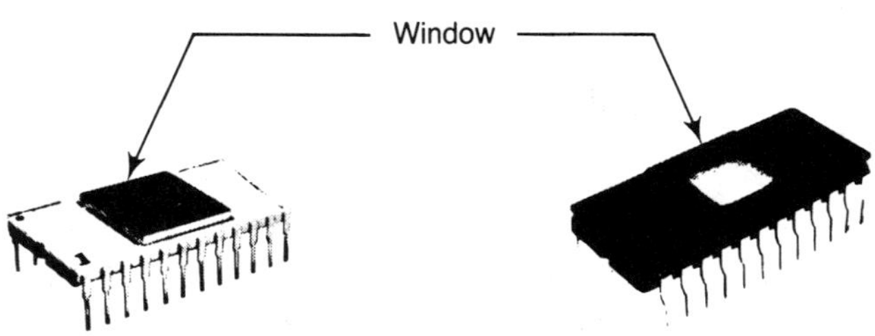

Figure 7-1 Two different ways of packaging an EPROM. The window in each package admits ultraviolet light, which is used to erase stored data. © Intel, 1979.

By using an ultraviolet light we now have a means of erasing or altering the data within an EPROM. Note that there are special ultraviolet light set-ups that can be purchased for the sole purpose of erasing data contained within an EPROM. For anyone planning to do much work involving the use of EPROMs, this type of light source is highly recommended. Figure 7–2 shows a block diagram of a typical setup for erasing the data in an EPROM.

As we have stated, when the 2708 device is erased all the data go to logical 1s. This is a helpful fact to note because we can use this criterion as an electrical check for complete erasure of the data contained within the EPROM. That is, if we are not sure that the device is completely erased, we can electrically read the device at every address and check to insure that the data at all locations are equal to logical 1. This particular aspect of checking an EPROM is discussed in Chapter 9, where we will be considering the software needed to control the hardware we will be building in Chapter 8. We mention the fact now so that we are aware of what the data within an EPROM are like when it is erased. Different EPROMs contain different data values when erased—that is, one device may erase to all logical 0s. Refer to manufacturers' data sheets for this explicit information.

The remainder of this chapter is devoted to the exact details needed to understand how data in an EPROM can be electrically programmed or stored. When we electrically program a 2708 EPROM, we are changing the internal characteristics of the device in a specified way. The change results in a logical 0 being stored at the selected location. Once a logical 0 has been stored in the EPROM, the only way to change it to logical 1 is by erasing the data with the ultraviolet light source.

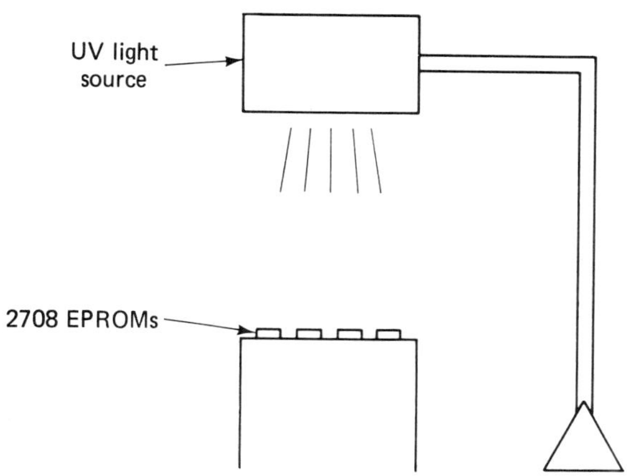

Figure 7-2 Block diagram of a typical setup for erasing EPROMs.

The mechanism for changing the internal characteristics of the 2708 device is by *charge transfer*. When we program a 2708 EPROM we are forcing the charges within the silicon to collect in a certain way. This way that the charges collect changes data in the storage location from logical 1 to logical 0. When we erase an EPROM we disperse the collection of charges that were forced together when we were programming the device.

This is an overview of what actually happens at the atomic level within the silicon chip and the details of how to make it happen at the user level.

7-3 Programming a 2708 EPROM

We now discuss the events for programming the 2708 device with references to timing diagrams and voltage levels. The main idea in programming the 2708 device is that *we apply the data to be programmed at the device outputs*. We set an address on the address inputs. We then force certain pins of the device to specific voltage levels. These events are shown in the flowchart in Figure 7–3.

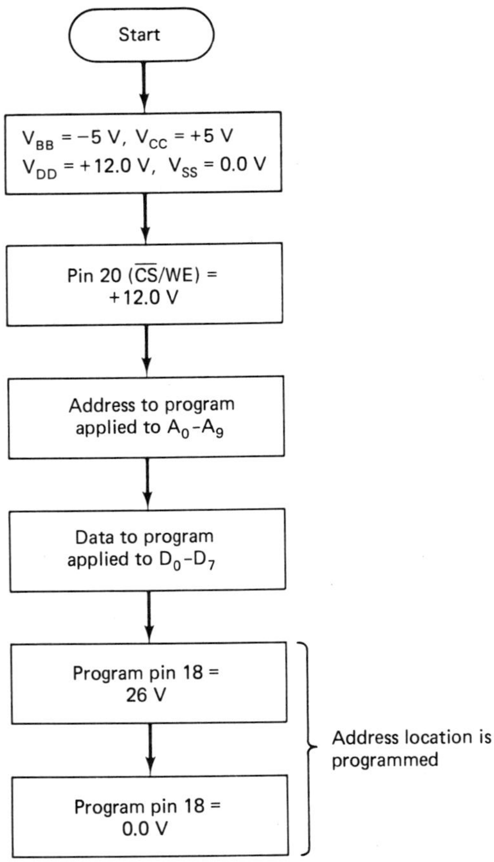

Figure 7-3 Flowchart showing the sequence of events to program a single location in an EPROM.

A.C. Programming Characteristics

Symbol	Parameter	Min.	Typ.	Max.	Units
t_{AS}	Address Setup Time	10			μs
t_{CSS}	$\overline{CS}$/WE Setup Time	10			μs
t_{DS}	Data Setup Time	10			μs
t_{AH}	Address Hold Time	1			μs
t_{CH}	$\overline{CS}$/WE Hold Time	.5			μs
t_{DH}	Data Hold Time	1			μs
t_{DF}	Chip Deselect to Output Float Delay	0		120	ns
t_{DPR}	Program To Read Delay			10	μs
t_{PW}	Program Pulse Width	.1		1.0	ms
t_{PR}	Program Pulse Rise Time	.5		2.0	μs
t_{PF}	Program Pulse Fall Time	.5		2.0	μs

NOTE: Intel's standard product warranty applies only to devices programmed to specifications described herein.

2704, 2708
Programming Waveforms

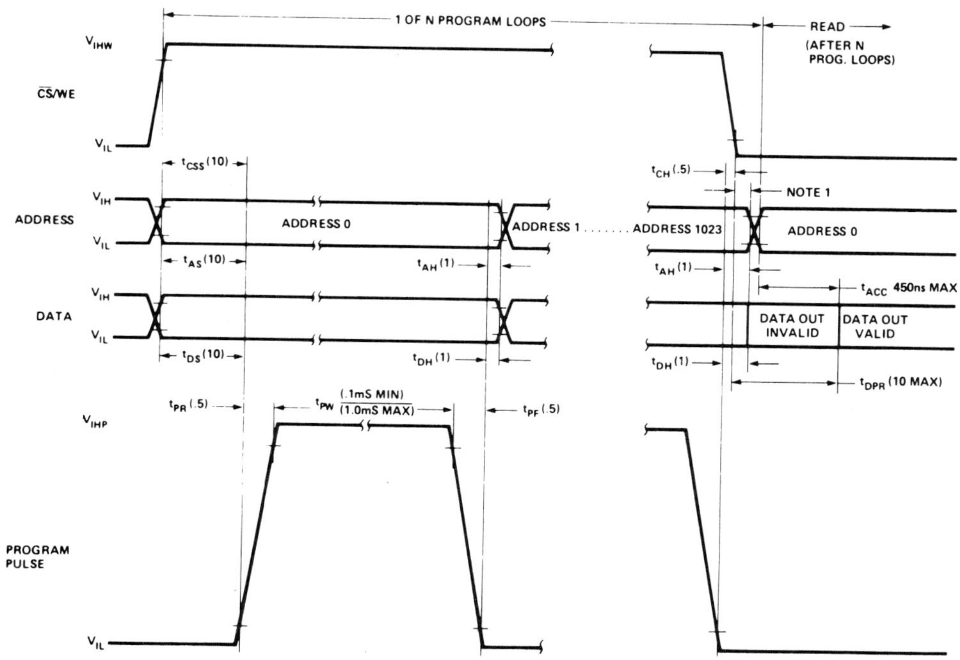

NOTE 1. THE $\overline{CS}$/WE TRANSITION MUST OCCUR AFTER THE PROGRAM PULSE TRANSITION AND BEFORE THE ADDRESS TRANSITION.

NOTE 2. NUMBERS IN ( ) INDICATE MINIMUM TIMING IN μS UNLESS OTHERWISE SPECIFIED.

Figure 7-4 Excerpted specifications for the 2708 EPROM showing the important timing characteristics. © Intel, 1979.

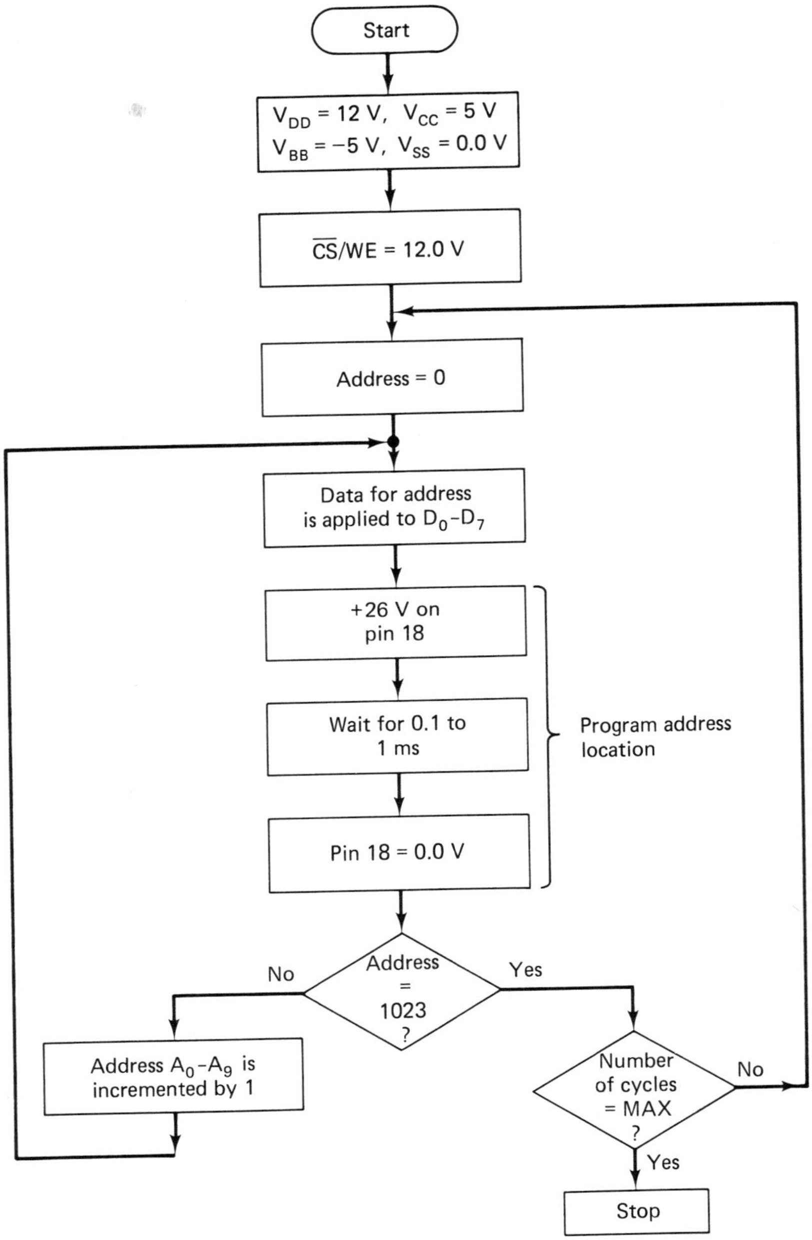

Figure 7-5 Flowchart showing the sequence of events required to program an entire EPROM.

The timing diagram of Figure 7–4 shows the relationship between the data applied, the addresses applied, and the programming pulses applied to the device. Referring to the manufacturers' data sheets, we see that the address inputs are standard TTL voltage-level inputs. The data inputs to the device are also standard TTL voltage inputs. The $\overline{CS}$/WE signal on Pin 20 of the 2708 device is forced to +12 volts during the EPROM programming mode. The programming pulse Pin 18 of the 2708 EPROM is taken from 0 V to 26 V typically. The program pulse is taken high, 26 volts, and then low at every address location we want to program. In programming the 2708, we must apply only one program pulse per address. Also, we must cycle through all 1024 addresses when programming the device.

Figure 7–5 shows a flowchart for the sequence of events required when programming a 2708 EPROM. The flowchart in Figure 7–5 shows the events for a single programming pass or loop.

In this figure, we see that the $\overline{CS}$/WRITE ENABLE signal equals +12 V prior to data being applied to the outputs of the device. This action forces the 2708 outputs into the input mode. If this were not the case, the data outputs of the 2708 would conflict with the data we are trying to input to the 2708. Also, the data input is applied to all bits of the 2708 in parallel. The 2708 EPROM can program 8 bits internally on the EPROM at the same time.

7-4 The Program Pulse for the 2708 EPROM

When programming a 2708 EPROM the maximum time the programming pulse can be at +26 V is 1 millisecond. The minimum time the pulse can be at +26 V is 0.1 msec. However, the actual value of the pulse width can be anywhere between these limits. Although the pulse width can be any value between the limits, it is important, as we will show later, to know that the exact value of the programming pulse width.

Another important characteristic of the programming pulse is the rise and fall time. The rise and fall time of the programming pulse must be between 0.5 and 2.0 microseconds. These specifications are shown in the waveform of Figure 7–6. For programming the 2708 according to the specifications, we must keep the product of the programming pulse width and the number of programming passes through the memory greater than or equal to 100 msec. A pass through the memory consists of applying the programming pulse at each address location in succession. This means we base the number of programming passes needed (NP) on the formula:

$$NP = \frac{100 \text{ msec}}{\text{Program Pulse Time in msec}}$$

For our system we have a program pulse time of 0.5 msec. This means we must make:

$$NP = \frac{100 \text{ msec}}{0.5 \text{ msec}} = 200$$

We must make 200 passes through the entire memory if we are to program the device as specified. More than 200 passes may be made if we wish. No damage to the device will result; only the overall programming time is increased. Once we have adequately programmed the device with 200 complete passes through the memory as specified, more programming *will not* make the device better programmed. This point is mistaken many times. Users feel that if they program longer than the specified period of time, the device will be much better programmed. This is just not the case. The specification for the device is written such that the EPROM is well programmed if all the rules are followed. The bottom line is: do not waste extra programming time where it will not provide substantial gain.

There is a point to be stressed in programming the device, however. The EPROM may give all indications of being fully programmed before the required number of passes through the memory is complete. For example, we program

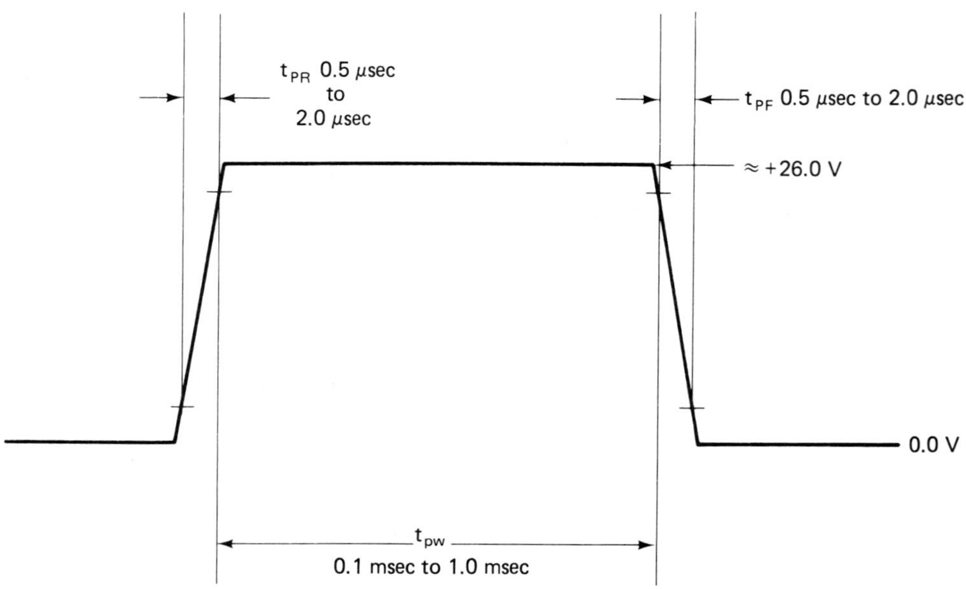

Figure 7-6 Waveform of the programming pulse for the 2708 EPROM.

the device for 200 complete passes through the memory. After 20 passes the device has all the data stored in it either as logical 1 or logical 0. In this case, however, it is wise to let the device continue programming until the specified number of passes through the memory have been completed, because the device may lose stored data if it is not programmed for the specified length of time.

We mentioned earlier that as the 2708 device is programmed it essentially collects charges in such a way as to change the internal characteristics of the device. If a large enough collection of charges is obtained to barely change these characteristics (analogous to short programming time), then some of the charges may disperse and the device characteristics may revert to the nonprogrammed mode as the device is used. So if we do not program the device for the time specified, the EPROM, in normal operation, may lose data. That is, if a 0 were stored within the device, the 0 may fade to a 1. So always, when you are writing data into the EPROM, program the device for the length of time specified.

When there is a very large collection of charges stored as a logical corresponding to adequate programming time, some of these charges may disperse during normal use. There will be a sufficient number left to keep the device characteristics in the programmed state. It is best not to sacrifice EPROM reliability for speed in programming time.

In the system to be discussed in Chapter 8, we will realize the programming flowchart shown in Figure 7–7. There we see that data to be programmed into memory is stored in an external RAM and then applied to the data inputs of the 2708 EPROM. When the required number of programming loops have been completed, we compare the contents of the external RAM data against the contents that we read from the EPROM. If each data output of the address of the RAM matches the data output in the equivalent address of the EPROM, then the device has been successfully programmed.

7-5 Summary

In this chapter we presented some of the important characteristics of the 2708 EPROM. We explained how the 2708 device is programmed. In the next chapter we use these details to design a microprocessor-controlled system to program 2708 EPROMs automatically. When we understand how one EPROM is programmed, it is easier to understand how other types of these devices are programmed, because we know what essentials to look for when reading the characteristics of programming a specific unit.

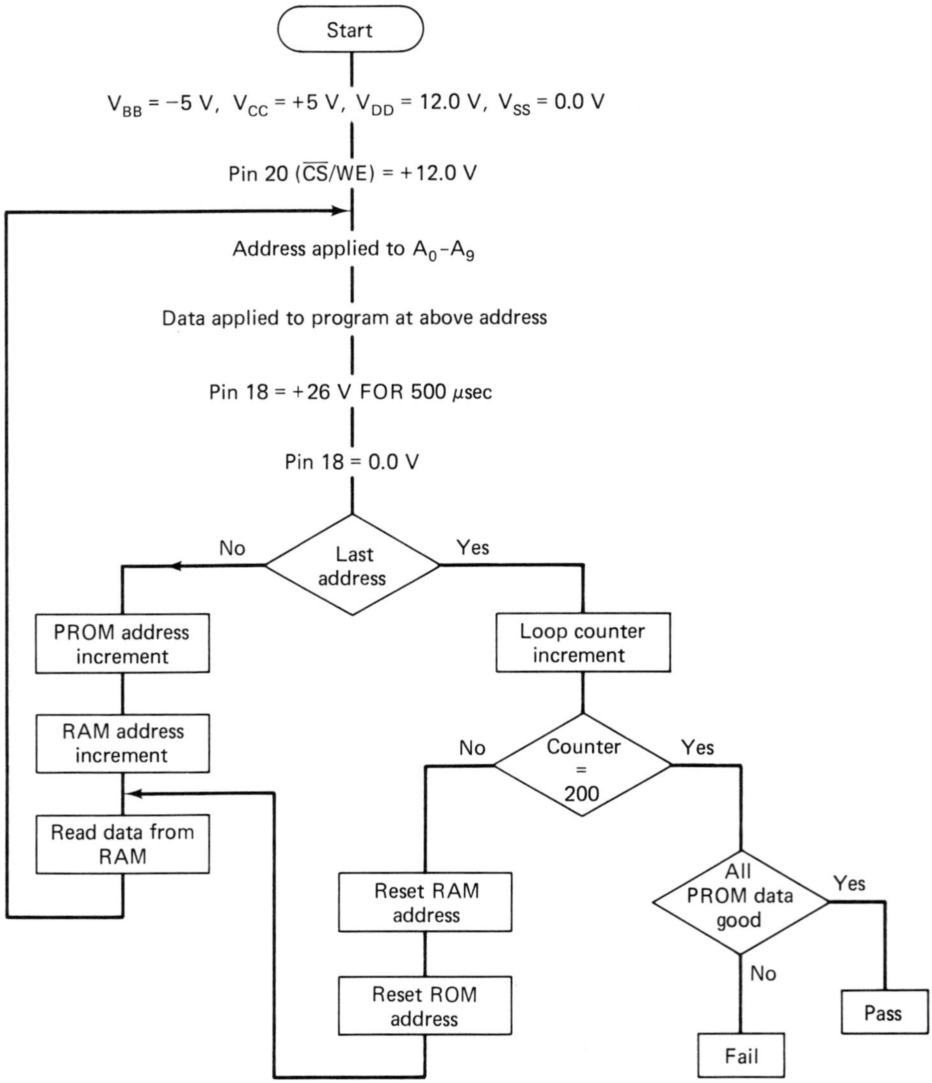

Figure 7-7 Flowchart showing major sequence of events for programming an EPROM (2708), assuming data to be programmed is in a RAM.

8

PROM PROGRAMMER HARDWARE DETAILS

In this chapter we will present the hardware for a microprocessor system that can be used to program a 2708 EPROM automatically. We discussed the details of programming the 2708 device earlier in Chapter 7, but not an automatic system to accomplish the job. Our system will be realized by using four different microprocessors. We shall first present systems that use the 8080, 8085, and Z80 microprocessors; then we shall discuss the system that uses the 6800 device.

This chapter will cover only the hardware aspects of the design. The software for all systems—8080, 8085, Z80, and 6800—will be discussed in Chapter 9. In Chapter 10 we shall discuss system debugging by using the static stimulus testing technique.

8-1 Overview of the System

Before we can discuss any of the details of the system we must first decide what we want the system to do. Once this is decided, we can turn our attention to how to do it. The main function of the system under discussion is to program a 2708 EPROM. This broad function brings to mind further questions.

The first question is, where is the data that are to be written or programmed? For this system we will first store the data in a RAM. Once we assume this, the next question is, "How does the data get into the RAM?" The answer is: we will be entering data into the RAM via a keyboard.

If we plan to enter data into a RAM via a keyboard what means can be used to examine the data visually? For this we will use a 6-digit hexadecimal display.

We now have some general blocks of our system defined. Just how to realize these blocks has yet to be decided. The major system blocks are shown in Figure 8-1. There we see the overall function for our system defined as: (a) entering data into RAM via a keyboard, and (b) programming this data into a 2708 EPROM.

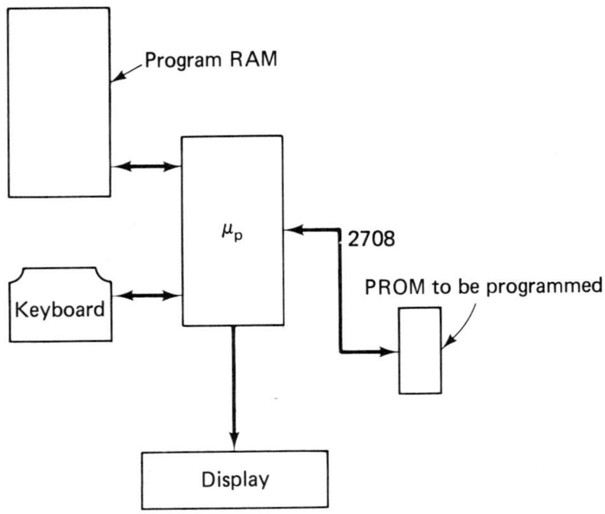

Figure 8-1 Block diagram of the hardware for an automatic PROM programmer system.

8-2 Specific Functions of the System

The broad function of entering data by means of a keyboard necessitates nine specific key functions. These are:

1. Data Keys 0–F (Actual data to be entered)
2. Enter Key
3. Clear Entry Key
4. Address Set Key
5. Clear RAM Key
6. Start Program Key
7. Verify (VFY) Key
8. Copy Key
9. Reset System Key

An explanation of the reason for each of these keys follows:

DATA KEYS: These 16 unique data keys are used to enter data into the system. They have values 0–F.

ENTER KEY: The ENTER key is used to "qualify" data input by the data keys. That is, when inputting data to the system we have an opportunity to check the data before it is entered.

CLEAR ENTRY KEY: The CLEAR ENTRY key is used to clear data that was loaded by the data keys or the function of address set.

CLEAR RAM KEY: The CLEAR RAM key prepares the internal RAM. That is, it sets the data to all 1s.

START PROGRAM KEY: The START PROGRAM key puts the system into programming mode so the data in the RAM will be transferred into the 2708 device. The display will indicate that the programming mode has been entered. When the start key is pressed, the only way to stop system execution is by pressing the *reset key*.

VERIFY KEY (VFY): When the VFY key is pushed, the system compares the data in the 2708 in the socket against the data stored in the RAM. If a mismatch is detected, the display shows the failed address and the data in the 2708 EPROM.

COPY KEY: When the COPY key is pushed the system duplicates the data in the 2708 EPROM installed in the socket onto an internal RAM. This is useful when we have a programmed EPROM and want another EPROM, identical to the first.

RESET KEY: When the RESET key is pushed, the system stops executing any command in progress and begins to execute software from the initial power-up sequence.

When the system first has power applied it executes the same sequence of instructions as if one had pressed the reset key.

8-3 Support Hardware

Now that we have an understanding of what the system will do, we can design hardware to realize the functions.

The 2708 EPROM requires power supply voltages of +12, +5, and −5 V when the EPROM is operating *in the read mode*, where the device is operating like a ROM. The 2708 requires an additional +26-V programming pulse when operating *in the programming mode*. The voltages needed are +26, +12, +5, and −5.

The +5 V is also needed for the TTL devices in the system, so this should be a fairly high, current-rated supply. We will have to calculate the current required by the +5 V supply. There are many "off the shelf" +5-V power supplies available that can do the job. Let us say we use a +5-V supply rated at 3 amperes.

The −5-V supply must sink very little current—a typical amount is less than 200 milliamperes. From a data sheet of the 2708 it can be seen that the V_{BB} supply current maximum is 60 mA. We plan to use three 2708s in our system—two for controlling the system, and one to be programmed. Our system is designed to accommodate possible future expansion. This could include as many as four 2708 EPROMs, in which case the maximum V_{BB} current would be 5 × 60 mA or 240 mA. We select a power supply rated for −5 V at 500 mA; again, this is an "off the shelf" item.

The +12-volt supply must provide current required for the two 2708s that are running the present system plus the one that is to be programmed. Again, if we installed four such units in the system at some future date, and one 2708 were being programmed, then the +12-volt source would need to supply 5 × 65 mA or 325 mA. The 65 mA represents the "worst case" supply current I_{DD} in a data sheet for the 2708 EPROM.

Since we need a +26-V supply for programming, we can tap off the +26-V supply with a +12-V regulator to obtain the +12 V of power needed for the system. The worst case power dissipation of the +12 V regulator would be (26 V − 12 V) × I_{DD} (system):

$$P_D = 14 \text{ V} \times 325 \text{ mA} = 4.55 \text{ watts}$$

We will use an LM340C-12 for the +12-V regulator. The required power supplies are now selected and shown in Figure 8-2.

If we were using an 8080 microprocessor, both the +12-V and −5-V supply currents would have to be increased, because the 8080 requires +12 and −5 volts. An 8224 clock generator also requires +12 V for its own operation.

"Off the shelf" power supplies are manufactured in a variety of voltages and currents. After estimating the system requirements we can usually find a ready-made power supply that meets and probably exceeds the specifications. If we decide to construct rather than purchase ready-made system power supplies, there are a number of inexpensive, high quality, three-terminal voltage regulators available to use in designing the power supply. It is usually better to buy an "off the shelf" supply if possible, however.

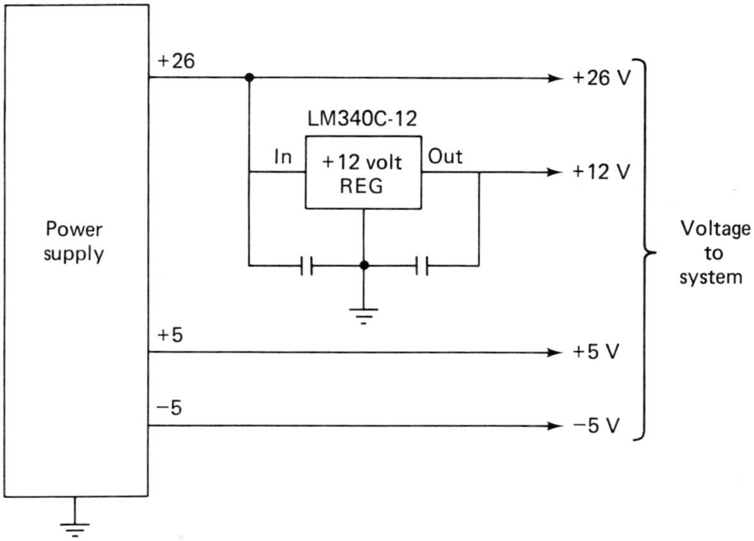

Figure 8-2 Block diagram showing how the power supplies are generated for the system.

8-4 Keyboard Input and Output Device

For the keyboard circuit we will use the hardware that was presented in Chapter 4. The circuit is shown in Figure 8-3. Note that 24 keys are required. The calculation is:

16 Data Keys } (To accommodate numbers 0–F_{16})

1 Enter Key
1 Clear Entry Key
1 Address Set Key
1 Clear RAM Key
1 Start Program Key
1 Verify Key
1 Copy Key
1 Reset Key

} Function Keys

Total keys = 24

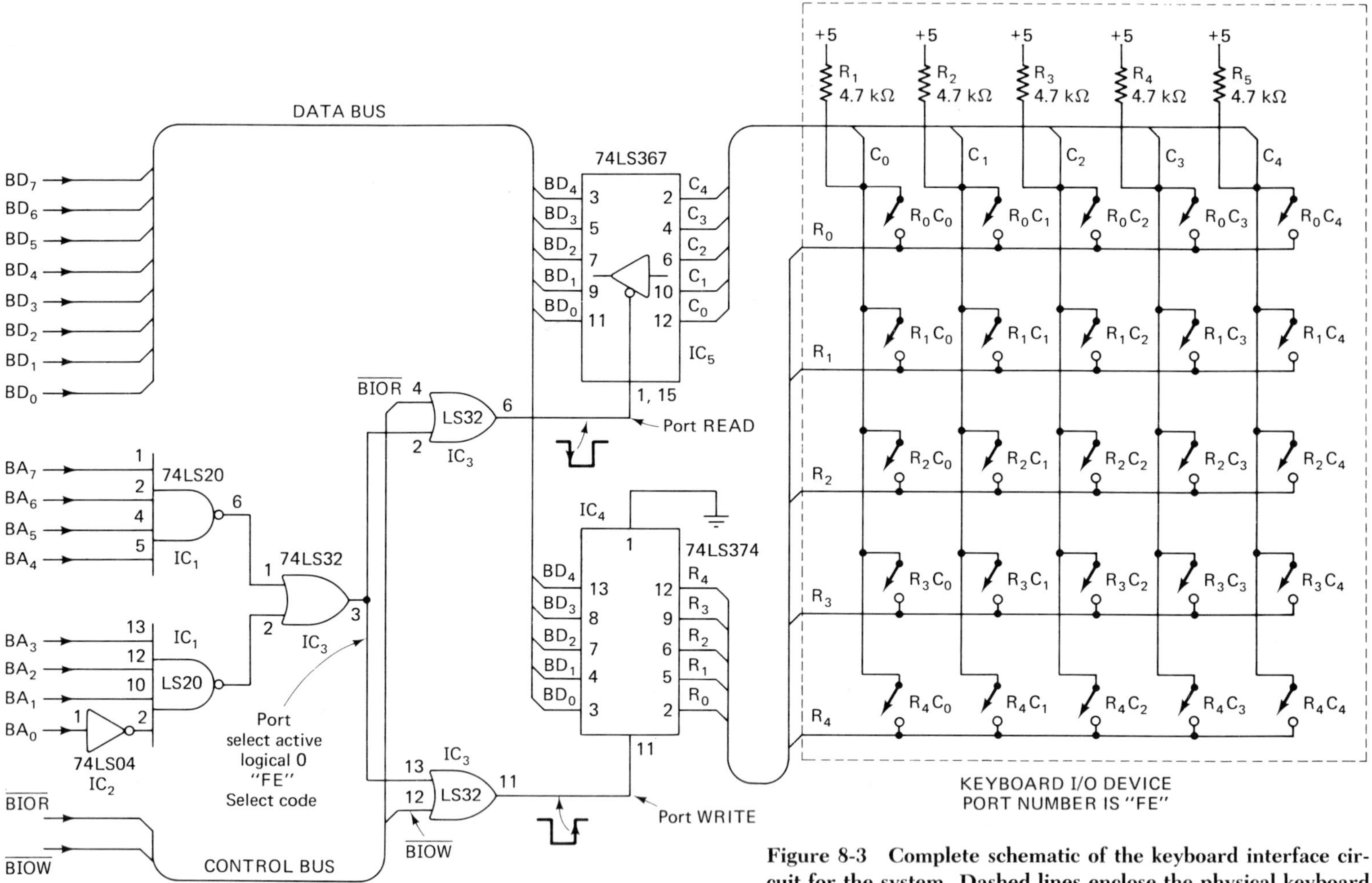

Figure 8-3 Complete schematic of the keyboard interface circuit for the system. Dashed lines enclose the physical keyboard switches.

The Reset System key is not part of the keyboard matrix. The reset function is asynchronous and is realized by a switch not contained in the keyboard matrix. The exact switch type and location in the system is shown later in this chapter when we examine all of the system hardware.

8-5 Display Hardware

The display will be the same system display that we discussed in Chapter 4. A schematic diagram of this circuit is shown in Figure 8-4.

8-6 System Read-Only Memory

The system ROM can be realized by using the 2708 EPROM. Two 2708s are used to realize all system commands; however, the system is designed to accept four 2708 EPROMs to accommodate future expansion. The memory map for the system ROM is:

Address Space		
0000–03FF	ROM 0	These two ROMs contain the software.
0400–07FF	ROM 1	
0800–0BFF	ROM 2	These ROMs are not used; they are intended for system expansion
0C00–0FFF	ROM 3	

8-7 System Random Access Memory

Data storage for programming the 2708 is provided by 1K (1024 bytes) of RAM. This system requires additional space in RAM for use with the microprocessor for the "stack" and temporary storage of data. The RAM used in this sytem consists of four 2114 1K static devices. Two of the 2114 units comprise a 1K × 8 RAM. The memory map for the complete system RAM is:

Address Space	
1000–13FF	System RAM for use with the microprocessor
1400–17FF	Storage RAM for the 2708 program data
1800–1BFF	Not used, left for future expansion.

We notice in both the ROM and RAM that additional space is designed into the system at the beginning. This preplanning feature makes it easier to add memory for future applications that may require it. Note here, too, that the memory map shown for the system ROM and RAM is used only for the 8080, 8085, and Z80 microprocessors. The 6800 device requires a new memory map due to the way it handles the reset function. Realization of this system, using a 6800 device, is discussed later.

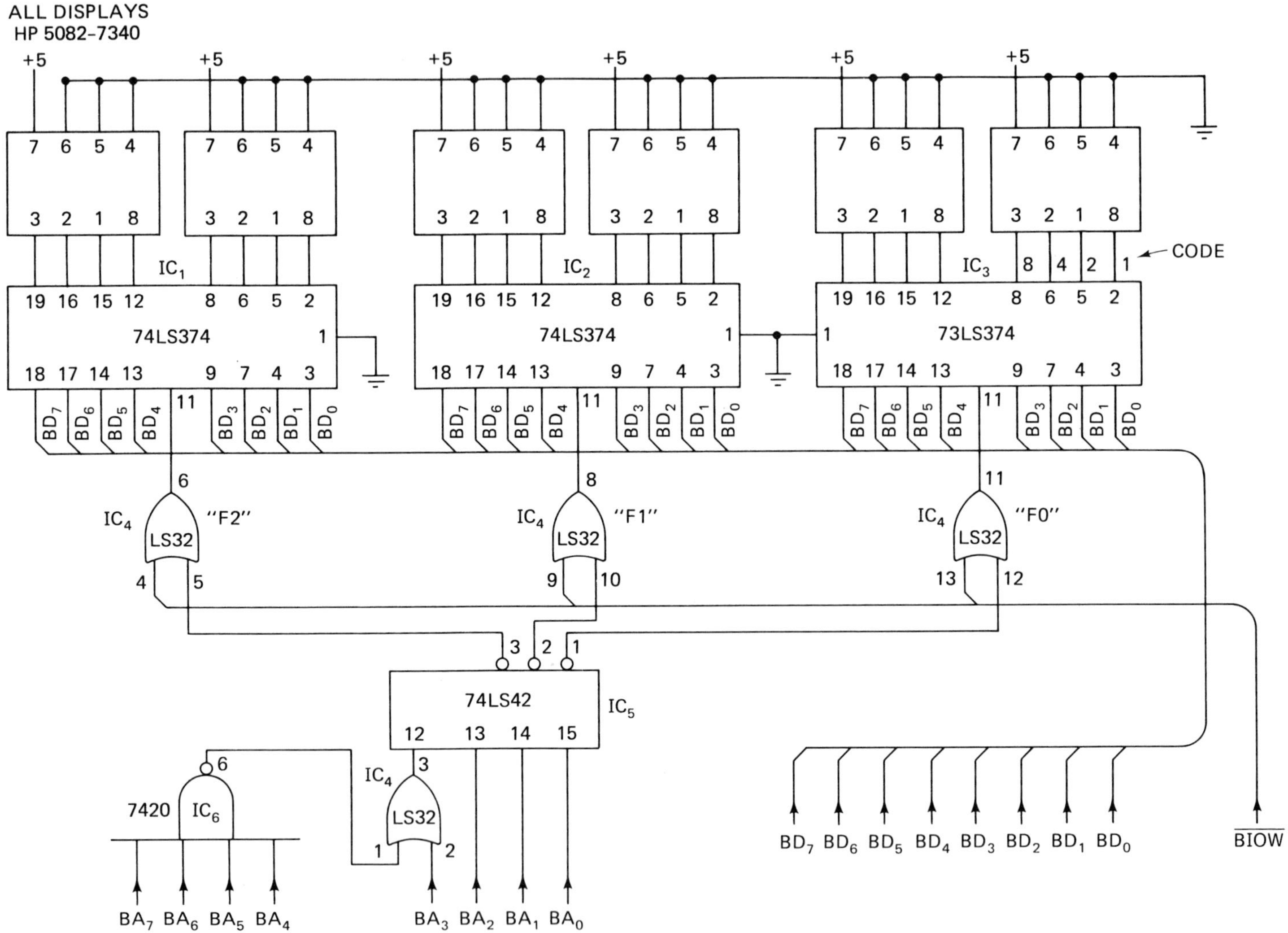

Figure 8-4 Complete schematic of the general display circuit for the system.

8-8 Interface to Programming 2708

We shall now discuss the hardware required to provide the 2708 to be programmed with the correct inputs. The first topic will be the address lines. The 2708 has 10 address lines. We shall treat the address input to the 2708 as two separate output ports. One output port will be for address inputs A_0–A_7. The other output port will be for address inputs A_8 and A_9. Further, we shall use an 8-bit latch 74LS374 and a 4-bit latch 74LS175 to realize these output ports. The output addresses of these devices will be 00_{16} and 01_{16}, in which output 00_{16} will constitute the 2708 device address lines A_0–A_7, and 01_{16} will be for the 2708 device address lines A_8–A_9.

The hardware required for this addressing function is shown in Figure 8-5.

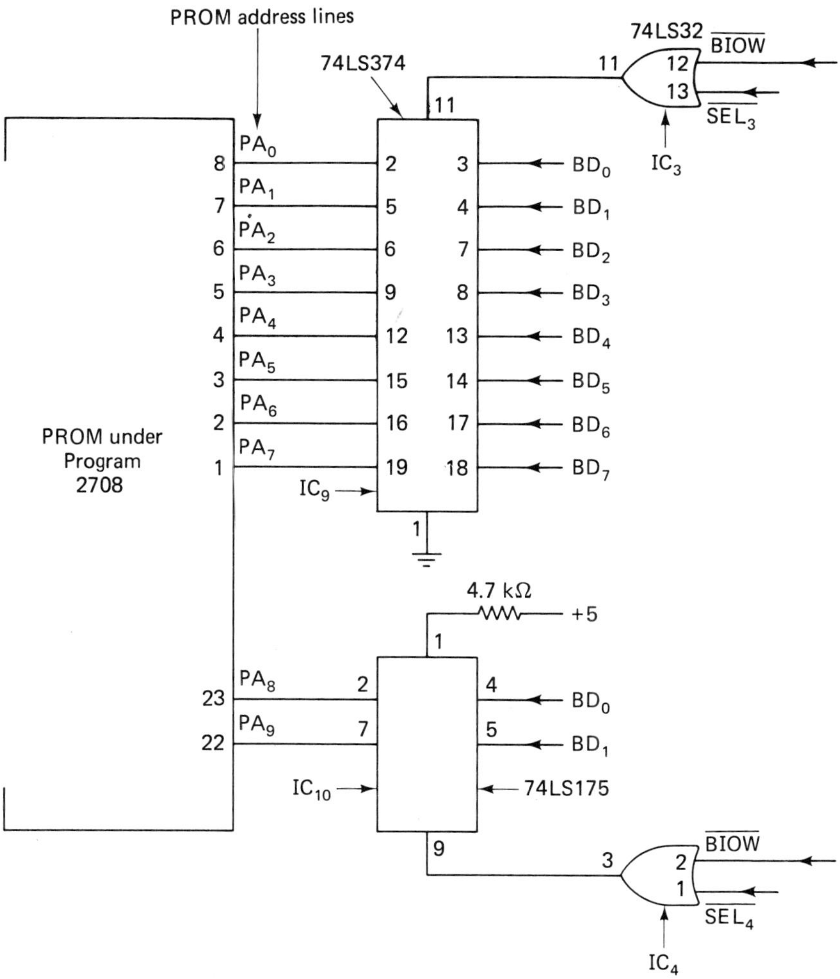

Figure 8-5 Schematic of the hardware required to input the address to the PROM under program.

8-9 Data Input and Output Hardware

To program the 2708 EPROM we must apply data to the data output pins. When checking to insure that the 2708 device has been programmed correctly, we must read the data out of the EPROM. Sometimes we are inputting data to the 2708 EPROM and sometimes we are outputting data from it. To input data to the 2708 device we use system output address 02_{16}. When reading data from this EPROM we use system input address 02_{16}.

When we apply data to the EPROM we must leave the other data that has been applied to the device outputs. However, when we read data, we do not want the system to interfere with the output data of the 2708. This is shown in block diagram form in Figure 8-6(a) and (b).

In order to insure that hardware blocks A and B in Figures 8-6(a) and (b) do not interfere with one another, we need a control line that can determine whether data is traveling into or out of the 2708. This control line will be an output device to the microprocessor system. The output select code for this control device is 03_{16}. Hardware realization for this control function is shown in Figure 8-7.

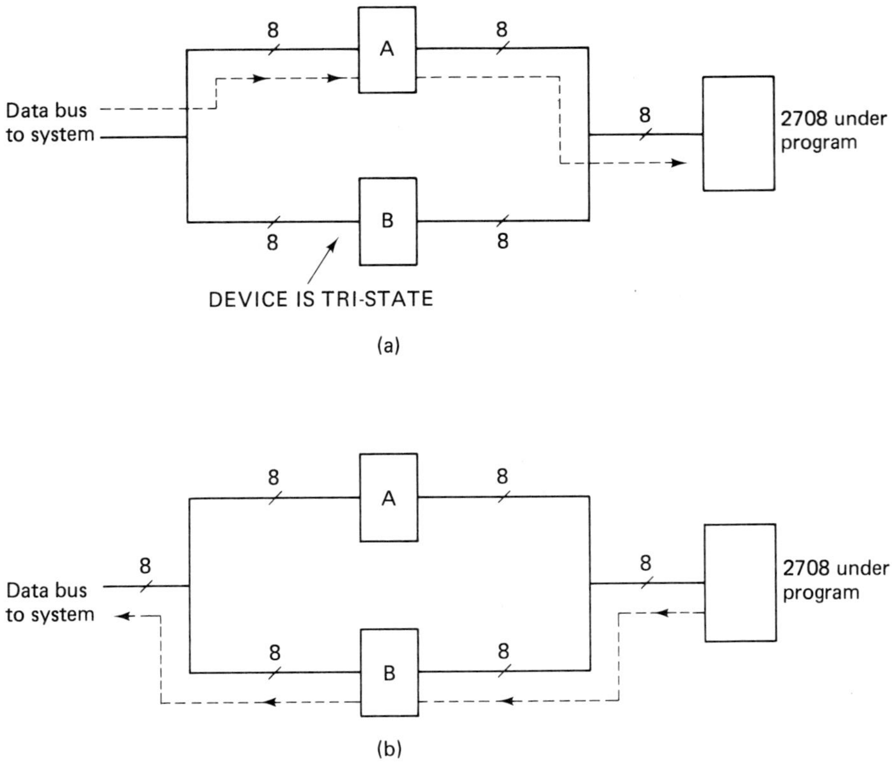

Figure 8-6 (a) Block diagram showing the data flow from the system to the PROM under program. (b) Block diagram showing the data flow from the PROM under program to the system.

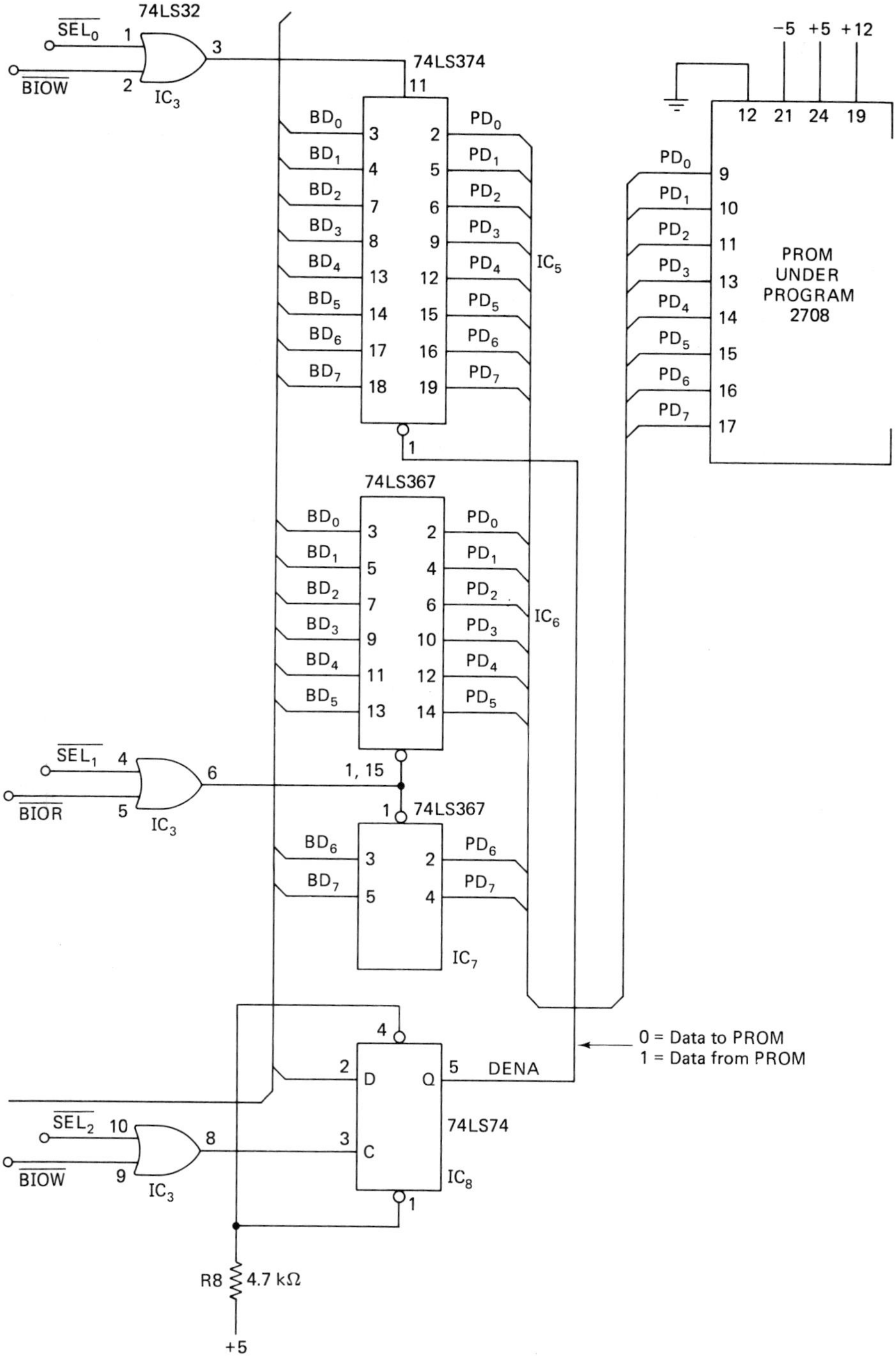

Figure 8-7 Complete schematic of the hardware required to realize bi-directional data flow to and from the PROM under program. This concept was shown in block diagram form in Figure 8-6.

8-10 Program Pulse Hardware

The program pulse pin 18 of the 2708 EPROM must be pulsed between +26 volts and 0 V. The pulse width is approximately 0.5 millisecond. The control signal for the pulse high level (+26 V) and pulse low level (0.0 V) must be a TTL level. These facts about the programming pulse are shown in Figure 8-8(a) and (b).

In Figure 8-8(b) we see that we must design a voltage level shifter from TTL to +26 V. The microprocessor will provide a correctly timed TTL pulse to control the programming pulse. The schematic for generating the high-level pulse is shown in Figure 8-9 where the enable signal is the TTL control signal. The $\overline{\text{ENABLE}}$ signal is the complement of the TTL enable signal. Later in the chapter we shall discuss how the enable and $\overline{\text{ENABLE}}$ signals are generated. When the enable signal of Figure 8-9 is logical 1, the 7406 open collector inverter

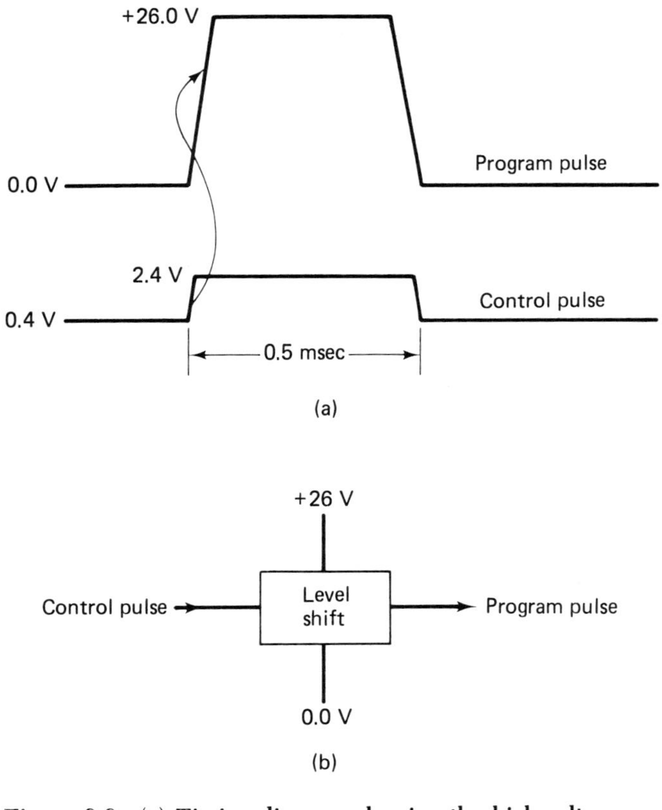

Figure 8-8 (a) Timing diagram showing the high-voltage programming pulse in relation to the TTL control pulse. (b) Block diagram of the level-shift circuit that will convert the TTL control pulse into the high-level programming pulse needed for the PROM under program.

output pin 2 is logical 0. This logical 0 provides a current path from the +26 V through resistors $R_1$and R_2 to ground. Under these conditions the transistor T_1 turns on. When T_1 turns on, the collector voltage is pulled toward +26 V. The $\overline{\text{ENABLE}}$ signal is a logical 0. Pin 4 of the 7406 is open collector. This allows the voltage at the point A to rise toward +26 V. Resistor R_3 and capacitor C_1 control the rise time of the wave form.

Let us assume that the enable signal of Figure 8-9 is logical 0. This would mean that the $\overline{\text{ENABLE}}$ signal is logical 1. The 7406 collector inverter output pin 2 would be open due to the logical 0 input from the enable line. Therefore, transistor T_1 turns off. The 7406 inverter output pin 4 is logical 0 due to the $\overline{\text{ENABLE}}$ input being logical 1. This tends to pull the voltage at output A toward 0.0 V. Now resistor R_4 and capacitor C_1 control the fall time of the output voltage.

This is how the program pulse input voltage controlled by a TTL logic level generates a +26 V programming pulse.

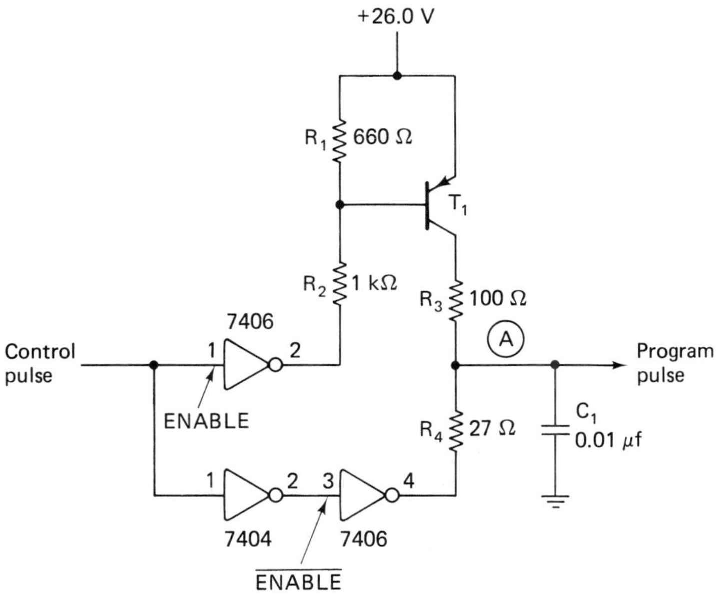

Figure 8-9 Complete schematic for the level shift circuit shown in the block diagram of Figure 8-8(b).

8-11 $\overline{CS}$/WE Voltage Control Hardware

During programming of the 2708 EPROM the $\overline{CS}$/WE pin 20 must be connected to +12 V. Here, again, the voltage must be controlled by a TTL input. We shall use the same technique that was shown for generating the program pulse. The schematic for the signal is shown in Figure 8-10. Note here that the

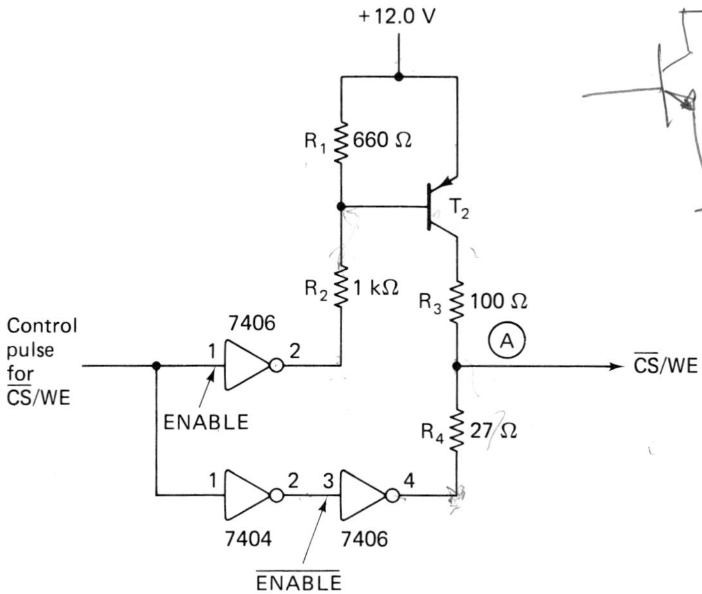

Figure 8-10 Complete schematic showing the circuit for generating the +12-volt $\overline{CS}$/WE signal for the PROM under program.

voltage of the emitter of transistor T_2 is +12 V. There is no capacitor to control the rise and fall time of this signal.

We have shown how the $\overline{CS}$/WE signals are generated and how the program pulse is generated. Next we shall discuss how the microprocessor system controls the enable signals to these circuits. To do this, these circuits are treated like an output device. The address of the output device is $04_{(16)}$. Data bit D_0 controls the program pulse. Data bit D_1 controls the $\overline{CS}$/WE pulse. The schematic for this output device is shown in Figure 8-11.

8-12 Power Supply for the 2708 EPROM

The 2708 EPROM to be programmed will require DC power supplied as follows: +12 V to pin 19, +5 V to pin 24, −5 V to pin 21, and 0.0 V, or ground, connected to pin 12. These supplies will always be connected to the programming socket. Each supply pin will have a 0.1 μF bypass capacitor connected between the supply pin and the system ground.

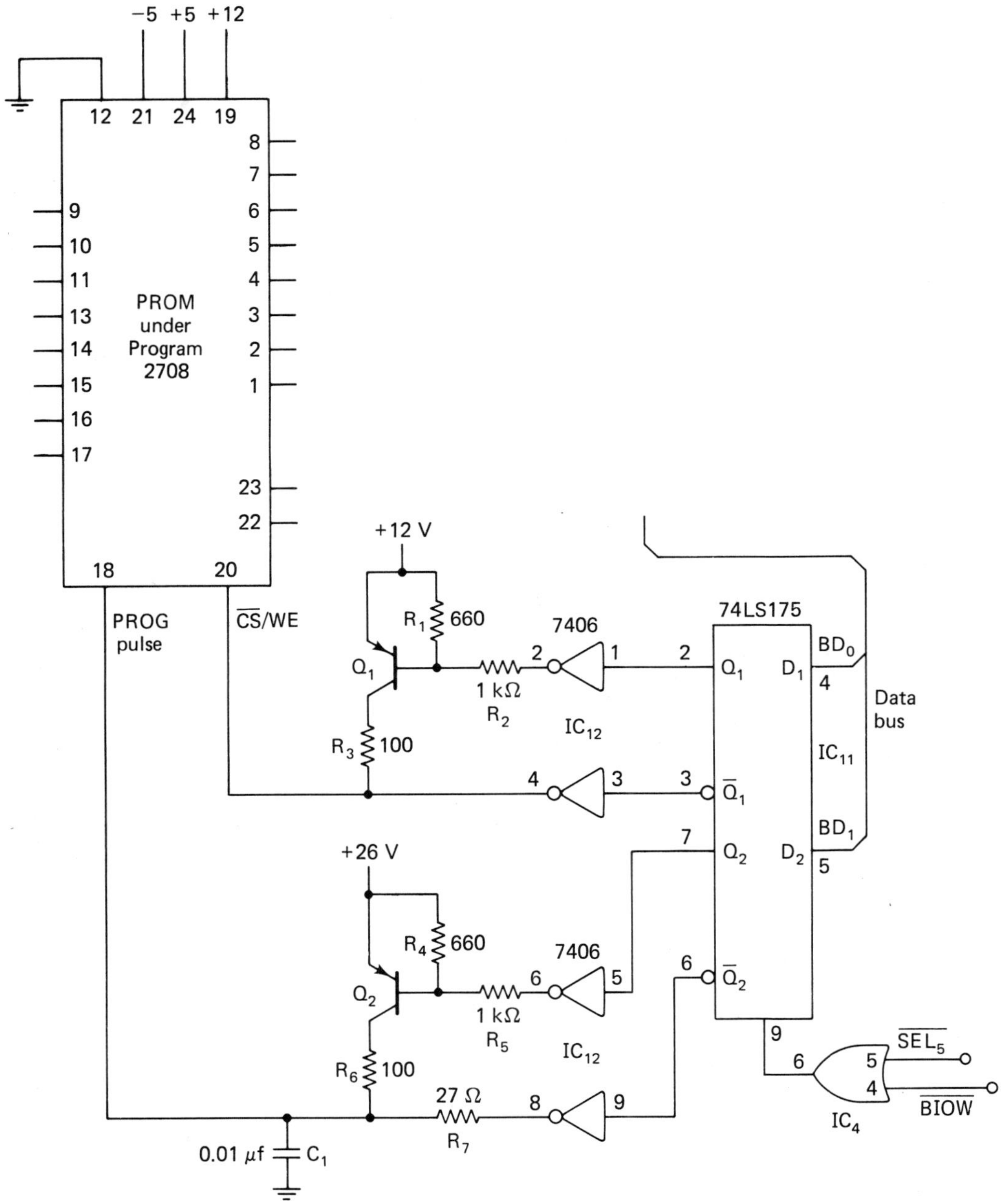

Figure 8-11 Complete schematic showing interface to the system for the programming pulse and the $\overline{CS}$/WE pulse for the PROM under program.

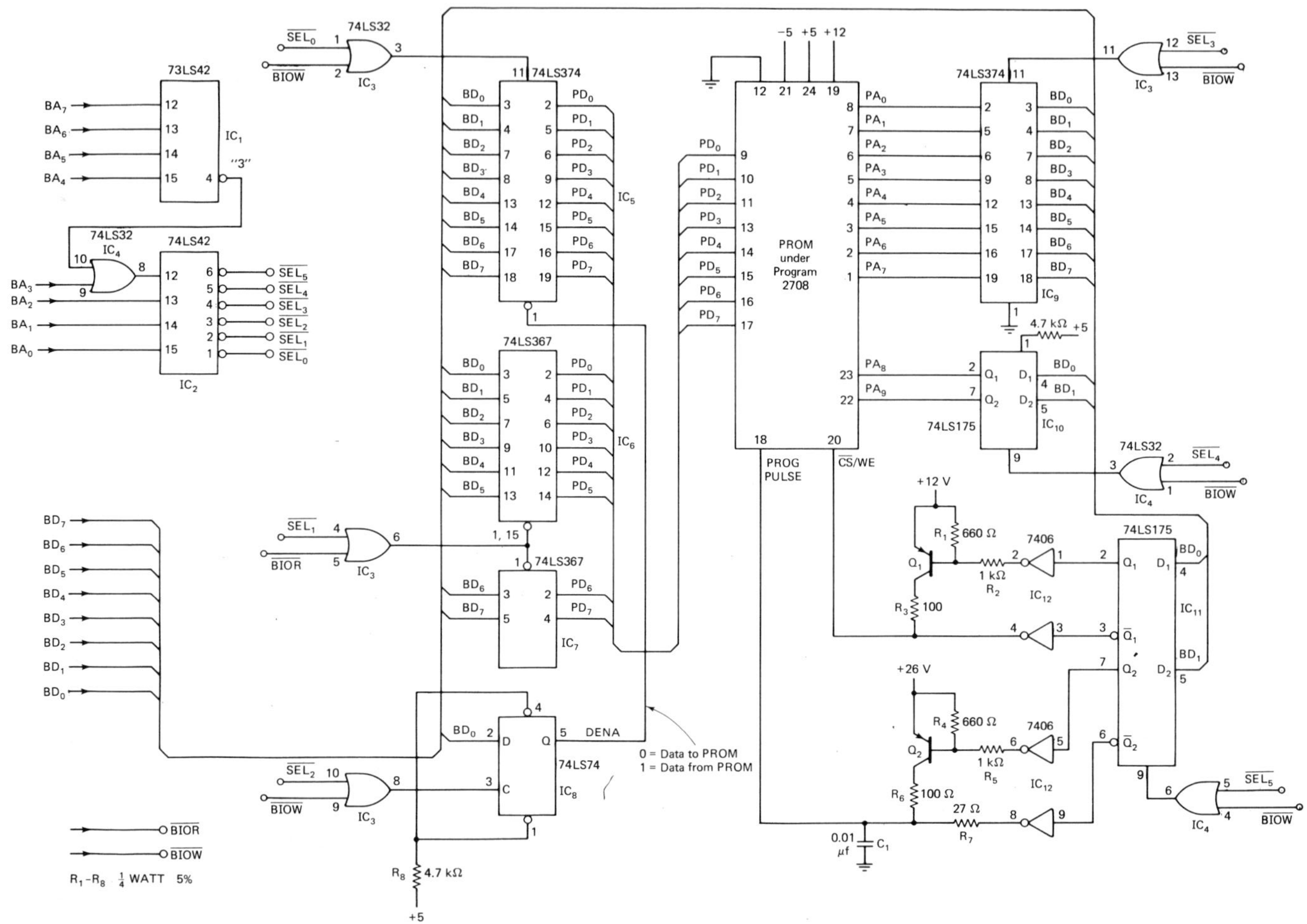

Figure 8-12 Complete schematic for interfacing the PROM under program to the system address, data, and control busses.

8-13 Connecting the Programming Socket to the System

Figure 8-12 shows the entire hardware schematic for interfacing the Programmable Read Only Memory to an 8080, 8085, or Z80 microprocessor. This schematic does not show the microprocessor keyboard or display circuits.

8-14 The 6800 as the Control Microprocessor

When using the 6800 system we must map our memories differently than for the 8080, 8085, or Z80 microprocessors. The memory map for a system using the 6800 microprocessor is shown in Figure 8-13. The memory map here is such that when the system is reset it uses data at memory addresses FFFE and FFFF. Therefore, we must have a ROM in the uppermost address space.

The I/O itself is memory mapped. When the address is between E000 and E3FF the 6800 system is performing an I/O operation. Further, we can keep all input-output select codes the same as we had assigned in the 8085 system. Instead of the display being at F0, F1, F2 as they are in the 8080 system, the display is now at E0F0, E0F1, E0F2 for the 6800 system.

FC00 – FFFF	ROM_1	SYSTEM PROGRAM
F800 – FBFF	ROM_0	
F400 – F7FF	ROM_2	NOT USED
F000 – F3FF	ROM_3	NOT USED
EC00 – EFFF	RAM_1	SYSTEM RAM
E800 – EBFF	RAM_2	PROGRAMMING RAM
E400 – E7FF	RAM_3	NOT USED
E000 – E3FF	SYSTEM	I/O

Figure 8-13 Memory map of the system for using a 6800 microprocessor as the system controller.

Figure 8-14 shows how the memory select lines are generated. Also shown in Figure 8-14 is the $\overline{IO}/M$ signal that is used to help form the control bus.

Figure 8-15 shows the control bus schematic. Notice that the $\overline{IO}/M$ signal used is the signal generated in Figure 8-14. Also note that some control bus signals are "qualified" by the Phase 2 clock.

The complete schematic for the 6800 system is shown in Figures 8-16, 8-17, and 8-18.

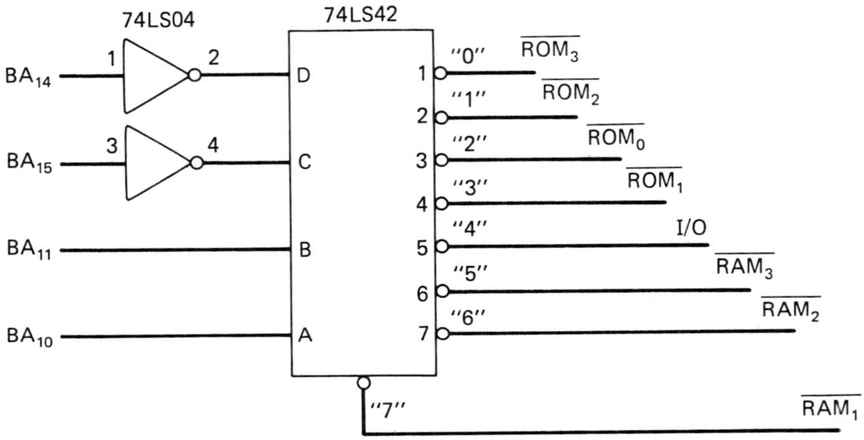

(a)

A_{15}	A_{14}	A_{11}	A_{10}	FUNCTION	74LS42 STATE
1	1	0	0	$\overline{ROM_3}$	0
1	1	0	1	$\overline{ROM_2}$	1
1	1	1	0	$\overline{ROM_0}$	2
1	1	1	1	$\overline{ROM_1}$	3
0	1	0	0	I/O	4
0	1	0	1	$\overline{RAM_3}$	5
0	1	1	0	$\overline{RAM_2}$	6
0	1	1	1	$\overline{RAM_1}$	7

(b)

Figure 8-14 Schematic showing how select codes are generated for the 6800 system. Note the generation of the I/O enable signal.

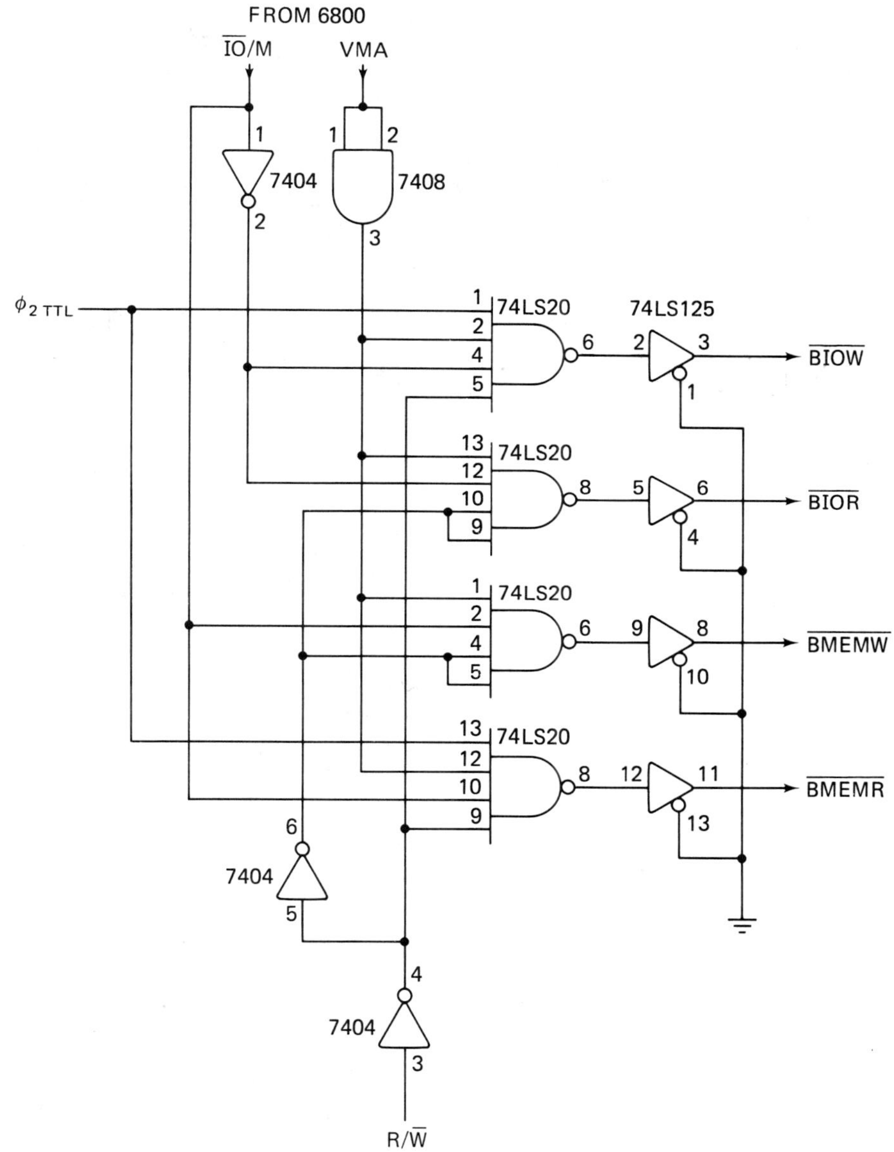

Figure 8-15 Complete schematic for realizing the 6800 system control bus signals.

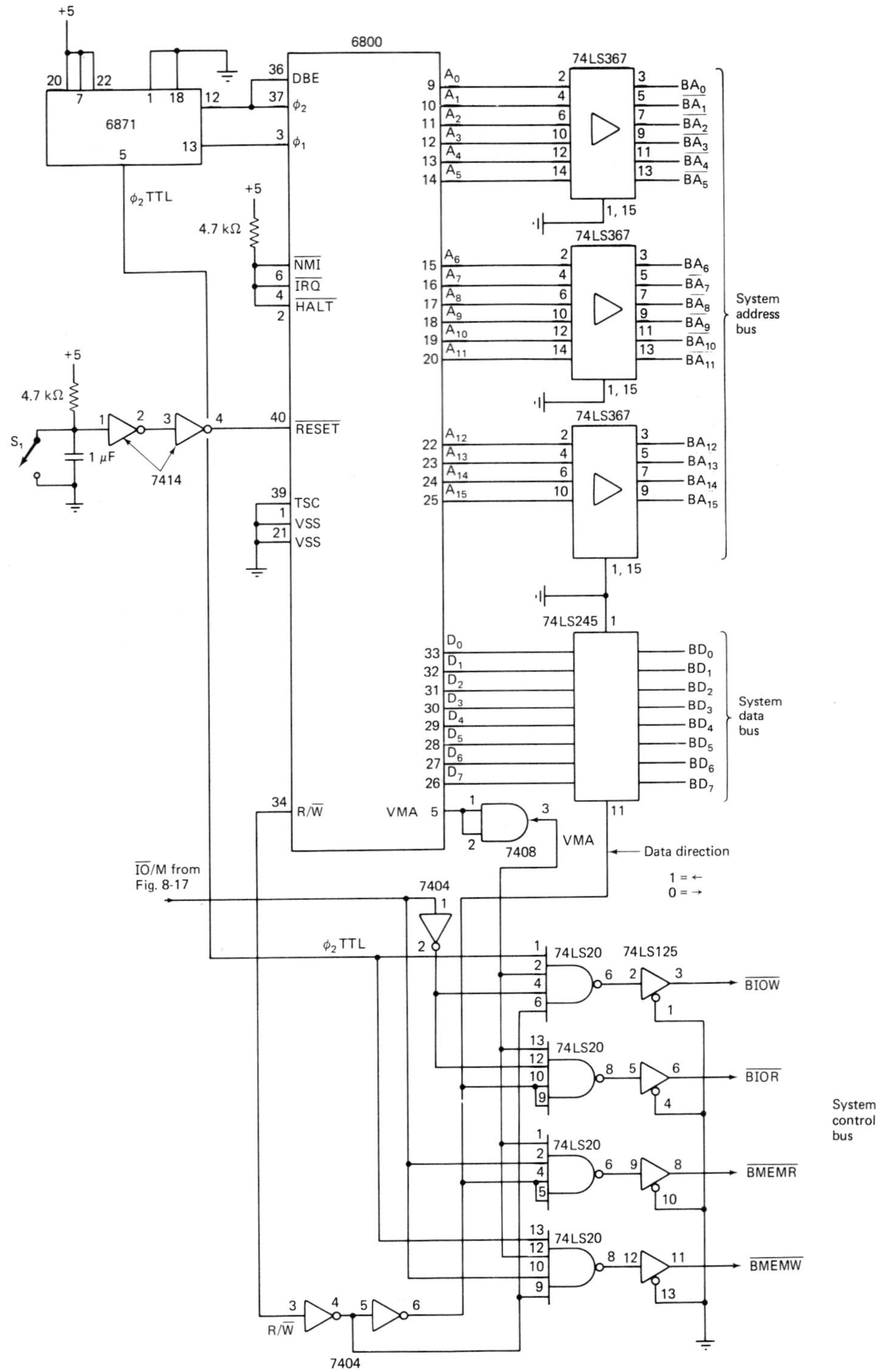

Figure 8-16 Complete schematic for using the 6800 microprocessor as a system controller for the automatic PROM programmer.

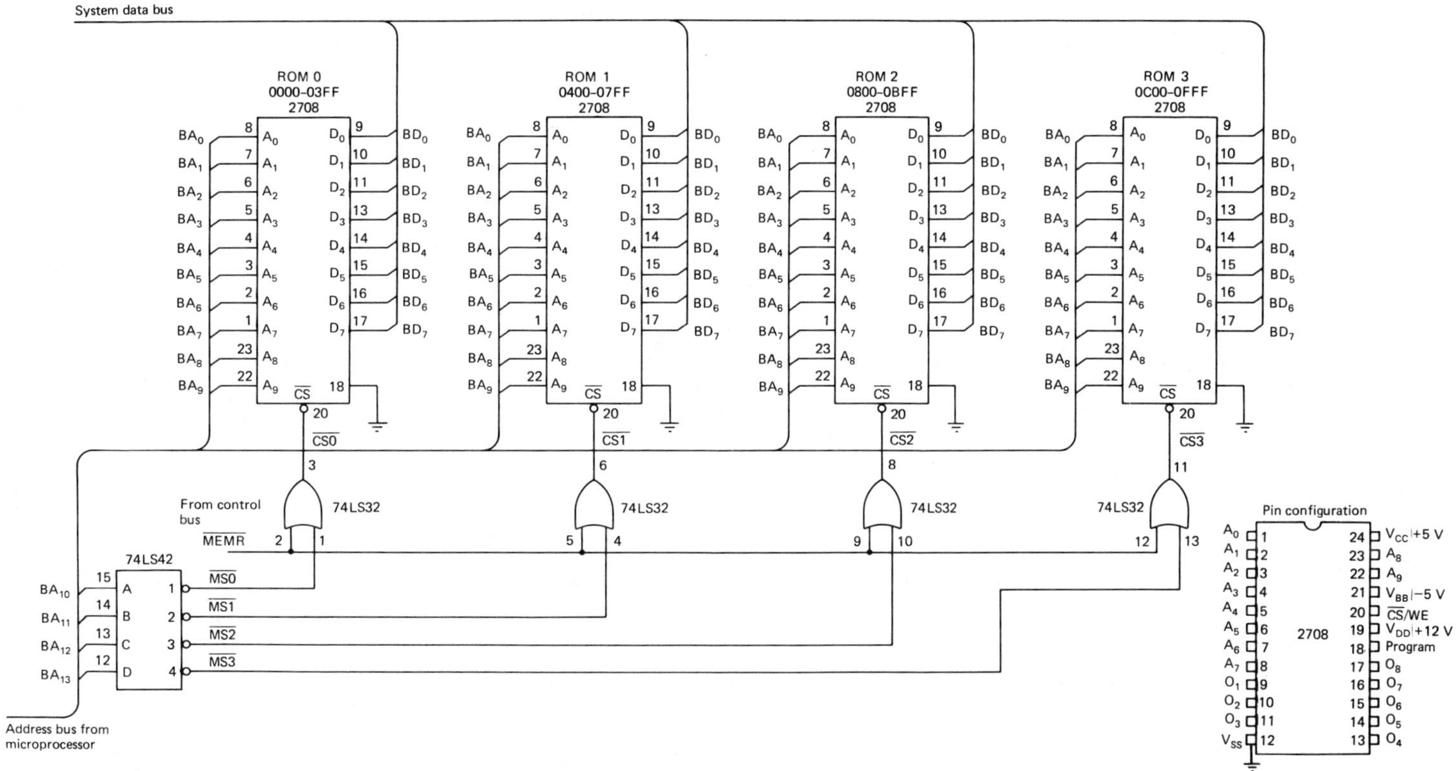

Figure 8-17 Complete schematic for the system ROM interface when using a 6800 microprocessor as the system controller.

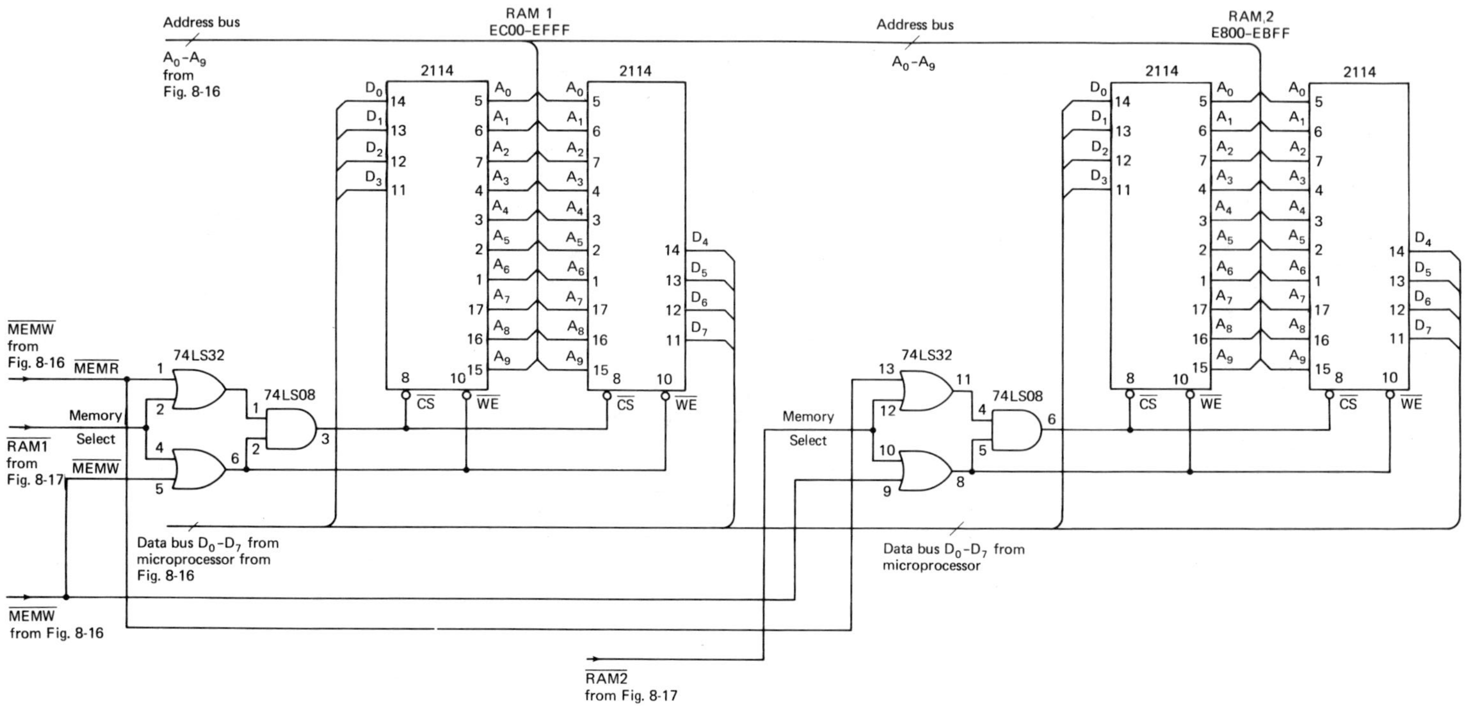

Figure 8-18 Complete schematic for the system RAM interface when using a 6800 as the system controller.

8-15 Summary of the Hardware

In this chapter we have shown the hardware necessary to construct a microprocessor controlled system. We chose the function of the system to be a PROM programmer. However, in the discussion of the design of this system we have introduced many standard interfacing techniques that are applicable to general microprocessor-controlled systems.

The complete hardware schematics have been shown and discussed to realize the PROM programmer for using four different microprocessors. If we can understand the details of how these hardware systems interact with the microprocessor, then the design of another system for some other purpose will be just a different application of these details.

In Chapter 9 we shall discuss the software to control the hardware that we developed in this chapter. Finally, in Chapter 10 we shall present a discussion of debugging this system if it fails to operate correctly.

9

DESIGNING SOFTWARE TO CONTROL A MICROPROCESSOR SYSTEM

In this chapter we shall present the software required to control the system hardware described in Chapter 8. Each separate function of the software will be shown by a flowchart. We shall realize the flowchart with actual object (binary) code for the 6800 and the 8085 microprocessors. Finally, an entire program listing will be given for each microprocessor.

After understanding the various discussions presented in this chapter, we will have a good idea of where to start when writing software to control the microprocessor hardware for these devices. These discussions are designed to allow us to see exactly why the program is written the way it is, by showing the relationship between the final objective and the detailed machine functions that are available to accomplish it.

9-1 Getting Started

Before we can write *any* software a few preliminary details need to be discussed. One of these is a software layout of the system; another is what hardware must be initialized, or set to a particular starting point, when the system is first powered up. Let us discuss each of the two points in detail.

The software layout is a mapping of all of the address space and of the corresponding function of each block of address space in the system. This is the first level of a software layout. The mapping for the system presented in Chapter 8 is shown in Figure 9-1. We see in Figure 9-1 that we have a very precise guide as to exactly where and what address in memory and I/O the microprocessor must use to communicate electrically with all system hardware. In writing the controlling software we assume that the hardware will work properly, that a failure to execute a program properly will be due to an error in the program as written and not due to a hardware fault.

In effect, when we are writing the software we do not even have to know what the hardware physically looks like. We are given a specification for how the hardware operates, based on system addresses and data bits. From this information *we can accurately write* the software that will control the hardware without reference to hardware details at all.

The opposite is also true. When we are designing the hardware it is not necessary to know the specific details of the software. *We can design the hardware such that the microprocessor can communicate reliably with all hardware elements in the system without reference to software (program) details at all*. The fact is, when these communication paths are properly established in hardware, the software makes use of the communication paths needed to achieve the overall programming objectives.

If we are knowledgeable in both software and hardware, many times system designs (hardware and software) become simpler and more elegant as a result.

Address Space	Function	
0000 – 03FF	ROM_0	All control software
0400 – 07FF	ROM_1	in these two ROMS
0800 – 0BFF	ROM_2	Not used now,
0C00 – 0FFF	ROM_3	for expansion
1000 – 13FF	RAM_1	– System RAM
1400 – 17FF	RAM_2	– Storage RAM for 2708
1800 – 1BFF	RAM_3	– Not used

I/O

F_0, F_1, F_2	Display
FE	Keyboard
30,31,32,33,34,35	Program Board

Figure 9-1 System address mapping space for the hardware system of Chapter 8.

The hardware engineer, for example, can design the system around special software features of a certain microprocessor. The hardware can also be designed so that specific details of a certain microprocessor's software do not create a system problem. On the other hand, the software writer who knows hardware can modify a software task to take advantage of the hardware capabilities. When two specialists are involved, the best results are obtained when the person writing the software and the person designing the hardware communicate well and closely with each other. In this way each will have a good feel for where the other is heading. Often much design effort on the part of either the hardware or software engineer can be minimized, or even eliminated, by performing a certain function in either hardware or software a particular way, a way that might not have emerged without this collaboration.

Ideally, the person working in microprocessor systems hardware or software should have an understanding of both areas. This understanding does not have to be extreme, but just enough to appreciate the problems of both areas and enable effective communication between the two disciplines.

In industry there seems to be a very definite split in hardware and software. The split is necessary in some instances in order to get the job done. But for the person designing microprocessor-controlled systems today, at the engineering level or the technician level, an understanding of both hardware and software is extremely valuable.

Returning to the memory map of our system shown in Figure 9-1, we see that some details are not shown. These details correspond to the data bits D0-D7 that provide the exact control over the hardware. For the system RAM and ROM this is a very straightforward question to answer. The 2708 ROM has output 0_1 connected to D0 and this is consistent through output 0_8 which is connected to D_7.

The same question relating to system RAM is also very easy to answer. The answer is, it really does not matter which data bits on the RAM are connected to which data bits of the system data bus. This is because the microprocessor will write the data into the RAM, and as long as the microprocessor provides the input data, the data returned from the RAM will be in the correct position on the data bus. What all of this really means is that we do not need to concern ourselves with the data bits for either the system ROM or RAM. The data bits do become important when we are communicating with the I/O devices, however.

For example, consider the case when the microprocessor is electrically communicating with the output display. Here, the software person needs to know exactly which data bits are connected to which inputs to activate a particular display digit. This type of information is provided by the system hardware. Figure 9-2 removes the uncertainties noted in the preceding paragraph by showing the details of the data bits for each input and output device in the system.

ADDRESS Space	Data Bits	Function	
ADDRESS Space	Data Bits	Function	
ADDRESS Space	Data Bits	Function	
FE (OUTPUT)	D_0	R_0	Keyboard
	D_1	R_1	
	D_2	R_2	
	D_3	R_3	
	D_4	R_4	
	D_5, D_6, D_7	Not used	
FE (INPUT)	D_0	C_0	
	D_1	C_1	
	D_2	C_2	
	D_3	C_3	
	D_4	C_4	
	D_5, D_6, D_7	Not used	
F_2 (OUTPUT)	D_7	MSD (8 bit)	Output Display
	D_6	MSD (4 bit)	
	D_5	MSD (2 bit)	
	D_4	MSD (1 bit)	
	D_3	(MSD − 1) 8 bit	
	D_2	(MSD − 1) 4 bit	
	D_1	(MSD − 1) 2 bit	
	D_0	(MSD − 1) 1 bit	

Figure 9-2 Detailed data bit usage chart for all system input and output ports. Note that all data bits are not used for each input and output port.

F_1 Output	D_7	MSD − 2 (8 bit)	OUTPUT DISPLAY
	D_6	MSD − 2 (4 bit)	
	D_5	MSD − 2 (2 bit)	
	D_4	MSD − 2 (1 bit)	
	D_3	LSD + 2 (8 bit)	
	D_2	LSD + 2 (4 bit)	
	D_1	LSD + 2 (2 bit)	
	D_0	LSD + 2 (1 bit)	
F_0 Output	D_7	LSD + 1 (8 bit)	
	D_6	LSD + 1 (4 bit)	
	D_5	LSD + 1 (2 bit)	
	D_4	LSD + 1 (1 bit)	
	D_3	LSD (8 bit)	
	D_2	LSD (4 bit)	
	D_1	LSD (2 bit)	
	D_0	LSD (1 bit)	
30 OUTPUT	$D_0 - D_7$	Data to program EPROM	
31 INPUT	$D_0 - D_7$	Data from EPROM outputs	
32 OUTPUT	$D_0 = 1$	Read data from EPROM	
	$D_0 = 0$	WRITE data to EPROM	
	$D_1 - D_7$	Not used	
33 Output	D_0–D_7	PA_0–PA_7 Address to EPROM	
34 Output	D_0, D_1	PA_8–PA_9 Address to EPROM	
	$D_2 - D_7$	Not used	
35 Output	$D_0 = 1$	$\overline{\text{CS/WE}}$ = +12 V	
	$D_0 = 0$	CS/WE = 0.0 V	
	$D_1 = 1$	Program pulse = +26 V	
	$D_1 = 0$	Program pulse = 0.0 V	
	$D_2 - D_7$	Not used	

From Figure 9-2 we see that the exact function of each data bit for each input and output port is defined. The data bits not listed for a particular input or output device are either not used or "don't care." The information shown in Figure 9-2 may appear in system documentation in many different forms. Regardless of the form, *this is* the specific information we need before attempting to write the software.

The additional information we need before writing the software is which input and output devices must be set up in a certain way, or initialized, when the power is first applied to the system. In general, we must always initialize the system stack pointer. Also, if a system uses interrupts, we must initialize interrupt masks, and enable or disable the interrupt function as required. After these general initializations are done we turn our attention to the specific information needed to initialize the rest of the hardware of a system.

For the system we are discussing, the following must be initialized.

1. Program pulse = 0.0V
2. $\overline{CS}$/WE voltage = 0.0V
3. Control port $32_{(16)}$This step sets up the data path from the EPROM to the system. D0 = 1. (From Figure 9-2)
4. The system display is set to F00000.
5. Interrupts are not used in our system.
6. Stack pointer = $03FF_{(16)}$. From memory map in Figure 9-1.

These are the major hardware initializations that are required for this system. There may be more software initialization needed, such as variables preset to certain values. These types of initializations will surface as we write the software for the system. We now have all of the information needed to start our software programming for this problem.

9-2 Overview of the Software

Before proceeding into the details of writing the software program, let us examine the overall structure of our software. Since the system is interactive with a keyboard, the system must wait for a particular key to be input before executing certain routines in the program. The main idea is this: The system inputs a key. Then, based on what the function of that particular key is, the system executes certain specified software. After execution of that software, the system pauses and waits for another key input.

To enable the user to enter the correct information, the system must prompt the user via the display. It is by intelligent use of the keyboard and display that we can realize the functions listed in Chapter 8 for this system.

A general flowchart of the software is shown in Figure 9-3 that displays the direction in which we are heading when writing the software.

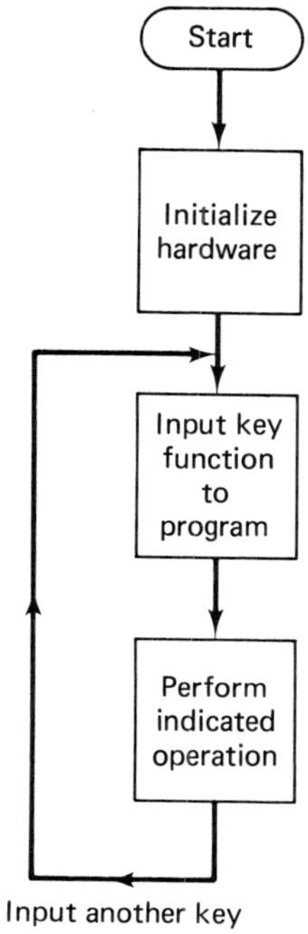

Figure 9-3 General flowchart of overall system operation. This is the basic operations chart showing what takes place within the system software. Details of each major block are presented in this chapter.

9-3 Keyboard Input Software

A major part of the system success lies in its ability to detect a unique key from among those that make up the keyboard I/O device. In Chapter 4, we discussed in detail how we can implement this function with software. Here we once again use the keyboard input routine shown in Chapter 4. This subroutine is repeated in Figure 9-4 for convenience. Notice that the variable returned or set by the routine in Figure 9-4 is the decimal value of the key weight in the keyboard matrix. This means we can show the function of the keyboard subroutine in the general flowchart of Figure 9-5.

Notice in Figure 9-5 that the keyboard routine does not return to the main program until a valid key is detected and the decimal weight of the key is set in a memory location KWGT. The decimal weight for each key in the keyboard matrix is shown in Figure 9-6 where we see that when the program returns from the keyboard input routine, the value of KWGT becomes an integer between 0-24 inclusive.

Recall that we have not yet assigned any function to the keys in the matrix. We now assign these functions as shown in Figure 9-7. Note that the KWGT

```
0000                ***************************************************************
0000                *
0000                *   8080 PROGRAM FOR INPUTTING A KEY AND WRITE TO DISPLAY
0000                *
0000                *******  PROGRAMMER: JIM COFFRON    8-28-79   ****************
0000                *
0000                *
0000                    ORG   00         SET STARTING ADDRESS IN MEM
0000                *
0000                *   WE FIRST MUST INITIALIZE ALL VARIABLES
0000                *
0000 31 FF 13           LXI   SP,13FFH   INITAILIZE STACK POINTER
0003 AF                 XRA   A          RESET FLAGS, ZERO ACC
0004 FB                 EI               ENABLE INTERRUPTS
0005 D3 F0              OUT   0F0H       ZERO OUT DISPLAY
0007 D3 F1              OUT   0F1H
0009 D3 F2              OUT   0F2H       SET DISPLAY=000000
000B 32 00 10           STA   KTIME      KTIME=0
000E 32 01 10           STA   CFLAG      CFLAG=0
0011 32 02 10           STA   KWGHT      KWGHT=0
0014 32 03 10           STA   KCOMP      KCOMP=0
0017 3C                 INR   A          ACC=1
0018 32 04 10           STA   KROW       KROW=00000001
001B                *
001B                *
001B                *   NOW TO SET MEMORY ADDRESS OF VARIABLES
001B                *
001B                KTIME EQU   1000H
001B                CFLAG EQU   KTIME+1
001B                KWGHT EQU   CFLAG+1
001B                KCOMP EQU   KWGHT+1
001B                KROW  EQU   KCOMP+1
001B                NROW  EQU   KROW+1
001B                *
001B                *
001B                ******  NOW TO START THE PROGRAM   *********
001B                *
001B                *   START OF FIGURE 4-20
001B                *
001B CD EB 00       SROW   CALL  OROW     OUTPUT THE ACTIVE ROW
001E CD DB 00              CALL  COLM     CALL COLUMN ROUTINE
0021 3A 01 10              LDA   CFLAG    NEED TO CHECK THE COLUMN FLAG
0024 FE 00                 CPI   00H      CHECK FOR ACTIVE COLUMN
0026 CA 1B 00              JZ    SROW     NO ACTIVE COLUMN LOOP AGAIN
0029 CD B1 00              CALL  KEYW     ACTIVE COLUMN, WHICH ONE???
002C                *
002C                *   END OF FIGURE 4-20
002C                *
002C                *   START OF FIGURE 4-21
002C                *
002C                ***** WE HAVE AN ACTIVE KEY *******
002C                *
002C                *****(STEP 1)
002C                *
002C 3A 00 10              LDA   KTIME    RECALL KTIME FROM MEM
002F                *
002F                *
002F                *****(STEP 2)
002F                *
002F FE 00                 CPI   00H      KTIME=0??
```

Figure 9-4 8080 program for inputting a key and write to display.

```
0031 CA 5B 00           JZ   KCLO1      YES THIS IS FIRST TIME
0034                *
0034                *** NOT THE FIRST TIME *****
0034                *
0034                *****(STEP 7)
0034                *
0034 3A 02 10           LDA  KWGHT      WHAT KEY VALUE WAS PUSHED???
0037 4F                 MOV  C,A        C REG = KWGHT
0038 3A 03 10           LDA  KCOMP      A REG = COMPARE VALUE
003B B9                 CMP  C          KCOMP=KWGHT?
003C CA 46 00           JZ   KCLO2      YES THEY DO!!!!!!
003F                *
003F                *****(STEP 8)
003F                *
003F AF                 XRA  A          THEY ARE NOT EQUAL
0040 32 00 10           STA  KTIME      RESET THE KTIME VARIABLE
0043 C3 66 00           JMP  KCLO3      GOTO RESET ACTIVE ROW
0046                *
0046                ****(STEP 9)
0046                *
0046 3A 00 10       KCLO2 LDA KTIME     RECALL KTIME FROM MEM
0049 3C                 INR  A          KTIME=KTIME+1
004A 32 00 10           STA  KTIME      KTIME=KTIME+1
004D                *
004D                *****(STEP 10)
004D                *
004D FE 32              CPI  50         KTIME=50??
004F C2 66 00           JNZ  KCLO3      NOT 50 YET
0052 CD 6E 00           CALL KOPN       CHECK FOR KEY OPEN
0055 CD A7 00           CALL KOUT       OUTPUT THE KEY
0058 C3 1B 00           JMP  SROW       BACK TO THE START
005B                *
005B                *****(STEP 3)
005B                *
005B 3A 02 10       KCLO1 LDA KWGHT
005E 32 03 10           STA  KCOMP      KCOMP=KWGHT
0061                *
0061                *****(STEP 4)
0061                *
0061 3E 01              MVI  A,01
0063 32 00 10           STA  KTIME      UP DATE KTIME=1
0066                *
0066                ****(STEP 5)
0066                *
0066 3E 01          KCLO3 MVI A,01
0068 32 04 10           STA  KROW       RESET ACTIVE ROW=00000001
006B                *
006B                *****(STEP 6)
006B                *
006B C3 1B 00           JMP  SROW       GOTO START OF PROGRAM
006E                *
006E                *
006E                ***************************************************************
006E                *
006E                ******   START OF SUBROUTINES    ************
006E                *
006E                ***************************************************************
006E                *
006E                *
006E                *  FIGURE 4-22
```

Figure 9-4 (Cont'd.)

```
006E                 *   KEY OPEN SUBROUTINE
006E                 *
006E                 ******************************************************************
006E                 *
006E                 ******(STEP 1)
006E                 *
006E 3E 01           KOPN   MVI   A,01
0070 32 04 10               STA   KROW       SET KROW=00000001
0073 3D                     DCR   A
0074 32 05 10               STA   NROW       SET NROW=00000000
0077                 *
0077                 *****(STEP 2)
0077                 *
0077 32 00 10               STA   KTIME      KTIME=0
007A                 *
007A                 *****(STEP 3)
007A                 *
007A CD EB 00        KOPN1  CALL  OROW       OUTPUT THE ROW
007D                 *
007D                 *****(STEP 4)
007D                 *
007D CD DB 00               CALL  COLM       INPUT THE COLUMN DATA
0080                 *
0080                 *****(STEP 5)
0080                 *
0080 3A 01 10               LDA   CFLAG      INPUT THE CFLAG DATA
0083 FE 00                  CPI   00         CFLAG=0??
0085 C2 6E 00               JNZ   KOPN       KEY NOT RELEASED YET
0088                 *
0088                 *****(STEP 9)
0088                 *
0088 3A 05 10               LDA   NROW       INPUT THE ACTIVE ROW
008B 3C                     INR   A
008C 32 05 10               STA   NROW       UPDATE THE ACTIVE ROW
008F                 *
008F                 *****(STEP 10)
008F                 *
008F FE 05                  CPI   05
0091 C2 7A 00               JNZ   KOPN1      NOT A COMPLETE SCAN
0094                 *
0094                 *****(STEP 6)
0094                 *
0094 3A 00 10               LDA   KTIME
0097 3C                     INR   A
0098 32 00 10               STA   KTIME
009B 47                     MOV   B,A        B REG=KTIME
009C                 *
009C                 ******(STEP 6A)
009C                 *
009C AF                     XRA   A
009D 32 05 10               STA   NROW       ROW VALUE =0
00A0                 *
00A0                 *****(STEP 7)
00A0                 *
00A0 3E 32                  MVI   A,50
00A2 B8                     CMP   B          KTIME=50???
00A3 C2 7A 00               JNZ   KOPN1      NO, TRY ANOTHER SCAN
00A6                 *
00A6                 ******(STEP 8)
00A6                 *
```

Figure 9-4 (Cont'd.)

```
00A6 C9                  RET            RETURN FROM THIS OPEN ROUTINE
00A7                 *
00A7                 *
00A7                 **************************************************************
00A7                 *
00A7                 *     SUBROUTINE KOUT
00A7                 *
00A7                 *   THIS SUBROUTINE WILL OUTPUT THE KEY TO THE DISPLAY
00A7                 *
00A7                 **************************************************************
00A7                 *
00A7 3A 02 10        KOUT   LDA   KWGHT     VALUE OF KEY IN ACC
00AA D3 F0                  OUT   0F0H
00AC D3 F1                  OUT 0F1H
00AE D3 F2                  OUT 0F2H
00B0 C9                     RET
00B1                 *
00B1                 **************************************************************
00B1                 *
00B1                 *   SUBROUTINE KEYW
00B1                 *
00B1                 *   THIS SUBROUTINE WILL COMPUTE THE VALUE OF THE KEY PUSHED
00B1                 *
00B1                 **************************************************************
00B1                 *
00B1                 ***** THIS ROUTINE IS FROM FIGURE 4-18
00B1                 *
00B1                 ******(STEP 1)
00B1                 *
00B1 AF              KEYW   XRA   A           ZERO FLAGS AND ACC
00B2 3A 01 10               LDA   CFLAG     GET COLUMN FLAG FROM MEM
00B5                 *
00B5                 *****(STEP 2)
00B5                 *
00B5 06 00                  MVI   B,00      ZERO THE COUNTER
00B7                 *
00B7                 ****(STEP 3)
00B7                 *
00B7 1F              KEYW1 RAR              SHIFT RIGHT 1 BIT,0 INTO D7
00B8 FE 00                  CPI   00
00BA                 *
00BA                 ****(STEP 4)
00BA                 *
00BA CA C1 00               JZ    KEYW2     BREG=0,1,2,3,4 (STEP 6)
00BD                 *
00BD                 *****(STEP 5)
00BD                 *
00BD 04                     INR   B
00BE C3 B7 00               JMP   KEYW1     INCREMENT COUNTER GO AGAIN
00C1                 *
00C1                 *****(STEP 7)
00C1                 *
00C1 AF              KEYW2 XRA    A         ZERO THE FLAGS
00C2 3A 04 10               LDA   KROW      RECALL ACTIVE ROW
00C5                 *
00C5                 *****(STEP 8)
00C5                 *
00C5 0E 00                  MVI   C,00      ZERO THE COUNTER T2
00C7                 *
00C7                 ******(STEP 9)
```

Figure 9-4 (Cont'd.)

```
00C7           *
00C7 1F        KEYW3 RAR             SHIFT RIGHT 1 BIT,0 INTO D7
00C8 FE 00           CPI   00
00CA           *
00CA           *******(STEP 10)
00CA           *
00CA CA D1 00        JZ   KEYW4      IF ZERO THEN DONE
00CD           *
00CD           *****(STEP 14)
00CD           *
00CD 0C              INR  C          INCREMENT THE COUNTER
00CE C3 C7 00        JMP  KEYW3      GO AGAIN
00D1           *
00D1           *****(STEP 11)
00D1           *
00D1 AF        KEYW4 XRA  A          ZERO THE FLAGS
00D2 78              MOV  A,B        ACC=COLUMN COUNT(T1)
00D3 17              RAL             B*2
00D4 17              RAL             B*4
00D5 80              ADD B           B*5
00D6 81              ADD C           (B*5)+C=0 - 24
00D7           *
00D7           *******(STEP 12)
00D7           *
00D7 32 02 10        STA  KWGHT
00DA           *
00DA           *******(STEP 13)
00DA           *
00DA C9              RET             RETURN FROM THIS SUBROUTINE
00DB           *
00DB           ***************************************************************
00DB           *
00DB           *  COLM SUBROUTINE
00DB           *
00DB           *   THIS SUBROUTINE WILL DETERMINE THE ACTIVE COLUMN
00DB           *   IF THERE IS ONE.
00DB           *
00DB           ***************************************************************
00DB           *
00DB           *   THIS SUBROUTINE IS FIGURE 4-15
00DB           *
00DB           ***************************************************************
00DB           *
00DB           ******(STEP 1)
00DB           *
00DB AF        COLM  XRA  A
00DC 32 01 10        STA  CFLAG      SET THE COLUMN FLAG=0
00DF           *
00DF           ******(STEP 2)
00DF           *
00DF DB FE           IN   0FEH       INPUT DATA FROM PORT FE
00E1           *
00E1           ******(STEP 3)
00E1           *
00E1 F6 E0           ORI  0E0H       SET BITS D5,D6,D7=1
00E3           *
00E3           *******(STEP 4)
00E3           *
00E3 FE FF           CPI  0FFH
00E5 C8              RZ              STEP(4A)
```

Figure 9-4 (Cont'd.)

```
00E6              *
00E6              *****(STEP 5)
00E6              *
00E6 2F                CMA             INVERT THE DATA
00E7              *
00E7              ******(STEP 6)
00E7              *
00E7 32 01 10          STA   CFLAG     SET THE COLUMN FLAG
00EA C9                RET             RETURN FROM THIS SUB
00EB              *
00EB              ****************************************************************
00EB              *
00EB              * SUBROUTINE TO OUTPUT THE ACTIVE ROW TO THE KEYBOARD
00EB              *
00EB              *  OROW IS THE NAME OF THIS SUBROUTINE
00EB              *
00EB              *
00EB              *
00EB              ****************************************************************
00EB              ****************************************************************
00EB              *
00EB              *                        8080 MNEMONICS FOR FIGURE 4-10
00EB              *
00EB              ****************************************************************
00EB              *
00EB              *
00EB 3A 04 10 OROW     LDA KROW   RECALL ACTIVE ROW
00EE              *
00EE              * STEP  2
00EE              *
00EE FE 10             CPI   10H       COMPLETE ROW SCAN????
00F0 C2 F8 00          JNZ   OROW1     IF NOT THEN STEP 2B
00F3              *
00F3              * STEP  2A
00F3              *
00F3 3E 01             MVI   A,01H     RESET THE ACTIVE ROW
00F5 C3 F9 00          JMP   ST3       GOTO STEP 3
00F8              *
00F8              * STEP  2B
00F8              *
00F8 07           OROW1 RLC            SHIFT DATA LEFT,0 INTO D0
00F9              *
00F9              * STEP 3
00F9              *
00F9 32 04 10 ST3      STA   KROW      SAVE ACTIVE ROW IN MEM
00FC              *
00FC              *  STEP 4
00FC              *
00FC 2F                CMA             INVERT ROW WORD
00FD              *
00FD              * STEP 5
00FD              *
00FD D3 FE             OUT 0FEH        OUTPUT ACTIVE ROW TO PORT FE
00FF              *
00FF              *STEP 6
00FF              *
00FF C9                RET
0100              *
0100              *
0100              ****************************************************************
```

Figure 9-4 (Cont'd.)

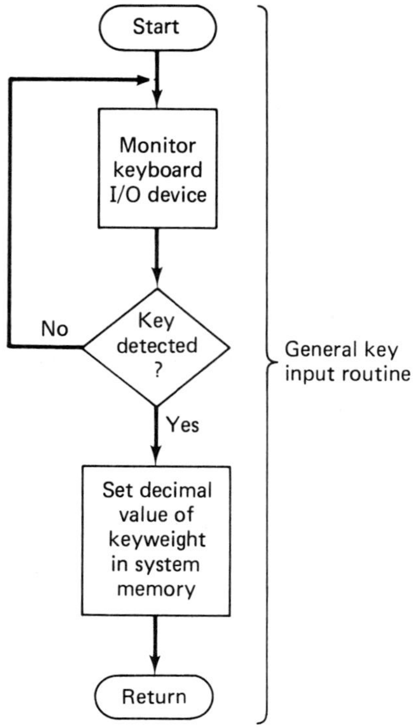

Figure 9-5 Flowchart showing the overall function of inputting a key from the keyboard. This action pattern occurs each time the software code shown in Figure 9-4 is executed.

	C_0	C_1	C_2	C_3	C_4
R_0	X 0	X 1	X 2	X 3	X 4
R_1	X 5	X 6	X 7	X 8	X 9
R_2	X 10	X 11	X 12	X 13	X 14
R_3	X 15	X 16	X 17	X 18	X 19
R_4	X 20	X 21	X 22	X 23	X 24

Figure 9-6 This is the same as Figure 4-17, showing the decimal weight value assigned to each switch position in the 5 × 5 keyboard matrix.

value for all data keys corresponds to the value of the data key. This means that if we press the data key labeled "B" on the keyboard, the KWGT value is set to 1011 (binary). This is the value of decimal 11 of B_{16}. Thus, with software, we do not have to compute a binary value for the data keys. The value is already set in memory location KWGT.

Based on the keyboard assignments of Figure 9-7, the physical keyboard will appear as shown in Figure 9-8 where we see that the reset key is not part of the keyboard matrix. This key is an asyncronous and resets the system immediately, regardless of the function that the system is executing.

In Figure 9-4 we showed the 8085 software required to realize the function of the KEYIN subroutine. This program was discussed in detail in Chapter 4. Refer to this discussion if the details of Figure 9-4 are unclear.

Function		Keyweight returned from Key Input routine
0	Data keys	0
1		1
2		2
3		3
4		4
5		5
6		6
7		7
8		8
9		9
A		10
B		11
C		12
D		13
E		14
F		15
ENTER		16
CLEAR ENTER		17
ADDRESS SET		18
CLEAR RAM		19
START PROG		20
VERIFY		21
COPY		22
NOT ASSIGNED		23, 24

Figure 9-7 The key weight is shown in the right-hand column, and the actual function of the key for the system is shown in the left-hand column.

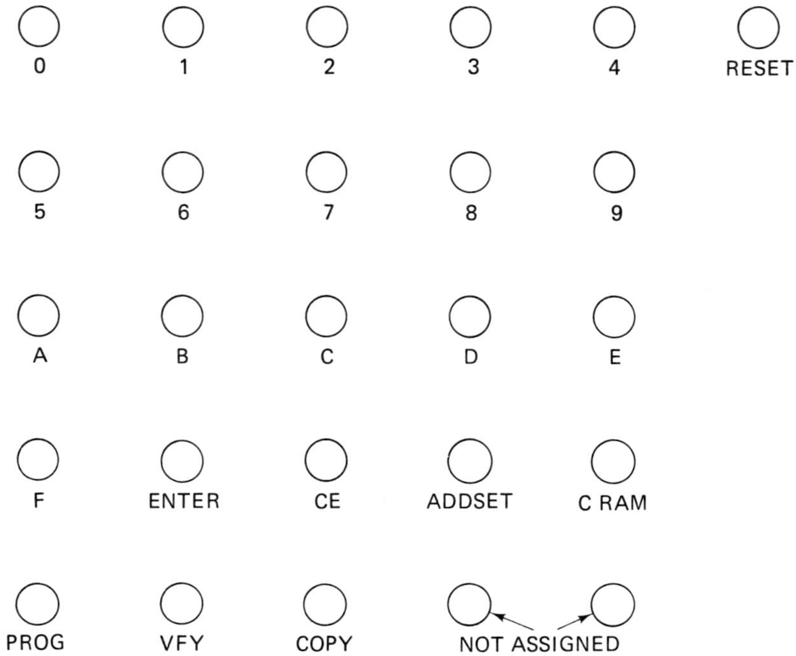

Figure 9-8 Physical layout of the keyboard with all key functions shown. Notice that the reset key is not part of the keyboard matrix. This key is asynchronous to the microprocessor and is used simply to reset it.

9-4 Main Calling Program

Let us now discuss the details of the main calling program. This main program directs the system execution based on the key that is input. When a particular system function is completed, program execution returns to this main calling program. We gave a brief flowchart for this main operational program in Figure 9-3. We now present a more detailed flowchart of the main calling program in Figure 9-9.

There we see that one of the first events to occur in the main program is to call to the subroutine for inputting a key, Step (1a). We recall that the system will not return from this subroutine until a valid key has been input to the system. When the system returns from the input key subroutine it checks the KWGT value of the key input. If this KWGT value corresponds to a legal function key, then the system continues to step (5).

The system expects a function key to be input. If a data key is input, it will be meaningless to the system at this point in the program. From the assigned

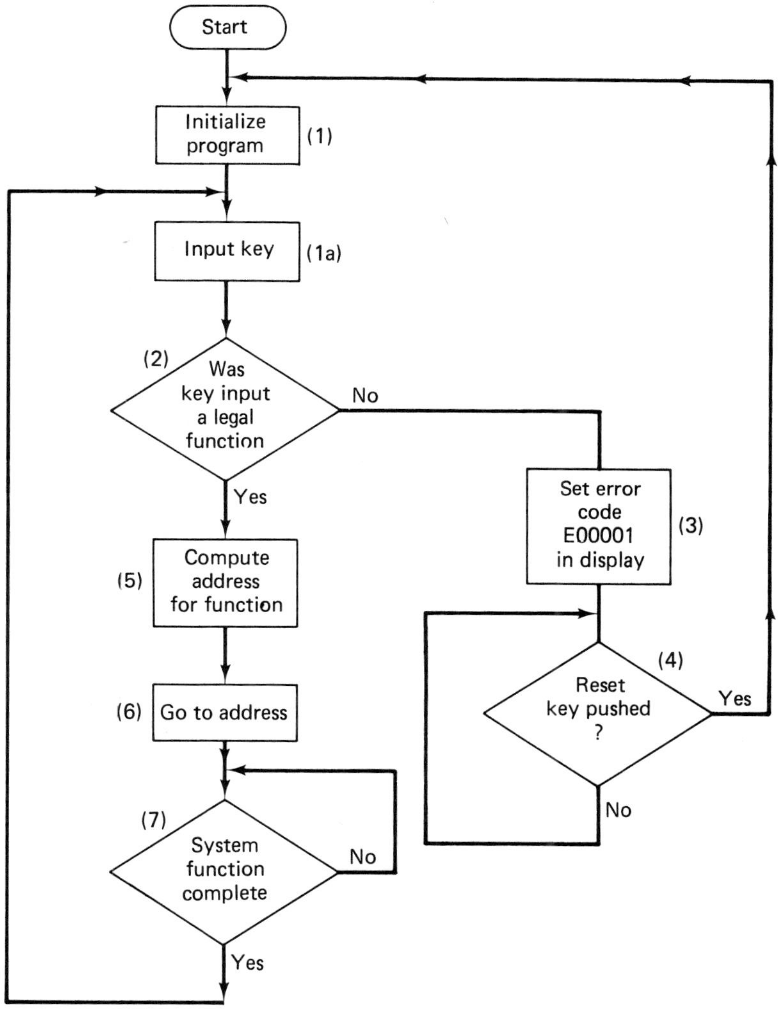

Figure 9-9 Expanded flowchart of the main calling program for the system.

KWGT values of the function keys, we note that any KWGT value greater than 15 is a legal function. In step 2 of the flowchart of Figure 9-9 we shall logically decide if the KWGT value is greater than 15.

If the KWGT value is not greater than 15, we shall display a system ERROR. This particular error number assigned will be 1. We can set the system display to read $E00001_{(16)}$. This display, which indicates that an illegal key (Error) has been input, remains until the reset key is pressed. Since we will be generating other error codes as we proceed through the writing of the software, we should start a list of ERROR codes and their meaning now, so that this may be included with the documentation.

In step 5 of Figure 9-9 we will compute the address of the section of software that will control the system for a specific function. The technique of this computation follows. First, we will make a table of jump statements that will be referenced to labels in the system, as shown in Figure 9-10. The address that we will compute (based on the KWGT input) will be to one of the JMP instructions listed in Figure 9-10; this instruction will then direct the software to the address location for execution of a specific subsection of software for the key that was input.

The JMP instruction in Figure 9-10 that will be pointed to is referenced to a particular KWGT value. For example, if the KWGT value is 16_{10}, then JMP "ENTER" will be executed. If the KWGT value is $17_{(10)}$, then the JMP CENTY will be executed. Notice that, as the KWGT value input from the KEYIN routine increases by one, the JMP instruction to be executed in Figure 9-10 relative to the first JMP instruction is increased by one.

We can calculate the proper JMP instruction relative to the first by this relationship:

$$\text{JMP relative to JMP ENTER} = \text{KWGT} - 16_{(10)}$$

To illustrate this, let us suppose that the value of KWGT were obtained from the KEYIN routine $19_{(10)}$. This corresponds to a CLEAR RAM key. We would compute the JMP instruction to be executed by this formula:

$$\begin{aligned}\text{JMP relative to JMP ENTER} &= \text{KWGT} - 16\\ &= 19 - 6\\ &= 3\end{aligned}$$

```
TABLE   JMP   ENTER
        JMP   CENTY
        JMP   ADDSE
        JMP   CLRAM
        JMP   PROG
        JMP   VFY
        JMP   COPY
        JMP   NA1
        JMP   NA2
```

Figure 9-10 Table of jump statements that direct the program to the proper section of code for execution of the function indicated.

We would execute the third JMP instruction away from the JMP ENTER instruction. Execution of the JMP CLRAM instruction would force the software to execute the code for controlling the system in performance of the clear RAM function.

However, the relationship given does not tell the whole story. If the section of program shown in Figure 9-10 were assembled, it would appear as in Figure 9-11 which shows the absolute address for the location of each JMP instruction in the table. Now, if we use the given relationship just as it stands, with no modification, the following happens.

Suppose we assign the address of the first JMP instruction in the table as a base address. Next, we compute the new address (NEWA) pointer in the table as a function of the base address and the variable (V_1). If we were to use the relationship that we presented earlier,

$$\text{NEWA} = \text{Base Address} + (\text{KWGT} - 16),$$

we would be in trouble because the assigned base address is $0100_{(16)}$ as shown in Figure 9-11. We let KWGT = 19 as it did before. And what we want is an address NEWA that points to the JMP CLRAM instruction. This address is 010B, according to Figure 9-11. Using the present relationship, we would compute the address as:

$$\text{NEWA} = \text{BASE ADDRESS} + (\text{KWGT} - 16)$$
$$\text{NEWA} = 0100 + (19_{10} - 16_{10})$$
$$\text{NEWA} = 0100 + 0003$$
$$\text{NEWA} = 0103$$

```
0000             *
0100                   ORG   0100H     SET THE ORIGIN OF THE TABLE
0100             *
0100             **** START THE TABLE ******
0100             *
0100 C3 33 0F          JMP   ENTER
0103 C3 34 0F          JMP   CENTY
0106 C3 35 0F          JMP   ADDSE
0109 C3 36 0F          JMP   CLRAM
010C C3 37 0F          JMP   PROG
010F C3 38 0F          JMP   VFY
0112 C3 39 0F          JMP   COPY
0115 C3 3A 0F          JMP   NA1
0118 C3 3B 0F          JMP   NA2
011B             *
011B             *****END OF THE TABLE ***
011B             *
```

Figure 9-11 This is the jump table of Figure 9-10 in assembled form. The starting location of the table is memory address 0100 (hexadecimal). Note that each jump instruction requires 3 bytes of memory.

But we wanted 010B, not 0103! What happened? We point to the JMP CENTY instruction address (0103) instead of the JMP CLRAM instruction (010B). This situation is even worse if we have KWGT $= 17_{(10)}$. Making use of the same relationship as before for computing the jump address pointer, we calculate a value of NEWA $= 0101_{(16)}$. This is a total system disaster. We are now pointing to an absolute system address that is in the middle of a 3-byte instruction. Where did we go wrong? The factor we did not take into consideration is that *each JMP instruction requires 3 bytes of memory*, not 1 byte, as we assumed. Therefore, the second JMP instruction is actually three relative addresses away from the base address instead of 1. The JMP instructions may be assembled in different ways for different microprocessors. The point is: great caution must be exercised when computing jump addresses in this fashion within the system software.

Fortunately, this particular error can be remedied easily by changing the relationship for computing the jump address to:

$$\text{NEWA} = \text{BASE ADDRESS} + [\text{KWGT} - 16] \times 3$$

To illustrate how this works, we use the example that failed so miserably before. The value of KWGT $= 19_{(10)}$. The base address is 0100 $_{(16)}$ as shown in Figure 9-11. The value of the new address is:

$$\begin{aligned}
\text{NEW A} &= \text{BASE ADDRESS} + [\text{KWGT} - 16] \times 3 \\
\text{NEW A} &= 0100_{16} + [19_{10} - 16_{10}] \times 3_{10} \\
\text{NEW A} &= 0100_{16} + [3_{10} \times 3_{10}] \\
\text{NEW A} &= 0109_{10}
\end{aligned}$$

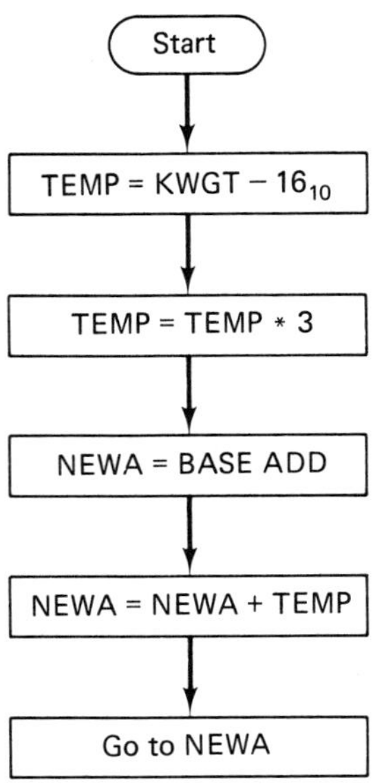

Figure 9-12 Flowchart for realizing the correct computation of the jump address for entering the look-up table.

```
0000                      ORG   00
0000 3A 00 10             LDA   KWGHT      ACC=KWGHT
0003 D6 10                SUI   16         ACC=KWGHT-16
0005 47                   MOV   B,A        STORE IN B REG
0006               *
0006               *
0006 87                   ADD A            ACC*2
0007 80                   ADD B            ACC*3
0008               *
0008               *
0008 01 00 00             LXI B,00         ZERO OUT B,C REGISTERS
000B 4F                   MOV  C,A         STORE IN C REG
000C 21 00 01             LXI H,TABLE       LOAD THE BASE ADDRESS OF TABLE
000F               *
000F               *
000F 09                   DAD B            NEWA=BASE ADD+TEMP(BREG)
0010               *
0010               *
0010 E9                   PCHL             JMP TO THE TABLE ADDRESS
0011               *
0011               *************************************************************
0011               *
0100                      ORG   0100H      SET THE ORIGIN OF THE TABLE
0100               *
0100               **** START THE TABLE ******
0100               *
0100 C3 33 0F      TABLE JMP   ENTER
0103 C3 34 0F            JMP   CENTY
0106 C3 35 0F            JMP   ADDSE
0109 C3 36 0F            JMP   CLRAM
010C C3 37 0F            JMP   PROG
010F C3 38 0F            JMP   VFY
0112 C3 39 0F            JMP   COPY
0115 C3 3A 0F            JMP   NA1
0118 C3 3B 0F            JMP   NA2
011B               *
011B               *****END OF THE TABLE ***
```

Figure 9-13 8080 mnemonics for realizing the flowchart of Figure 9-12.

From Figure 9-11 we see that absolute address 0109 is indeed the correct location to enter the table for a KWGT of 19. The 8085 flowchart for realizing this computation is given in Figure 9-12. Software for realizing this flowchart is given in Figure 9-13.

9-5 Software for the SET ADDRESS Function

Now that we have a means through software of executing any function, the software for performing each function will be discussed. In the following parts of this chapter we shall discuss how each function is performed.

Note here that the KEY INPUT subroutine can be used anywhere in the program. By using the KEY INPUT routine, certain functions obtain the data required at that point.

The first function we shall discuss is the SET ADDRESS function that may be described as follows. The address set function will set a memory address 0000-03FF$_{(16)}$. This address is the starting address for examining data in PROG RAM$_2$, or for entering data into RAM. When the SET ADDRESS function key is pressed, the system automatically waits for three hexadecimal digits to be entered. When this operation is completed, the system uses these digits as an address to RAM$_2$.

At this point the system displays the RAM address 0000-03FF and the data stored at that location. If we wish to change the data, two new hexadecimal digits must be entered. The new data is written into the RAM$_2$ when the ENTER key is pushed.

If we wish only to examine the data, then repeated pushes of the ENTER key increment the address and rewrite the same data. A flowchart for this function is shown in Figure 9-14.

There we see that the first event to occur is that the display is set to A30000$_{(16)}$. This alerts the user, indicating that the system is waiting for three address digits or nibbles. Next, the program inputs the three nibbles. Notice that the major block of the flowchart, indicated as step 2, simply states that the program will input three nibbles. It will be shown in the actual software how the program inputs a digit and displays it. If we were to show all the details now of the major block in step 2 the flowchart would be too confusing to convey the major flow.

When we present the actual 8085 mnemonics for major step 2, we will comment on this section of code so that the actual details will be exposed. This preliminary type of simplification in flowcharting is often done to promote understanding of major ideas. Of course, the exact details are needed to make a program function. This text puts the details in the software realization of the flowcharts. This is where we should expect to see them throughout the explanations given to this text.

The next step in the flowchart of Figure 9-14 occurs when the system uses the address entered by the user and reads the data at that address in RAM$_2$. The system must calculate an absolute system address because memory location 0000 for RAM2 is actually system address 1400$_{(16)}$. We obtain this system address from the memory map of Figure 9-1. Therefore, if we had entered an address of 103$_{(16)}$, the system would perform a memory read from absolute system address of 1400$_{(16)}$ + 0103$_{(16)}$ = 1503. This is the reason we need to have a good memory map before we start writing software.

After the system reads the data from the RAM$_2$ address it displays the address and its data as indicated by block 4 of the flowchart in Figure 9-14.

Next the system gets another key input. If the CENTY key is entered, the overall system function is terminated and the system jumps to the main calling program. If the ENTER key is pushed, the system simply increments the RAM$_2$

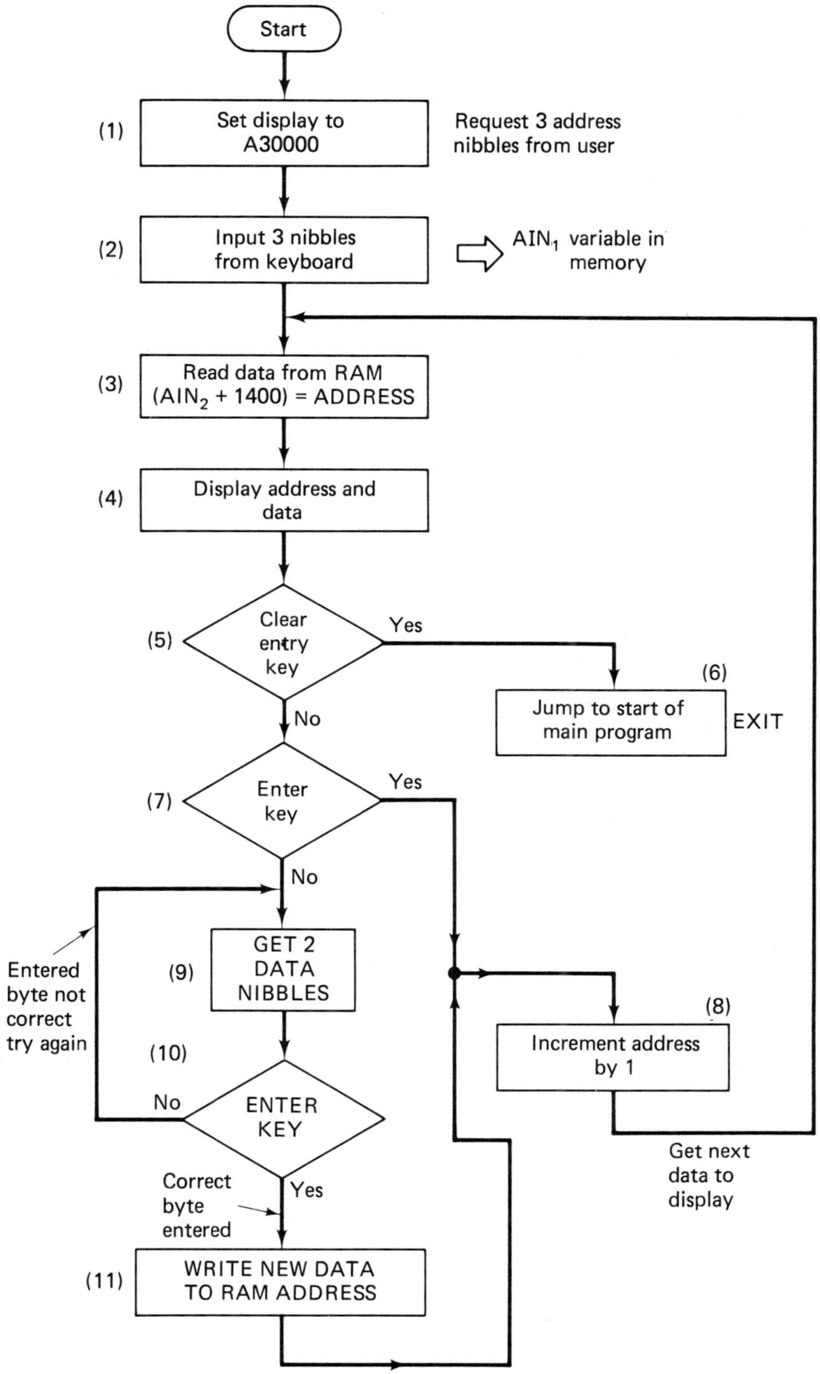

Figure 9-14 Flowchart showing the system operation for the set address function.

address, step 8, and displays the new RAM address and the data stored at that address. In this way we can step through the RAM_2 program memory and examine the data.

If the key input is a data key 0-F (step 9), then the program will assume that new data is to be entered into the RAM_2 address. The program waits for two digits to be input. After the two digits are input, the program checks for the ENTER key to be pushed (step 10). The ENTER key "qualifies" the data just entered. If any key except ENTER, the system will not continue downward in the flow. This is shown by the "no" condition on step 10.

When the ENTER key is input to the system, the new data input in step 9 is written to RAM_2, as shown by step 11. After this data has been written, the program jumps to step 8 where the address to RAM_2 is incremented. From step 8, the program begins again at step 3.

Actual software for realizing this function of SET ADDRESS is shown in Figure 9-15.

```
0000                ****************************************************************
0000                *
0000                *     SUBROUTINE ADDSE.
0000                *     THIS ROUTINE WILL INPUT A 3 DIGIT ADDRESS FROM THE
0000                *     THE KEYBOARD AND DISPLAY THE ADDRESS AND THE DATA
0000                *     STORED IN THE PROGRAM RAM AT THE DISPLAYED ADDRESS
0000                *
0000                ****************************************************************
0000                *
0000                      ORG 00          SET THE FIRST BYTE
0000 3E A3          ADDSE MVI  A,0A3H
0002 D3 F2                OUT 0F2H
0004 AF                   XRA  A
0005 D3 F1                OUT 0F1H
0007 D3 F0                OUT 0F0H        SET DISPLAY = A30000
0009                *
0009                *
0009 CD C3 00             CALL KDET       GET THE FIRST NIBBLE FROM KEYBOARD
000C 3A C2 00             LDA  KWGHT      ACC=VALUE OF FIRST NIBBLE
000F D3 F0                OUT  0F0H       DISPLAY THE FIRST DIGIT
0011 32 BF 00             STA  AIN1       SAVE THE FIRST DIGIT
0014                *
0014                *
0014 CD C3 00             CALL KDET       GET THE SECOND NIBBLE FROM KEYBOARD
0017 3A C2 00             LDA  KWGHT      ACC=SECOND NIBBLE
001A 32 BF 00             STA  AIN2       SAVE THE SECOND NIBBLE
001D 3A BE 00             LDA  AIN1       GET THE FIRST NIBBLE FROM MEM
0020 17                   RAL
0021 17                   RAL
0022 17                   RAL
0023 17                   RAL             SHIFT LEFT 4 BITS
0024 E6 F0                ANI  0F0H       MASK OFF LOWER 4 BITS
0026 32 C1 00             STA  AIN4       SAVE TEMP
0029 3A BF 00             LDA  AIN2       ACC =SECOND NIBBLE IN LOWER 4 BITS
002C 21 C1 00             LXI  H,AIN4     SET H,L = TO MEM LOC AIN4
```

Figure 9-15(a) 8085 mnemonics for realizing the flowchart of Figure 9-14.

```
002F B6                 ORA   M         OR ACC WITH FIRST NIBBLE IN AIN4
0030 D3 F0              OUT  0F0H       UPDATE THE DISPLAY  XXXX--
0032             *
0032             *
0032 CD C3 00           CALL KDET       GET THE THIRD NIBBLE
0035 3A C2 00           LDA   KWGHT     ACC=3RD NIBBLE
0038 32 C0 00           STA   AIN3      SAVE TEMP IN MEM
003B 3A BF 00           LDA   AIN2      RECALL SECOND NIBBLE
003E 17                 RAL
003F 17                 RAL
0040 17                 RAL
0041 17                 RAL             SHIFT THE NIBBLE LEFT 4 BITS
0042 E6 F0              ANI  0F0H       MASK OFF THE LOWER 4 BITS
0044 21 C0 00           LXI   H,AIN3
0047 B6                 ORA   M         OR THE 2ND AND THIRD NIBBLE
0048 D3 F1              OUT   0F1H      OUTPUT THE NIBBLE TO DISPLAY XX--XX
004A 32 BF 00           STA   AIN2      2ND AND 3RD NIBBLE IN AIN2
004D             *
004D             *
004D AF                 XRA   A
004E D3 F0              OUT   0F0H      DISPLAY= XX--00
0050             *
0050             *
0050 3A BE 00           LDA   AIN1      RECALL THE FIRST MSN
0053 D3 F2              OUT   0F2H      DISPLAY=0XXX00 WHERE XXX=ADDRESS
0055             *
0055             *
0055             * NOW TO READ DATA FROM THE MEMORY LOCATION
0055             * UPPER ADDRESS=AIN1, LOWER ADDRESS=AIN2
0055             *
0055 21 00 14           LXI H,1400H     H,L=STARTING ADDRESS OF RAM
0058 3A BF 00           LDA   AIN2
005B 5F                 MOV   E,A
005C 3A BE 00           LDA   AIN1
005F 57                 MOV   D,A       D,E= THE ADDRESS OF RAM
0060 D5                 PUSH  D         SAVE VALUE
0061 19                 DAD   D         H,L=OFFSET +STARTING ADDRESS
0062             *
0062             *
0062 7E          NRED   MOV   A,M       LOAD ACC WITH DATA FROM RAM
0063 D3 F0              OUT  0F0H       SET DISPLAY =0XXXDD  WHERE DD=DATA
0065             *
0065             *
0065             *  WE HAVE JUST FINISHED STEP 4 OF THE FLOW CHART
0065             *
0065             *
0065 E5                 PUSH H          SAVE THE ADDRESS
0066 CD C3 00           CALL KDET       GET THE NEXT KEY PUSH
0069 3A C2 00           LDA KWGHT       ACC=KEY VALUE
006C FE 11              CPI   17        CLEAR KEY ???
006E CA B9 00           JZ   ADEX       YES GOT TO EXIT OF THIS ROUTINE
0071 FE 10              CPI   16        ENTER KEY ??
0073 CA AB 00           JZ   STP8       YES GOTO STEP 8 OF FLOW CHART
0076             *
0076             *
0076             *  WE NEED TO GET 2 NEW NIBBLES FOR NEW DATA IN RAM
0076             *
0076 CD C3 00    TNIB   CALL  KDET      GET THE FIRST NIBBLE
0079 3A C2 00           LDA   KWGHT     ACC=KEY VALUE
007C 32 C1 00           STA   AIN4      TEMP SAVE
007F D3 F0              OUT   0F0H      UP DATA THE DISPLAY
0081 CD C3 00           CALL  KDET      GET THE NEXT NIBBLE
0084 3A C2 00           LDA   KWGHT
0087             *
```

```
0087 32 C0 00          STA   AIN3       SAVE TEMP IN MEM
008A 3A C1 00          LDA   AIN4       RECALL FIRST NIBBLE
008D 17                RAL
008E 17                RAL
008F 17                RAL
0090 17                RAL              SHIFT LEFT 4 BITS
0091 21 C0 00          LXI   H,AIN3
0094 B6                ORA   M          OR THE FIRST AND SECOND NIBBLE
0095 32 C0 00          STA   AIN3       SAVE THE DATA IN MEM
0098 D3 F0             OUT   0F0H       UPDATE THE DISPLAY
009A             *
009A             *
009A             *   NOW TO CHECK IF THIS DATA IS OK
009A             *
009A CD C3 00          CALL  KDET       GET THE KEY
009D 3A C2 00          LDA   KWGHT      ACC= KEY VALUE
00A0 FE 10             CPI   16         ENTER KEY???
00A2 C2 76 00          JNZ   TNIB       NO ASK FOR THE NEW DATA AGAIN
00A5             *
00A5             *
00A5             *   NOW TO WRITE THE DATA INTO THE MEMORY
00A5             *
00A5 3A C0 00          LDA   AIN3       RECALL THE DATA
00A8 E1                POP   H          RESTORE THE MEM ADDRESS
00A9 77                MOV   M,A        DATA TO MEM
00AA E5                PUSH  H
00AB             *
00AB             *
00AB E1          STP8  POP   H
00AC 23                INX   H          INCREMENT THE ADDRESS
00AD D1                POP   D          RESTORE THE RAM ADDRESS
00AE 13                INX   D
00AF D5                PUSH  D          SAVE THE VALUE
00B0 7B                MOV   A,E
00B1 D3 F1             OUT   0F1H       UPDATE THE ADDRESS IN DISPLAY
00B3 7A                MOV   A,D
00B4 D3 F2             OUT   0F2H       UPDATE THE ADDRESS IN DISPLAY
00B6 C3 62 00          JMP   NRED       START THE OPERATION OVER
00B9             *
00B9             *
00B9 E1          ADEX  POP   H
00BA D1                POP   D
00BB C3 C4 00          JMP   BEGIN      GO TO START OF THE CONTROL SECTION
00BE             *
00BE             *
00BE             *
00BE             *
00BE             *   NEED TO INSTALL DUMMY LOCATIONS FOR REFERENCED VARIABLES
00BE             *
00BE 00          AIN1  NOP
00BF 00          AIN2  NOP
00C0 00          AIN3  NOP
00C1 00          AIN4  NOP
00C2 00          KWGHT NOP
00C3 00          KDET  NOP
00C4 00          BEGIN NOP
00C5                   END              END STATEMENT FOR ASSEMBLER


    0 ERRORS             12 SYMBOLS
```

Figure 9-15 (Cont'd.)

9-6 Software for the CLEAR RAM Function

We shall now discuss the software required to realize the CLEAR RAM system function. First, in words, let us define CLEAR RAM. The CLEAR RAM function writes all 1s ($FF_{(16)}$) into each memory location of RAM_2.

Figure 9-16 shows the flowchart for the major sequence of events for the CLEAR RAM function. After the system writes the 1s into the RAM_2 locations, it jumps back to the main program and waits for a new function to be entered. The actual 8085 mnemonics for realizing the flowchart of Figure 9-16 are shown in Figure 9-17.

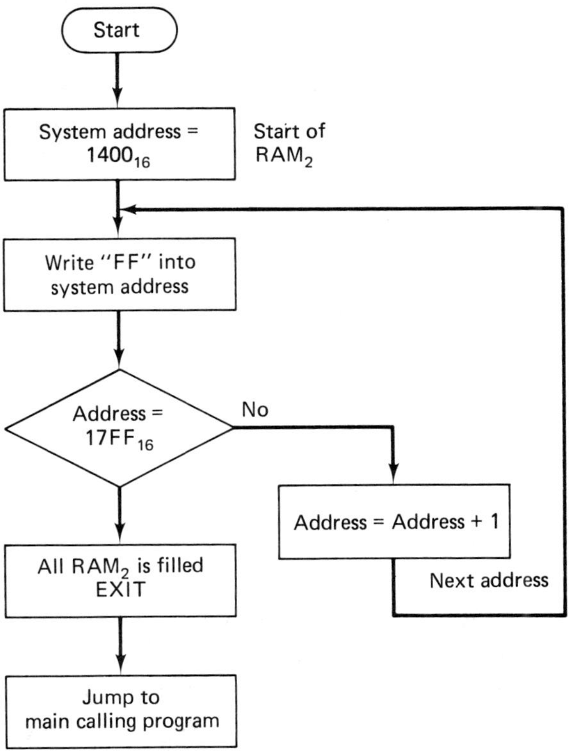

Figure 9-16 Flowchart showing the system operation for the clear RAM function.

```
0000                 *************************************************************
0000                 *
0000                 *    THIS IS CLEAR RAM SUBROUTINE
0000                 *
0000                 *
0000                 *************************************************************
0000                       ORG 0000        SET THE STARTING ADDRESS
0000 3E FF           CLRAM MVI  A,0FFH     ACC=FF
0002 21 00 14              LXI  H,1400H    SET H,L TO STARTING RAM ADD
0005 77              CL1   MOV  M,A        FF TO MEMORY
0006 F5                    PUSH PSW        SAVE ACC
0007 3E 17                 MVI  A,17H
0009 BC                    CMP  H          CHECK FOR UPPER BYTE LIMIT
000A CA 12 00              JZ LCHK         YES CHECK FOR LOWER BYTE LIMIT
000D F1                    POP  PSW        RESTORE ACC
000E 23                    INX  H          INCREMENT RAM ADDRESS
000F C3 05 00              JMP  CL1        DO THE NEXT ADDRESS
0012 F1              LCHK  POP  PSW        RESTORE THE ACC
0013 BD                    CMP  L          CHECK FOR LOWER BYTE=FF
0014 CA 1B 00              JZ   BEGIN      END OF THIS SUBROUTINE
0017 23                    INX  H          NOT END INCREMENT ADDRESS
0018 C3 05 00              JMP  CL1        GO AGAIN AT A DIFFERENT ADDRESS
001B                 *
001B                 *
001B                 *
001B                 *   NEED DUMMY ADDRESS FOR BEGIN
001B                 *
001B 00              BEGIN NOP             THIS IS A DUMMY FOR THE ASSEMBLER
001C                 *
001C                       END             END STATEMENT FOR THE ASSEMBLER


      0 ERRORS              4 SYMBOLS
```

Figure 9-17 8085 mnemonics for realizing the flowchart of Figure 9-16.

9-7 Software for the Programming Function

Programming of an EPROM is undertaken when the need exists to store information (a fixed program) that will and can be used over and over without reprogramming. Such nonvolatile memory storage has value in a wide variety of applications. EPROMs have the additional attractive feature that they can be erased when the need for a particular stored program has passed, then reprogrammed to meet new needs as desired. In programming an EPROM, the desired program is first stored in another location, in this case RAM_2, and then transferred in the programming operation to the EPROM, where it resides until erased.

We will now discuss the software required to program the EPROM. The system sets the EPROM into programming mode. Data from RAM_2 is applied to the EPROM's data output lines. The system pulses the programming pin on the EPROM. The system repeats the programming pulse at each successive address location, $0000\text{-}03FF_{(16)}$.

After 200 programming passes through address 0000-03FF, the system then does a compare operation. The compare operation matches the data now in the EPROM just programmed against the original data stored in RAM_2. If all data now in EPROM compares at each address location with the original data in RAM_2, then the program function was successful. If data at any address of the EPROM does not compare exactly with that of RAM_2, then the system displays the address and data of the EPROM that did not compare. This overall system flowchart is shown in Figure 9-18.

There we see that the first event to occur is that the display is set to $DDDDDD_{(16)}$. This is done to indicate that the system is executing the programming routine. It takes more than a minute to fully program the EPROM, and we need an indication that the system is actively running.

The system then sets up the EPROM in the programming mode (step 2). We recall that this is accomplished by forcing the $\overline{CS}$/WE pin of the 2708 to +12 volts. The system then executes a loop of steps 3, 4, 5, 6. This is where the 2708 is actually being programmed with the data stored in RAM_2.

After one complete pass at programming all 1024 locations, the system checks whether 200 loops have been made on the EPROM. This is shown in step 7 of Figure 9-18. If 200 passes have not been made, the system continues back to step 3. If 200 loops have been made, the system verifies if the data programmed was good; this is shown in steps 8 and 9.

If the data does not compare, then this programming was unsuccessful or invalid. The system then sets the display to show (a) the first nonvalid compare address and (b) the data in the EPROM at that address. This is shown in steps 10 and 12. If the data does compare, then the system indicates a good programming of the EPROM, the display is set to FDDDDD, and the system jumps back to the start of the main program. This is shown in Step 11 of Figure 9-18.

The actual 8085 mnemonics for realizing the flowchart of Figure 9-18 are shown in Figure 9-19.

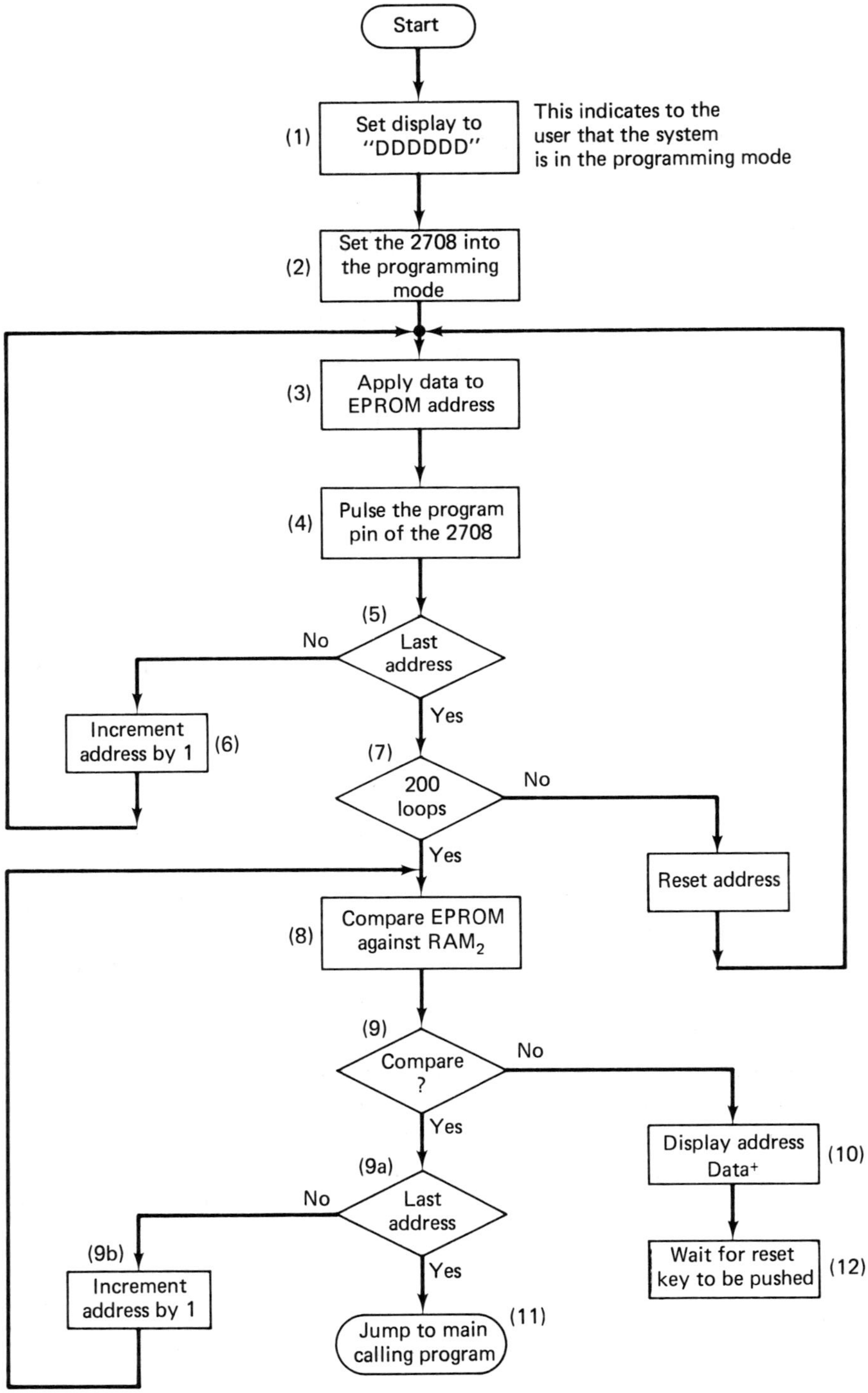

Figure 9-18 Flowchart showing system operation for programming.

```
0000            ************************************************************
0000            *
0000            *  88080 PROGRAM FOR THE PROG COMMAND
0000            *  THIS ROUTINE WILL PERFORM THE ELECTRICAL FUNCTION
0000            *  OF PROGRAMMING THE 2708 EPROM.  THE RAM DATA IS
0000            *  STORED AT MEMORY LOCATION 1400H.  THE EPROM ADDRESS
0000            *  WILL START AT LOCATION 0000.
0000            *
0000            **************** PROGRAMMER:  JIM COFFRON  *****************
0000            *
0000                  ORG  0000       SET THE ORIGIN FOR THE ASSEMBLER
0000            *
0000 3E DD      PROG  MVI  A,0DDH
0002 D3 F0            OUT  0F0H
0004 D3 F1            OUT  0F1H
0006 D3 F2            OUT  0F2H       SET DISPLAY TO DDDDDD
0008 3E 00            MVI  A,00
000A D3 32            OUT  32H        ENABLE THE DATA TO PROM
000C 32 03 14         STA  CNT1       ZERO THE LOOP COUNTER
000F 3C               INR  A
0010 D3 34            OUT  34H        CS/WE = 12 VOLTS
0012            *
0012 11 00 00   PROG3 LXI  D,0000H    SET THE PROM ADDRESS
0015 21 00 14         LXI  H,1400H    SET THE RAM ADDRESS
0018            *
0018 7E         PROG2 MOV  A,M        DATA FROM RAM  TO ACC
0019 D3 30            OUT  30H        DATA TO PROM
001B 7B               MOV  A,E        A0-A7 TO ACC
001C D3 33            OUT  33H        A0-A7 TO PROM
001E 7A               MOV  A,D        A8-A9 TO ACC
001F D3 34            OUT  34H        A8-A9 TO PROM
0021            *
0021            * NOW TO APPLY THE PROGRAMMING PULSE
0021            *
0021 06 08            MVI  B,08
0023 3E 03            MVI  A,03
0025 D3 35            OUT  35H        TURN ON CS/WE AND PROG PULSE
0027 05         PULSE DCR  B
0028 C2 27 00         JNZ  PULSE      PULSE WIDTH
002B 3E 01            MVI  A,01
002D D3 35            OUT  35H        TURN OFF PROG PULSE
002F            *
002F            * NOW TO CHECK IF LAST ADDRESS PROGRAMMED
002F            *
002F 7B               MOV  A,E
0030 FE FF            CPI  0FFH       LAST BYTE A0-A7
0032 C2 3B 00         JNZ  PROG1
0035 7A               MOV  A,D
0036 FE 03            CPI  03         LAST BYTE A8-A9
0038 CA 40 00         JZ   LOPC       LAST ADDRESS (YES)
003B 23         PROG1 INX  H
003C 13               INX  D          BUMP THE RAM AND PROM ADDRESS
003D C3 18 00         JMP  PROG2      DO THE NEXT ADDRESS
0040            *
0040            * NOW TO CHECK IF LAST TIME THROUGH THE 1024 ADDRESSES
0040            *
0040 3A 03 14   LOPC  LDA  CNT1       GET THE COUNT
0043 3C               INR  A
0044 32 03 14         STA  CNT1
0047 FE C8            CPI  200        200 LOOPS YET ??
```

Figure 9-19 8085 mnemonics for realizing the flowchart of Figure 9-18.

```
0049 C2 12 00          JNZ   PROG3     NOT 200 LOOPS START OVER
004C              *
004C              *  FINISHED PROGRAMMING NOW TO VERIFY
004C              *
004C 3E 01             MVI A,01        DISABLE DATA TO PROM
004E D3 32             OUT 32H
0050 3D                DCR   A         ACC=0
0051 D3 35             OUT 35H         CS/WE = 0.0 V
0053              *
0053              * INITIALIZE THE ADDRESS OF PROM AND RAM
0053              *
0053 11 00 00          LXI   D,00
0056 21 78 05          LXI   H,1400    RAM ADDRESS
0059              *
0059 7B           PROG4 MOV   A,E       A0-A7 TO ACC
005A D3 33             OUT   33H       ADDRESS TO PROM
005C 7A                MOV   A,D       A8-A9 TO ACC
005D D3 34             OUT   34H       A8-A9 TO PROM
005F DB 31             IN   31H        READ THE PROM DATA TO ACC
0061 BE                CMP   M         CHECK FOR VALID DATA IN PROM
0062 C2 76 00          JNZ   PROGF     NOT EQUAL FAIL
0065              *
0065              * IF HERE THEN PASSED AT ABOVE LOCATION
0065              *
0065              * NOW TO CHECK FOR LAST ADDRESS
0065              *
0065 7B                MOV   A,E
0066 FE FF             CPI   0FFH      LAST A0-A7?
0068 C2 71 00          JNZ   PROG5     NOT LAST ONE
006B 7A                MOV   A,D       A8-A9 LAST
006C FE 03             CPI   03
006E CA 02 14          JZ   BEGIN      LAST ONE START NEW COMMAND
0071              *
0071              * INCREMENT THE RAM AND PROM ADDRESS
0071              *
0071 23           PROG5 INX   H
0072 13                INX   D
0073 C3 59 00          JMP   PROG4     NEXT ADDRESS FOR COMPARE
0076              *
0076              * THIS IS THE FAIL SECTION
0076              *
0076 7B           PROGF MOV   A,E       A0-A7 TO ACC
0077 D3 F0             OUT   0F0H
0079 7A                MOV   A,D       A8-A9 TO ACC
007A D3 F1             OUT   0F1H       TO DISPLAY
007C DB 31             IN   31H        GET PROM DATA
007E D3 F2             OUT   0F2H      TO DISPLAY
0080              *
0080              * NOW TO LOOP UNTIL CE KEY HIT
0080              *
0080 CD 00 14     PROG6 CALL  KDET
0083 3A 01 14          LDA   KWGT
0086 FE 16             CPI   16H       IS THE KEY CLEAR ENTRY??
0088 C2 80 00          JNZ   PROG6
008B C3 02 14          JMP   BEGIN     RETURN AND DO ANOTHER COMMAND
008E              *
008E              *  NOW TO INSERT THE DUMMY VARIABLES FOR NOW
008E              *
008E              ****************************************************************
008E              *
```

Figure 9-19 (Cont'd.)

```
008E          *  DUMMY EQUATES AND VARIABLES FOR NOW
008E          *
008E          ***************************************************
008E          *
008E          KDET  EQU  1400H
008E          KWGT  EQU  1401H
008E          BEGIN EQU 1402H
008E          CNT1  EQU  1403H
008E          *
008E          *
008E                END          END FOR ASSEMBLER


   0 ERRORS          14 SYMBOLS
```

Figure 9-19 (Cont'd.)

9-8 Software for the VERIFY Function

The next function we shall discuss is VERIFY. This function compares EPROM data against the RAM_2 data. If any data fails to compare, then the failed address and data are displayed. This function is especially useful if we are unsure if an EPROM has been programmed correctly. It is also useful for verifying if an EPROM is fully erased. To do this the RAM_2 is cleared and then the erased EPROM is checked by using the VERIFY key.

The flowchart for the verify function is given in Figure 9-20 where we see that the system first sets the compare address equal to 0000 in step 1. The system then compares RAM_2 data at address 0 to EPROM data at address 0. If these data do not compare, the system displays the failed address and its data. This is shown in steps 3 and 4. If these data compare, then the system increments to the next address, as shown in step 6.

The addresses are incremented and the data is compared at each address. If the data at all addresses compare successfully, the system jumps to the main program, as shown in step 7. The 8085 mnemonics required to realize this VERIFY function are given in Figure 9-21.

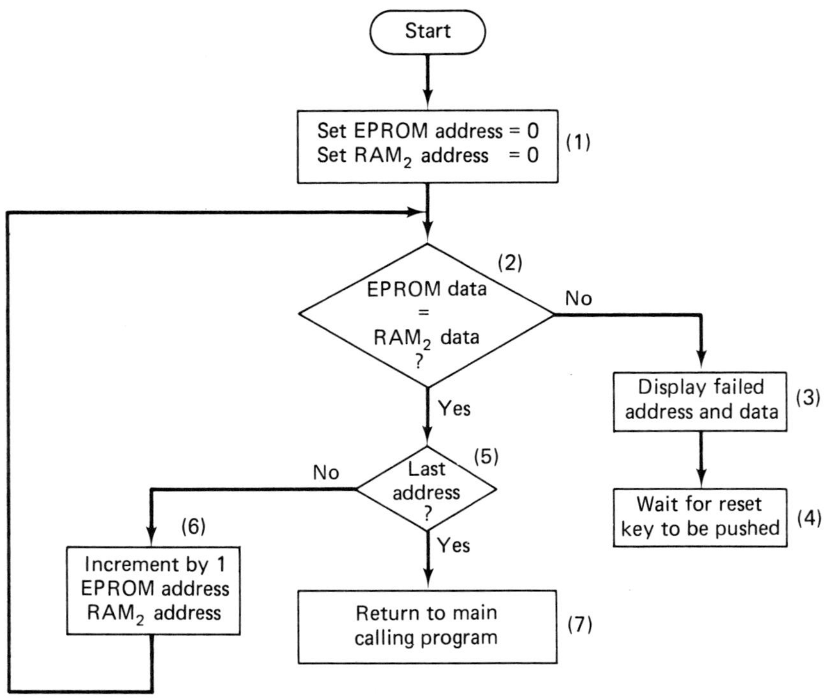

Figure 9-20 Flowchart showing system operation for VERIFY.

```
0000                 ************************** ***********************************
0000                 *
0000                 *  FIGURE 9-21  PROGRAM TO REALIZE THE FLOW CHART OF
0000                 *  FIGURE 9 - 20.
0000                 *  PROGRAMMER:    JIM COFFRON
0000                 *
0000                 **************************************************************
0000                 *
0000                        ORG 0000       SET THE ORIGIN FOR THE ASSEMBLER
0000                 *
0000                 *  SET UP THE PROM TO BE READ
0000                 *
0000 AF              VFY    XRA  A
0001 3C                     INR  A
0002 D3 32                  OUT 32H        ENABLE THE DRIVERS IN THE RIGHT DIRECTIO
0004 AF                     XRA  A
0005 D3 35                  OUT  35H       CS=0.0V,PGM=0.0V
0007 D3 33                  OUT  33H       ADDRESS A0-A7=0
0009 D3 34                  OUT  34H       ADDRESS A8-A9=0
000B 11 00 00               LXI  D,0000    SET UP PROM ADDRESS
000E 21 00 14               LXI  H,1400H   RAM ADDRESS OFFSET
0011                 *
0011                 *  NOW TO START THE READ AND VERIFY LOOP
0011                 *
0011 DB 31           VFY1   IN   31H       READ THE PROM DATA
0013 BE                     CMP  M         PROM DATA =RAM DATA??
0014 C2 31 00               JNZ  VFAIL     VFAIL IF NOT EQUAL
0017 3E 13                  MVI  A,13H
0019 BA                     CMP  D         UPPER BYTE MATCH, LAST ADDRESS
001A C2 26 00               JNZ  VNEX      NO MATCH GET NEXT ADDRESS
001D 3E FF                  MVI  A,0FFH
001F BB                     CMP  E         LOWER BYTE MATCH??
0020 C2 26 00               JNZ  VNEX      NO, GET THE NEXT ADDRESS
0023 C3 3C 00               JMP  START     BACK TO MAIN PROGRAM..PASS
0026 13              VNEX   INX  D
0027 7A                     MOV  A,D       NEW PROM ADDRESS
0028 D3 34                  OUT  34H       DATA TO HARDWARE
002A 7B                     MOV  A,E
002B D3 33                  OUT  33H       DATA TO HARDWARE
002D 23                     INX  H         NEW RAM ADDRESS
002E C3 11 00               JMP  VFY1      COMPARE THE NEXT DATA
0031 D3 F0           VFAIL  OUT  0F0H      SET DISPLAY----XX
0033 7B                     MOV  A,E
0034 D3 F1                  OUT  0F1H      LOWER ADDRESS TO DISPLAY
0036 7A                     MOV  A,D
0037 D3 F2                  OUT  0F2H      UPPER ADDRESS TO DISPLAY
0039 C3 39 00        VOUT   JMP  VOUT      WAIT FOR INTERRUPT
003C                 *
003C                 *
003C                 ****** NOW TO PUT IN THE DUMMY VARIABLES ***
003C                 *
003C 00              START  NOP
003D                        END            END FOR THE ASSEMBLER


0 ERRORS                 6 SYMBOLS
```

Figure 9-21 8085 mnemonics for realizing the flowchart of Figure 9-20.

9-9 Software for the COPY Function

The final function we will discuss is COPY, in which data stored in an EPROM is copied electrically into the address locations of the RAM_2. This COPY function is useful if we wish to duplicate an already existing EPROM. The flowchart for this function is given in Figure 9-22. There we see that the system reads the data from the EPROM in step 2 and writes that data into the RAM in step 3. This action is repeated for all address locations $0000\text{-}03FF_{(16)}$. Figure 9-23 shows the 8085 mnemonics needed to realize the COPY function.

9-10 Summary of the Software

In this chapter we have discussed all major aspects of designing and writing software for a microprocessor-controlled system. We have used a specific example to show the details. In this, many universal points were covered that can be applied to different problems. We have shown and discussed the use of flowcharting to help us organize and communicate thoughts. In addition, in order to fully show the process, the mnemonics were presented to realize the flowcharts.

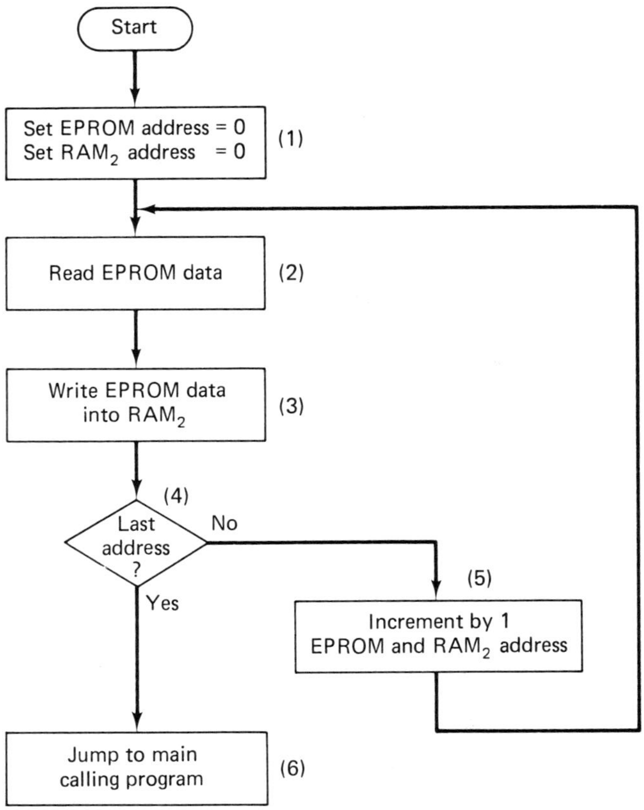

Figure 9-22 Flowchart showing the system operation for COPY.

```
ØØØØ              ****************************************************************
ØØØØ              *
ØØØØ              *   FIGURE 9-23   PROGRAM TO REALIZE THE COPY FLOWCHART
ØØØØ              *   OF FIGURE 9-22
ØØØØ              *
ØØØØ              *   PROGRAMMER:   JIM COFFRON
ØØØØ              *
ØØØØ              ****************************************************************
ØØØØ              *
ØØØØ                     ORG   ØØØØ
ØØØØ              *
ØØØØ              *   SET UP THE PROM TO READ DATA
ØØØØ              *
ØØØØ AF           COPY   XRA   A
ØØØ1 3C                  INR   A            ACC=1
ØØØ2 D3 32               OUT   32H
ØØØ4 AF                  XRA   A
ØØØ5 D3 35               OUT   35H          CS=Ø.ØV,PGM=Ø.ØV
ØØØ7 11 ØØ ØØ            LXI   D,ØØØØ       PROM ADDRESS=Ø
ØØØA 21 ØØ 14            LXI   H,14ØØH      SET THE RAM OFFSET ADD
ØØØD 7B           COPY1  MOV   A,E
ØØØE D3 33               OUT   33H          ADDRESS AØ-A7 SET
ØØ1Ø 7A                  MOV   A,D
ØØ11 D3 34               OUT   34H          ADDRESS A8-A9 SET
ØØ13 DB 31               IN   31H           READ THE DATA FROM THE PROM
ØØ15 77                  MOV   M,A          OUTPUT THE DATA TO RAM
ØØ16 3E 13               MVI   A,13H
ØØ18 BA                  CMP   D            CHECK FOR LAST ADDRESS
ØØ19 C2 22 ØØ            JNZ   CNEX         CNEX IF NOT LAST ADDRESS
ØØ1C 3E FF               MVI   A,ØFFH
ØØ1E BB                  CMP   E            LAST ADDRESS LOWER BYTE
ØØ1F CA 27 ØØ            JZ   START         IF LAST ADDRESS.. THE END
ØØ22 23           CNEX   INX   H            NEXT RAM ADDRESS
ØØ23 13                  INX   D            NEXT PROM ADDRESS
ØØ24 C3 ØD ØØ            JMP   COPY1        GET THE NEXT DATA
ØØ27              *
ØØ27              *   NOW TO PUT IN THE DUMMY VARIABLES
ØØ27              *
ØØ27 ØØ           START  NOP
ØØ28                     END                END STATEMENT FOR THE ASSEMBLER


    Ø ERRORS               4 SYMBOLS
```

Figure 9-23 8085 mnemonics for realizing the flowchart of Figure 9-22.

We have shown step by step in this chapter how to approach a software problem. The correct choice of a starting point will usually get us headed in the right direction. Important questions that need to be answered before the actual software can be written were pointed out and stressed. By understanding the flow of events covered in this sample problem, we will gain some useful insights that will be of value for other microprocessor applications that are of personal interest.

Figure 9-24 shows the full software program for the 8085 to realize the system control.

```
0000              *************************************************************
0000              *
0000              *  8080 PROGRAM FOR CONTROLLING THE PROM PROGRAMMER
0000              *
0000              *******  PROGRAMMER: JIM COFFRON ****************************
0000              *
0000              *
0000                    ORG   00        SET STARTING ADDRESS IN MEM
0000              *
0000              *  WE FIRST MUST INITIALIZE ALL VARIABLES
0000              *
0000 31 FF 13           LXI   SP,13FFH  INITAILIZE STACK POINTER
0003 AF           BEGIN XRA   A         RESET FLAGS, ZERO ACC
0004 FB                 EI              ENABLE INTERRUPTS
0005 D3 F0              OUT   0F0H      ZERO OUT DISPLAY
0007 D3 F1              OUT   0F1H
0009 D3 F2              OUT   0F2H      SET DISPLAY=000000
000B 32 00 10           STA   KTIME     KTIME=0
000E 32 01 10           STA   CFLAG     CFLAG=0
0011 32 02 10           STA   KWGHT     KWGHT=0
0014 32 03 10           STA   KCOMP     KCOMP=0
0017 3C                 INR   A         ACC=1
0018 32 04 10           STA   KROW      KROW=00000001
001B              *
001B              *
001B              *  NOW TO SET MEMORY ADDRESS OF VARIABLES
001B              *
001B              KTIME EQU   1000H
001B              CFLAG EQU   KTIME+1
001B              KWGHT EQU   CFLAG+1
001B              KCOMP EQU   KWGHT+1
001B              KROW  EQU   KCOMP+1
001B              NROW  EQU   KROW+1
001B              CNT1  EQU   NROW+1
001B              AIN1  EQU   CNT1+1
001B              AIN2  EQU   AIN1+1
001B              AIN3  EQU   AIN2+1
001B              AIN4  EQU   AIN3+1
001B              *
001B              * START OF THE MAIN PROGRAM FOR INPUTTING A COMMAND
001B              *
001B CD 64 00           CALL   KDET     GET A KEY
001E              *
001E 3A 02 10           LDA   KWGHT     GET THE KEY WEIGHT
0021 FE 16              CPI   16H       IS THE KEY A COMMAND???
0023 CA 2C 00           JZ   BEGN1
0026 DA 2C 00           JC   BEGN1      IF THESE JUMPS THEN LEGAL COMMAND
0029 C3 03 00           JMP BEGIN     IGNORE THE ENTRY
002C              *
002C              * NOW TO COMPUTE THE JMP ADDRESS
002C              *  FIGURE  9-13
002C              *
002C 3A 02 10     BEGN1 LDA   KWGHT
002F D6 10              SUI   16        ACC= KWGHT-16
0031 47                 MOV   B,A
0032 87                 ADD   A         ACC*2
0033 80                 ADD   B         ACC*3
0034              *
0034 01 00 00           LXI   B,00
```

Figure 9-24 The complete 8085 software program for realizing the complete system operation.

```
0037 4F                 MOV   C,A        COMPUTED OFFSET IN C REG
0038 21 3D 00           LXI   H,TABLE    LOAD BASE ADDRESS OF TABLE
003B 09                 DAD   B          ADD OFFSET TO BASE ADDRESS
003C E9                 PCHL             JUMP TO COMPUTED ADDRESS OF TABLE
003D              *
003D              *
003D              *   TABLE FOR JUMP ADDRESSES
003D              *
003D C3 58 00     TABLE JMP   ENTER
0040 C3 5B 00           JMP   CENTY
0043 C3 44 01           JMP   ADDSE
0046 C3 02 02           JMP   CLRAM
0049 C3 1D 02           JMP   PROG
004C C3 AB 02           JMP   VFY
004F C3 F2 02           JMP   COPY
0052 C3 5E 00           JMP   NA1
0055 C3 61 00           JMP   NA2
0058              *
0058              *** END OF TABLE ENTRYS *****
0058              *
0058              *   THIS IS FOR THE ENTRY, CENTRY,NA1,NA2 COMMANDS
0058              *
0058 C3 03 00     ENTER JMP   BEGIN
005B C3 03 00     CENTY JMP   BEGIN
005E C3 03 00     NA1   JMP   BEGIN
0061 C3 03 00     NA2   JMP   BEGIN
0064              *
0064              *
0064              ******  START OF THE KEY DETECT KDET ROUTINE  *****
0064              *
0064              *   START OF FIGURE 4-20
0064              *
0064 CD 2F 01     KDET  CALL  OROW      OUTPUT THE ACTIVE ROW
0067 CD 1F 01           CALL  COLM      CALL COLUMN ROUTINE
006A 3A 01 10           LDA   CFLAG     NEED TO CHECK THE COLUMN FLAG
006D FE 00              CPI   00H       CHECK FOR ACTIVE COLUMN
006F CA 64 00           JZ    KDET      NO ACTIVE COLUMN LOOP AGAIN
0072 CD F5 00           CALL  KEYW      ACTIVE COLUMN, WHICH ONE???
0075              *
0075              *   END OF FIGURE 4-20
0075              *
0075              *   START OF FIGURE 4-21
0075              *
0075              ***** WE HAVE AN ACTIVE KEY *******
0075              *
0075              *****(STEP 1)
0075              *
0075 3A 00 10           LDA   KTIME     RECALL KTIME FROM MEM
0078              *
0078              *
0078              *****(STEP 2)
0078              *
0078 FE 00              CPI   00H       KTIME=0??
007A CA 9F 00           JZ    KCL01     YES THIS IS FIRST TIME
007D              *
007D              *** NOT THE FIRST TIME *****
007D              *
007D              *****(STEP 7)
007D              *
007D 3A 02 10           LDA   KWGHT     WHAT KEY VALUE WAS PUSHED???
```

```
0080 4F               MOV   C,A       C REG = KWGHT
0081 3A 03 10         LDA   KCOMP     A REG = COMPARE VALUE
0084 B9               CMP   C         KCOMP=KWGHT?
0085 CA 8F 00         JZ   KCLO2      YES THEY DO!!!!!!
0088            *
0088            *****(STEP 8)
0088            *
0088 AF               XRA   A         THEY ARE NOT EQUAL
0089 32 00 10         STA   KTIME     RESET THE KTIME VARIABLE
008C C3 AA 00         JMP   KCLO3     GOTO RESET ACTIVE ROW
008F            *
008F            ****(STEP 9)
008F            *
008F 3A 00 10   KCLO2 LDA   KTIME     RECALL KTIME FROM MEM
0092 3C               INR A           KTIME=KTIME+1
0093 32 00 10         STA   KTIME     KTIME=KTIME+1
0096            *
0096            *****(STEP 10)
0096            *
0096 FE 32            CPI   50        KTIME=50??
0098 C2 AA 00         JNZ   KCLO3     NOT 50 YET
009B CD B2 00         CALL KOPN       CHECK FOR KEY OPEN
009E C9               RET             END OF THIS ROUTINE
009F            *
009F            *****(STEP 3)
009F            *
009F 3A 02 10   KCLO1 LDA   KWGHT
00A2 32 03 10         STA   KCOMP     KCOMP=KWGHT
00A5            *
00A5            *****(STEP 4)
00A5            *
00A5 3E 01            MVI   A,01
00A7 32 00 10         STA   KTIME     UP DATE KTIME=1
00AA            *
00AA            ****(STEP 5)
00AA            *
00AA 3E 01      KCLO3 MVI   A,01
00AC 32 04 10         STA   KROW      RESET ACTIVE ROW=00000001
00AF            *
00AF            *****(STEP 6)
00AF            *
00AF C3 64 00         JMP   KDET      GOTO START OF PROGRAM
00B2            *
00B2            *
00B2            ************************************************************
00B2            *
00B2            ******    START OF SUBROUTINES     ************
00B2            *
00B2            ************************************************************
00B2            *
00B2            *
00B2            *  FIGURE 4-22
00B2            *  KEY OPEN SUBROUTINE
00B2            *
00B2            ************************************************************
00B2            *
00B2            ******(STEP 1)
00B2            *
00B2 3E 01      KOPN  MVI   A,01
00B4 32 04 10         STA   KROW      SET KROW=00000001
```

```
0087 3D                DCR   A
00B8 32 05 10          STA   NROW      SET NROW=00000000
00BB                   *
00BB                   *****(STEP 2)
00BB                   *
00BB 32 00 10          STA   KTIME     KTIME=0
00BE                   *
00BE                   *****(STEP 3)
00BE                   *
00BE CD 2F 01 KOPN1 CALL  ORCW      OUTPUT THE ROW
00C1                   *
00C1                   *****(STEP 4)
00C1                   *
00C1 CD 1F 01          CALL  COLM      INPUT THE COLUMN DATA
00C4                   *
00C4                   *****(STEP 5)
00C4                   *
00C4 3A 01 10          LDA   CFLAG     INPUT THE CFLAG DATA
00C7 FE 00             CPI   00        CFLAG=0??
00C9 C2 B2 00          JNZ   KOPN      KEY NOT RELEASED YET
00CC                   *
00CC                   *****(STEP 9)
00CC                   *
00CC 3A 05 10          LDA   NROW      INPUT THE ACTIVE ROW
00CF 3C                INR   A
00D0 32 05 10          STA   NROW      UPDATE THE ACTIVE ROW
00D3                   *
00D3                   *****(STEP 10)
00D3                   *
00D3 FE 05             CPI   05
00D5 C2 BE 00          JNZ   KOPN1     NOT A COMPLETE SCAN
00D8                   *
00D8                   *****(STEP 6)
00D8                   *
00D8 3A 00 10          LDA   KTIME
00DB 3C                INR   A
00DC 32 00 10          STA   KTIME
00DF 47                MOV   B,A       B REG=KTIME
00E0                   *
00E0                   ******(STEP 6A)
00E0                   *
00E0 AF                XRA   A
00E1 32 05 10          STA   NROW      ROW VALUE =0
00E4                   *
00E4                   *****(STEP 7)
00E4                   *
00E4 3E 32             MVI   A,50
00E6 B8                CMP   B         KTIME=50???
00E7 C2 BE 00          JNZ   KOPN1     NO, TRY ANOTHER SCAN
00EA                   *
00EA                   ******(STEP 8)
00EA                   *
00EA C9                RET             RETURN FROM THIS OPEN ROUTINE
00EB                   *
00EB                   *
00EB                   ****************************************************************
00EB                   *
00EB                   *    SUBROUTINE KOUT
00EB                   *
00EB                   *  THIS SUBROUTINE WILL OUTPUT THE KEY TO THE DISPLAY
```

```
00EB                 *
00EB                 ***************************************************************
00EB                 *
00EB 3A 02 10 KOUT   LDA   KWGHT     VALUE OF KEY IN ACC
00EE D3 F0           OUT   0F0H
00F0 D3 F1           OUT 0F1H
00F2 D3 F2           OUT 0F2H
00F4 C9              RET
00F5                 *
00F5                 ***************************************************************
00F5                 *
00F5                 *  SUBROUTINE KEYW
00F5                 *
00F5                 *  THIS SUBROUTINE WILL COMPUTE THE VALUE OF THE KEY PUSHED
00F5                 *
00F5                 ***************************************************************
00F5                 *
00F5                 ***** THIS ROUTINE IS FROM FIGURE 4-18
00F5                 *
00F5                 ******(STEP 1)
00F5                 *
00F5 AF       KEYW    XRA   A           ZERO FLAGS AND ACC
00F6 3A 01 10        LDA   CFLAG     GET COLUMN FLAG FROM MEM
00F9                 *
00F9                 *****(STEP 2)
00F9                 *
00F9 06 00           MVI   B,00      ZERO THE COUNTER
00FB                 *
00FB                 ****(STEP 3)
00FB                 *
00FB 1F       KEYW1 RAR              SHIFT RIGHT 1 BIT,0 INTO D7
00FC FE 00           CPI   00
00FE                 *
00FE                 ****(STEP 4)
00FE                 *
00FE CA 05 01        JZ   KEYW2      BREG=0,1,2,3,4 (STEP 6)
0101                 *
0101                 *****(STEP 5)
0101                 *
0101 04              INR   B
0102 C3 FB 00        JMP   KEYW1     INCREMENT COUNTER GO AGAIN
0105                 *
0105                 *****(STEP 7)
0105                 *
0105 AF       KEYW2 XRA   A          ZERO THE FLAGS
0106 3A 04 10        LDA   KROW      RECALL ACTIVE ROW
0109                 *
0109                 *****(STEP 8)
0109                 *
0109 0E 00           MVI   C,00      ZERO THE COUNTER T2
010B                 *
010B                 ******(STEP 9)
010B                 *
010B 1F       KEYW3 RAR              SHIFT RIGHT 1 BIT,0 INTO D7
010C FE 00           CPI   00
010E                 *
010E                 *******(STEP 10)
010E                 *
010E CA 15 01        JZ   KEYW4      IF ZERO THEN DONE
0111                 *
```

```
0111            *****(STEP 14)
0111            *
0111 0C                 INR   C        INCREMENT THE COUNTER
0112 C3 0B 01           JMP   KEYW3    GO AGAIN
0115            *
0115            *****(STEP 11)
0115            *
0115 AF         KEYW4 XRA   A          ZERO THE FLAGS
0116 78               MOV   A,B        ACC=COLUMN COUNT(T1)
0117 17               RAL              B*2
0118 17               RAL              B*4
0119 80               ADD B            B*5
011A 81               ADD C            (B*5)+C=0 - 24
011B            *
011B            *******(STEP 12)
011B            *
011B 32 02 10         STA   KWGHT
011E            *
011E            *******(STEP 13)
011E            *
011E C9               RET              RETURN FROM THIS SUBROUTINE
011F            *
011F            ***********************************************************
011F            *
011F            *  COLM SUBROUTINE
011F            *
011F            *   THIS SUBROUTINE WILL DETERMINE THE ACTIVE COLUMN
011F            *   IF THERE IS ONE.
011F            *
011F            ***********************************************************
011F            *
011F            *   THIS SUBROUTINE IS FIGURE 4-15
011F            *
011F            ***********************************************************
011F            *
011F            ******(STEP 1)
011F            *
011F AF         COLM  XRA   A
0120 32 01 10         STA   CFLAG      SET THE COLUMN FLAG=0
0123            *
0123            ******(STEP 2)
0123            *
0123 DB FE            IN    0FEH       INPUT DATA FROM PORT FE
0125            *
0125            ******(STEP 3)
0125            *
0125 F6 E0            ORI   0E0H       SET BITS D5,D6,D7=1
0127            *
0127            *******(STEP 4)
0127            *
0127 FE FF            CPI   0FFH
0129 C8               RZ               STEP(4A)
012A            *
012A            *****(STEP 5)
012A            *
012A 2F               CMA              INVERT THE DATA
012B            *
012B            ******(STEP 6)
012B            *
012B 32 01 10         STA   CFLAG      SET THE COLUMN FLAG
```

```
012E C9                RET            RETURN FROM THIS SUB
012F                *
012F                ***************************************************************
012F                *
012F                * SUBROUTINE TO OUTPUT THE ACTIVE ROW TO THE KEYBOARD
012F                *
012F                *  OROW IS THE NAME OF THIS SUBROUTINE
012F                *
012F                *  THIS IS FIGURE 4-12
012F                *
012F                ***************************************************************
012F                ***************************************************************
012F                *
012F                *  FIGURE  4-12     8080 MNEMONICS FOR FIGURE 4-10
012F                *
012F                ***************************************************************
012F                *
012F                *
012F 3A 04 10 OROW  LDA KROW   RECALL ACTIVE ROW
0132                *
0132                * STEP  2
0132                *
0132 FE 10             CPI   10H      COMPLETE ROW SCAN????
0134 C2 3C 01          JNZ   OROW1    IF NOT THEN STEP 2B
0137                *
0137                * STEP  2A
0137                *
0137 3E 01             MVI   A,01H    RESET THE ACTIVE ROW
0139 C3 3D 01          JMP   ST3      GOTO STEP 3
013C                *
013C                * STEP  2B
013C                *
013C 07             OROW1 RLC         SHIFT DATA LEFT,0 INTO D0
013D                *
013D                * STEP 3
013D                *
013D 32 04 10 ST3   STA   KROW     SAVE ACTIVE ROW IN MEM
0140                *
0140                *  STEP 4
0140                *
0140 2F                CMA            INVERT ROW WORD
0141                *
0141                * STEP 5
0141                *
0141 D3 FE             OUT 0FEH       OUTPUT ACTIVE ROW TO PORT FE
0143                *
0143                *STEP 6
0143                *
0143 C9                RET
0144                *
0144                *
0144                ***************************************************************
0144                ***************************************************************
0144                *
0144                *    SUBROUTINE ADDSE.  FIGURE 9-15
0144                *    THIS ROUTINE WILL INPUT A 3 DIGIT ADDRESS FROM THE
0144                *    THE KEYBOARD AND DISPLAY THE ADDRESS AND THE DATA
0144                *    STORED IN THE PROGRAM RAM AT THE DISPLAYED ADDRESS
0144                *
0144                ***************************************************************
```

```
Ø144                  *
Ø144 3E A3      ADDSE MVI  A,ØA3H
Ø146 D3 F2            OUT ØF2H
Ø148 AF               XRA  A
Ø149 D3 F1            OUT ØF1H
Ø14B D3 FØ            OUT ØFØH        SET DISPLAY = A3ØØØØ
Ø14D                  *
Ø14D                  *
Ø14D CD 64 ØØ         CALL KDET       GET THE FIRST NIBBLE FROM KEYBOARD
Ø15Ø 3A Ø2 1Ø         LDA  KWGHT      ACC=VALUE OF FIRST NIBBLE
Ø153 D3 FØ            OUT  ØFØH       DISPLAY THE FIRST DIGIT
Ø155 32 Ø7 1Ø         STA  AIN1       SAVE THE FIRST DIGIT
Ø158                  *
Ø158                  *
Ø158 CD 64 ØØ         CALL KDET       GET THE SECOND NIBBLE FROM KEYBOARD
Ø15B 3A Ø2 1Ø         LDA  KWGHT      ACC=SECOND NIBBLE
Ø15E 32 Ø8 1Ø         STA  AIN2       SAVE THE SECOND NIBBLE
Ø161 3A Ø7 1Ø         LDA  AIN1       GET THE FIRST NIBBLE FROM MEM
Ø164 17               RAL
Ø165 17               RAL
Ø166 17               RAL
Ø167 17               RAL             SHIFT LEFT 4 BITS
Ø168 E6 FØ            ANI  ØFØH       MASK OFF LOWER 4 BITS
Ø16A 32 ØA 1Ø         STA  AIN4       SAVE TEMP
Ø16D 3A Ø8 1Ø         LDA  AIN2       ACC =SECOND NIBBLE IN LOWER 4 BITS
Ø17Ø 21 ØA 1Ø         LXI  H,AIN4     SET H,L = TO MEM LOC AIN4
Ø173 B6               ORA  M          OR ACC WITH FIRST NIBBLE IN AIN4
Ø174 D3 FØ            OUT ØFØH        UPDATE THE DISPLAY  XXXX--
Ø176                  *
Ø176                  *
Ø176 CD 64 ØØ         CALL KDET       GET THE THIRD NIBBLE
Ø179 3A Ø2 1Ø         LDA  KWGHT      ACC=3RD NIBBLE
Ø17C 32 Ø9 1Ø         STA  AIN3       SAVE TEMP IN MEM
Ø17F 3A Ø8 1Ø         LDA  AIN2       RECALL SECOND NIBBLE
Ø182 17               RAL
Ø183 17               RAL
Ø184 17               RAL
Ø185 17               RAL             SHIFT THE NIBBLE LEFT 4 BITS
Ø186 E6 FØ            ANI ØFØH        MASK OFF THE LOWER 4 BITS
Ø188 21 Ø9 1Ø         LXI  H,AIN3
Ø18B B6               ORA  M          OR THE 2ND AND THIRD NIBBLE
Ø18C D3 F1            OUT  ØF1H       OUTPUT THE NIBBLE TO DISPLAY XX--XX
Ø18E 32 Ø8 1Ø         STA  AIN2       2ND AND 3RD NIBBLE IN AIN2
Ø191                  *
Ø191                  *
Ø191 AF               XRA  A
Ø192 D3 FØ            OUT  ØFØH       DISPLAY= XX--ØØ
Ø194                  *
Ø194                  *
Ø194 3A Ø7 1Ø         LDA  AIN1       RECALL THE FIRST MSN
Ø197 D3 F2            OUT  ØF2H       DISPLAY=ØXXXØØ WHERE XXX=ADDRESS
Ø199                  *
Ø199                  *
Ø199                  * NOW TO READ DATA FROM THE MEMORY LOCATION
Ø199                  * UPPER ADDRESS=AIN1, LOWER ADDRESS=AIN2
Ø199                  *
Ø199 21 ØØ 14         LXI H,14ØØH     H,L=STARTING ADDRESS OF RAM
Ø19C 3A Ø8 1Ø         LDA  AIN2
Ø19F 5F               MOV  E,A
Ø1AØ 3A Ø7 1Ø         LDA  AIN1
```

```
Ø1A3 57                 MOV  D,A       D,E= THE ADDRESS OF RAM
Ø1A4 D5                 PUSH D         SAVE VALUE
Ø1A5 19                 DAD  D         H,L=OFFSET +STARTING ADDRESS
Ø1A6             *
Ø1A6             *
Ø1A6 7E          NRED   MOV  A,M       LOAD ACC WITH DATA FROM RAM
Ø1A7 D3 FØ              OUT ØFØH       SET DISPLAY =ØXXXDD  WHERE DD=DATA
Ø1A9             *
Ø1A9             *
Ø1A9             *   WE HAVE JUST FINISHED STEP 4 OF THE FLOW CHART
Ø1A9             *
Ø1A9             *
Ø1A9 E5                 PUSH H         SAVE THE ADDRESS
Ø1AA CD 64 ØØ           CALL KDET      GET THE NEXT KEY PUSH
Ø1AD 3A Ø2 1Ø           LDA KWGHT      ACC=KEY VALUE
Ø1BØ FE 11              CPI  17        CLEAR KEY ???
Ø1B2 CA FD Ø1           JZ   ADEX      YES GOT TO EXIT OF THIS ROUTINE
Ø1B5 FE 1Ø              CPI  16        ENTER KEY ??
Ø1B7 CA EF Ø1           JZ   STP8      YES GOTO STEP 8 OF FLOW CHART
Ø1BA             *
Ø1BA             *
Ø1BA             *   WE NEED TO GET 2 NEW NIBBLES FOR NEW DATA IN RAM
Ø1BA             *
Ø1BA CD 64 ØØ    TNIB   CALL KDET      GET THE FIRST NIBBLE
Ø1BD 3A Ø2 1Ø           LDA  KWGHT     ACC=KEY VALUE
Ø1CØ 32 ØA 1Ø           STA  AIN4      TEMP SAVE
Ø1C3 D3 FØ              OUT  ØFØH      UP DATA THE DISPLAY
Ø1C5 CD 64 ØØ           CALL KDET      GET THE NEXT NIBBLE
Ø1C8 3A Ø2 1Ø           LDA  KWGHT
Ø1CB             *
Ø1CB 32 Ø9 1Ø           STA  AIN3      SAVE TEMP IN MEM
Ø1CE 3A ØA 1Ø           LDA  AIN4      RECALL FIRST NIBBLE
Ø1D1 17                 RAL
Ø1D2 17                 RAL
Ø1D3 17                 RAL
Ø1D4 17                 RAL            SHIFT LEFT 4 BITS
Ø1D5 21 Ø9 1Ø           LXI  H,AIN3
Ø1D8 B6                 ORA  M         OR THE FIRST AND SECOND NIBBLE
Ø1D9 32 Ø9 1Ø           STA  AIN3      SAVE THE DATA IN MEM
Ø1DC D3 FØ              OUT  ØFØH      UPDATE THE DISPLAY
Ø1DE             *
Ø1DE             *
Ø1DE             *   NOW TO CHECK IF THIS DATA IS OK
Ø1DE             *
Ø1DE CD 64 ØØ           CALL KDET      GET THE KEY
Ø1E1 3A Ø2 1Ø           LDA  KWGHT     ACC= KEY VALUE
Ø1E4 FE 1Ø              CPI  16        ENTER KEY???
Ø1E6 C2 BA Ø1           JNZ  TNIB      NO ASK FOR THE NEW DATA AGAIN
Ø1E9             *
Ø1E9             *
Ø1E9             *   NOW TO WRITE THE DATA INTO THE MEMORY
Ø1E9             *
Ø1E9 3A Ø9 1Ø           LDA  AIN3      RECALL THE DATA
Ø1EC E1                 POP  H         RESTORE THE MEM ADDRESS
Ø1ED 77                 MOV  M,A       DATA TO MEM
Ø1EE E5                 PUSH H
Ø1EF             *
Ø1EF             *
Ø1EF E1          STP8   POP  H
Ø1FØ 23                 INX  H         INCREMENT THE ADDRESS
```

```
01F1 D1                 POP   D          RESTORE THE RAM ADDRESS
01F2 13                 INX   D
01F3 D5                 PUSH  D          SAVE THE VALUE
01F4 7B                 MOV   A,E
01F5 D3 F1              OUT   0F1H       UPDATE THE ADDRESS IN DISPLAY
01F7 7A                 MOV   A,D
01F8 D3 F2              OUT   0F2H       UPDATE THE ADDRESS IN DISPLAY
01FA C3 A6 01           JMP   NRED       START THE OPERATION OVER
01FD           *
01FD           *
01FD E1        ADEX     POP   H
01FE D1                 POP   D
01FF C3 03 00           JMP   BEGIN      GO TO START OF THE CONTROL SECTION
0202            *
0202           *
0202           *
0202           *
0202           **********************************************************
0202           *
0202           *   THIS IS CLEAR RAM SUBROUTINE
0202           *
0202           *   FIGURE 9-17
0202           **********************************************************
0202 3E FF     CLRAM MVI   A,0FFH     ACC=FF
0204 21 00 14           LXI   H,1400H    SET H,L TO STARTING RAM ADD
0207 77        CL1      MOV   M,A        FF TO MEMORY
0208 F5                 PUSH  PSW        SAVE ACC
0209 3E 17              MVI   A,17H
020B BC                 CMP   H          CHECK FOR UPPER BYTE LIMIT
020C CA 14 02           JZ LCHK          YES CHECK FOR LOWER BYTE LIMIT
020F F1                 POP   PSW        RESTORE ACC
0210 23                 INX   H          INCREMENT RAM ADDRESS
0211 C3 07 02           JMP   CL1        DO THE NEXT ADDRESS
0214 F1        LCHK     POP   PSW        RESTORE THE ACC
0215 BD                 CMP   L          CHECK FOR LOWER BYTE=FF
0216 CA 03 00           JZ    BEGIN      END OF THIS SUBROUTINE
0219 23                 INX   H          NOT END INCREMENT ADDRESS
021A C3 07 02           JMP   CL1        GO AGAIN AT A DIFFERENT ADDRESS
021D           *
021D           *
021D           *
021D           **********************************************************
021D           *
021D           *  ROUTINE PROGRAM FOR THE PROG COMMAND
021D           *  THIS ROUTINE WILL PERFORM THE ELECTRICAL FUNCTION
021D           *  OF PROGRAMMING THE 2708 EPROM.  THE RAM DATA IS
021D           *  STORED AT MEMORY LOCATION 1400H.  THE EPROM ADDRESS
021D           *  WILL START AT LOCATION 0000.
021D           *
021D           *
021D           **********************************************************
021D           *
021D           *
021D 3E DD     PROG     MVI   A,0DDH
021F D3 F0              OUT   0F0H
0221 D3 F1              OUT   0F1H
0223 D3 F2              OUT   0F2H       SET DISPLAY TO DDDDDD
0225 3E 00              MVI   A,00
0227 D3 32              OUT   32H        ENABLE THE DATA TO PROM
0229 32 06 10           STA   CNT1       ZERO THE LOOP COUNTER
```

```
022C 3C                  INR   A
022D D3 34               OUT   34H       CS/WE = 12 VOLTS
022F                   *
022F 11 00 00    PROG3 LXI   D,0000H   SET THE PROM ADDRESS
0232 21 00 14          LXI   H,1400H   SET THE RAM ADDRESS
0235                   *
0235 7E          PROG2 MOV   A,M       DATA FROM RAM  TO ACC
0236 D3 30             OUT   30H       DATA TO PROM
0238 7B                MOV   A,E       A0-A7 TO ACC
0239 D3 33             OUT   33H       A0-A7 TO PROM
023B 7A                MOV   A,D       A8-A9 TO ACC
023C D3 34             OUT   34H       A8-A9 TO PROM
023E                   *
023E                   * NOW TO APPLY THE PROGRAMMING PULSE
023E                   *
023E 06 08             MVI   B,08
0240 3E 03             MVI   A,03
0242 D3 35             OUT   35H       TURN ON CS/WE AND PROG PULSE
0244 05          PULSE DCR   B
0245 C2 44 02          JNZ   PULSE     PULSE WIDTH
0248 3E 01             MVI   A,01
024A D3 35             OUT   35H       TURN OFF PROG PULSE
024C                   *
024C                   * NOW TO CHECK IF LAST ADDRESS PROGRAMMED
024C                   *
024C 7B                MOV   A,E
024D FE FF             CPI   0FFH      LAST BYTE A0-A7
024F C2 58 02          JNZ   PROG1
0252 7A                MOV   A,D
0253 FE 03             CPI   03        LAST BYTE A8-A9
0255 CA 5D 02          JZ    LOPC      LAST ADDRESS (YES)
0258 23          PROG1 INX   H
0259 13                INX   D         BUMP THE RAM AND PROM ADDRESS
025A C3 35 02          JMP   PROG2     DO THE NEXT ADDRESS
025D                   *
025D                   * NOW TO CHECK IF LAST TIME THROUGH THE 1024 ADDRESSES
025D                   *
025D 3A 06 10    LOPC  LDA   CNT1      GET THE COUNT
0260 3C                INR   A
0261 32 06 10          STA   CNT1
0264 FE C8             CPI   200       200 LOOPS YET ??
0266 C2 2F 02          JNZ   PROG3     NOT 200 LOOPS START OVER
0269                   *
0269                   *  FINISHED PROGRAMMING NOW TO VERIFY
0269                   *
0269 3E 01             MVI A,01        DISABLE DATA TO PROM
026B D3 32             OUT 32H
026D 3D                DCR   A         ACC=0
026E D3 35             OUT 35H         CS/WE = 0.0 V
0270                   *
0270                   * INITIALIZE THE ADDRESS OF PROM AND RAM
0270                   *
0270 11 00 00          LXI   D,00
0273 21 78 05          LXI   H,1400    RAM ADDRESS
0276                   *
0276 7B          PROG4 MOV   A,E       A0-A7 TO ACC
0277 D3 33             OUT   33H       ADDRESS TO PROM
0279 7A                MOV   A,D       A8-A9 TO ACC
027A D3 34             OUT   34H       A8-A9 TO PROM
027C DB 31             IN   31H        READ THE PROM DATA TO ACC
```

```
027E BE                  CMP  M         CHECK FOR VALID DATA IN PROM
027F C2 93 02            JNZ  PROGF     NOT EQUAL FAIL
0282               *
0282               * IF HERE THEN PASSED AT ABOVE LOCATION
0282               *
0282               * NOW TO CHECK FOR LAST ADDRESS
0282               *
0282 7B                  MOV  A,E
0283 FE FF               CPI  0FFH      LAST A0-A7?
0285 C2 8E 02            JNZ  PROG5     NOT LAST ONE
0288 7A                  MOV  A,D       A8-A9 LAST
0289 FE 03               CPI  03
028B CA 03 00            JZ  BEGIN      LAST ONE START NEW COMMAND
028E               *
028E               * INCREMENT THE RAM AND PROM ADDRESS
028E               *
028E 23            PROG5 INX  H
028F 13                  INX  D
0290 C3 76 02            JMP  PROG4     NEXT ADDRESS FOR COMPARE
0293               *
0293               * THIS IS THE FAIL SECTION
0293               *
0293 7B            PROGF MOV  A,E       A0-A7 TO ACC
0294 D3 F0               OUT  0F0H
0296 7A                  MOV  A,D       A8-A9 TO ACC
0297 D3 F1               OUT  0F1H       TO DISPLAY
0299 DB 31               IN   31H       GET PROM DATA
029B D3 F2               OUT  0F2H      TO DISPLAY
029D               *
029D               * NOW TO LOOP UNTIL CE KEY HIT
029D               *
029D CD 64 00      PROG6 CALL KDET
02A0 3A 02 10            LDA  KWGHT
02A3 FE 16               CPI  16H       IS THE KEY CLEAR ENTRY??
02A5 C2 9D 02            JNZ  PROG6
02A8 C3 03 00            JMP  BEGIN     RETURN AND DO ANOTHER COMMAND
02AB               *
02AB               ************************* **********************************
02AB               *
02AB               *  FIGURE 9-21  PROGRAM TO REALIZE THE FLOW CHART OF
02AB               *  THE FIGURE 20.
02AB               *
02AB               ***********************************************************
02AB               *
02AB               *
02AB               *  SET UP THE PROM TO BE READ
02AB               *
02AB AF            VFY    XRA  A
02AC 3C                   INR  A
02AD D3 32                OUT 32H       ENABLE THE DRIVERS IN THE RIGHT DIRECTIO
02AF AF                   XRA  A
02B0 D3 35                OUT   35H     CS=0,0V,PGM=0,0V
02B2 D3 33                OUT   33H     ADDRESS A0-A7=0
02B4 D3 34                OUT   34H     ADDRESS A8-A9=0
02B6 11 00 00             LXI   D,0000  SET UP PROM ADDRESS
02B9 21 00 14             LXI   H,1400H RAM ADDRESS OFFSET
02BC               *
02BC               *  NOW TO START THE READ AND VERIFY LOOP
02BC               *
02BC DB 31         VFY1   IN   31H      READ THE PROM DATA
```

```
02BE BE                CMP M          PROM DATA =RAM DATA??
02BF C2 DC 02          JNZ  VFAIL     VFAIL IF NOT EQUAL
02C2 3E 13             MVI  A,13H
02C4 BA                CMP  D         UPPER BYTE MATCH, LAST ADDRESS
02C5 C2 D1 02          JNZ  VNEX      NO MATCH GET NEXT ADDRESS
02C8 3E FF             MVI  A,0FFH
02CA BB                CMP  E         LOWER BYTE MATCH??
02CB C2 D1 02          JNZ  VNEX      NO, GET THE NEXT ADDRESS
02CE C3 03 00          JMP  BEGIN     BACK TO MAIN PROGRAM..PASS
02D1 13          VNEX  INX  D
02D2 7A                MOV  A,D       NEW PROM ADDRESS
02D3 D3 34             OUT  34H       DATA TO HARDWARE
02D5 7B                MOV  A,E
02D6 D3 33             OUT  33H       DATA TO HARDWARE
02D8 23                INX  H         NEW RAM ADDRESS
02D9 C3 BC 02          JMP  VFY1      COMPARE THE NEXT DATA
02DC D3 F0       VFAIL OUT  0F0H      SET DISPLAY----XX
02DE 7B                MOV  A,E
02DF D3 F1             OUT  0F1H      LOWER ADDRESS TO DISPLAY
02E1 7A                MOV  A,D
02E2 D3 F2             OUT  0F2H      UPPER ADDRESS TO DISPLAY
02E4 CD 64 00    VOUT  CALL KDET      GET A KEY
02E7 3A 02 10          LDA  KWGHT
02EA FE 16             CPI  16H       IS IT THE CE KEY??
02EC CA 03 00          JZ   BEGIN
02EF C2 E4 02          JNZ  VOUT      WAIT UNTIL THE KEY IS PUSHED
02F2                   *
02F2                   *
02F2                   ***********************************************************
02F2                   *
02F2                   *  FIGURE 9-23  PROGRAM TO REALIZE THE COPY FLOWCHART
02F2                   *  OF FIGURE 9-22
02F2                   *
02F2                   *
02F2                   ***********************************************************
02F2                   *
02F2                   *
02F2                   *  SET UP THE PROM TO READ DATA
02F2                   *
02F2 AF          COPY  XRA  A
02F3 3C                INR  A         ACC=1
02F4 D3 32             OUT  32H
02F6 AF                XRA  A
02F7 D3 35             OUT  35H       CS=0.0V,PGM=0.0V
02F9 11 00 00          LXI  D,0000    PROM ADDRESS=0
02FC 21 00 14          LXI  H,1400H   SET THE RAM OFFSET ADD
02FF 7B          COPY1 MOV  A,E
0300 D3 33             OUT  33H       ADDRESS A0-A7 SET
0302 7A                MOV  A,D
0303 D3 34             OUT  34H       ADDRESS A8-A9 SET
0305 DB 31             IN   31H       READ THE DATA FROM THE PROM
0307 77                MOV  M,A       OUTPUT THE DATA TO RAM
0308 3E 13             MVI  A,13H
030A BA                CMP  D         CHECK FOR LAST ADDRESS
030B C2 14 03          JNZ  CNEX      CNEX IF NOT LAST ADDRESS
030E 3E FF             MVI  A,0FFH
0310 BB                CMP  E         LAST ADDRESS LOWER BYTE
0311 CA 03 00          JZ   BEGIN     IF LAST ADDRESS.. THE END
0314 23          CNEX  INX  H         NEXT RAM ADDRESS
0315 13                INX  D         NEXT PROM ADDRESS
0316 C3 FF 02          JMP  COPY1     GET THE NEXT DATA
0319                   *
0319                   END            END STATEMENT FOR THE ASSEMBLER

    0 ERRORS              60 SYMBOLS
```

10

DEBUGGING THE SYSTEM HARDWARE

In this chapter we will discuss different concepts for trouble-shooting and debugging a microprocessor-controlled system. The system we will discuss will be the PROM programmer described in Chapters 8 and 9. The techniques for trouble-shooting will be similar to those discussed in Chapter 5. We will show exactly how we can verify the hardware operation of a particular system.

We will again discuss debugging the system hardware via a technique known as static stimulus testing. This debugging method provides a solid, direct approach to hardware trouble-shooting that is powerful and effective, yet relatively inexpensive. Because of its basic simplicity and other advantages over dynamic testing for most hardware problems, we shall again discuss the concept and application of static stimulus testing at some length.

10-1 Static Stimulus Testing

We introduced the concept of static stimulus testing in Chapter 5. Static stimulus testing was used to "checkout" or debug the initial system hardware. In this chapter, static stimulus testing is again used to debug the hardware of the PROM programmer system. Before we install the microprocessor in the system, by using this procedure we can insure that all hardware of the input/output circuits and memory is functioning properly.

The static stimulus tester we will use is shown in Figure 10-1. Before we explain exactly how to checkout the 8085 system with the static stimulus tester, let us briefly review some important points concerning static stimulus testing. The

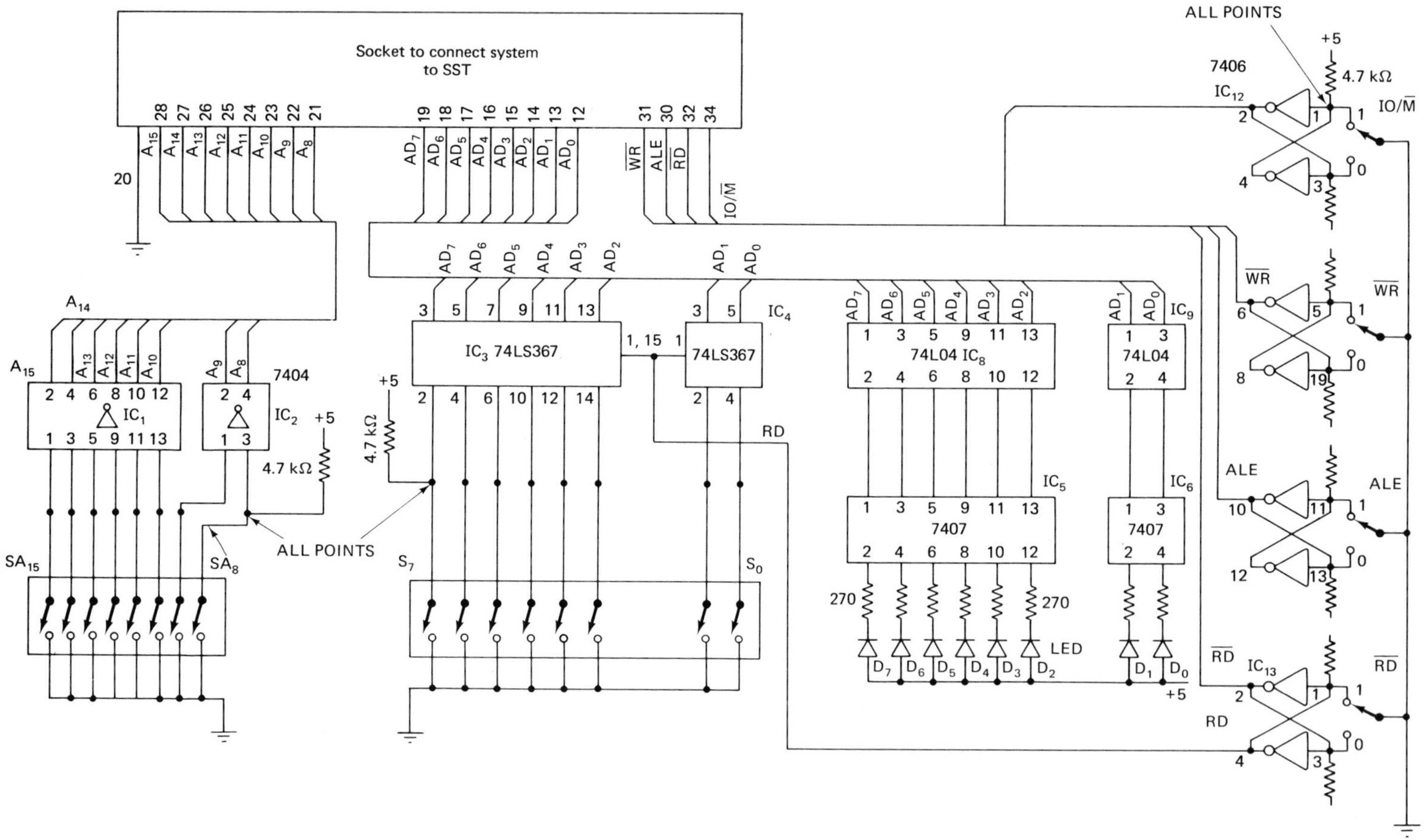

Figure 10-1 Complete schematic for the 8085 Static Stimulus Tester.

first point is that *the hardware of the static stimulus tester is simple*. The static stimulus tester can be constructed by using standard logic devices. From Figure 10-1 we see that only five different ICs are used in the construction of a static stimulus tester.

The second point about static stimulus testing is that *it is extremely easy to use*. We recall that the SST implements system control in the same way that the microprocessor does. In order to use the SST we need only to understand how the microprocessor controls the system hardware.

The third point about the SST is the fact that *it can be "tailored" to fit an individual system's needs*. Since the hardware is simple, we can modify the SST to perform any special function that is unique to an individual system. The user can put as many "bells and whistles" on the SST as desired. This point is emphasized by the fact that an automated version of the SST for any of the microprocessors discussed in this text is available from CMS.*

10-2 The 8085 Static Stimulus Tester

Let us now discuss the operation of the SST shown in Figure 10-1. We will examine in detail the function of each component in the circuit. Referring to Figure 10-1, we notice the switches SA_{15}–SA_8. These eight switches are SPST toggle switches. One side of each switch is connected to ground. The other side of each switch is connected to a 4.7 Ω pull-up resistor, as shown in Figure 1-10 for SA_8 only.

The toggle switches are the inputs to IC_1 and IC_2 of Figure 10-1. The output of the 7404 IC_1 and IC_2 are the A_{15}–A_8 address outputs for the 8085. When the toggle switches are open, the input pin to IC_1 or IC_2 is logical 1. This logical 1 is the result of the input being pulled up to +5 volts via the 4.7k Ω resistor. When the toggle switches are closed, the input to IC_1 or IC_2 is connected to ground. This corresponds to a logical 0 input.

The operation of the switches SA_{15}–SA_8 can be summed up as follows. In one position the switches produce a logical 1 on the respective output pins of IC_1 or IC_2. In the other position the switches produce a logical 0 on the respective output pins of IC_1 or IC_2. In this way we can force, stimulate, or set the address output lines A_{15}–A_8 to logical 0 or logical 1 whenever we wish. The output level we have set will be input to the system in exactly the same manner the 8085 would output the address lines. The one important exception is that we may leave the logic level at the address output pin for *as long as we desire* (static) for debugging purposes.

The next portion of the SST that we will discuss is the data output section. This section is excerpted from Figure 10-1 and is shown in Figure 10-2. Notice that the switches S_0–S_7 are connected in exactly the same fashion as the switches

*Creative Microprocessor Systems, Inc., P.O. Box 1538, Los Gatos, CA 95030

SA_{15}–SA_8 we discussed earlier. These switches S_0–S_7 are inputs to the 74LS367 IC_3, IC_4. This IC was chosen because we must use some type of tri-state device for the data output. A tri-state device is necessary because sometimes the data must be input to the SST. This case is exactly the same as when data are being input to the 8085. When data is input to the 8085 the data pins become inputs. Therefore, we must disable the data out drivers 74LS367 IC_3, IC_4 on the SST during a read operation by the SST to avoid interfering with the data input function.

Disabling of the data out drivers is accomplished via the control signal labeled RD. Notice that RD is shown as a line at right in Figure 10-2. Later in our discussion we will show where this signal originates. For now it is important to

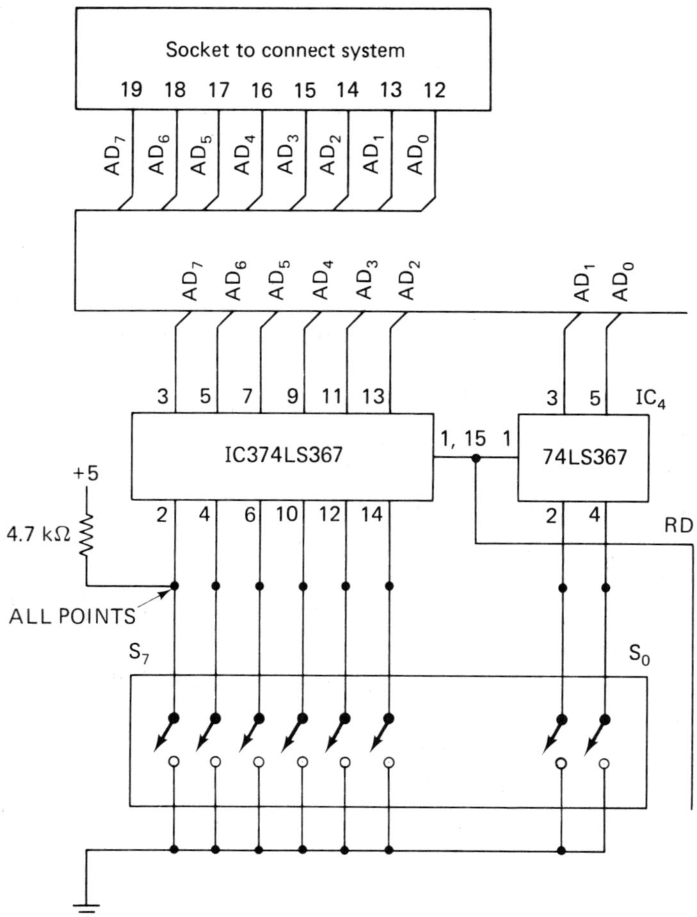

Figure 10-2 Partial schematic excerpted from Figure 10-1. This portion shows the data output section of the 8085 SST.

understand that the data out drivers must be disabled during a read operation of the SST.

During a read operation with the SST, data are input to the SST from the system under test. In order to verify that the data input is correct, the SST has LED indicators. The circuit for the LED indicators is shown in Figure 10-3. Notice that IC_8 and IC_9, 74L04, have each of their inputs connected to a unique line of the data bus. The logic level present on the data lines is then reflected by the LEDs shown in the figure.

When the input to IC_8 and IC_9 is logical 1, the output of the corresponding 74L04 is logical 0. The output of the 74L04 is connected to the input of the 7407, IC_5 and IC_6, which is an open collector buffer. If the input to the 7407 is logical 0, the output is logical 0. We recall from our knowledge of open collector devices that the output structure of the 7407 is as shown in Figure 10-4.

There we see that if the output of the 7407 is logical 0, the transistor is turned on. This provides a current path to ground from the collector to the emitter. Referring again to Figure 10-3 we see that the LED has the anode connected to +5 volts and the cathode connected through a 270-ohm resistor to the output of the 7407. When the output of the 7407 is logical 0, the resistor is connected

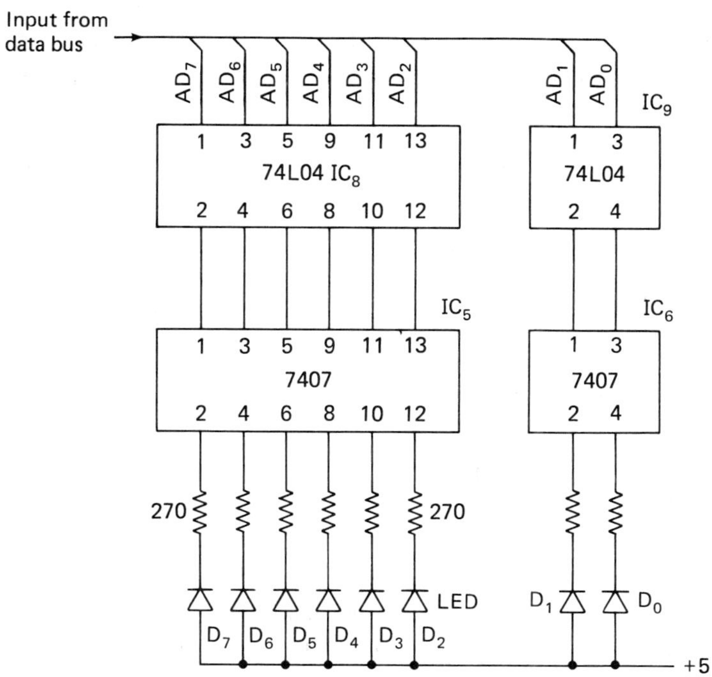

Figure 10-3 Partial schematic excerpted from Figure 10-1. This portion shows the LED output section of the 8085 SST.

effectively to ground. This causes current to flow through the LED from the +5-Volt supply to the anode and out the cathode. Under these conditions the LED becomes forward biased and lights up.

When the output of the 7407, IC_5 and IC_6, is logical 1, the transistor of Figure 10-4 is off. This causes the resistor connected to the collector to be disconnected from ground. Under these conditions there is no current flow in the LED, and the LED turns off.

From the preceding discussion we see that the LED is on when logical 1 is present on the respective line of the data bus. The LED is off when logical 0 is present on the respective line of the data bus. In this way we can obtain a visual indication of the logical condition present on the data bus at any time.

Note here that internally the SST has a 74L04 as an input from the data bus. This is seen in Figure 10-3. We may ask: Why use an inverter as an input and then use a 7407? Why not use a 7406 to realize the function of the 74L04 and the 7407? The answer is this: The 74L04 has an input current of 0.1 milliampere in logical 0 state and 4 microamperes in logical 1 state. This current must be sunk and sourced by the output controlling the data bus.

In effect, the input of whatever device we use in the SST is an additional load on the data bus. For a monitor the additional load should be as small as possible. If we realize the input monitor with the 7406, we would induce a greater load on the system data bus than with the 74L04. The 7406 has an input current of 1.6 mA in logical 0 state and 40 mA in logical 1 state. Thus, by using

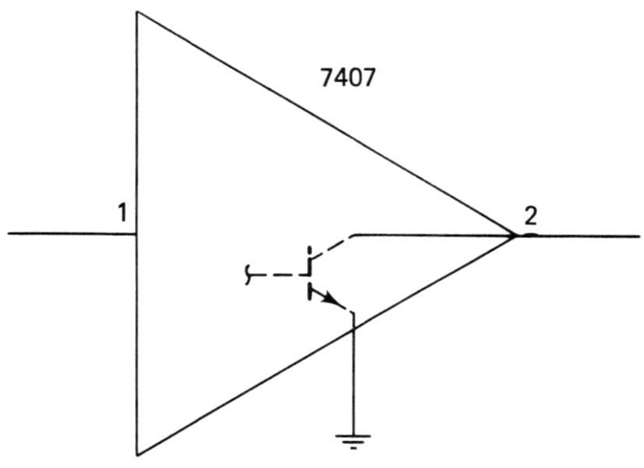

Figure 10-4 Block diagram of the 7407 showing the output transistor that will sync the current that is required to turn on the LED.

the 74L04 and 7407 instead of a single 7406 the loading effect of the SST on the data bus is reduced by a factor of 10. The trade-off between additional circuitry and reduced loading is well worth it in this case.

Notice from Figure 10-3 that the LEDs always monitor and display the logical condition of the data bus lines. This display monitors both during a READ operation and during a WRITE operation. During READ the "system" data is displayed by the LEDs. During WRITE the SST data out is displayed. This is possible because we disable the data out drivers, IC_3 and IC_4, during a READ operation.

Let us examine how the data out drivers are disabled during a READ operation. In the schematic of Figure 10-5 we show the section of the SST that is used to manipulate the logic levels of certain control output pins of the 8085. These specific pins are labeled $\overline{RD}$, $\overline{WR}$, $IO/\overline{M}$, ALE. There are other control output pins on the 8085 such as S_0 and S_1; however, we chose not to use these pins in our system. If other 8085 control pins are used in a system we design or build, then we would want to provide a similar means for controlling the logical state with an SST.

When we contemplate the electrical events that occur during a READ operation of the 8085, one of the main events is the assertion of the $\overline{RD}$ signal. When the $\overline{RD}$ signal on the 8085 goes to logical 0, the 8085 is performing either a memory read or an input device read. The logical state of the $IO/\overline{M}$ signal determines which. This information also indicates to the SST that when $\overline{RD}$ goes to logical 0 the data out drivers IC_3 and IC_4 must be disabled.

The 74LS367 is tri-stated, or disabled, when input pins 1 and 15 are logical 1. This means we must force these input pins of the 74LS367 to logical 1 whenever the $\overline{RD}$ signal is logical 0. We can accomplish this by connecting disable pins 1 and 15 of IC_3 and IC_4 in Figure 10-2 to the RD signal shown in Figure 10-5. This connection is made whenever $\overline{RD}$ is logical 0, indicating a READ operation for the 8085 SST; the LEDs reflect the data being input to the microprocessor.

The control signals for the SST are all connected to an anti-bounce latch circuit, as shown in Figure 10-6. This circuit is used so that mechanical switch bounce can be eliminated from all control signal outputs. A natural question at this point might be: Why not use anti-bounce circuits on all switches? The answer is that the address and data lines of the microprocessor have no effect on the system communication until the communication is qualified by the control signals. It is really the control signals that strobe the data into external circuits. We want only one strobe signal per toggle of the switch. We could install anti-bounce circuits on all switches if we wish, but it is an unnecessary addition of hardware.

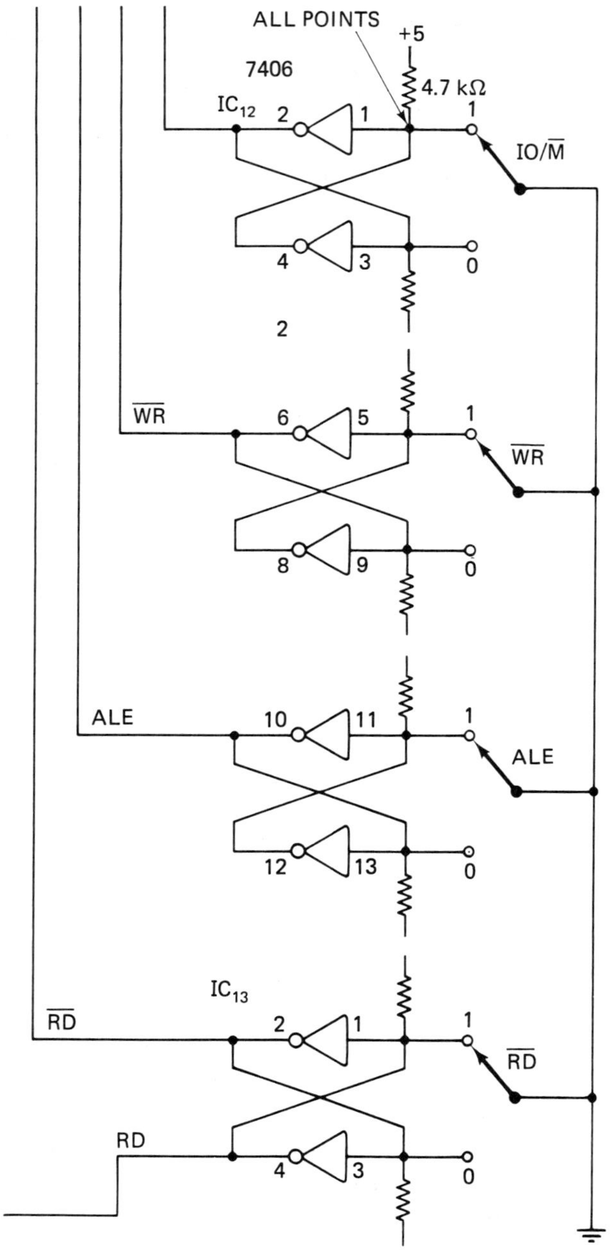

Figure 10-5 Partial schematic excerpted from Figure 10-1. This portion shows the section of the SST used to manipulate the logic level of the control bits for the 8085.

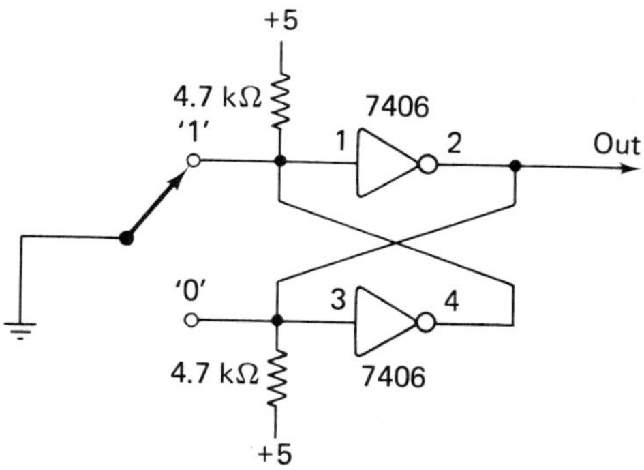

Figure 10-6 Schematic showing how an anti-bounce circuit can be constructed by using two 7406 open collector inverters.

10-3 Comments on System Hardware Debugging

Now that we have seen the details of SST circuitry, let us give an overview of the approach to be used for effective system hardware debugging. The main idea behind our approach is this: We want to determine if all logic communication paths in the system are valid. At this point in our hardware debugging we are not concerned about timing parameters. We are just trying to determine if it is electrically possible for the microprocessor to communicate with all logic devices required in the system. If we can verify this, then we will have made great progress in the overall system hardware debugging.

Static stimulus testing provides the means by which all of the electrical communication paths within the system can be verified. This is part of the elegance associated with static stimulus testing. We do not have to design special test circuits to be used with a specific test setup into the microprocessor system initially. Further, the basics of static stimulus testing can be realized with hardware for very minimal cost. This allows virtually anyone who is trouble-shooting or designing microprocessor-based systems to obtain a powerful debugging aid.

In using the SST we connect it to the system under test via cable, as shown in Chapter 5. We then proceed, in a straightforward and orderly manner, to check the *entire* system hardware. Here, we are using the SST as a means for debugging an 8085-based system. However, enough details have been given to construct an SST for checking out virtually any microprocessor system.*

*Complete schematics for SST circuits for the 8085, 8080, Z80, and 6800 microprocessors are given in the appendix.

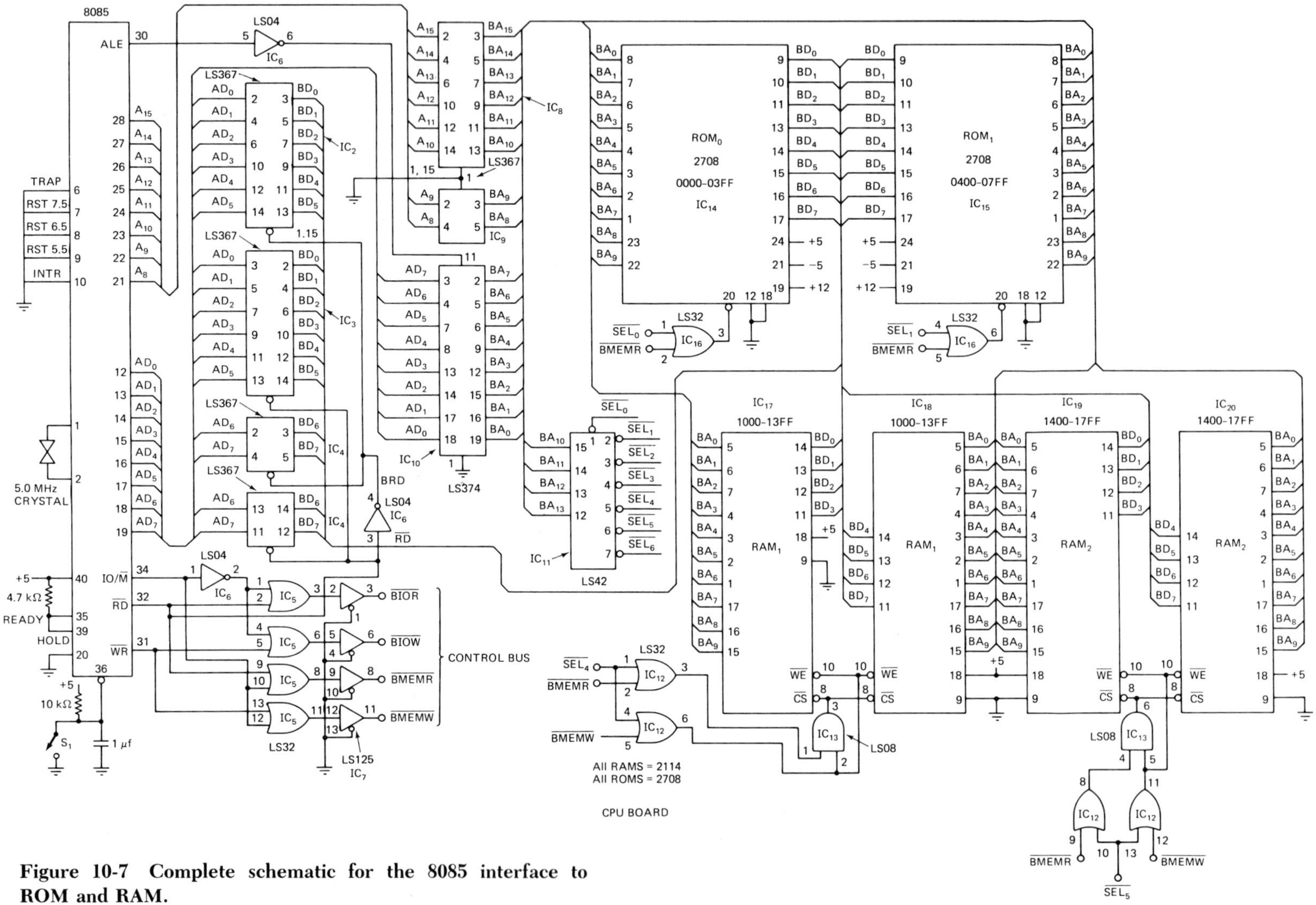

Figure 10-7 Complete schematic for the 8085 interface to ROM and RAM.

10-4 Debugging the System Address Bus

The complete schematic for the 8085 microprocessor interface to ROM and RAM is shown in Figure 10-7. We refer to Figure 10-7 quite often in the following discussion, and because we will need to use it frequently, it may be helpful if we put some type of external marking on that figure. For example, we might attach a paper clip to the page. This allows easy access for finding and studying Figure 10-7 as it is referenced in the text.

The system address bus is the first part of the EPROM programmer system that we will check electrically. We will determine if the BA_0–BA_{15} address lines are electrically capable of switching to both a logical 0 and a logical 1. To do this, we install our SST system of Figure 10-1 into the system being checked by removing the microprocessor and plugging our SST connecting plug into the microprocessor socket. The easiest address lines to check are BA_8–BA_{15} because these address lines are not "time multiplexed" as are address lines BA_0–BA_7.

Procedure for checking BA_8–BA_{15} with SST

1. Set switches on SST labeled SA_8–SA_{15} to the position corresponding to logical 0 output.
2. Connect one end of a scope probe, logic probe, DVM, or VOM to ground.
3. Connect the other end of the voltage probe to output pin 5 of IC_9 of the system (Figure 10-7).
4. The voltage should indicate a valid logical 0.
5. Toggle the switch on the SST labeled SA_8 to logical 1 position.
6. The voltage at output pin 5 of IC_9 of Figure 10-7 should now indicate a valid logical 1.
7. We have now insured that the BA_8 address line to the system will toggle from logical 0 to logical 1.
8. We repeat steps 3–7 for each address line BA_9–BA_{15}, checking for proper voltage levels at appropriate device pin numbers.
9. If at any time the address output fails to toggle as it should, we investigate statically to determine the cause.
10. We have now determined that all address lines BA_8–BA_{15} do toggle from logical 0 to logical 1 under microprocessor control. Or, we have found that some lines do not toggle and must be investigated further. (Trace each circuit from schematic, locating and checking strategic points for proper voltage level from origin to destination of signal path.)

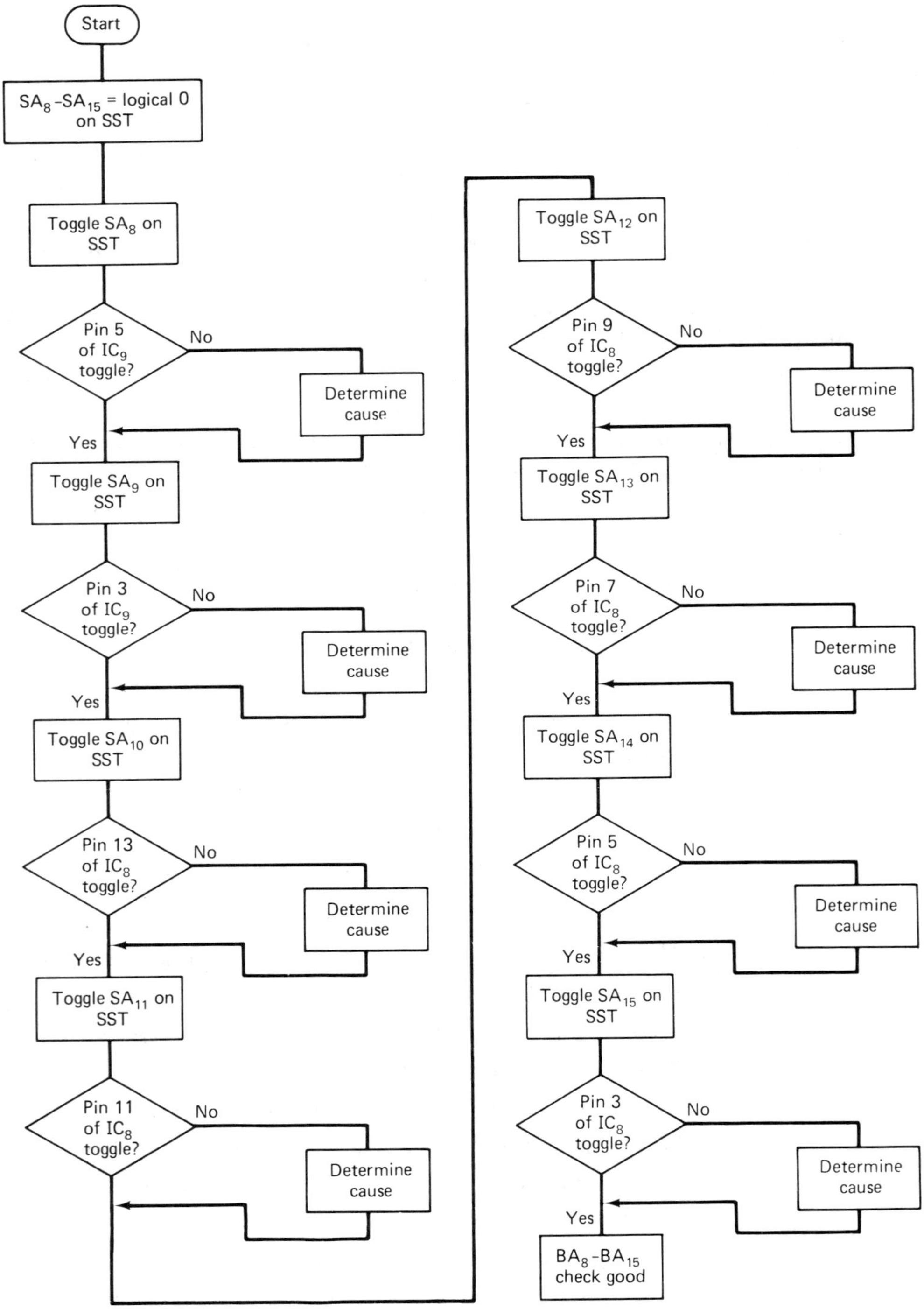

Figure 10-8 Flowchart showing the sequence of events for checking the 8085 address line outputs BA_8–$BA_1$5.

Figure 10-8 shows a flow chart of the events listed for checking the address lines BA_8–BA_{15}. Remember that we have not determined if the address lines BA_8–BA_{15} are connected to the correct places throughout the entire system at this point. This check will be discussed later in this chapter.

We will now determine if the address lines BA_0–BA_7 are electrically capable of toggling from logical 1 to logical 0 level. This procedure is a little more difficult than the previous procedure for checking the BA_8–BA_{15} address lines. However, it is very straightforward.

Procedure for checking the BA_0–BA_7 address line:

1. Set the switches labeled S_0–S_7 to the position indicating logical 0.
2. Set the control switches on the SST to the following:
   a. $\overline{WR}$ = logical 1 (unasserted)
   b. $\overline{RD}$ = logical 1 (unasserted)
   c. $IO/\overline{M}$ = logical 1 (don't care)
   d. ALE = logical 0 (unasserted)
3. With the $\overline{RD}$ signal equal to logical 0, the LEDs will (or should) reflect the data set up by the switches S_0–S_7.
4. Set up the S_0 switch to logical 1 position. The D_0 LED should be lighted.
5. Change the ALE control switch from logical 0 to logical 1.
6. Set the ALE control switch back to logical 0. The action of steps 5 and 6 should latch the address bits.
7. Measure the voltage on output pin 19 of IC_{10}. This voltage should correspond to valid logical 1 output.
8. Reset the S_0 switch to logical 1.
9. Repeat steps 4–8 for each address BA_0–BA_7. If, at step 7, the output does not reflect the correct data, then we may start the procedure from step 3 and measure the voltages at each step to determine if the signals are logically correct before proceeding to the next step.

The objective is to perform the overall function of "latching" the address data. Then, if the overall function fails to perform correctly, we can "micro-step" through each part of the function to determine where in the sequence and the hardware the system failed to respond. A flowchart showing the major steps for checking the address lines BA_0–BA_7 is shown in Figure 10-9.

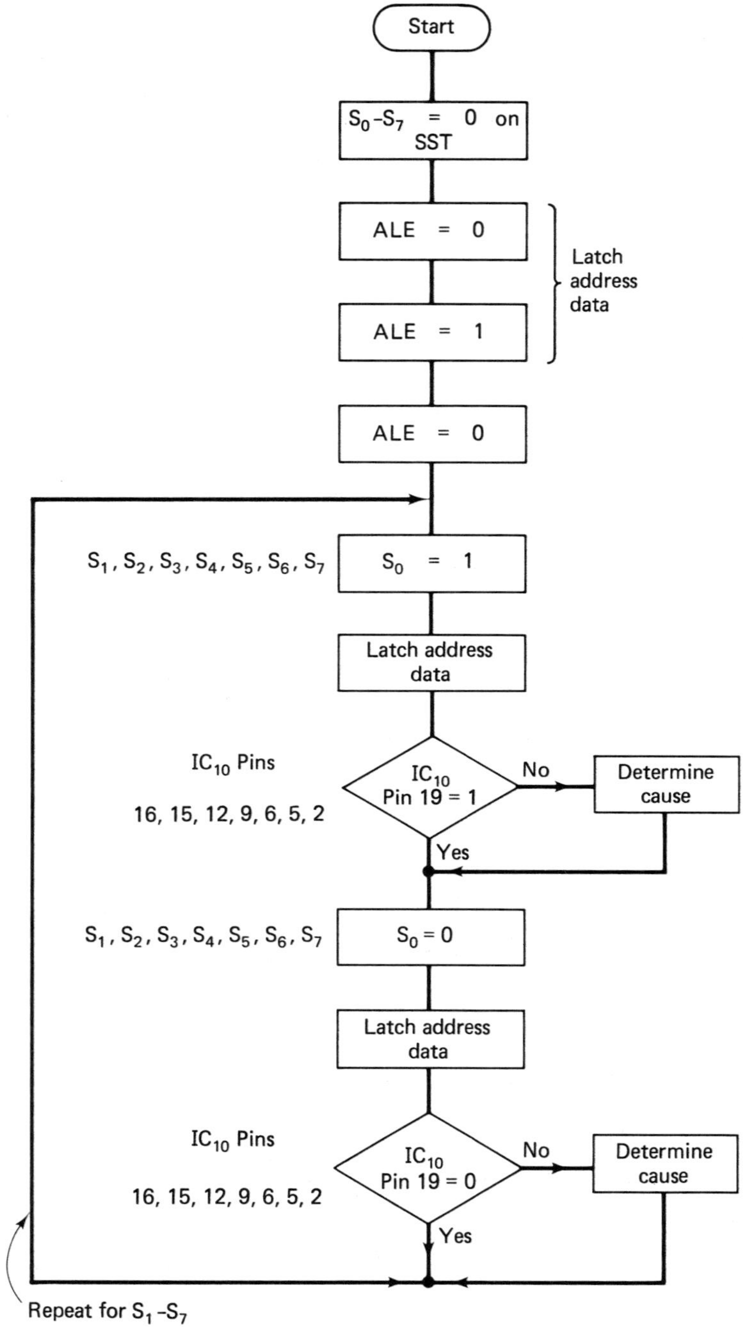

Figure 10-9 Flowchart showing the sequence of events for checking the address line outputs BA_0–BA_7.

10-5 Debugging the System Control Bus

We will now turn our attention to the checkout of the system control bus with the SST. The control bus, as shown in the schematic of Figure 10-10, is excerpted from the overall schematic of Figure 10-7. This excerpting was done in order to promote easier understanding. Following our discussion we should restudy Figure 10-7 to make certain that we have gained an understanding of how the control bus circuit of Figure 10-10 "fits" into the system.

In debugging the system control bus we will use the control switches on the SST labeled $\overline{RD}$, $\overline{WR}$, $IO/\overline{M}$. We see from Figure 10-10 that these three signals are the inputs to the combinational logic circuits that comprise the system control bus. The OR gates of IC_5 and the single inverter IC_6 generate the control signals. The 74LS125 IC7 buffers these signals for outputting to the system. The following procedure may be used in conjunction with the SST to debug the system control bus.

Procedure for Debugging the system control bus:

1. Set the control switches labeled $\overline{RD}$, $\overline{WR}$, $IO/\overline{M}$ to the following position:

   a. $\overline{RD}$ = logical 1 (unasserted)
   b. $\overline{WR}$ = logical 0 (unasserted)
   c. $IO/\overline{M}$ = logical 1 (I/O mode)

2. With the switches set as in step 1, all system control bus outputs should measure a valid logical 1. Verify that the 74LS125 IC_7 pins 3, 6, 8, and 11 all equal logical 1 voltage level.
3. Set switch labeled $\overline{WR}$ to logical 0. This asserts the $\overline{BIOW}$ control signal. Verify that IC_7 pin 6 ($\overline{BIOW}$) is logical 0 voltage level.
4. Verify that IC_7 pins 3, 8, and 11 are equal to logical 1 voltage level (unasserted).
5. As we check the functioning of each control bus line we recall from previous discussions that those signal lines are *mutually exclusive*. This means that no two control lines should be asserted at the same time.
6. Set $\overline{WR}$ switch to logical 1 position.
7. Set the $\overline{RD}$ switch to logical 0 position. This asserts the $\overline{BIOR}$ control signal.
8. Verify that the $\overline{BIOR}$ control signal IC_7 pin 3 is the only one that is at logical 0 voltage level.

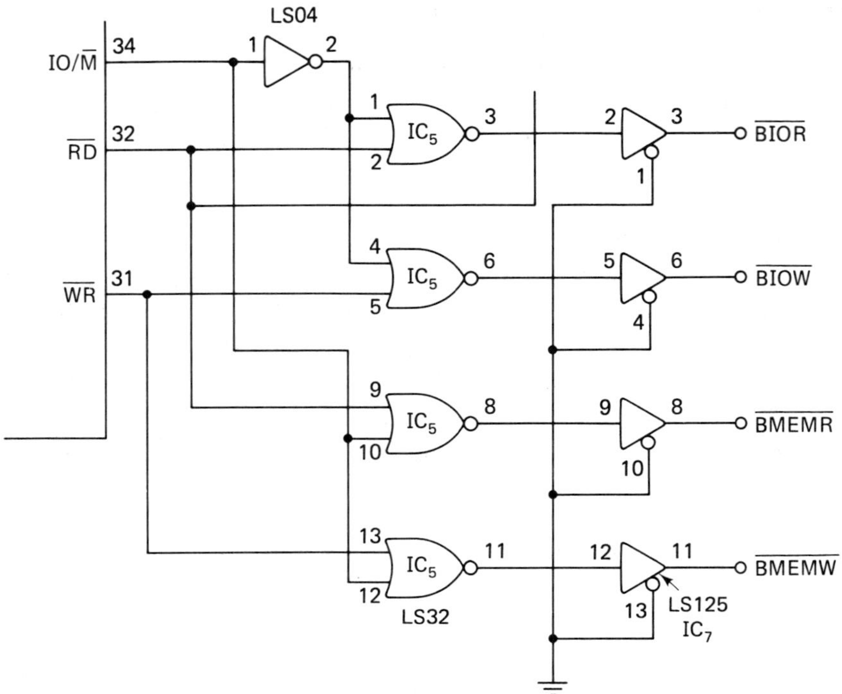

Figure 10-10 Partial schematic excerpted from Figure 10-7. This portion shows the system control bus.

9. Set the $\overline{RD}$ switch to logical 1.
10. We have now verified that the $\overline{BIOW}$ and $\overline{BIOR}$ signals are operating correctly.
11. Set the control switch labeled IO/$\overline{M}$ to logical 0. This puts the control bus into memory mode.
12. Set the $\overline{WR}$ switch to logical 0. This asserts the $\overline{BMEMW}$ control signal. Verify that the $\overline{BMEMW}$ IC_7 pin 11 signal is a valid logical 0 voltage level.
13. Verify that the $\overline{BIOR}$, $\overline{BIOW}$, $\overline{BMEMR}$ signals are at valid logical 1 voltage level.
14. Set the $\overline{WR}$ switch to logical 1 position.
15. Set the $\overline{RD}$ switch to logical 0 position. This asserts the $\overline{BMEMR}$ signal. Verify that the $\overline{BMEMR}$ control signal IC_7 pin 8 is at valid logical 0 voltage level.

16. Verify that the $\overline{BMEMW}$, $\overline{BIOW}$, $\overline{BIOR}$ control signals are at valid logical 1 voltage level.
17. Set the $\overline{RD}$ switch to logical 1 position.

We have now cerified that the system control signal outputs are responding correctly to inputs provided by the 8085 microprocessor. If at any step in the procedure these outputs do not respond correctly, then static checks of the logic signals can be performed easily. We can statically check the system and pinpoint any malfunction in hardware whenever needed.

10-6 Debugging the System Data Bus

We will now discuss debugging of the system data bus by using the SST. In this procedure we will determine if the system data bus is capable of bi-directional data movement. We will be checking all data bus buffering and input devices.

Procedure for checking data output path

1. Set the $\overline{RD}$, $\overline{WR}$ control switches on the SST to:

   a. $\overline{RD}$ = logical 1
   b. $\overline{WR}$ = logical 1

   Under these conditions the data path is from the 8085 SST to the system under test. The SST is in the output mode exactly as the 8085 microprocessor would be in the output mode.

2. Set the SST switches labeled S_0–S_7 to logical 0 output position.
3. Set the SST switch labeled S_0 to logical 1.
4. Verify that BD_0 output, IC_3 pin 2, is at logical 1 voltage level.
5. Set the SST switch labeled S_0 to logical 0. Verify that the BD_0 output, IC_3 pin 2, is at logical 0 voltage level.
6. Repeat steps 3–5 for all data bus lines DB_1–DB_7.
7. At each step verify the correct operation of the data bus output lines by checking for proper logical voltage levels.

If the data bus outputs do not respond correctly at any time in the procedure, then we may statically check DC voltage levels to determine the cause. This is accomplished by performing static electrical checks all along the data path in question.

When this procedure is finished we have verified that the system data bus will *output* data correctly. The data bus must output data corresponding to the correct stimulus from the 8085. Next, we verify the correct operation of the data bus in the input mode, and show how the input data path from the system under test to the SST can be checked to insure proper operation.

Procedure for checking the data bus input path

1. Set the SST switches labeled S_0–S_7 to logical 0 output position.
2. Set system address lines BA_0–BA_{15} to 0s.
3. Set the control switches to:
   a. $\overline{RD}$ = logical 1
   b. $\overline{WR}$ = logical 1
   c. IO/$\overline{M}$ = logical 1 (I/O mode)

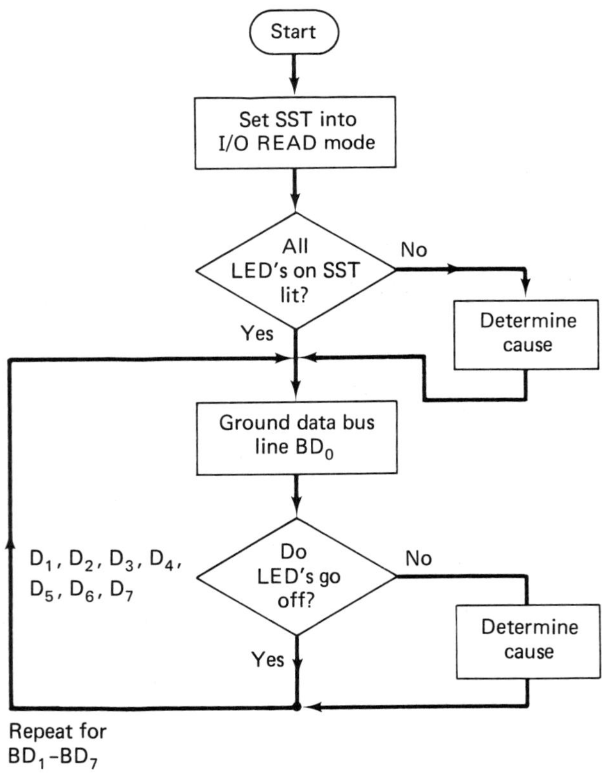

Figure 10-11 Flowchart showing the major events for checking the system data bus signal lines BD_0–BD_7.

4. With control switches $\overline{RD}$ and $\overline{WR}$ in this mode, the LEDs should be off.
5. Set the RD switch to logical 0 position. All LEDs should now be lighted, because the data bus is floating. That is, no output device is controlling the data bus lines. The 74L04 IC_8 and IC_9 of the SST have floating inputs. A floating TTL input corresponds to logical 1.
6. With a jumper wire, we connect one end of the wire to ground.
7. Connect the other end of the jumper wire to system data bus bit BD_0. This is on IC_3 pin 2. What we are doing is forcing a logical 0 level (ground) on the data bus.
8. Verify that the LED labeled D_0 on the SST is off.
9. One at a time, ground the data bus lines BD_1–BD_7. Each time, insure that the LED corresponding to that data bus line goes off. Figure 10-11 shows a flowchart of this procedure.

Now we have completed the procedure for checking the system address bus, the data bus, and the control bus. We have insured that these three system busses do perform correctly if the 8085 provides proper inputs to them. But we have not verified that each system bus is connected properly throughout the remainder of the system. This will be verified as we proceed through the system checkout.

10-7 Verifying Memory Select Decoding

The next section of the system to be checked is the hardware that decodes the memory. In the system shown in Figure 10-7, IC_{11} provides the memory select decoding logic. IC_{11} is a 74LS42. The main idea behind the 74LS42 device is this: the device outputs a logical 0 on an output pin corresponding to a unique binary input. That is, output pins 1, 2, 3, 4, 5, 6, 7 correspond to binary input codes 0, 1, 2, 3, 4, 5, 6, respectively. Now assume a binary input code of $0011_{(2)}$ on pins 12, 13, 14, 15 of the 74LS42, respectively. (This corresponds to a binary 3 input.) Output pin 4 of the 74LS42 is now logical 0.

Procedure for checking the 74LS42

1. Set SST switches labeled SA_{10}–SA_{13} to logical 0 position. Notice in Figure 10-7 that address inputs BA_{10}–BA_{13} are inputs to the 74LS42.
2. Verify that pin 1 of IC_{11} is at logical 0 voltage.

3. Set switches SA_{10}–SA_{13} to:

   a. $SA_{10} = 1$
   b. $SA_{11} = 0$
   c. $SA_{12} = 0$
   d. $SA_{13} = 0$

   Verify that pin 2 of IC_{11} is at logical 0 voltage.

4. Set SST switches SA_{10}–SA_{13} to binary input values 2–6. Each binary input value insures that the corresponding output pin of the 74LS42 IC_{11} goes to logical 0 level. Output pins of the 74LS42 that remain to be checked for logical 0 are:

Binary Input Numbers		*Output Pin = 0*
0010	2	3
0011	3	4
0100	4	5
0101	5	6
0110	6	7

When all output pins go to the proper logic level for all of the preceding steps, we have now verified that the memory select decoding logic is operating correctly. If at any point in the checkout procedure we fail to verify the output pin, then the system may be checked in a static way to determine the cause. Note that we have not so far verified that the memory select lines are connected in the system correctly. We will do this later in the procedure.

10-8 Verifying the System ROM Interface

In verifying the system ROM interface, we must insure that:

1. the address input to the ROM is correct,
2. the data outputs of the ROM are correct,
3. the chip-select input to the ROM is correct, and that
4. the power supply input to the ROM is correct.

The discussion of the ROM interface is divided into four sections. Each section covers one of the four topics listed above.

First: Address Inputs to the ROM: We must insure that the address inputs BA_0–BA_9 to the system ROM are valid. To do this the following procedure may be used:

1. Set address switches SA_8–SA_{15} to logical 0 position.
2. Set control-bit switches $\overline{RD}$, $\overline{WR}$, IO/$\overline{M}$ to the following positions.

   a. $\overline{RD}$ = logical 1
   b. $\overline{WR}$ = logical 1
   c. IO/$\overline{M}$ = logical 0.

3. Set switches S_0–S_7 to logical 0 position.
4. Set switch S_0 to logical 1 position.
5. Toggle the ALE switch to logical 1, then to logical 0 position. This action latches the address bits BA_0–BA_7 into the 74LS374 IC_{10}.
6. Verify that BA_0 pin 8 of IC_{14} and IC_{15} is at logical 1 voltage level.
7. Repeat steps 3–6 for address inputs BA_1–BA_7. Verify that the corresponding address input pin on the 2708, IC_{14}, IC_{15} responds when the address bus is set to logical 1.
8. We now verify the address inputs BA_8 and BA_9 to the system ROM. Sęt the switch labeled SA_8 to logical 1. Verify that the BA_8 address input to IC_{14}, IC_{15} pin 22 goes to logical 1. Repeat this step for address BA_9.

If at any point in this procedure the address inputs to the system ROM IC_{14}, IC_{15} fail to respond correctly, the trouble-shooter may "freeze" the system under code condition and check statically for proper operation.

Checking the System ROM Data Outputs

In checking the ROM outputs we will be following this procedure: To begin, the system will be set up in an input read mode. However, no input device will be selected. Essentially we are enabling the system data bus in the input mode. This allows us to use the LEDs on the SST to give a quick visual check of the data bus lines. We then connect the ROM output pins to ground, one at a time, via a clip lead. As we ground each output pin of the ROM, the corresponding LED indicator should go off.

We note that it is electrically valid to ground the ROM outputs, because these outputs are in tri-state mode. We insured that they would be in the tri-state mode by setting the system to input device READ mode via the system control bus. In making this check we are verifying that the data bus is physically connected to the ROM data outputs of IC_{14}, IC_{15} correctly. The procedure for performing this check follows:

1. Set the IO/$\overline{M}$ switch on the SST to the I/O position. (This puts the system into the input, output mode).

2. Set the $\overline{WR}$ switch to logical 1.

3. Set the $\overline{RD}$ switch to logical 0. This puts the system to input device READ mode.

4. Set the system address BA_0–BA_{15} = 0000. With this address, we have insured that no input device is selected.

5. The LEDs on the SST box should now all be on.

6. With one end of a clip lead connected to ground, attach the other end of the clip lead to the ROM_0 and ROM_1 outputs. We do this one at a time. Each time we ground a ROM_0 or ROM_1 output, the corresponding LED on the SST should go off. For example, suppose we connect pin 8 of IC_{14} or IC_{15}, ROM_0 or ROM_1, to ground via the clip lead. The LED labeled D_0 on the SST should go off. In this way we get quick visual verification that the hardware path from the system ROM output to the 8085 microprocessor is electrically good.

Checking Chip Select Inputs to the ROM

Next we show how to verify that the chip select input to the ROM is working correctly. As you recall, the function of a chip-select operation is to place the outputs of one ROM chip at a time on the system data bus. Let us first discuss how to check the chip select of IC_{14} ROM.

The chip select for ROM, pin 20, of IC_{14} will be logical 0 when the output pin 3 of IC_{16} is logical 0. Output pin 3 will be logical 0 when pin 1, $\overline{SEL_0}$, and pin 2 $\overline{BMEMR}$, are both logical 0. This is consistent because the $\overline{BMEMR}$ signal goes to logical 0 when the system is reading memory data. The $\overline{SEL_0}$ signal goes to logical 0 when the system address is pointing to ROM, IC_{14}.

To insure that the chip select is operating correctly, we must force the system into the mode of reading memory data from ROM.

Procedure to read memory data from ROM

1. Set system address BA_0–BA_{15} to 0000. From the memory map of the system we know that ROM_0 is contained in the address space 0000–03FF. This step forces the system to generate $\overline{SEL_0}$ to equal logical 0.

2. Set the control bit switches as follows:

   a. $\overline{WR}$ = logical 1

b. IO/$\overline{M}$ = logical 0. This puts the system into the memory mode.
c. $\overline{RD}$ = logical 0. This forces the system into memory-read mode. That is, $\overline{BMEMR}$ is logical 0.

3. After step 2c, verify that chip select input pin 20 on IC_{14} is logical 0 as it should be. (This chip is selected.)
4. Verify that chip select input pin 20 in IC_{15} is logical 1. (The chip is *not* selected.) If steps 3 or 4 are not correct, then we may trace the decoding problem statically while the system is "frozen" in the correct mode.

Procedure to verify that chip select input pin 20 of IC_{15} is operating correctly

5. Set the system address bus BA_0–BA_{15} equal to 0400. We know from our memory map that ROM_1 has valid addresses located in the address space from $0400_{(16)}$–$07FF_{(16)}$. This forces the system to enable $\overline{SEL_1}$ to logical 0.
6. The system should already be in the mode where $\overline{BMEMR}$ is logical 0.
7. We now verify that pin 20 of IC_{15} is logical 0 (selected) as it should be.
8. We verify that pin 20 of IC_{14} is logical 1 (not selected). If steps 7 or 8 do not verify correctly, we can trace the problem statically while the system is in this particular electrical mode.

We have now verified that the hardware will properly decode the correct ROM_0 or ROM_1 based on the electrical condition of the system address bus BA_0–BA_{15} and control bus. The last section of the ROM hardware we must verify is the ROM power supply.

The 2708 EPROM requires three power supplies. These are +12 volts, +5 V, and −5 V. We should electrically verify that these three power supplies are connected to the following pins:

1. +12 V—pin 19 (IC_{14}, IC_{15})
2. +5 V—pin 24 (IC_{14}, IC_{15})
3. −5 V—pin 21 (IC_{14}, IC_{15})

These voltages should exist on both IC_{14} and IC_{15}. We are now finished verifying that the entire system ROM electrical interface to the system is correct, and that the hardware is functional.

10-9 Verifying System RAM Interface

In verifying the RAM interface we must check the following five major hardware categories:

1. the data bus interface to the RAM,
2. the address bus interface to the RAM,
3. the chip select interface to the RAM,
4. the write enable interface to the RAM, and
5. the power supplies to the RAM

You will recall that when we were verifying the ROM interface we had only four categories to verify. In the RAM interface we have five major areas to verify. The additional area is the WRITE ENABLE interface. Note that the write enable interface exists on the RAM because the system is electrically capable of writing data to the RAM, not just reading data as it was with the ROM.

Verifying Address Inputs to RAM

In verifying the RAM inputs we will perform the checks in exactly the same way that we verified ROM inputs. That is, we stimulate each address input via the Static Stimulus Tester and then monitor the corresponding address inputs on the RAM. The system RAM consists of IC_{17}, IC_{18}, IC_{19}, and IC_{20}. Therefore, when we verify the address inputs, we much check to insure that the correct address line is connected and responding to all four of these ICs. We will not repeat the exact procedure for verifying the RAM address inputs because we have done this in a very detailed manner for the address inputs for the system ROM.

Verifying Data Bus Inputs to RAM

To verify the data bus inputs to the RAM we again perform this in exactly the same way we did for the ROM inputs. The difference is in the fact that two RAM chips here comprise a 1K × 8 RAM. The reason being that the RAMs we have chosen are 2114s, which are organized as 1K × 4 static RAMs. We connect two 2114s in parallel to give us a 1K × 8 system RAM. Referring again to the system schematic of Figure 10-7 notice that IC_{17} and IC_{18} comprise one 1K × 8 system RAM, and IC_{19} and IC_{20} comprise another 1K × 8 system RAM.

Data bus bits BD_0–BD_3 are input to IC_{17}, and data bus bits BD_4–BD_7 are input to IC_{18}. Data bus bits BD_0–BD_3 are inputs to IC_{19}, and data bus bits BD_4–BD_7 are inputs to IC_{20}, as shown in Figure 10-7.

To verify that these data bus bits are connected to the correct RAM chips we follow the same procedure used to verify the system ROM data bus bits. That is, we set the system into an I/O READ mode with address 0000 on address bus bits BA_0–BA_{15}. We then ground the data bus bits of the RAM BD_0–BD_7, one at a time, and verify that the corresponding LED on the SST goes to logical 0 for all data lines. Note that data bus bits BD_0–BD_3 are connected to IC_{17} and IC_{19}. Therefore, when verifying data bus bits BD_0–BD_3 we ground pin 14 of IC_{17} and verify that the LED labeled D_0 goes off. Next we ground pin 14 of IC_{19} and verify that the LED labeled D_0 goes off. We continue this procedure until all data bus bits BD_0–BD_7 have been verified that they are indeed connected to the correct system RAM chip.

Verifying WRITE ENABLE Input to RAM

Next we discuss the technique for verifying the WRITE ENABLE signal to the system RAM. Note first that the write enable signal is connected to pin 10 of IC_{17} and IC_{18} in parallel. Further, the WRITE ENABLE signal pin 10 of IC_{19} and IC_{20} is also connected in parallel. This is because one RAM organized as 1K × 8 uses two smaller RAM chips in parallel. The conditions for the WRITE ENABLE signal to be asserted follow: The system must be in a memory write mode, and the address bus must be addressing the particular RAM to be written into. For example, the system address bus must be addressing IC_{17} and IC_{18} in order for the WRITE ENABLE signal to be asserted successfully to these two devices. This means the address bus must have an address of 1000–13FF on address lines BA_0–BA_{15}.

Procedure to check the WRITE ENABLE signal of IC_{17} and IC_{18},

1. First set address bus BA_0–BA_{15} to 1000. This forces the system to enable the signal $\overline{SEL_4}$ to logical 0. The $\overline{SEL_4}$ signal is connected to IC_{12} pins 1 and 4.
2. Next, set the control bits on the SST to the mode in which $IO/\overline{M}$ becomes logical 0. This puts the system into the memory mode. The $\overline{RD}$ signal should be a logical 1 (unasserted). The $\overline{WR}$ signal should be logical 0. This is the asserted mode for the WRITE ENABLE. This condition on the control bits asserts the $\overline{BMEMW}$ signal. This is the buffered memory WRITE signal to the system. The buffered memory WRITE signal goes to IC_{12}, pin 5. Note that the $\overline{SEL_4}$ signal is logical 0, based on the electrical conditions of the address bus. The buffered memory WRITE signal is logical 0,

based on the electrical conditions of the control bus. Under these conditions, IC_{12} pin 6 will be logical 0. We note that pin 6 of IC_{12} is also connected to pin 10 of IC_{17} and IC_{18}, because these devices are in parallel, as described earlier.

3. We next verify that pin 10 of IC_{17} and IC_{18} is indeed logical 0 as it should be.
4. We verify that pin 10 of IC_{19} and IC_{20} is logical 1. This logical 1 indicates that the WRITE ENABLE signal of IC_{19} and IC_{20} is unasserted.

   If either step 3 or step 4 fail to verify correctly, then we must retrace the signal path from the 8085 SST to the RAM chip to determine where the break in the electrical path occurred.
5. We next verify that the WRITE ENABLE signal to IC_{19} and IC_{20} will be asserted. Notice from our memory map that the memory space for IC_{19} and IC_{20}, RAM 2, is 1400–17FF. We set the address switches so that the condition 1400_{16} will exist on the address bus lines BA_0–BA_{15}. This condition forces the $\overline{SEL_5}$ signal from IC_{11} pin 6 to logical 0. The $\overline{SEL_5}$ signal is connected to IC_{12} pins 10 and 13.
6. Now the system is still asserting the $\overline{BMEMW}$ signal. With pin 13 and pin 12 of IC_{12} at logical 0, pin 11 of IC_{12} will be logical 0.
7. We now verify that pin 10 of IC_{19} and IC_{20} is logical 0. This is the asserted mode for the write enable of RAM_2.
8. We verify that pin 10 of IC_{17} and IC_{18} is logical 1. This is the unasserted mode for the write enable of RAM_1. If either step 7 or step 8 fails to verify correctly, we again retrace the path from the RAM back to the SST to find where the break in electrical path occurred.

We have verified that the memory WRITE signal to system RAM_1 and RAM_2 is electrically correct. We now verify that the chip select line to system RAM_1 and RAM_2 is electrically correct. The RAM chip select line must become active 0 whenever the system is reading data from RAM or writing data to RAM.

Next, we shall discuss checking the chip select line to the system RAM for correct operation. In Figure 10-7 we see that IC_{13} is a 74LS08 AND gate. The chip select line is connected to the output of one of the quad gates contained within the 74LS08. IC_{17} and IC_{18} are connected to pin 3 of IC_{13}. IC_{19} and IC_{20} are connected to pin 6 of IC_{13}. We notice that one input to the AND gates is the WRITE ENABLE signal to either RAM_1 or RAM_2. That is, pin 2 of IC_{13} is the WRITE ENABLE signal for RAM_1, and pin 5 of IC_{13} is the WRITE ENABLE signal for RAM_2.

We must verify that when the system RAM_1 or system RAM_2 WRITE ENABLE signal is asserted, then the chip select line into the particular RAM that is being selected is also asserted. This fact will allow us to check one mode of the chip select in exactly the same way that we checked the write enable signal to RAM_1 or RAM_2. That is, we set the system in the mode to check the write enable RAM_1 as we have previously described. We then insure that the chip select for RAM_1 is also logical 0. Further, we next set the system in the mode to assert the write enable of RAM_2 as we have previously described. We then verify that the chip select signal of RAM_2 is also logical 0, the asserted mode.

The chip select signal for RAM_1 and RAM_2 must also be logical 0 when the system is reading data from either RAM_1 or RAM_2. This means we must force the system into the mode so that it is in a READ condition for the RAM_1 or the RAM_2. To do this we may use the following procedure:

1. Set the system address BA_0–BA_{15} to 1000. This sets the $\overline{SEL_4}$ signal from IC_{11} pin 5 to logical 0. The $\overline{SEL_4}$ signal will select RAM_1.
2. Now set the system control bits on the Static Stimulus Tester to a condition for a memory READ. This is done by setting the IO/$\overline{M}$ signal to logical 0. The $\overline{RD}$ signal goes to a logical 0. The $\overline{WR}$ signal goes to a logical 1. Under these conditions the $\overline{BMEMR}$ signal should be logical 0.

   With the $\overline{BMEMR}$ signal equal to logical 0 and the SEL_4 signal also equal to logical 0, IC_{12} pin 3 should be logical 0. This is the condition for the system to read from system RAM_1.
3. We now verify that the chip select signal at pin 8 of IC_{17} and IC_{18} goes to logical 0. Notice that the chip select signal goes to logical 0 because IC_{13} pin 1 will be a logical 0 due to IC_{12} pin 3 being forced to logical 0.
4. We further verify that the chip select signal for RAM_2 is logical 1, or unasserted mode. If either step 3 or step 4 fails to verify, we must determine the trouble spot in the system.
5. Next we must verify that the chip select signal for RAM_2 will become asserted when the system is performing a memory READ from system RAM_2. We set the system address bus BA_0–BA_{15} to 1400 by using the Static Stimulus Tester.
6. The system should already be in the memory READ mode. Notice that when the system is in this mode and $\overline{SEL_5}$ is selected by the system address bus, pin 8 of IC_{12} will become logical 0. This forces a logical 0 on pin 4 of IC_{13}, which in turn forces the output of pin 6 of IC_{13} to logical 0. We verify that the chip select input of RAM_2 is logical 0.

7. We now verify that the chip select of RAM_1 is logical 1, or unasserted. If either steps 6 and 7 fail to verify correctly, we must determine the trouble spot in the hardware.

Assuming that the preceding checks have verified that the hardware is operating correctly, we have determined thereby that the system address bus is connected to RAM_1 and RAM_2 correctly. We have also determined that the system data bus is connected to RAM_1 and RAM_2 correctly. And we have finished verifying that the system control bus will select the correct RAM_1 and RAM_2 for either reading or writing from system memory.

The final hardware step to be verified is that the power supplies for RAM_1 and RAM_2 are correct. The 2114 static RAM uses only a +5-V power supply, so we now check to see that +5 V is on IC_{17}, IC_{18}, IC_{19}, and IC_{20} pin 18. When we have proved that the power supply is satisfactory, we have finished verifying that all hardware is correct for the ROM and RAM interfaces to the three-bus architecture of our 8085 microprocessor-based system.

10-10 Debugging the Keyboard Interface

We will not discuss debugging the system keyboard interface here as we are using the same keyboard described in Chapter 4. A detailed discussion was given for debugging this interface in Chapter 5, so it would be redundant to repeat that procedure here. If you are uncertain about how to debug the keyboard interface, refer to the Chapter 5 for refreshing. In Chapter 5 we discussed debugging the keyboard interface when a Z80 microprocessor was the base of the system. In this present system we are using an 8085 microprocessor as the base. However, we have enough details about the 8085 microprocessor SST at this point to perform the same type of test as described in Chapter 5 for debugging the Z80-based keyboard.

10-11 Debugging the Display Interface

A detailed description was given in Chapter 5 for debugging the system display interface. We are using the same display here that we used for the system in Chapter 4. If you are uncertain about the steps required to debug the display interface, refer to Chapter 5 where this discussion is presented in full. Here again, in Chapter 5 the discussion for debugging the system display interface dealt with a Z80 microprocessor. However, enough details have been given in Chapter 10 for using the static stimulus tester for the 8085 microprocessor to enable us to implement the same kind of checks with the 8085 that are presented in Chapter 5 for the Z80 microprocessor.

10-12 Debugging the EPROM Connection to the System

We will now discuss debugging of the I/O circuit for connection of the EPROM being programmed to this system. A complete schematic for this I/O circuit is given in Figure 10-12. There are five major areas for system hardware that we must cover in discussing the interface to the EPROM to be programmed for this particular system. These sections are:

1. the address to the EPROM under program,
2. the data input and output from the EPROM under program,
3. the system power supplies for the EPROM under program,
4. the programming pulse to the EPROM under programming, and
5. the chip select bar/WRITE ENABLE pulse

The last two items are covered in separate sections of this particular discussion. We first discuss the address to the EPROM under program.

In the schematic of Figure 10-12, notice that the address to the EPROM under program is supplied via two binary latches. These are IC_9 and IC_{10}. IC_9 is a 74LS374 octal latch, and IC_{10} is a 74LSI75 quad latch. Notice also that the data input to the 74LS374 is BD_0–BD_7. Data for the 74LS175 IC_{10} are data bits BD_0 and BD_1. These facts tell us that there will be a total of 10 bits of address for the EPROM under program. This is consistent because the PROM under program is a 1K × 8 EPROM, which requires 10 address lines. The 74LS374 IC_9 will form the lower data byte address lines to the EPROM. The 74LS175 will supply the upper two address lines to the PROM.

Notice that the 74LS374 octal latch is clocked from IC_3 pin 11. IC_3 pin 11 becomes logical 0 whenever $\overline{SEL_3}$ pin 12 and $\overline{BIOW}$ pin 13 are logical 0 at the same time. These conditions will exist when the address bus is forcing $\overline{SEL_3}$ to logical 0, and the control bus is generating a buffered I/O write ($\overline{BIOW}$) signal to the system. Let us now examine how the $\overline{SEL_3}$ signal is generated via the hardware.

Figure 10-13 is excerpted from Figure 10-12 and shows the select decoding for all output ports on the schematic of Figure 10-12. Notice that address bits BA_4–BA_7 are connected to a 74LS42 IC_1. Whenever BA_4–BA_7 represent binary 3, then pin 4 of IC_1 is logical 0. When pin 4 of IC_1 is logical 0, pin 10 of IC_4 is forced to logical 0. The logical 0 on pin 10 of IC_4 now enables this OR gate.

Notice that the lower address bits BA_0–BA_2 are connected to 74LS42 IC_2. Address bit BA_3 is connected to IC_4 pin 9. Whenever address bit BA_3 is logical 1, IC_4 pin 8 becomes logical 0. When IC_4 pin 8 is logical 0, pin 12 of IC_2 goes to logical 0. In effect, this action enables IC_2.

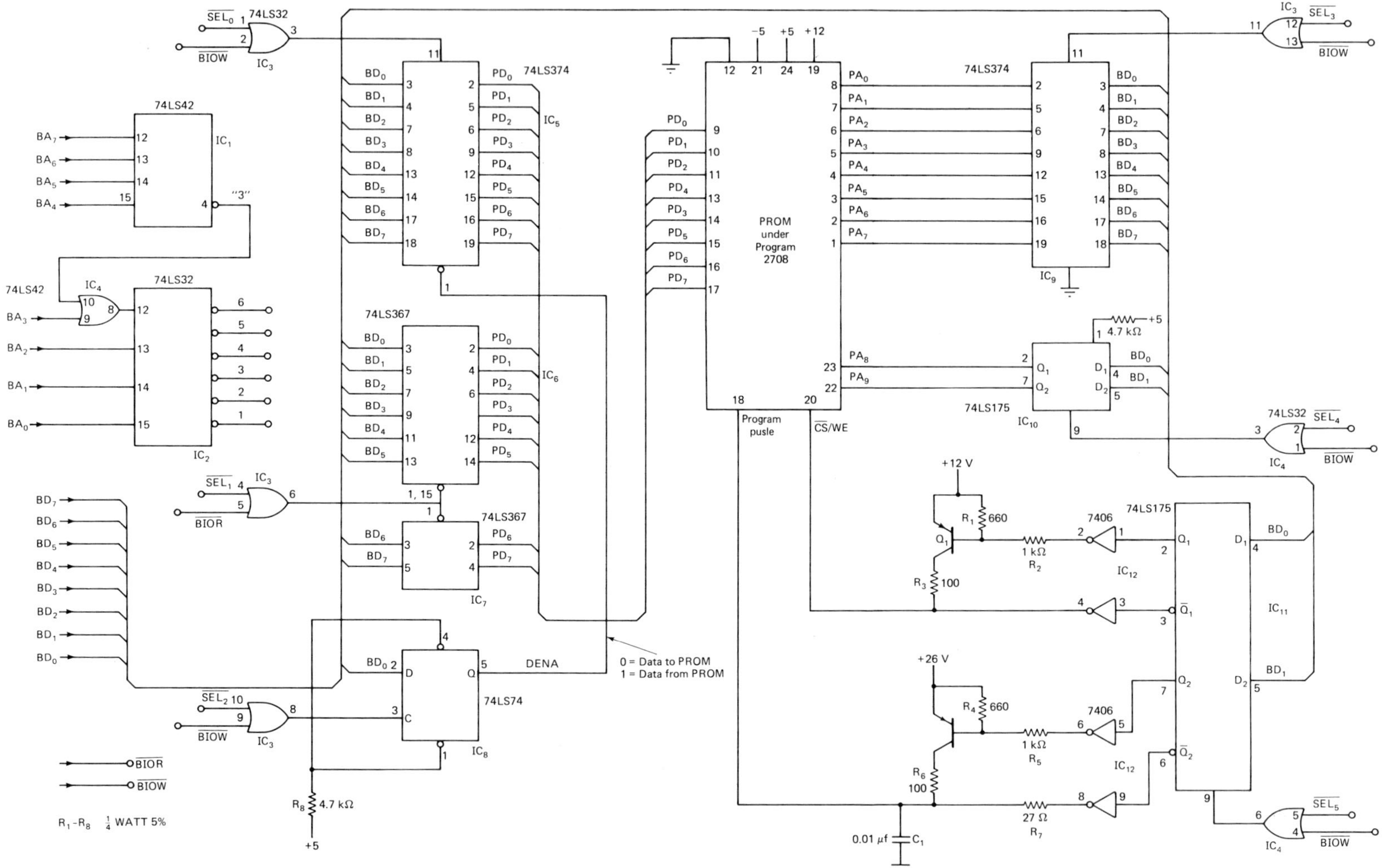

Figure 10-12 Complete schematic of the I/O circuit used for programming the EPROM.

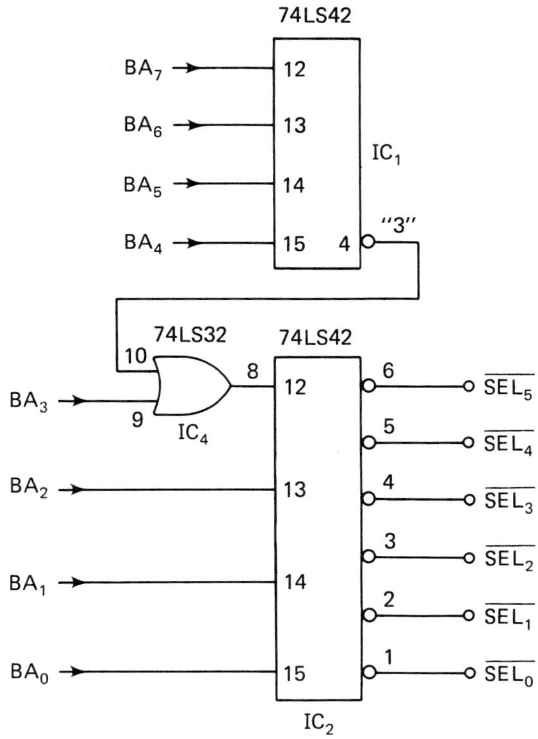

Figure 10-13 Partial schematic excerpted from Figure 10-12. This portion shows the generation of the select code.

The lower three address bits BA_0–BA_2 now determine which select line $\overline{SEL_0}$–$\overline{SEL_5}$ will become logical 0. This means that all $\overline{SEL}$ signals, $\overline{SEL_0}$–$\overline{SEL_5}$, are really a $30_{(16)}$, $31_{(16)}$, $32_{(16)}$, $33_{(16)}$, $34_{(16)}$, $35_{(16)}$ for the system address bus. The conditions for the address bus, and which select code will be selected, are shown in Figure 10-14. The select code for the particular select line is shown in quotes.

Referring again to Figure 10-12 notice that IC_9 will have data written into it whenever $\overline{SEL_3}$ is a logical 0 and the buffered I/O write signal is logical 0. Therefore, to check the hardware for this particular path we can do the following (If necessary, refer to itemized procedures given earlier in this chapter):

1. Set up the system such that $\overline{SEL_3}$ will be logical 0 based on the condition of the system address bus BA_0–BA_7.
2. Next, set the control switches on the SST to put the system into the mode that asserts the $\overline{BIOW}$ signal.
3. Then set the control bus into the condition where the $\overline{BIOW}$ signal becomes unasserted.

	IC_2						
Pin# 1	2	3	4	5	6	Select Code	ADDRESS
0	1	1	1	1	1	"0"	30_{16}
1	0	1	1	1	1	"1"	31_{16}
1	1	0	1	1	1	"2"	32_{16}
1	1	1	0	1	1	"3"	33_{16}
1	1	1	1	0	1	"4"	34_{16}
1	1	1	1	1	0	"5"	35_{16}

Figure 10-14 The logical conditions for the address bus for asserting the proper select code.

4. When the $\overline{BIOW}$ signal becomes unasserted, the data on the data bus will then be written into the octal latch IC_9. We can then verify that these data on the inputs to IC_9 were indeed transferred to the outputs of IC_9 by examining with a logic probe the voltage level on pins 1, 2, 3, 4, 5, 6, 7, and 8 of the EPROM socket to be programmed.

We will now verify that the 74LS175 IC_{10} is operating correctly within a system environment. To do this the following procedure may be used:

5. Put the address bus BA_0–BA_7 into the logical condition for the $\overline{SEL_4}$ signal to become active 0.
6. Next, set data BD_0–BD_1 on the inputs of the 74LS175 to logical 1.
7. Then, force the system such that the buffered I/O WRITE signal becomes asserted. Under these conditions pin 9 of IC_{10} should be logical 0.
8. We now unassert the buffered I/O write signal to the system.
9. We then verify that the data on pins 4 and 5 of the 74LS175 were transferred to the output pins 2 and 7 of IC_{10}. This may be done by looking at pins 22 and 23 of the EPROM socket to be programmed. If the data in step 9 failed to verify we must sequence through the procedure one step at a time to find out where in the hardware the procedure failed to respond correctly.

In effect, we are performing an overall system function and checking to see if that function performed correctly. If it does, we may move on to the next step of the procedure. If the function does not perform correctly, then we may step back through the procedure one step at a time. This will enable us to determine where the hardware failed to respond correctly.

We have now proved that the address to the EPROM under program can be written into via the hardware. Next, we will verify that data to the EPROM under program can be input via the microprocessor and can be read via the microprocessor and system hardware.

Note that during the programming of the EPROM the microprocessor sometimes inputs data from the EPROM under program; this is when the processor is reading data from the EPROM being programmed. At other times the microprocessor outputs data to the EPROM under program; this is when the microprocessor is generating data to be programmed into the EPROM. We must verify that under both conditions, data going into and that data coming out of the EPROM under program, is electrically capable of occurring in the system.

We will first discuss how data from the microprocessor is enabled for input to the EPROM under program. The hardware for doing this is mainly IC_5 of Figure 10-12. Figure 10-15 is excerpted from that schematic, and shows the data input path to the EPROM from the system data bus. Notice that pin 1 of IC_5 is connected to pin 5 on the 74LS74 latch. When pin 1 of IC_5 is logical 0, then the data at the output of IC_5 is enabled to the EPROM under program. We note that this data must be disabled whenever the EPROM under program is supplying data out to the system. This disabling action prevents a bus conflict between the data from the EPROM under program and the data being generated by IC_5.

Before we can write data to the EPROM under program we must insure that IC_5 is enabled via pin 1. This means we must write a logical 0 to the 74LS74 latch IC_8. This is accomplished via the data bus bit D_0. The D input to the latch and the clock input to the latch will be from IC_3 pin 8. Whenever $\overline{SEL_2}$ signal is asserted and the buffered I/O write signal is asserted *and* data bus bit BD_0 is logical 0, then IC_5 pin 1 becomes logical 0.

Let us assume that pin 1 of IC_5 is logical 0. We note that the data input to the 74LS374 octal latch, IC_5, is connected to the data bus BD_0–BD_7. This means the data bus carries whatever we wish to be programmed into the EPROM under program. Once the data is applied to the data bus we then perform an I/O write operation to IC_5. The I/O write operation will transfer the data from the data bus to the output of IC_5. This action will transfer the data to the EPROM under program.

Procedure to verify the operation of IC_5

1. Set the condition on the system address bits BA_0–BA_7 such that $\overline{SEL_0}$ is asserted.
2. Next, set the data bus bits BD_0–BD_7 to the data we wish transferred to the output of IC_5.

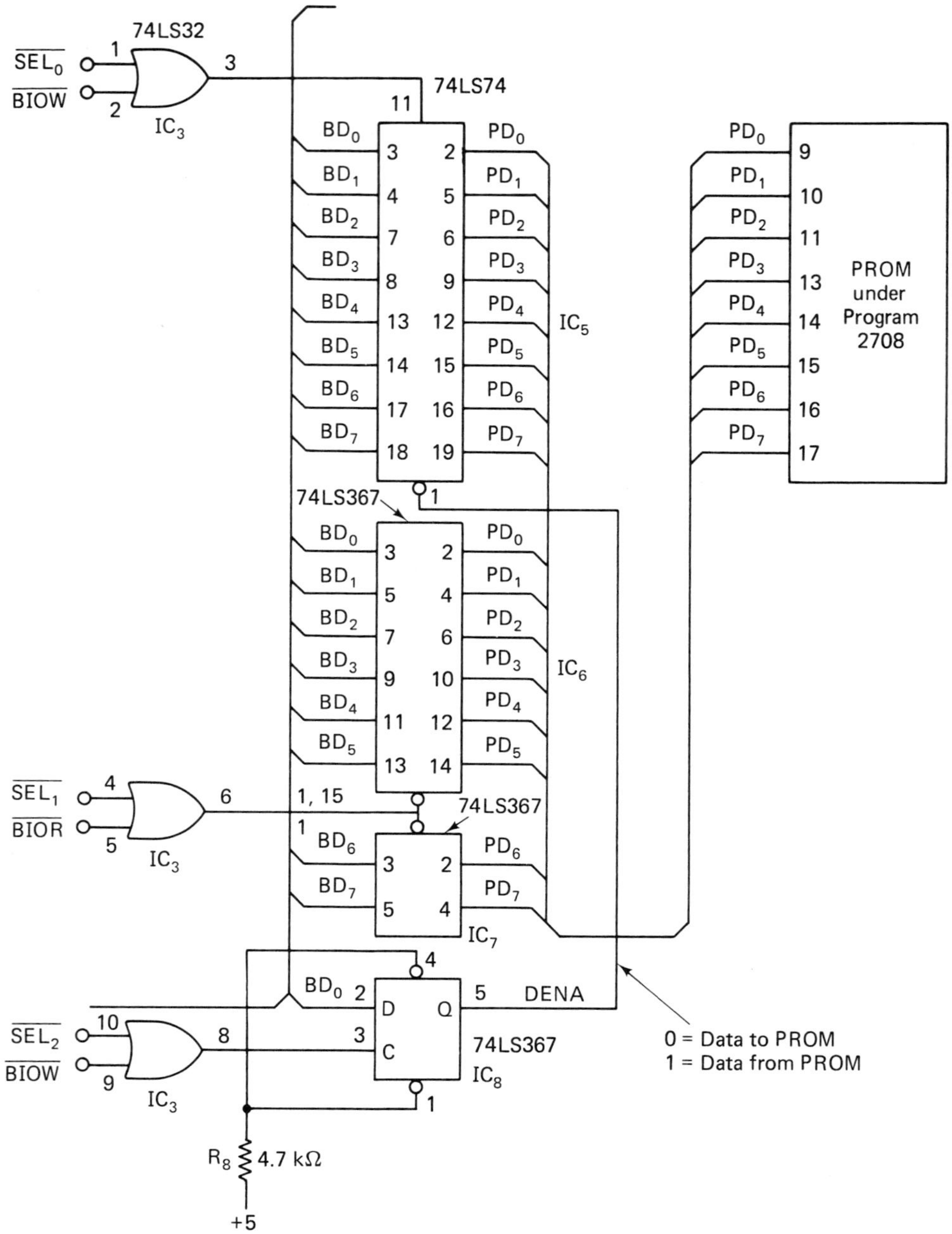

Figure 10-15 Partial schematic excerpted from Figure 10-12. This portion shows the data in and data out path for the EPROM under program.

3. Then set the conditions for the system control bus via the static stimulus tester such that the buffered I/O write signal will become a logical 0.
4. Next, set the condition on the control bits such that the $\overline{BIOW}$ signal will become unasserted. When this occurs the data on the data bus will be transferred to the output of IC_5.
5. We now verify that the data at the output of IC_5 is indeed the data that we wish transferred. If the data at output of IC_5 is not correct, we can step through the procedure for writing data to the output of IC_5 one step at a time via the SST to verify what hardware failed to respond correctly.

We will now discuss the technique for verifying that the data from the EPROM under program can be read by the microprocessor. This is the condition where the microprocessor will be determining if the EPROM under program did indeed get programmed correctly. In order for the data from the EPROM under program to be transferred to the microprocessor, the output pins of IC_5 PD_0–PD_7 must be disabled.

We recall that, in order to disable IC_5, pin 1 of IC_5 must be taken to logical 1 level. That means that we must perform an I/O WRITE operation to IC_8 with the data bus bit BD_0 set to logical 1. This forces a logical 1 on IC_5 and disables the 74LS374. Now the only data bits that could possibly control PD_0–PD_7 are the output pins from the EPROM under program.

After we have performed an I/O write to IC_8 and disabled IC_5 we may do the following. We set the system into a mode to perform an I/O read from IC_6 and IC_7. Then, one at a time, we ground the data output lines of the EPROM under program and see if the LED corresponding to that particular data bus bit does go to logical 0 on the SST.

Procedure to check for logical 0 on SST

1. Set the system address bus into the mode so that $\overline{SEL_1}$ is asserted.
2. Set the system control bus such that the buffered I/O read signal is asserted. This sets IC_3 pin 6 to logical 0. When IC_3 pin 6 is set to logical 0 the 74LS367 IC_6 and IC_7 are enabled. Under these conditions all LEDs on the Static Stimulus Tester should be on. This assumes, of course, that no device is in the EPROM under program socket. If there were an EPROM in the program socket, the LEDs would reflect the data stored in the device.

3. We next ground pin 9 of the EPROM under program, which is output 1, via a clip lead. This forces data bus bit BD_0 to logical 0, which forces the SST light labeled D_0 to go to logical 0.
4. We now force pins 10, 11, 13, 14, 15, 16, and 17 to logical 0 one at a time, and verify that the corresponding LED on the SST goes to logical 0. In this way we get a quick visual determination of the electrical path from the EPROM under program back to the 8085 microprocessor.

Now we have verified that the address to the PROM under program and the data bus to it is performing electrically as it should within the system environment. We must now determine if the power supplies to the EPROM under program are correct. This may be done by monitoring the voltages on pins 19, 24, 21 with a voltmeter or oscilloscope. These voltages should be +12 volts, +5 V, and −5 V, respectively. Once we have insured that these power supplies are correct, we may proceed to the next verification block for the EPROM under program.

10-13 Verifying Programming Pulse Hardware

Now we will verify that the hardware used to generate the programming pulse of +26 volts to 0 V is operating correctly. The hardware for performing the programming pulse is shown in Figure 10-16, which is excerpted from the Figure 10-12 schematic. In Chapter 8 we described how the circuit of Figure 10-16 operates electrically. We will now describe how this circuit is controlled via the microprocessor. Note in Figure 10-16 that the inputs to the 7406 IC_{12} are outputs of the 74LS175 quad latch IC_{11}. The inputs to 7406 pins 5 and 9 are the Q and $\overline{Q}$ outputs of a single bit of the 74LS175 latch. These Q and Q outputs are generated from the D_2 input of the 74LS175 latch. The D_2 input is connected to the data bus bit BD_1. This means that, whenever data bus bit BD_1 is transferred into the 74LS175 latch, the outputs Q2 and $\overline{Q2}$ will be affected.

Let us discuss how data from the data bus is transferred into the latch of IC_{11}. Whenever the system does an I/O write operation to the $\overline{SEL_5}$ select code, data on the bus will be transferred to latch IC_{11}. The $\overline{SEL_5}$ select will be asserted whenever the address bus BA_0–BA_7 is in the logical conditions for a 35_{16}. To check whether the programming pulse is working, we will transfer a logical 1 on data bus bit BD_1 to the Q2 output of IC_{11}. Under these conditions, programming pulse pin 18 of the EPROM under program will go to +26 V.

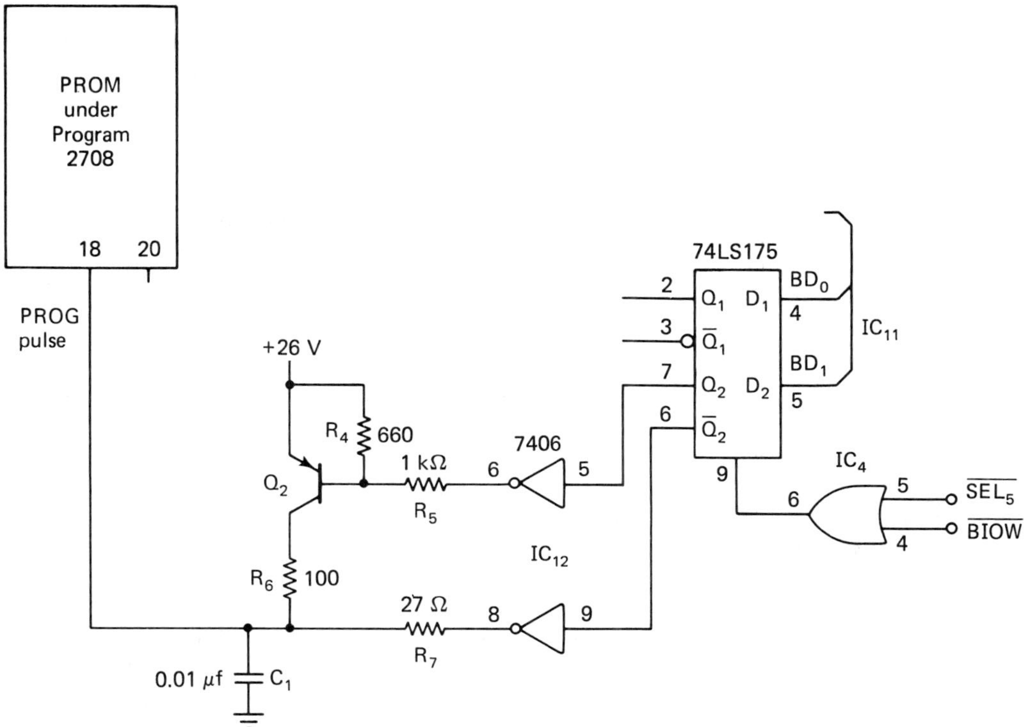

Figure 10-16 Partial schematic excerpted from Figure 10-12. This portion shows the hardware for controlling the programming pulse input to the EPROM under program.

Procedure to write a 1 into the D_2 input of IC_{11}

1. Set the system address bus BA_0–BA_7 into a condition such that $\overline{SEL_5}$ is asserted.
2. Then set a 1 on data bus bit BD_1.
3. Next set the system control bits via the SST in a condition such that the $\overline{BIOW}$ signal is asserted.
4. We now set the system control bus bits such that the buffered I/O write signal $\overline{BIOW}$ becomes unasserted. At this point, data that was on BD_1, a logical 1, is input to the 74LS175 latch.

5. The program pulse pin 18 of the EPROM under program should now go to +26 V. If this voltage is not +26 V, then we may retrace the hardware steps and determine exactly why the program pulse does not go to +26 V when a 1 is written into the D_2 input of IC_{11}.
6. We now write a logical 0 into the Q_2 of IC_{11} in exactly the same way that we wrote in the logical 1, except that the data bus bit at the time of the I/O write operation is a logical 0. After the I/O write operation is completed, the program pulse pin 18 of the PROM under program should be at logical 0. If steps 5 and 6 fail to verify correctly, then we must determine what hardware in the system is defective by stepping through the procedure and statically checking to see where the fault occurs.

10-14 Verifying CHIP SELECT and WRITE ENABLE Hardware Operation

We will now discuss the hardware that will allow the CHIP SELECT WRITE ENABLE line (pin 20 of the PROM under program) to go to +12 V under microprocessor control. Figure 10-17 is an excerpt of Figure 10-12 that shows the control circuit for the CHIP SELECT WRITE ENABLE pulse to the EPROM under program. This circuit operates very similarly to the programming pulse circuit described previously.

The major difference between the CHIP SELECT WRITE ENABLE hardware and the programming pulse hardware is that each is controlled by different bits of the data bus. The CHIP SELECT WRITE ENABLE hardware is controlled by data bus bit BD_0. Thus, we write a 1 into the Q_1 output of 74LS175 IC_1, the chip select write enable voltage should go to a +12 V via transistor T_1. When we write a 0 into Q_1, the chip select write enable voltage should go to 0 V. We can verify the operation of the chip select write enable hardware by performing an I/O WRITE operation with logical 1 set on data bus bit BD_0. This will force +12 V at the chip select write enable input. We then perform an I/O write operation with data bus bit BD_0 set to a logical 0, and the voltage on the chip select write enable will go to 0 V. If, during either of the two WRITE operations, the output of transistor T_1 fails to respond correctly, we must locate and correct the malfunction in the hardware before proceeding.

As we get further and further into the hardware the very rigorous procedures for checking the system that were given at the start of this chapter are being shortened. This is done because at this point we should have an understanding of what is meant to put the system into an I/O write mode or an I/O read mode via the Static Stimulus Tester. When information about putting the system into a particular mode is given, we assume that the reader knows how to do this now via the SST. If this assumption is not correct, a review of earlier procedures where the system is put into the I/O read, I/O write, memory read, or the memory write modes via the SST should be undertaken.

When we finish verifying the program pulse hardware and the chip select write enable hardware, we have verified that the entire I/O circuit for the EPROM under program is working correctly in an overall system environment. This is quite an achievement, considering that the only hardware tools we used to test with were the Static Stimulus Tester and a voltage monitoring device of some type. The major emphasis of what we have done is on understanding *exactly* how the communication processes take place within a certain microprocessor. That is, we must know how the 8085, or any other microprocessor, performs I/O

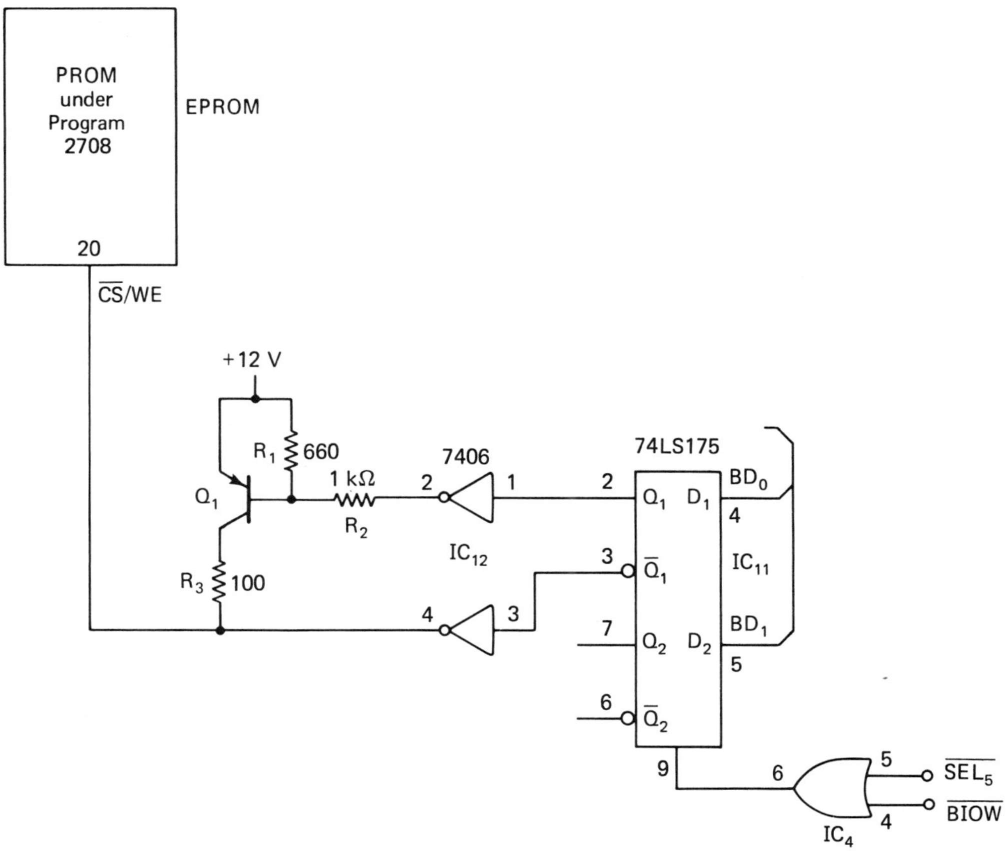

Figure 10-17 Partial schematic excerpted from Figure 10-12. This portion shows the hardware for controlling the $\overline{CS}$/WE pulse input to the EPROM under program.

Now that we are certain that the system hardware is operating correctly we can plug in our microprocessor and run the system at operating speed, confident that the system should indeed work correctly. Again, we stress that the SST will not verify timing errors. However, it has been the experience of this author that if the hardware will work without fault, using the Static Stimulus Tester, then there is high probability that when we install a microprocessor the hardware will also work without fault at normal system speed. This author has verified that the particular system described in Chapter 8 does indeed work with the 8080, 8085, Z80, and the 6800 microprocessors.

This brings up a point that we have not discussed: how to use the Static Stimulus Tester with the 6800 microprocessor. By going into detail on the Z80 and 8085 microprocessors we have developed a good feeling for how the SST must be built and used for debugging a microprocessor system. If we are to use the SST for debugging 6800 microprocessor-based equipment, we must build the 6800 static stimulus tester. The schematic is available from the publisher.

We then use this device to go through the entire checkout procedure described in this chapter, but when we indicate a memory-READ operation on the control bus it is a *6800 compatible* memory-read operation. When we indicate an I/O WRITE, an I/O READ, or a memory WRITE, the SST is put into the same mode that the 6800 would be in when performing these particular operations. These are the only differences between the SSTs used for different microprocessors. The tester used must be compatible with, and must emulate, the particular microprocessor it replaces in a system. It is this generalized attribute of the Static Stimulus Tester that allows us to modify an existing SST to checkout the hardware of any basic microprocessor system, whether it uses the 8080, 8085, Z80, 6800, or one of the other microprocessors in less common use.

10-15 Summary of the Text

In this text we have shown the steps required to design the hardware and construct the software program to allow us to use four different microprocessors to accomplish the same performance objective. These microprocessors were chosen because they describe general microprocessor architectures that are widely used throughout the industry.

We have also shown techniques for interfacing input and output devices and memories with common I/O or separate I/O to these four microprocessors. The input and output devices that we chose to interface to our system—the keyboard and the output display—were very general. These were chosen so that the overall concept of interfacing to input and output devices would be illustrated, rather than concentrating on unique peripheral devices that might be used only with a particular microprocessor, microprocessor system, or application.

The use of specific peripheral devices for a given microprocessor will reduce the can count of the system. We should become aware of the peripheral devices that are available for the microprocessor being used with the system. However, once we have been introduced to the concept of interfacing input and output devices, understanding the data sheets and specifications for specific peripheral devices becomes an easier matter. This is due to the fact that when we know "what should be there" we can look for those specific points in any peripheral device to be used.

We have further shown the technique for checking out, or debugging, the system hardware. The technique we introduced is called static stimulus testing. There are other techniques for checking system hardware, but static stimulus testing is perhaps the easiest debugging technique that can be applied, because it relies on the engineer's or technician's knowledge of how a specific microprocessor communicates with the memory and with the input and output devices. This particular information must be known in order to design the input and output devices and system memory into the microprocessor system. Beyond this, additional knowledge is not required to use the Static Stimulus Tester.

It is hoped that after studying this text readers will have an easier and more profitable time using, debugging, and designing with 8-bit microprocessors.

APPENDIX

PIN DESCRIPTION

The following describes the function of all of the 8080A I/O pins. Several of the descriptions refer to internal timing periods.

A_{15}-A_0 (output three-state)
ADDRESS BUS; the address bus provides the address to memory (up to 64K 8-bit words) or denotes the I/O device number for up to 256 input and 256 output devices. A_0 is the least significant address bit.

D_7-D_0 (input/output three-state)
DATA BUS; the data bus provides bi-directional communication between the CPU, memory, and I/O devices for instructions and data transfers. Also, during the first clock cycle of each machine cycle, the 8080A outputs a status word on the data bus that describes the current machine cycle. D_0 is the least significant bit.

SYNC (output)
SYNCHRONIZING SIGNAL; the SYNC pin provides a signal to indicate the beginning of each machine cycle.

DBIN (output)
DATA BUS IN; the DBIN signal indicates to external circuits that the data bus is in the input mode. This signal should be used to enable the gating of data onto the 8080A data bus from memory or I/O.

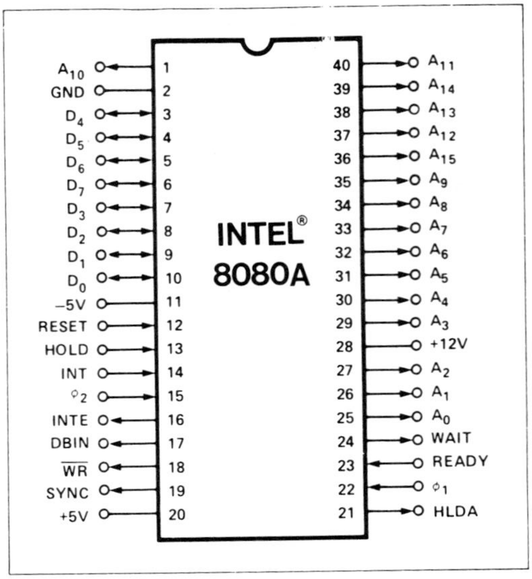

Figure 1. Pin Configuration

READY (input)
READY; the READY signal indicates to the 8080A that valid memory or input data is available on the 8080A data bus. This signal is used to synchronize the CPU with slower memory or I/O devices. If after sending an address out the 8080A does not receive a READY input, the 8080A will enter a WAIT state for as long as the READY line is low. READY can also be used to single step the CPU.

WAIT (output)
WAIT; the WAIT signal acknowledges that the CPU is in a WAIT state.

$\overline{WR}$ (output)
WRITE; the $\overline{WR}$ signal is used for memory WRITE or I/O output control. The data on the data bus is stable while the $\overline{WR}$ signal is active low ($\overline{WR}$ = 0).

HOLD (input)
HOLD; the HOLD signal requests the CPU to enter the HOLD state. The HOLD state allows an external device to gain control of the 8080A address and data bus as soon as the 8080A has completed its use of these buses for the current machine cycle. It is recognized under the following conditions:

- the CPU is in the HALT state.
- the CPU is in the T2 or TW state and the READY signal is active.

As a result of entering the HOLD state the CPU ADDRESS BUS (A_{15}-A_0) and DATA BUS (D_7-D_0) will be in their high impedance state. The CPU acknowledges its state with the HOLD ACKNOWLEDGE (HLDA) pin.

HLDA (output)
HOLD ACKNOWLEDGE; the HLDA signal appears in response to the HOLD signal and indicates that the data and address bus will go to the high impedance state. The HLDA signal begins at:

- T3 for READ memory or input.
- The Clock Period following T3 for WRITE memory or OUTPUT operation.

In either case, the HLDA signal appears after the rising edge of ϕ_1 and high impedance occurs after the rising edge of ϕ_2.

INTE (output)
INTERRUPT ENABLE; indicates the content of the internal interrupt enable flip/flop. This flip/flop may be set or reset by the Enable and Disable Interrupt instructions and inhibits interrupts from being accepted by the CPU when it is reset. It is automatically reset (disabling further interrupts) at time T1 of the instruction fetch cycle (M1) when an interrupt is accepted and is also reset by the RESET signal.

INT (input)
INTERRUPT REQUEST; the CPU recognizes an interrupt request on this line at the end of the current instruction or while halted. If the CPU is in the HOLD state or if the Interrupt Enable flip/flop is reset it will not honor the request.

RESET (input) [1]
RESET; while the RESET signal is activated, the content of the program counter is cleared. After RESET, the program will start at location 0 in memory. The INTE and HLDA flip/flops are also reset. Note that the flags, accumulator, stack pointer, and registers are not cleared.

V_{SS}	Ground Reference.
V_{DD}	+12 ± 5% Volts.
V_{CC}	+5 ± 5% Volts.
V_{BB}	-5 ±5% Volts (substrate bias).
ϕ_1, ϕ_2	2 externally supplied clock phases. (non TTL compatible)

ABSOLUTE MAXIMUM RATINGS*

Temperature Under Bias . . . . 0°C to +70° C
Storage Temperature . . . . -65°C to +150°C
All Input or Output Voltages
With Respect to V_{BB} . . . . -0.3V to +20V
V_{CC}, V_{DD} and V_{SS} With Respect to V_{BB} -0.3V to +20V
Power Dissipation 1.5W

**COMMENT:* *Stresses above those listed under "Absolute Maximum Ratings" may cause permanent damage to the device. This is a stress rating only and functional operation of the device at these or any other conditions above those indicated in the operational sections of this specification is not implied. Exposure to absolute maximum rating conditions for extended periods may affect device reliability.*

D.C. CHARACTERISTICS

T_A = 0°C to 70°C, V_{DD} = +12V ± 5%, V_{CC} = +5V ± 5%, V_{BB} = -5V ± 5%, V_{SS} = 0V, Unless Otherwise Noted.

Symbol	Parameter	Min.	Typ.	Max.	Unit	Test Condition
V_{ILC}	Clock Input Low Voltage	$V_{SS}-1$		$V_{SS}+0.8$	V	
V_{IHC}	Clock Input High Voltage	9.0		$V_{DD}+1$	V	
V_{IL}	Input Low Voltage	$V_{SS}-1$		$V_{SS}+0.8$	V	
V_{IH}	Input High Voltage	3.3		$V_{CC}+1$	V	
V_{OL}	Output Low Voltage			0.45	V	I_{OL} = 1.9mA on all outputs,
V_{OH}	Output High Voltage	3.7			V	I_{OH} = -150μA.
$I_{DD\,(AV)}$	Avg. Power Supply Current (V_{DD})		40	70	mA	Operation
$I_{CC\,(AV)}$	Avg. Power Supply Current (V_{CC})		60	80	mA	T_{CY} = .48 μsec
$I_{BB\,(AV)}$	Avg. Power Supply Current (V_{BB})		.01	1	mA	
I_{IL}	Input Leakage			±10	μA	$V_{SS} \leq V_{IN} \leq V_{CC}$
I_{CL}	Clock Leakage			±10	μA	$V_{SS} \leq V_{CLOCK} \leq V_{DD}$
I_{DL} [2]	Data Bus Leakage in Input Mode			-100 -2.0	μA mA	$V_{SS} \leq V_{IN} \leq V_{SS}+0.8V$ $V_{SS}+0.8V \leq V_{IN} \leq V_{CC}$
I_{FL}	Address and Data Bus Leakage During HOLD			+10 -100	μA	$V_{ADDR/DATA} = V_{CC}$ $V_{ADDR/DATA} = V_{SS} + 0.45V$

CAPACITANCE

T_A = 25°C $V_{CC} = V_{DD} = V_{SS}$ = 0V, V_{BB} = -5V

Symbol	Parameter	Typ.	Max.	Unit	Test Condition
C_ϕ	Clock Capacitance	17	25	pf	f_c = 1 MHz
C_{IN}	Input Capacitance	6	10	pf	Unmeasured Pins
C_{OUT}	Output Capacitance	10	20	pf	Returned to V_{SS}

NOTES:

1. The RESET signal must be active for a minimum of 3 clock cycles.
2. When DBIN is high and $V_{IN} > V_{IH}$ an internal active pull up will be switched onto the Data Bus.
3. ΔI supply / ΔT_A = -0.45%/°C.

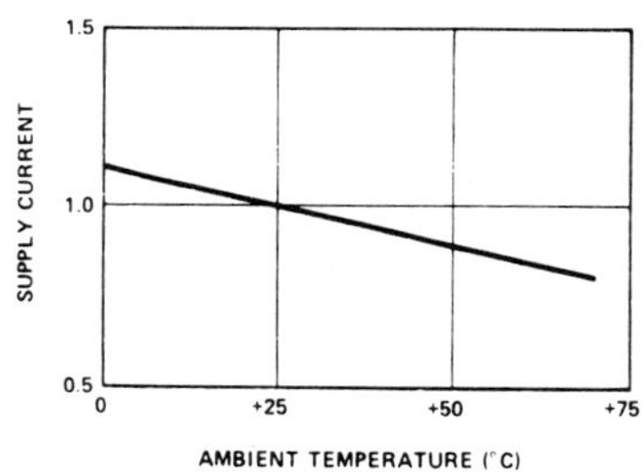

Figure 2. Typical Supply Current vs. Temperature, Normalized[3]

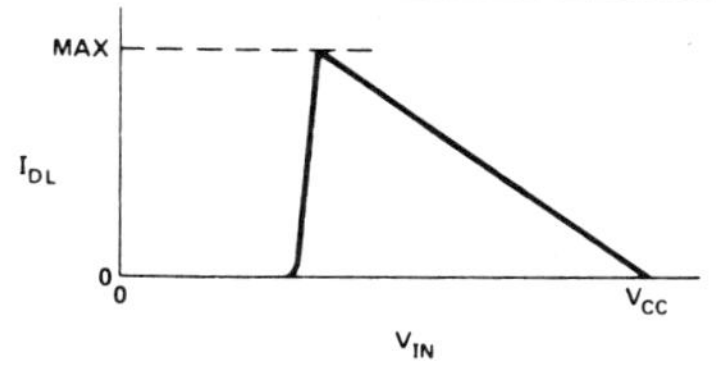

Figure 3. Data Bus Characteristic During DBIN

A.C. CHARACTERISTICS (8080A)

T_A = 0°C to 70°C, V_{DD} = +12V ± 5%, V_{CC} = +5V ± 5%, V_{BB} = -5V ± 5%, V_{SS} = 0V, Unless Otherwise Noted

Symbol	Parameter	Min.	Max.	-1 Min.	-1 Max.	-2 Min.	-2 Max.	Unit	Test Condition
t_{CY}[3]	Clock Period	0.48	2.0	0.32	2.0	0.38	2.0	μsec	
t_r, t_f	Clock Rise and Fall Time	0	50	0	25	0	50	nsec	
$t_{\varnothing 1}$	$\varnothing_1$ Pulse Width	60		50		60		nsec	
$t_{\varnothing 2}$	$\varnothing_2$ Pulse Width	220		145		175		nsec	
t_{D1}	Delay $\varnothing_1$ to $\varnothing_2$	0		0		0		nsec	
t_{D2}	Delay $\varnothing_2$ to $\varnothing_1$	70		60		70		nsec	
t_{D3}	Delay $\varnothing_1$ to $\varnothing_2$ Leading Edges	80		60		70		nsec	
t_{DA}[2]	Address Output Delay From $\varnothing_2$		200		150		175	nsec	C_L = 100 pF
t_{DD}[2]	Data Output Delay From $\varnothing_2$		220		180		200	nsec	
t_{DC}[2]	Signal Output Delay From $\varnothing_2$ or $\varnothing_2$ (SYNC, WR, WAIT, HLDA)		120		110		120	nsec	C_L = 50 pF
t_{DF}[2]	DBIN Delay From $\varnothing_2$	25	140	25	130	25	140	nsec	
t_{DI}[1]	Delay for Input Bus to Enter Input Mode		t_{DF}		t_{DF}		t_{DF}	nsec	
t_{DS1}	Data Setup Time During $\varnothing_1$ and DBIN	30		10		20		nsec	

WAVEFORMS

(Note: Timing measurements are made at the following reference voltages: CLOCK "1" = 8.0V "0" = 1.0V; INPUTS "1" = 3.3V, "0" = 0.8V; OUTPUTS "1" = 2.0V, "0" = 0.8V.)

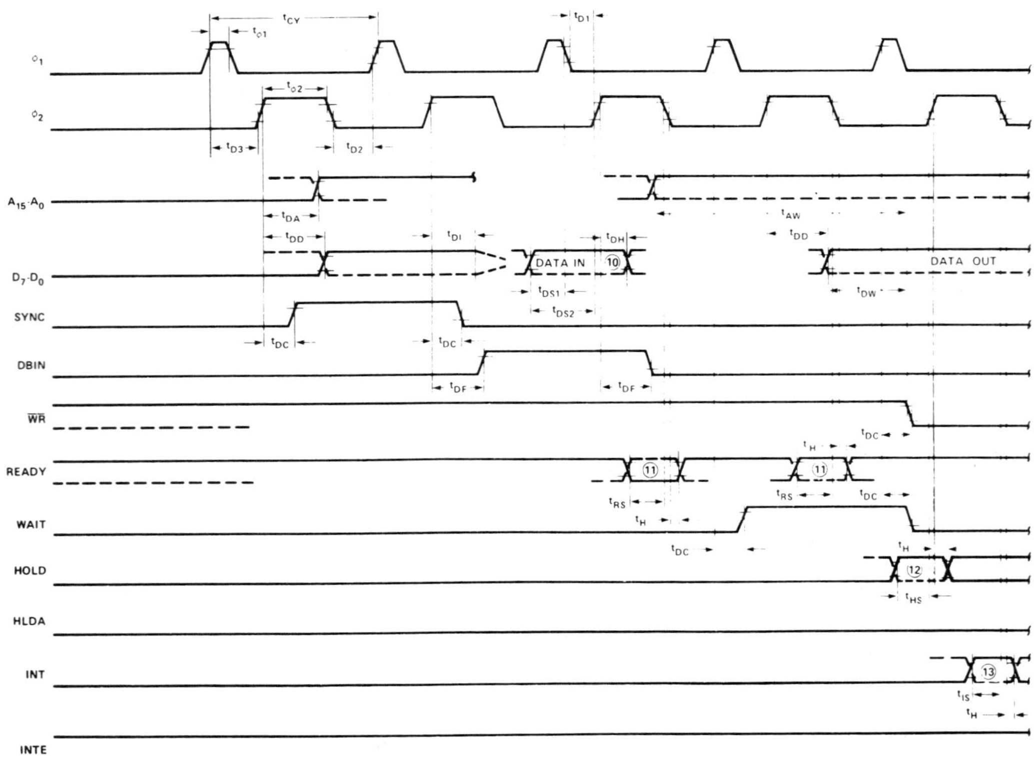

FUNCTIONAL DESCRIPTION

The 8085A is a complete 8-bit parallel central processor. It is designed with N-channel depletion loads and requires a single +5 volt supply. Its basic clock speed is 3 MHz (8085A) or 5 MHz (8085A-2), thus improving on the present 8080A's performance with higher system speed. Also it is designed to fit into a minimum system of three IC's: The cpu (8085A), a RAM/IO (8156), and a ROM or EPROM/IO chip (8355 or 8755A).

The 8085A has twelve addressable 8-bit registers. Four of them can function only as two 16-bit register pairs. Six others can be used interchangeably as 8-bit registers or as 16-bit register pairs. The 8085A register set is as follows:

Mnemonic	Register	Contents
ACC or A	Accumulator	8 bits
PC	Program Counter	16-bit address
BC,DE,HL	General-Purpose Registers; data pointer (HL)	8 bits x 6 or 16 bits x 3
SP	Stack Pointer	16-bit address
Flags or F	Flag Register	5 flags (8-bit space)

The 8085A uses a multiplexed Data Bus. The address is split between the higher 8-bit Address Bus and the lower 8-bit Address/Data Bus. During the first T state (clock cycle) of a machine cycle the low order address is sent out on the Address/Data bus. These lower 8 bits may be latched externally by the Address Latch Enable signal (ALE). During the rest of the machine cycle the data bus is used for memory or I/O data.

The 8085A provides $\overline{RD}$, $\overline{WR}$, S_0, S_1, and IO/$\overline{M}$ signals for bus control. An Interrupt Acknowledge signal ($\overline{INTA}$) is also provided. HOLD and all Interrupts are synchronized with the processor's internal clock. The 8085A also provides Serial Input Data (SID) and Serial Output Data (SOD) lines for simple serial interface.

In addition to these features, the 8085A has three maskable, vector interrupt pins and one nonmaskable TRAP interrupt.

INTERRUPT AND SERIAL I/O

The 8085A has 5 interrupt inputs: INTR, RST 5.5, RST 6.5, RST 7.5, and TRAP. INTR is identical in function to the 8080A INT. Each of the three RESTART inputs, 5.5, 6.5, and 7.5, has a programmable mask. TRAP is also a RESTART interrupt but it is nonmaskable.

The three maskable interrupts cause the internal execution of RESTART (saving the program counter in the stack and branching to the RESTART address) if the interrupts are enabled and if the interrupt mask is not set. The nonmaskable TRAP causes the internal execution of a RESTART vector independent of the state of the interrupt enable or masks. (See Table 1.)

There are two different types of inputs in the restart interrupts. RST 5.5 and RST 6.5 are *high level-sensitive* like INTR (and INT on the 8080) and are recognized with the same timing as INTR. RST 7.5 is *rising edge-sensitive*.

For RST 7.5, only a pulse is required to set an internal flip-flop which generates the internal interrupt request. (See Section 5.2.7.) The RST 7.5 request flip-flop remains set until the request is serviced. Then it is reset automatically. This flip-flop may also be reset by using the SIM instruction or by issuing a $\overline{\text{RESET IN}}$ to the 8085A. The RST 7.5 internal flip-flop will be set by a pulse on the RST 7.5 pin even when the RST 7.5 interrupt is masked out.

The status of the three RST interrupt masks can only be affected by the SIM instruction and $\overline{\text{RESET IN}}$. (See SIM, Chapter 5.)

The interrupts are arranged in a fixed priority that determines which interrupt is to be recognized if more than one is pending as follows: TRAP — highest priority, RST 7.5, RST 6.5, RST 5.5, INTR — lowest priority. This priority scheme does not take into account the priority of a routine that was started by a higher priority interrupt. RST 5.5 can interrupt an RST 7.5 routine if the interrupts are re-enabled before the end of the RST 7.5 routine.

The TRAP interrupt is useful for catastrophic events such as power failure or bus error. The TRAP input is recognized just as any other interrupt but has the highest priority. It is not affected by any flag or mask. The TRAP input is both *edge and level sensitive.* The TRAP input must go high and remain high until it is acknowledged. It will not be recognized again until it goes low, then high again. This avoids any false triggering due to noise or logic glitches. Figure 3 illustrates the TRAP interrupt request circuitry within the 8085A. Note that the servicing of any interrupt (TRAP, RST 7.5, RST 6.5, RST 5.5, INTR) disables all future interrupts (except TRAPs) until an EI instruction is executed.

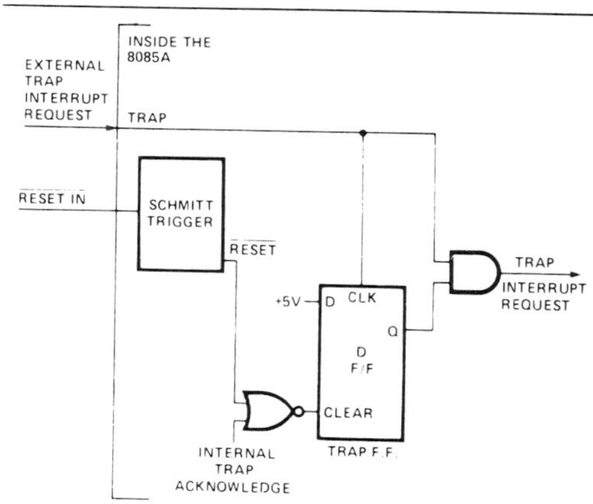

Figure 3. TRAP and $\overline{\text{RESET IN}}$ Circuit

The TRAP interrupt is special in that it disables interrupts, but preserves the previous interrupt enable status. Performing the first RIM instruction following a TRAP interrupt allows you to determine whether interrupts were enabled or disabled prior to the TRAP. All subsequent RIM instructions provide current interrupt enable status. Performing a RIM instruction following INTR, or RST 5.5–7.5 will provide current Interrupt Enable status, revealing that Interrupts are disabled. See the description of the RIM instruction in Chapter 5.

The serial I/O system is also controlled by the RIM and SIM instructions. SID is read by RIM, and SIM sets the SOD data.

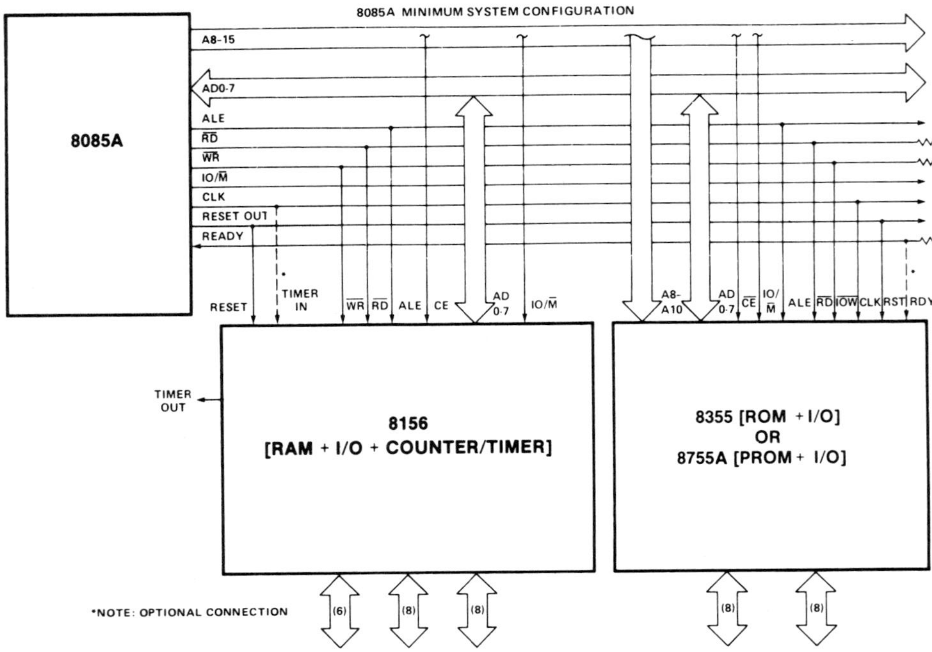

Figure 7. MCS-85™ Minimum System (Memory Mapped I/O)

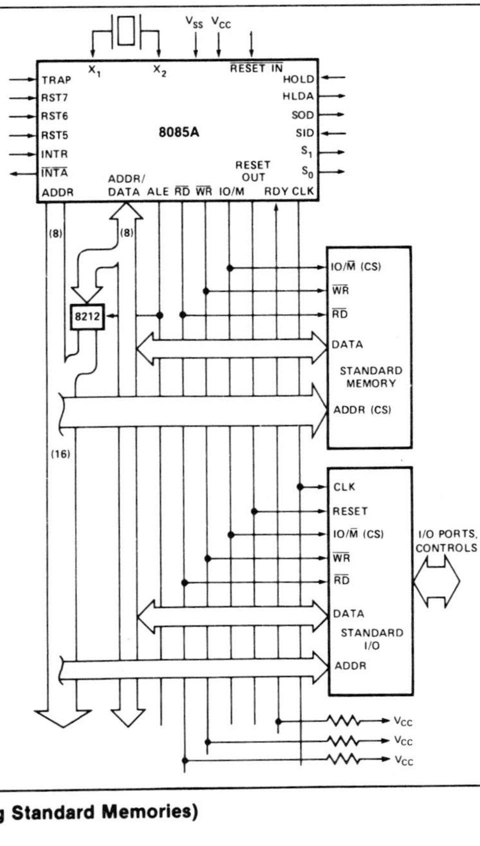

Figure 8. MCS-85™ System (Using Standard Memories)

TABLE 4. ABSOLUTE MAXIMUM RATINGS*

Ambient Temperature Under Bias. . . . . 0°C to 70°C
Storage Temperature . . . . −65°C to +150°C
Voltage on Any Pin
With Respect to Ground . . . . −0.5V to +7V
Power Dissipation . . . . 1.5 Watt

*COMMENT

Stresses above those listed under "Absolute Maximum Ratings" may cause permanent damage to the device. This is a stress rating only and functional operation of the device at these or any other conditions above those indicated in the operational sections of this specification is not implied. Exposure to absolute maximum rating conditions for extended periods may affect device reliability.

TABLE 5. D.C. CHARACTERISTICS

(T_A = 0°C to 70°C; V_{CC} = 5V ±5%; V_{SS} = 0V; unless otherwise specified)

Symbol	Parameter	Min.	Max.	Units	Test Conditions
V_{IL}	Input Low Voltage	-0.5	+0.8	V	
V_{IH}	Input High Voltage	2.0	V_{CC}+0.5	V	
V_{OL}	Output Low Voltage		0.45	V	I_{OL} = 2mA
V_{OH}	Output High Voltage	2.4		V	I_{OH} = -400μA
I_{CC}	Power Supply Current		170	mA	
I_{IL}	Input Leakage		±10	μA	$V_{in} = V_{CC}$
I_{LO}	Output Leakage		±10	μA	$0.45V \leqslant V_{out} \leqslant V_{CC}$
V_{ILR}	Input Low Level, RESET	-0.5	+0.8	V	
V_{IHR}	Input High Level, RESET	2.4	V_{CC} +0.5	V	
V_{HY}	Hysteresis, RESET	0.25		V	

Z80, Z80A-CPU Pin Description

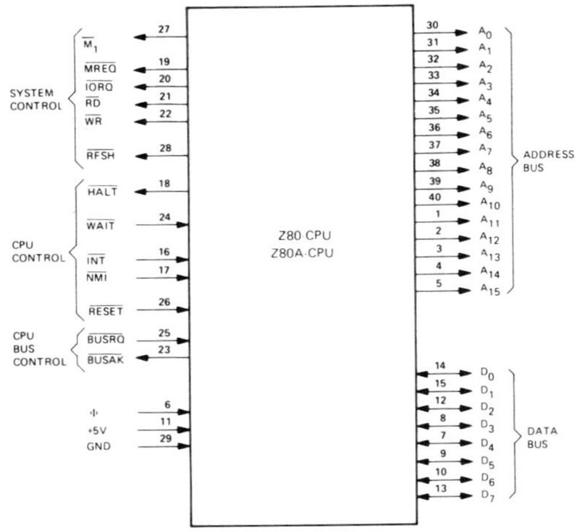

Z80, Z80A CPU PIN CONFIGURATION

A_0-A_{15} (Address Bus)
: Tri-state output, active high. A_0-A_{15} constitute a 16-bit address bus. The address bus provides the address for memory (up to 64K bytes) data exchanges and for I/O device data exchanges

D_0-D_7 (Data Bus)
: Tri-state input/output, active high. D_0 - D_7 constitute an 8-bit bidirectional data bus. The data bus is used for data exchanges with memory and I/O devices.

$\overline{M_1}$ (Machine Cycle one)
: Output, active low. $\overline{M_1}$ indicates that the current machine cycle is the OP code fetch cycle of an instruction execution.

$\overline{\text{MREQ}}$ (Memory Request)
: Tri-state output, active low. The memory request signal indicates that the address bus holds a valid address for a memory read or memory write operation.

$\overline{\text{IORQ}}$ (Input/ Output Request)
: Tri-state output, active low. The $\overline{\text{IORQ}}$ signal indicates that the lower half of the address bus holds a valid I/O address for a I/O read or write operation. An $\overline{\text{IORQ}}$ signal is also generated when an interrupt is being acknowledged to indicate that an interrupt response vector can be placed on the data bus.

$\overline{\text{RD}}$ (Memory Read)
: Tri-state output, active low. $\overline{\text{RD}}$ indicates that the CPU wants to read data from memory or an I/O device. The addressed I/O device or memory should use this signal to gate data onto the CPU data bus.

$\overline{\text{WR}}$ (Memory Write)
: Tri-state output, active low. $\overline{\text{WR}}$ indicates that the CPU data bus holds valid data to be stored in the addressed memory or I/O device.

$\overline{\text{RFSH}}$ (Refresh)
: Output, active low. $\overline{\text{RFSH}}$ indicates that the lower 7 bits of the address bus contain a refresh address for dynamic memories and the current $\overline{\text{MREQ}}$ signal should be used to do a refresh read to all dynamic memories.

$\overline{\text{HALT}}$ (Halt state)
: Output, active low. $\overline{\text{HALT}}$ indicates that the CPU has executed a HALT software instruction and is awaiting either a non-maskable or a maskable interrupt (with the mask enabled) before operation can resume. While halted, the CPU executes NOP's to maintain memory refresh activity.

$\overline{\text{WAIT}}$ (Wait)
: Input, active low. $\overline{\text{WAIT}}$ indicates to the Z-80 CPU that the addressed memory or I/O devices are not ready for a data transfer. The CPU continues to enter wait states for as long as this signal is active.

$\overline{\text{INT}}$ (Interrupt Request)
: Input, active low. The Interrupt Request signal is generated by I/O devices. A request will be honored at the end of the current instruction if the internal software controlled interrupt enable flip-flop (IFF) is enabled.

$\overline{\text{NMI}}$ (Non Maskable Interrupt)
: Input, active low. The non-maskable nterrupt request line has a higher priority than $\overline{\text{INT}}$ and is always recognized at the end of the current instruction, independent of the status of the interrupt enable flip-flop. $\overline{\text{NMI}}$ automatically forces the Z-80 CPU to restart to location 0066_H.

$\overline{\text{RESET}}$
: Input, active low. $\overline{\text{RESET}}$ initializes the CPU as follows: reset interrupt enable flip-flop, clear PC and registers I and R and set interrupt to 8080A mode. During reset time, the address and data bus go to a high impedance state and all control output signals go to the inactive state.

$\overline{\text{BUSRQ}}$ (Bus Request)
: Input, active low. The bus request signal has a higher priority than $\overline{\text{NMI}}$ and is always recognized at the end of the current machine cycle and is used to request the CPU address bus, data bus and tri-state output control signals to go to a high impedance state so that other devices can control these busses.

$\overline{\text{BUSAK}}$ (Bus Acknowledge)
: Output, active low. Bus acknowledge is used to indicate to the requesting device that the CPU address bus, data bus and tri-state control bus signals have been set to their high impedance state and the external device can now control these signals.

Timing Waveforms

INSTRUCTION OP CODE FETCH

The program counter content (PC) is placed on the address bus immediately at the start of the cycle. One half clock time later $\overline{MREQ}$ goes active. The falling edge of $\overline{MREQ}$ can be used directly as a chip enable to dynamic memories. $\overline{RD}$ when active indicates that the memory data should be enabled onto the CPU data bus. The CPU samples data with the rising edge of the clock state T_3. Clock states T_3 and T_4 of a fetch cycle are used to refresh dynamic memories while the CPU is internally decoding and executing the instruction. The refresh control signal $\overline{RFSH}$ indicates that a refresh read of all dynamic memories should be accomplished.

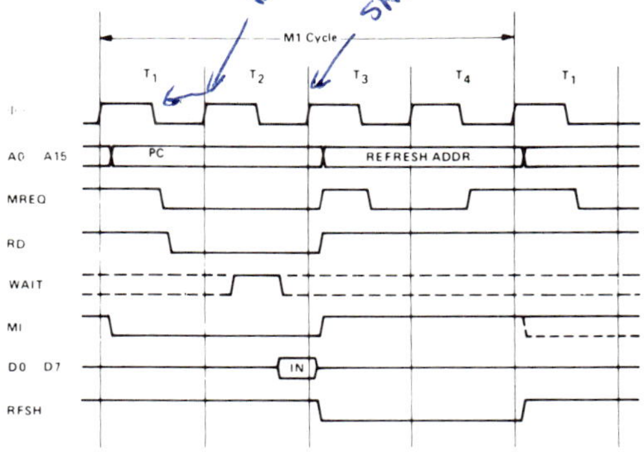

MEMORY READ OR WRITE CYCLES

Illustrated here is the timing of memory read or write cycles other than an OP code fetch (M_1 cycle). The $\overline{MREQ}$ and $\overline{RD}$ signals are used exactly as in the fetch cycle. In the case of a memory write cycle, the $\overline{MREQ}$ also becomes active when the address bus is stable so that it can be used directly as a chip enable for dynamic memories. The $\overline{WR}$ line is active when data on the data bus is stable so that it can be used directly as a R/W pulse to virtually any type of semiconductor memory.

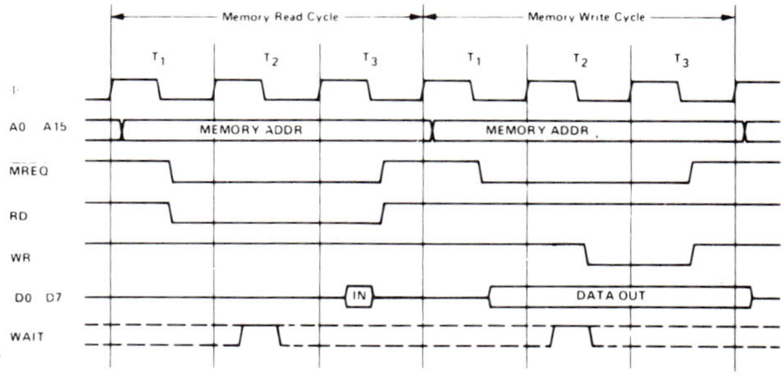

INPUT OR OUTPUT CYCLES

Illustrated here is the timing for an I/O read or I/O write operation. Notice that during I/O operations a single wait state is automatically inserted (Tw*). The reason for this is that during I/O operations this extra state allows sufficient time for an I/O port to decode its address and activate the $\overline{WAIT}$ line if a wait is required.

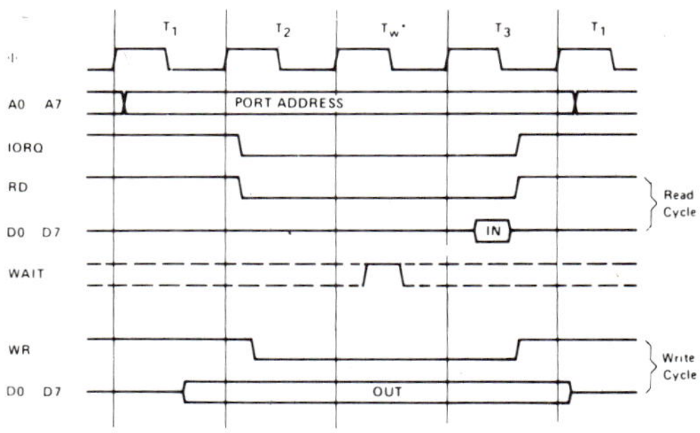

INTERRUPT REQUEST/ACKNOWLEDGE CYCLE

The interrupt signal is sampled by the CPU with the rising edge of the last clock at the end of any instruction. When an interrupt is accepted, a special M_1 cycle is generated. During this M_1 cycle, the $\overline{IORQ}$ signal becomes active (instead of $\overline{MREQ}$) to indicate that the interrupting device can place an 8-bit vector on the data bus. Two wait states (Tw*) are automatically added to this cycle so that a ripple priority interrupt scheme, such as the one used in the Z80 peripheral controllers, can be easily implemented.

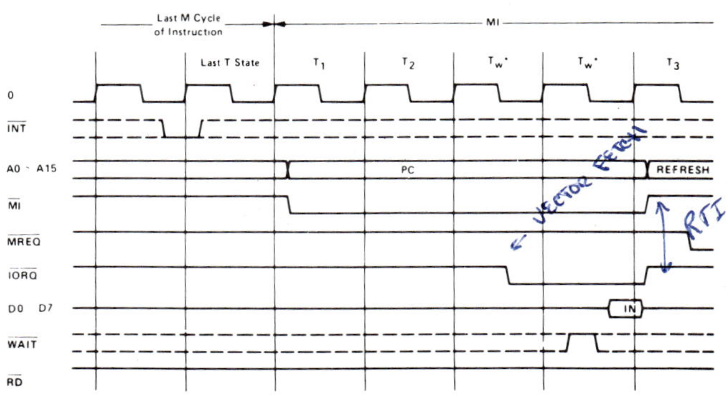

Absolute Maximum Ratings

Temperature Under Bias	Specified operating range.
Storage Temperature	-65°C to +150°C
Voltage On Any Pin with Respect to Ground	-0.3V to +7V
Power Dissipation	1.5W

*Comment

Stresses above those listed under "Absolute Maximum Rating" may cause permanent damage to the device. This is a stress rating only and functional operation of the device at these or any other condition above those indicated in the operational sections of this specification is not implied. Exposure to absolute maximum rating conditions for extended periods may affect device reliability.

Note

For Z80-CPU all AC and DC characteristics remain the same for the military grade parts except I_{cc}.

I_{cc} = 200 mA

Z80-CPU D.C. Characteristics

T_A = 0°C to 70°C, V_{cc} = 5V ± 5% unless otherwise specified

Symbol	Parameter	Min.	Typ.	Max.	Unit	Test Condition
V_{ILC}	Clock Input Low Voltage	-0.3		0.45	V	
V_{IHC}	Clock Input High Voltage	V_{cc} -.6		V_{cc}+.3	V	
V_{IL}	Input Low Voltage	-0.3		0.8	V	
V_{IH}	Input High Voltage	2.0		V_{cc}	V	
V_{OL}	Output Low Voltage			0.4	V	I_{OL}=1.8mA
V_{OH}	Output High Voltage	2.4			V	I_{OH} = -250μA
I_{CC}	Power Supply Current			150	mA	
I_{LI}	Input Leakage Current			10	μA	V_{IN}=0 to V_{cc}
I_{LOH}	Tri-State Output Leakage Current in Float			10	μA	V_{OUT}=2.4 to V_{cc}
I_{LOL}	Tri-State Output Leakage Current in Float			-10	μA	V_{OUT}=0.4V
I_{LD}	Data Bus Leakage Current in Input Mode			±10	μA	$0 \leq V_{IN} \leq V_{cc}$

Capacitance

T_A = 25°C, f = 1 MHz,
unmeasured pins returned to ground

Symbol	Parameter	Max.	Unit
C_Φ	Clock Capacitance	35	pF
C_{IN}	Input Capacitance	5	pF
C_{OUT}	Output Capacitance	10	pF

Z80A-CPU Ordering Information

C – Ceramic
P – Plastic
S – Standard 5V ±5% 0° to 70°C
E – Extended 5V ±5% -40° to 85°C
M – Military 5V ±10% -55° to 125°C

Z80A-CPU D.C. Characteristics

T_A = 0°C to 70°C, V_{cc} = 5V ± 5% unless otherwise specified

Symbol	Parameter	Min.	Typ.	Max.	Unit	Test Condition
V_{ILC}	Clock Input Low Voltage	-0.3		0.45	V	
V_{IHC}	Clock Input High Voltage	V_{cc} -.6		V_{cc}+.3	V	
V_{IL}	Input Low Voltage	-0.3		0.8	V	
V_{IH}	Input High Voltage	2.0		V_{cc}	V	
V_{OL}	Output Low Voltage			0.4	V	I_{OL}=1.8mA
V_{OH}	Output High Voltage	2.4			V	I_{OH} -250μA
I_{CC}	Power Supply Current		90	200	mA	
I_{LI}	Input Leakage Current			10	μA	V_{IN}=0 to V_{cc}
I_{LOH}	Tri-State Output Leakage Current in Float			10	μA	V_{OUT}=2.4 to V_{cc}
I_{LOL}	Tri-State Output Leakage Current in Float			-10	μA	V_{OUT}=0.4V
I_{LD}	Data Bus Leakage Current in Input Mode			±10	μA	$0 \leq V_{IN} \leq V_{cc}$

Capacitance

T_A = 25°C, f = 1 MHz,
unmeasured pins returned to ground

Symbol	Parameter	Max.	Unit
C_Φ	Clock Capacitance	35	pF
C_{IN}	Input Capacitance	5	pF
C_{OUT}	Output Capacitance	10	pF

Z80-CPU Ordering Information

C Ceramic
P Plastic
S Standard 5V ±5% 0° to 70°C

INDEX